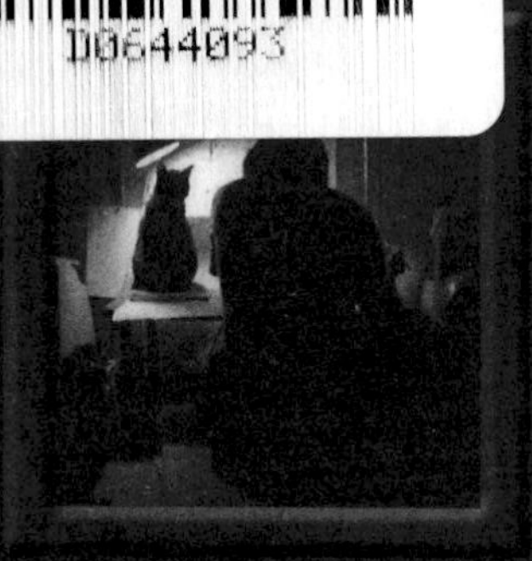

A picture of me and my cat, Moto-kyu, from a few years back when I was just starting out—taken by a friend who I thought was asleep. I might look quiet and lonely, but there's a battle going on inside my head... Some things never change.

– Yoshiyuki Nishi

Yoshiyuki Nishi was born in Tokyo. Two of his favorite manga series are *Dragon Ball* and the robot-cat comedy *Doraemon*. His latest series, *Muhyo & Roji's Bureau of Supernatural Investigation*, debuted in Japan's *Akamaru Jump* magazine in 2004 and went on to be serialized in *Weekly Shonen Jump*.

MUHYO & ROJI'S
BUREAU OF SUPERNATURAL INVESTIGATION

VOL. 12
The SHONEN JUMP Manga Edition

STORY AND ART BY
YOSHIYUKI NISH

Translation & Adaptation/Alexander O. Smith
Touch-up Art & Lettering/Brian Bilter
Design/Yukiko Whitle
Editor/Amy Yu

Editor in Chief, Books/Alvin Lu
Editor in Chief, Magazines/Marc Weidenbaum
VP, Publishing Licensing/Rika Inouye
VP, Sales & Product Marketing/Gonzalo Ferreyra
VP, Creative/Linda Espinosa
Publisher/Hyoe Narita

Printed in the U.S.A

Published by VIZ Media, LLC
P.O. Box 7701
San Francisco, CA 9410

SHONEN JUMP Manga Edition
10 9 8 7 6 5 4 3 2
First printing, August 2009

THE WORLD'S
MOST POPULAR MANGA

www.viz.com   www.shonenjump.com

SHONEN JUMP MANGA EDITION

Muhyo & Roji's Bureau of Supernatural Investigation

BSI

Vol. 12 Homecoming

Story & Art by Yoshiyuki Nishi

Dramatis Personae

Jiro Kusano (Roji)

Assistant at Muhyo's office, recently promoted from the lowest rank of "Second Clerk" to that of (provisional) "First Clerk." Roji has a gentle heart and has been known to freak out in the presence of spirits. Lately, he has been devoting himself to the study of magic law so that he can pull his own weight someday.

Toru Muhyo (Muhyo)

Young, genius magic law practitioner with the highest rank of "Executor." Always calm and collected (though sometimes considered cold), Muhyo possesses a strong sense of justice and even has a kind side. Sleeps a lot to recover from the exhaustion caused by his practice.

Yu Abiko (Biko)

Muhyo's classmate and an Artificer. Makes seals, pens, magic law books, and other accoutrements of magic law.

Yoichi Himukai (Yoichi)

Judge and Muhyo's former classmate. Expert practitioner of all magic law except execution.

Rio Kurotori (Rio)

Charismatic Artificer who turned traitor when the Magic Law Association stood by and let her mother die.

Soratsugu Madoka (Enchu)

Muhyo's former classmate and Executor-hopeful until one event turned him onto the traitor's path.

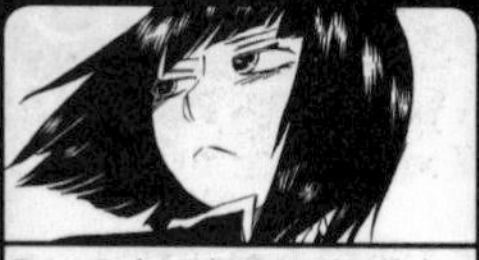

Brave Judge who joined Muhyo and gang during the fight against Face-Ripper Sophie.

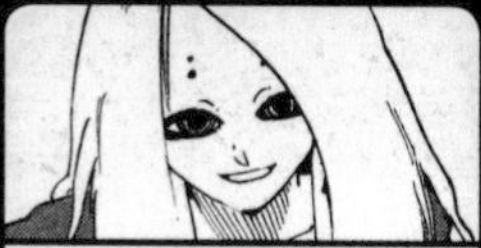

Forbidden magic law practitioner who made himself an envoy to obtain eternal life. Sole possessor of means to kill Teeki.

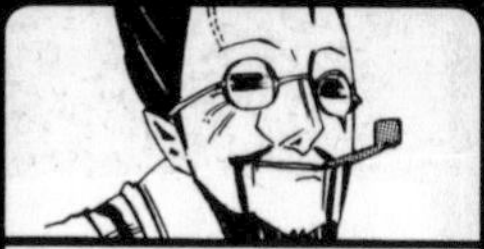

Chief Investigator for the Magic Law Association, Yoichi's boss, and Muhyo and Enchu's former instructor.

Seven-Faced Dog

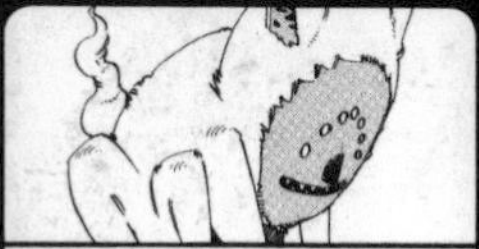

An envoy with the ability to change shape. Specialist at uncovering spectral crimes.

Umekichi Sasanoha

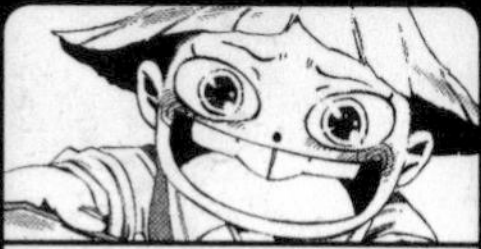

First clerk and Busujima's assistant. In his true envoy form he is called *Unryuso*. "Umekichi" is his human-form alias.

Harumi Busujima

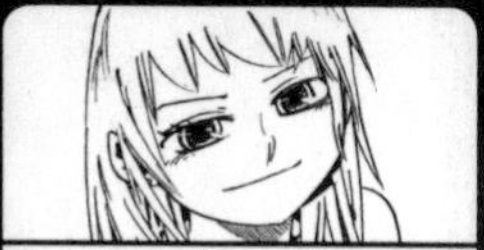

Executor and one of the only practitioners in the world capable of "remote magic law."

The Story

Magic law is a newly established practice for judging and punishing the increasing crimes committed by spirits; those who use it are called "practitioners."
Page and Yoichi contact Isabi to find a way to defeat Teeki and end up fighting for their very lives. They prevail, but now another battle rages in the Wailing Vale where Umekichi and Seven-Faced Dog are up against Mick. The Ark assassin proves to be a formidable foe, easily returning anything Umekichi throws at him. Brute force won't work, so the gang attempts strategy. Has Roji found a way past Mick's defenses?

Lili & Maril Mathias

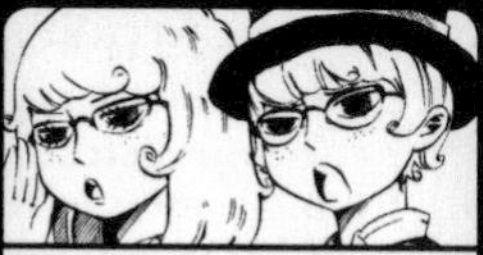

Twin siblings world-renowned for their research in magic law.

Mick

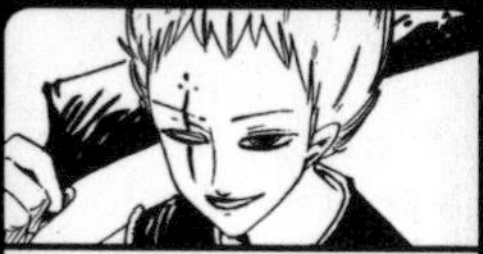

Member of the forbidden magic law group known as Ark. A heartless man who would as soon abandon a friend as kill a foe.

Teeki

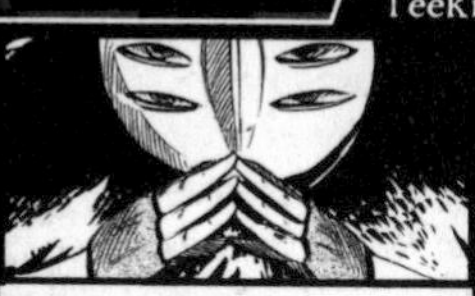

Dangerous entity marked as a traitor to the Magic Law Association for 800 years.

CONTENTS

Article 95: **Homecoming** 7

Article 96: **A Little Trick** 27

Article 97: **Aroropathy** 47

Article 98: **Writ of Passage** 67

Article 99: **Ginji** 87

Article 100: **It's Here** 107

Article 101: **The Bell** 127

Article 102: **Armor** 149

Article 103: **Bobby** 169

12

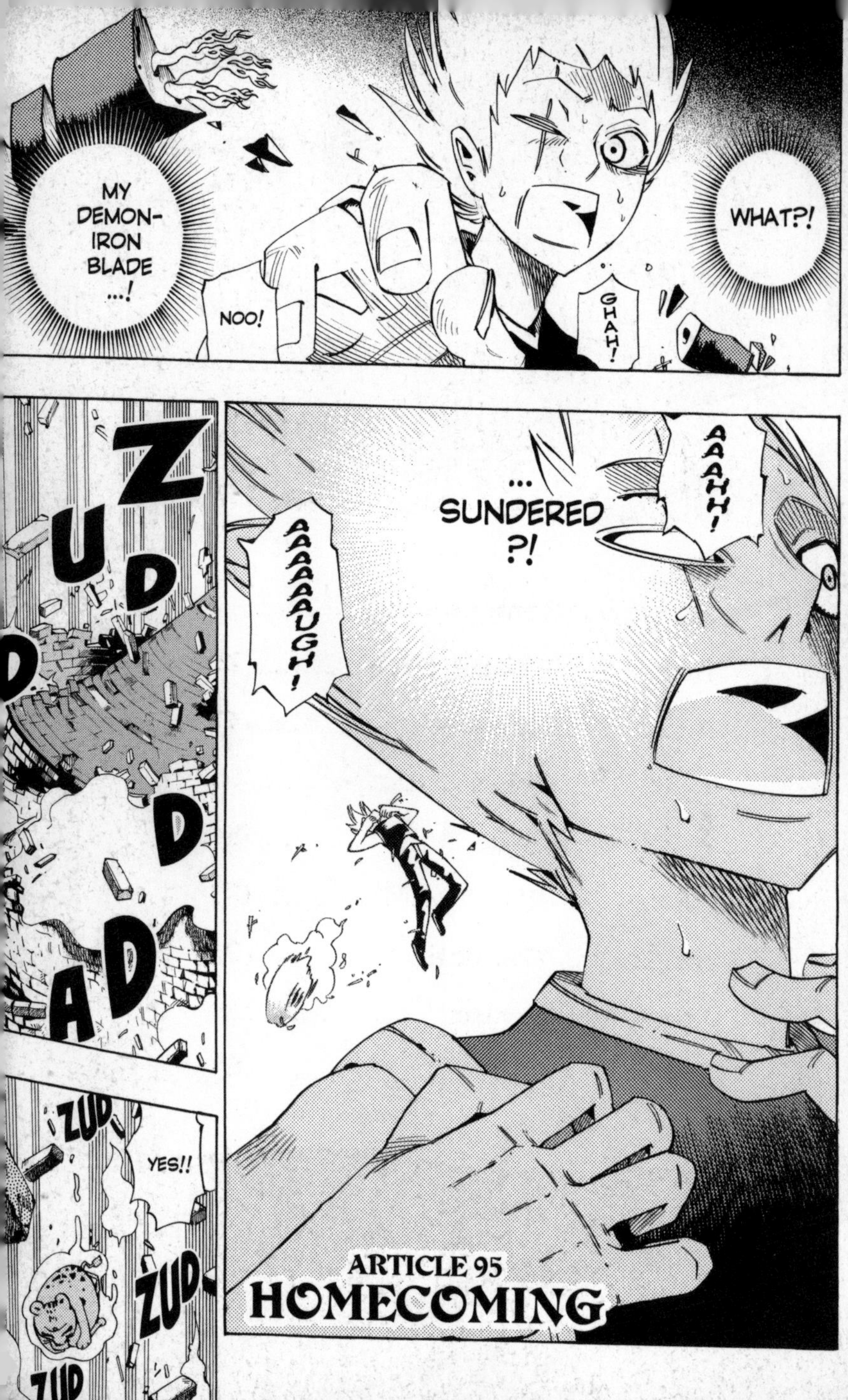
WHAT?!
GHAH!
MY DEMON-IRON BLADE ...!
NOO!
AAAHH!
... SUNDERED ?!
AAAAAAUGH!
ZUDDAD
YES!!
ZUD
ZUD
ZUD

ARTICLE 95
HOMECOMING

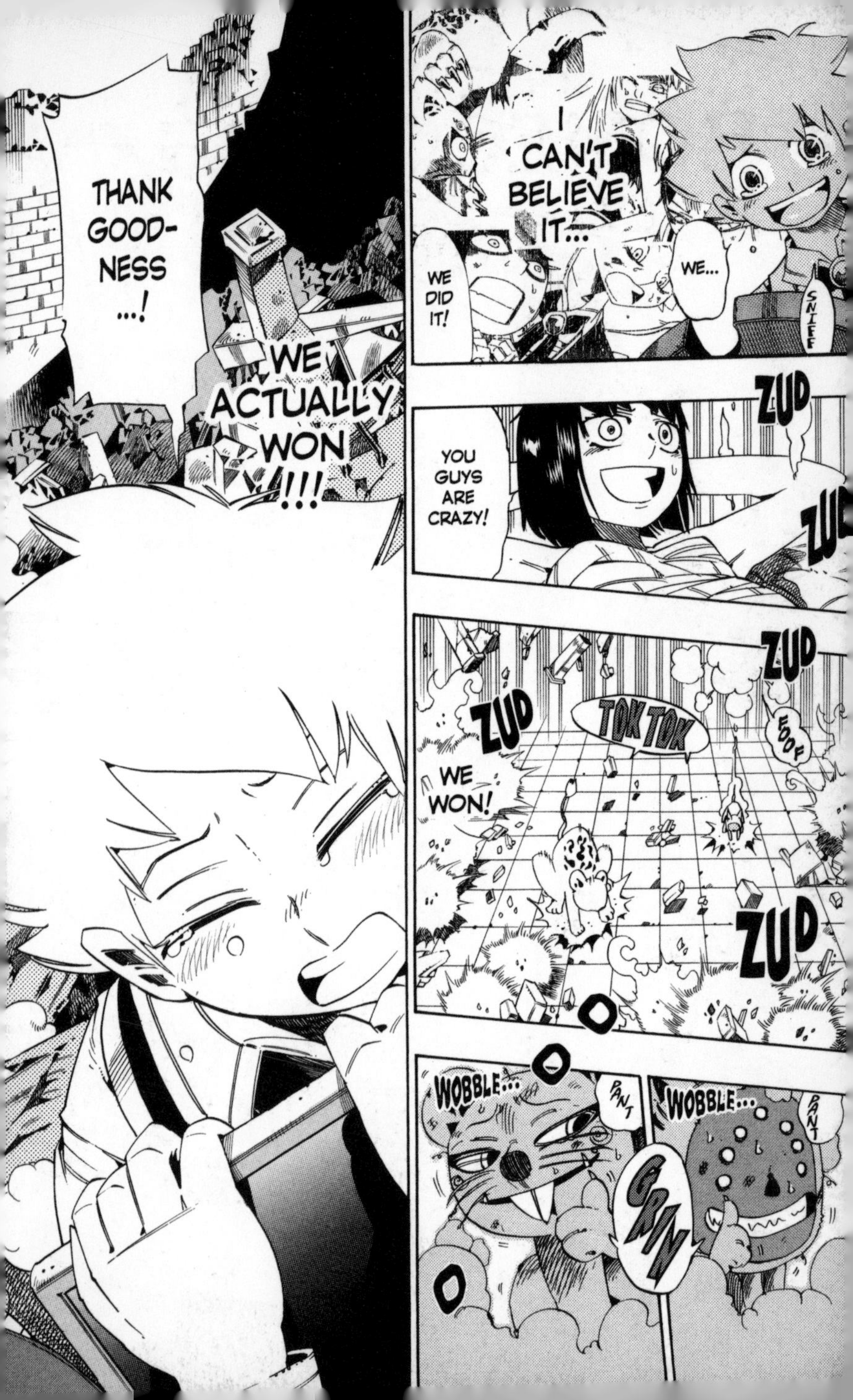
I CAN'T BELIEVE IT...
WE...
SNIFF
WE DID IT!
ZUD
ZU
YOU GUYS ARE CRAZY!
ZUD
FOOF
TOK TOK
ZUD
WE WON!
ZUD
WOBBLE...
PANT
WOBBLE...
PANT
GRIN
THANK GOODNESS...!
WE ACTUALLY WON!!!

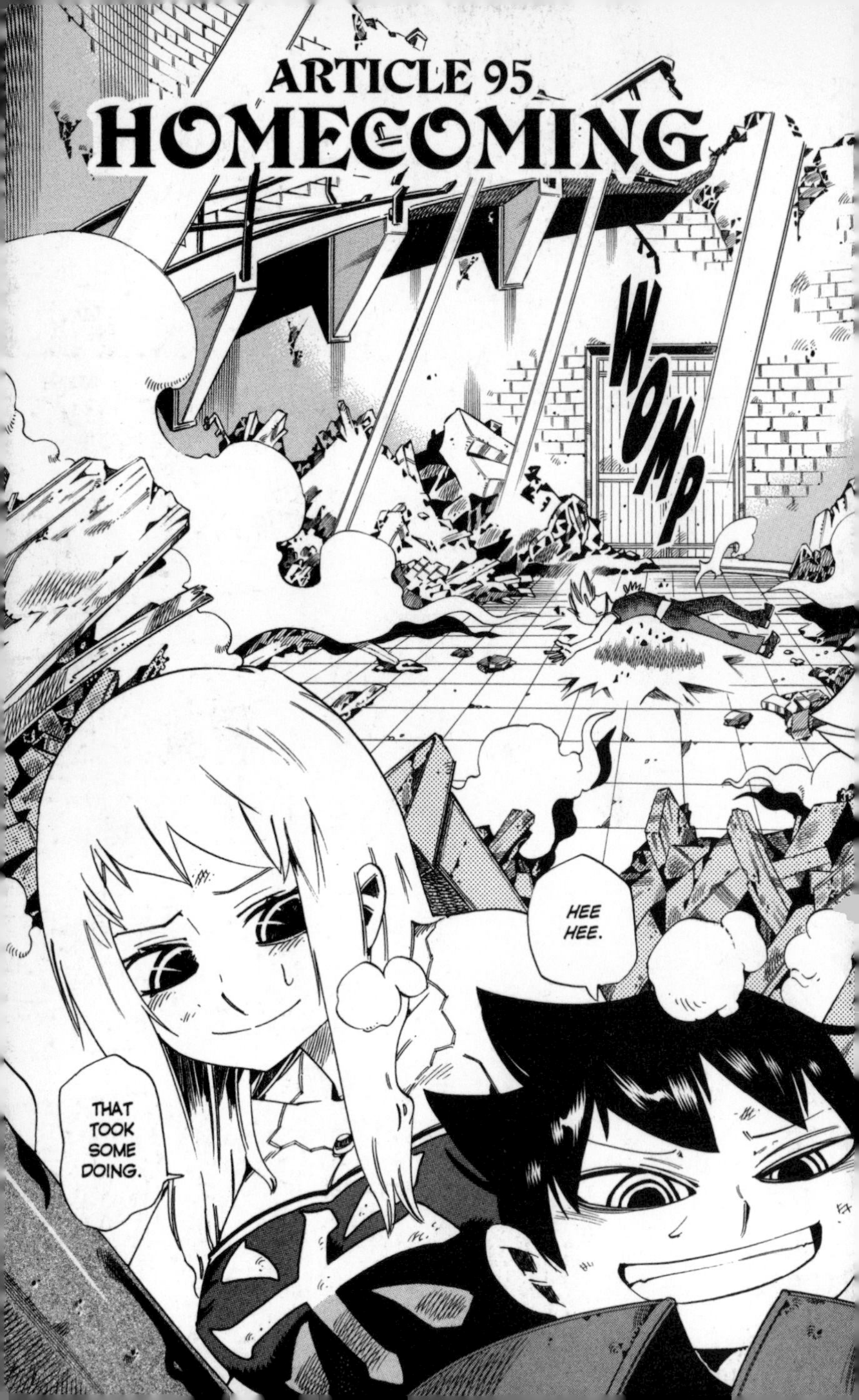
ARTICLE 95
HOMECOMING
WOMP
HEE HEE.
THAT TOOK SOME DOING.

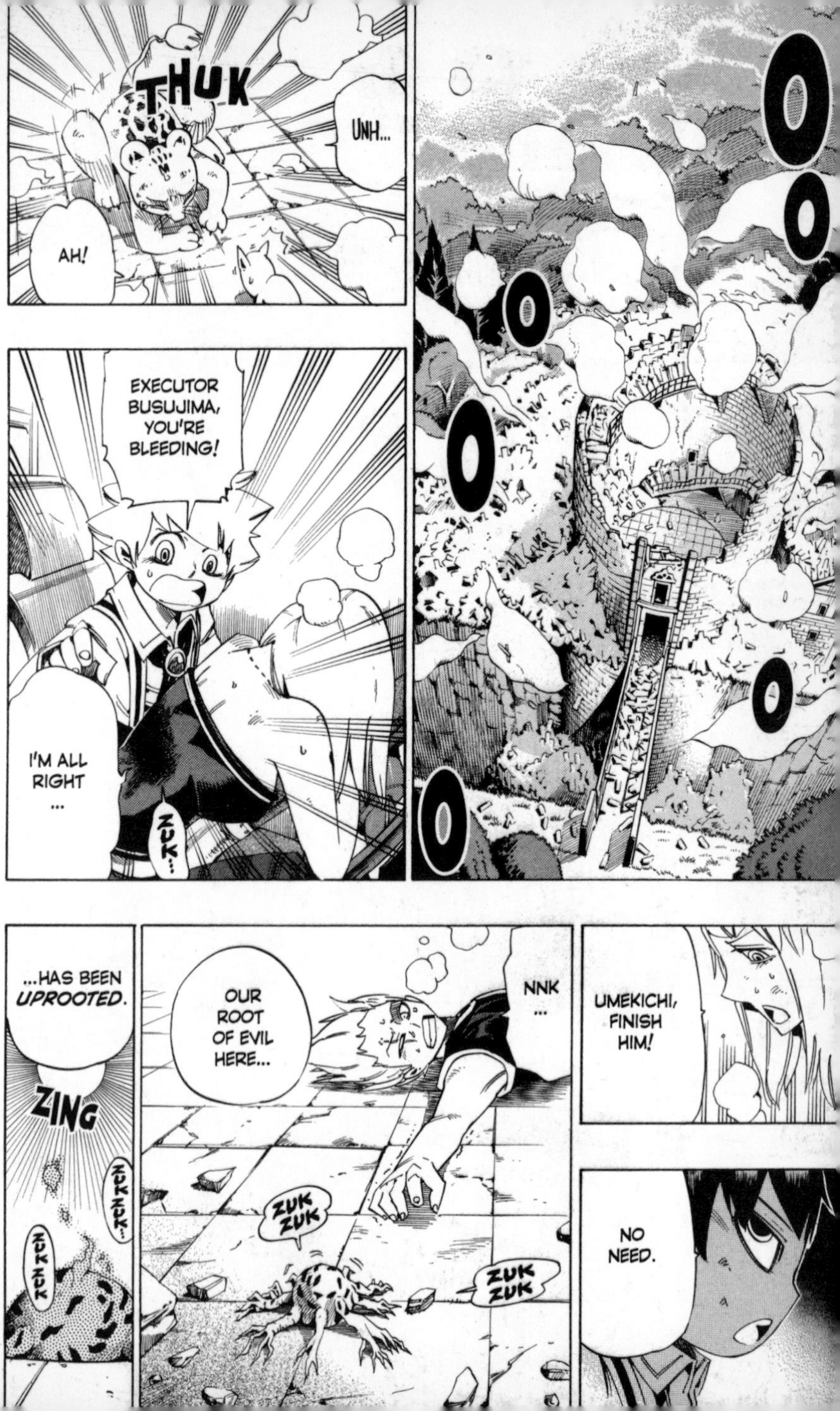
THUK
UNH...
AH!
EXECUTOR BUSUJIMA, YOU'RE BLEEDING!
I'M ALL RIGHT ...
ZUK...
UMEKICHI, FINISH HIM!
NO NEED.
NNK ...
OUR ROOT OF EVIL HERE...
ZUK ZUK
ZUK ZUK
...HAS BEEN UPROOTED.
ZING
ZUK ZUK...
ZUK ZUK

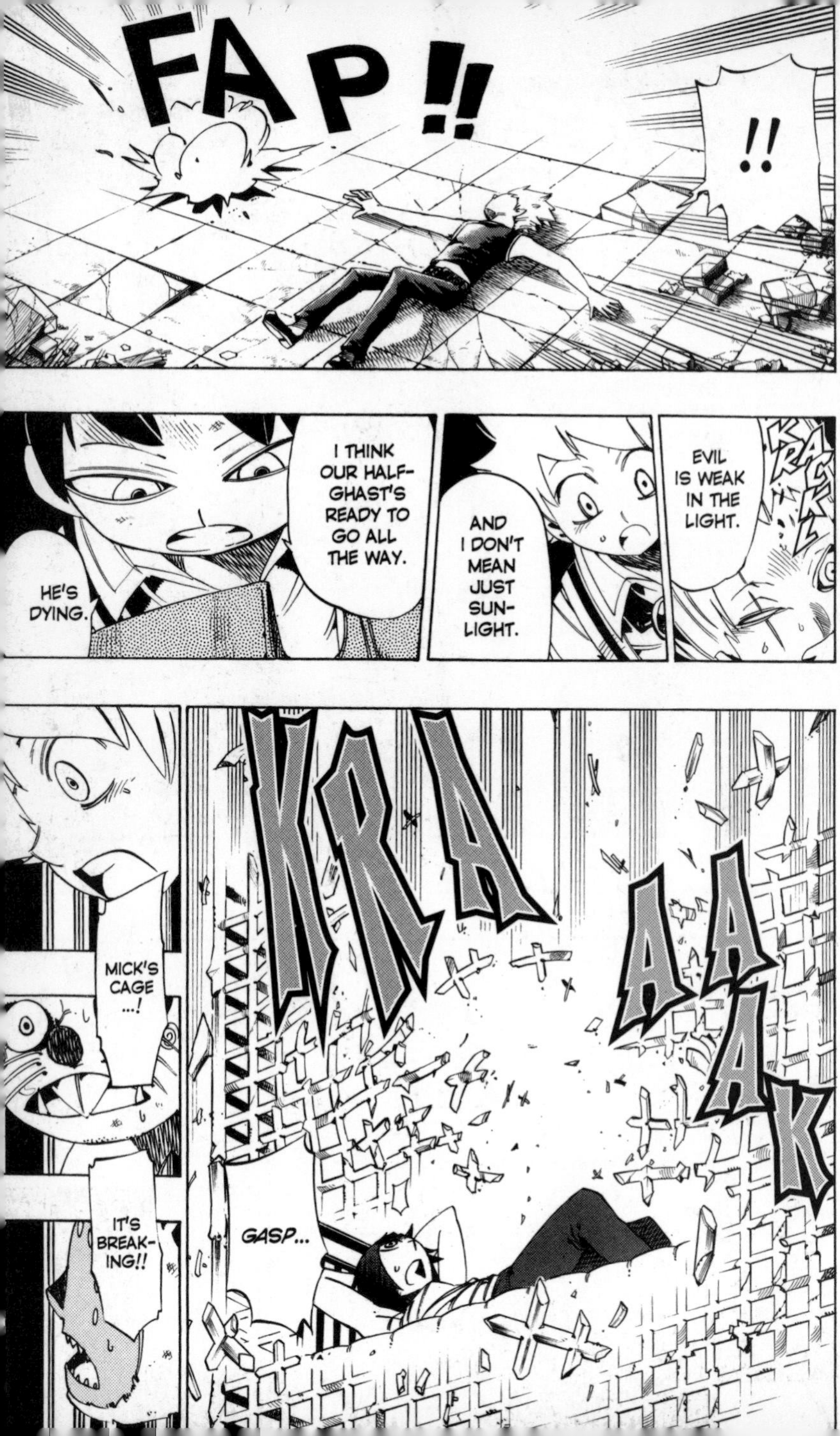
!!
FAP!!
KRACK
EVIL IS WEAK IN THE LIGHT.
AND I DON'T MEAN JUST SUN-LIGHT.
I THINK OUR HALF-GHAST'S READY TO GO ALL THE WAY.
HE'S DYING.
KRAAAAK
GASP...
MICK'S CAGE ...!
IT'S BREAKING!!

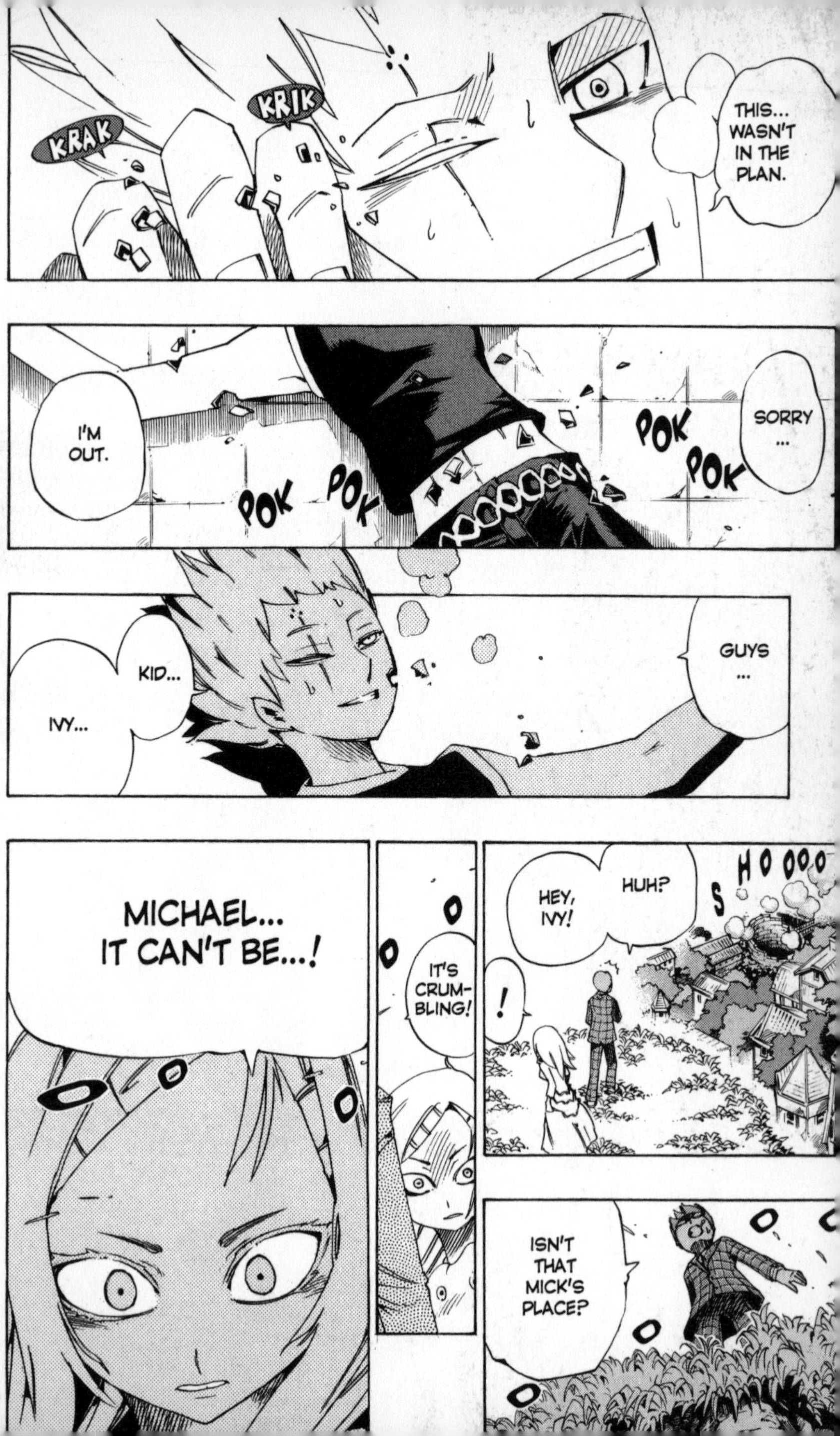
THIS... WASN'T IN THE PLAN.
KRIK
KRAK
SORRY...
POK POK
POK POK
I'M OUT.
GUYS...
KID...
IVY...
SHOOOO
HUH?
HEY, IVY!
!
ISN'T THAT MICK'S PLACE?
IT'S CRUM-BLING!
MICHAEL... IT CAN'T BE...!

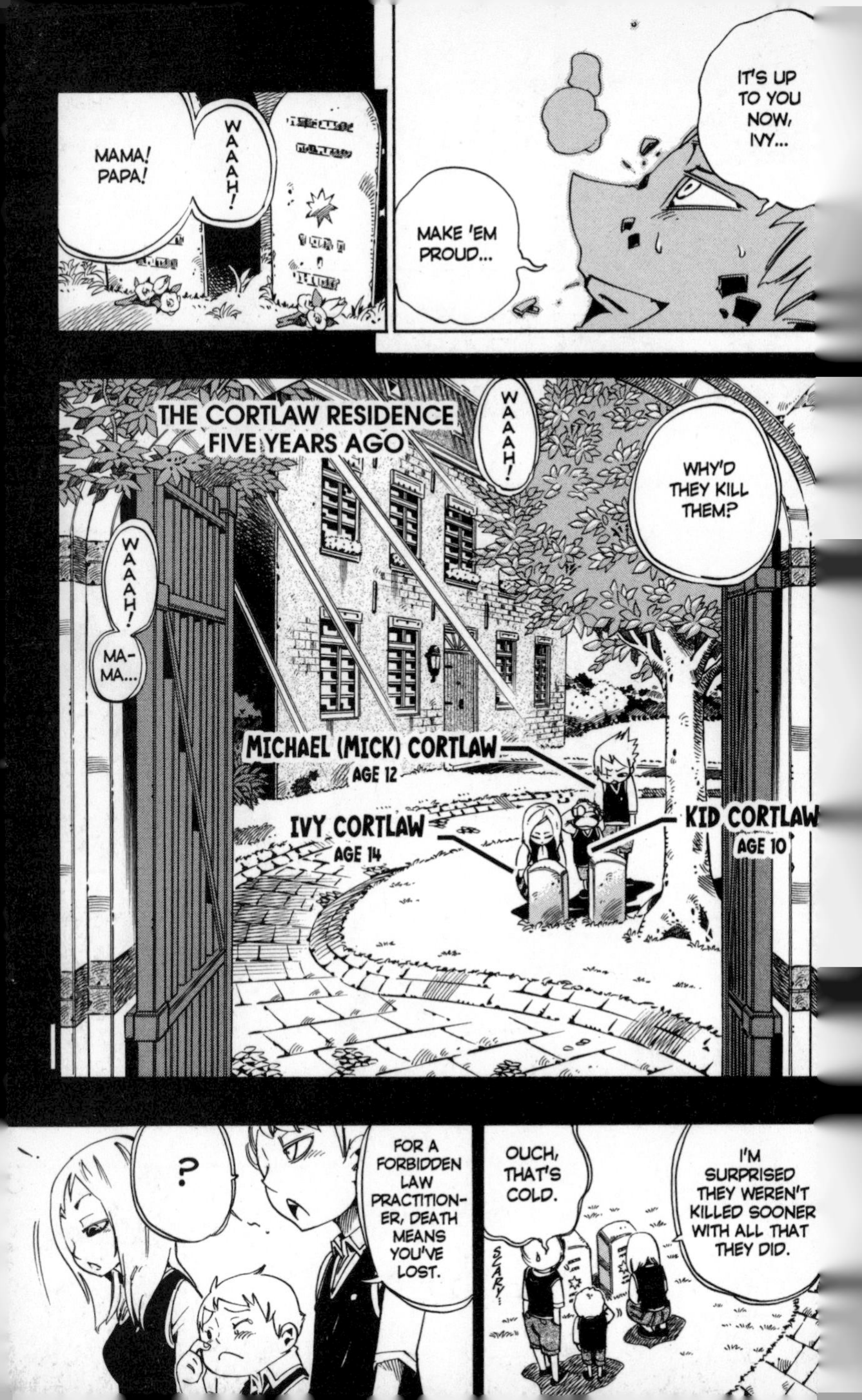

IT'S UP TO YOU NOW, IVY...
MAKE 'EM PROUD...
WAAAAH!
MAMA! PAPA!
THE CORTLAW RESIDENCE FIVE YEARS AGO
WAAAAH!
WHY'D THEY KILL THEM?
WAAAAH!
MA-MA...
MICHAEL (MICK) CORTLAW AGE 12
KID CORTLAW AGE 10
IVY CORTLAW AGE 14
I'M SURPRISED THEY WEREN'T KILLED SOONER WITH ALL THAT THEY DID.
OUCH, THAT'S COLD.
SCARY...
FOR A FORBIDDEN LAW PRACTITIONER, DEATH MEANS YOU'VE LOST.
?

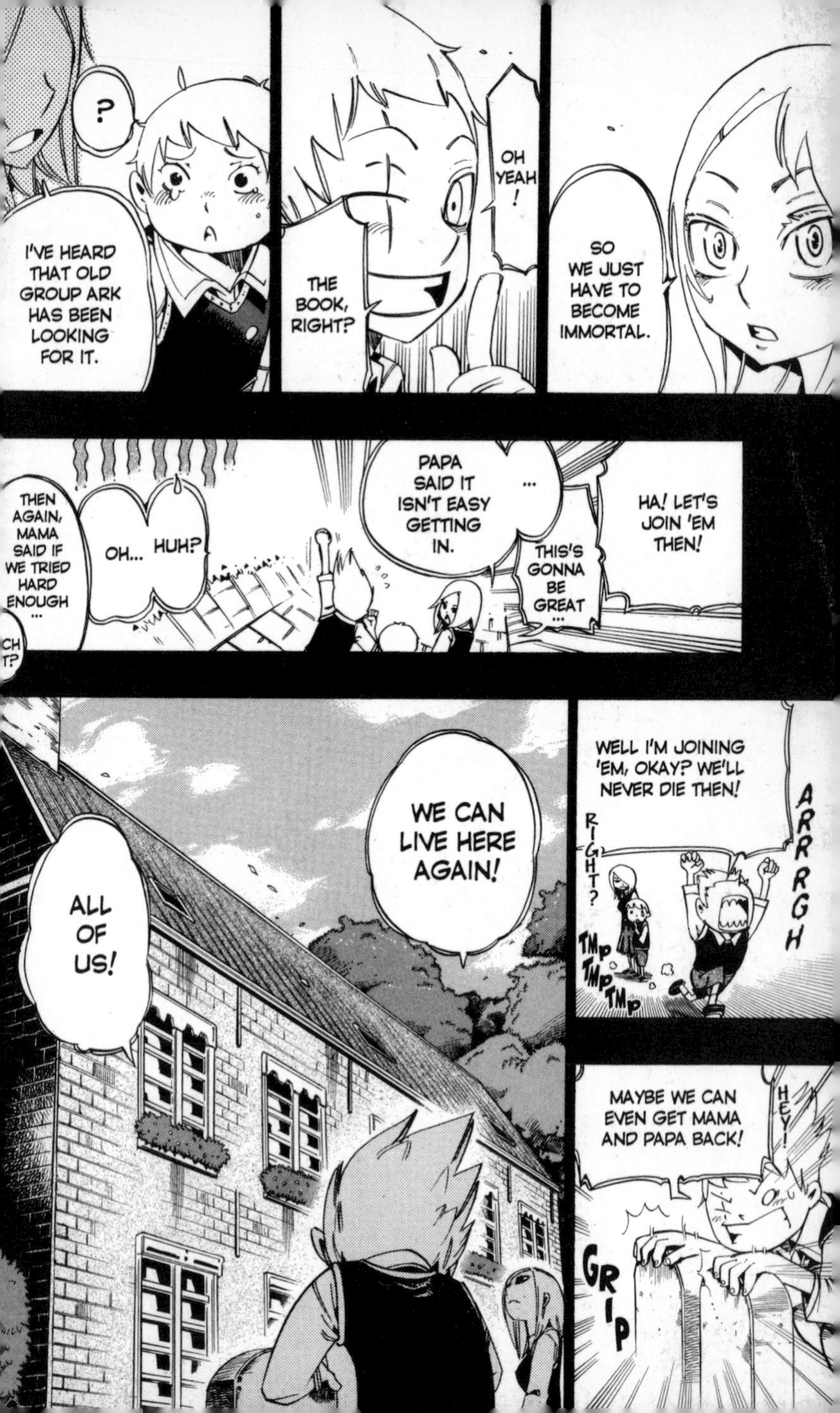
SO WE JUST HAVE TO BECOME IMMORTAL.
OH YEAH!
THE BOOK, RIGHT?
?
I'VE HEARD THAT OLD GROUP ARK HAS BEEN LOOKING FOR IT.
HA! LET'S JOIN 'EM THEN!
THIS'S GONNA BE GREAT...
...
PAPA SAID IT ISN'T EASY GETTING IN.
OH... HUH?
THEN AGAIN, MAMA SAID IF WE TRIED HARD ENOUGH...
WELL I'M JOINING 'EM, OKAY? WE'LL NEVER DIE THEN!
ARRRGH
RIGHT?
TMP TMP TMP TMP
MAYBE WE CAN EVEN GET MAMA AND PAPA BACK!
HEY!
GRIP
WE CAN LIVE HERE AGAIN!
ALL OF US!

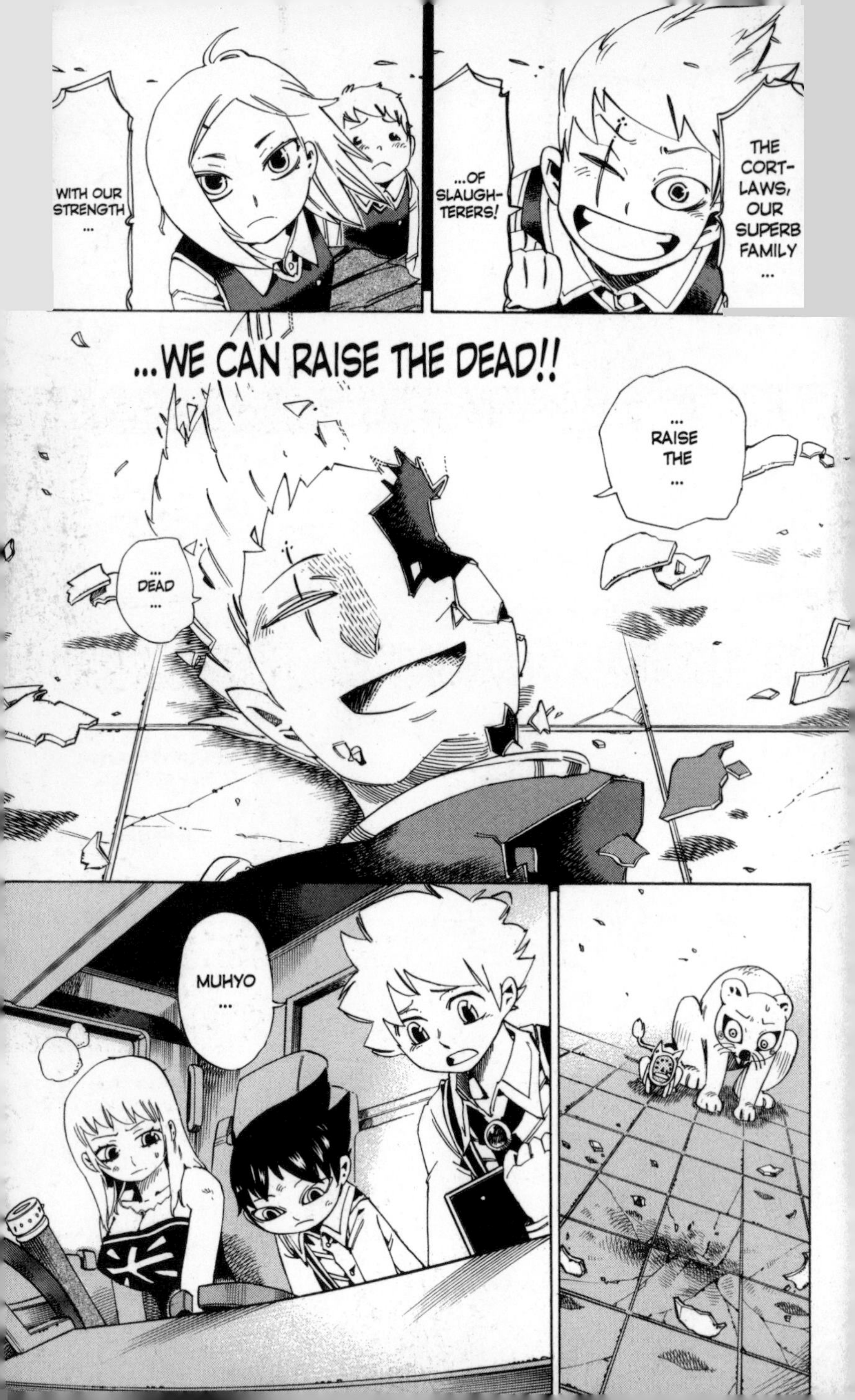
THE CORT-LAWS, OUR SUPERB FAMILY ...
...OF SLAUGHTERERS!
WITH OUR STRENGTH ...
...WE CAN RAISE THE DEAD!!
... RAISE THE ...
... DEAD ...
MUHYO ...

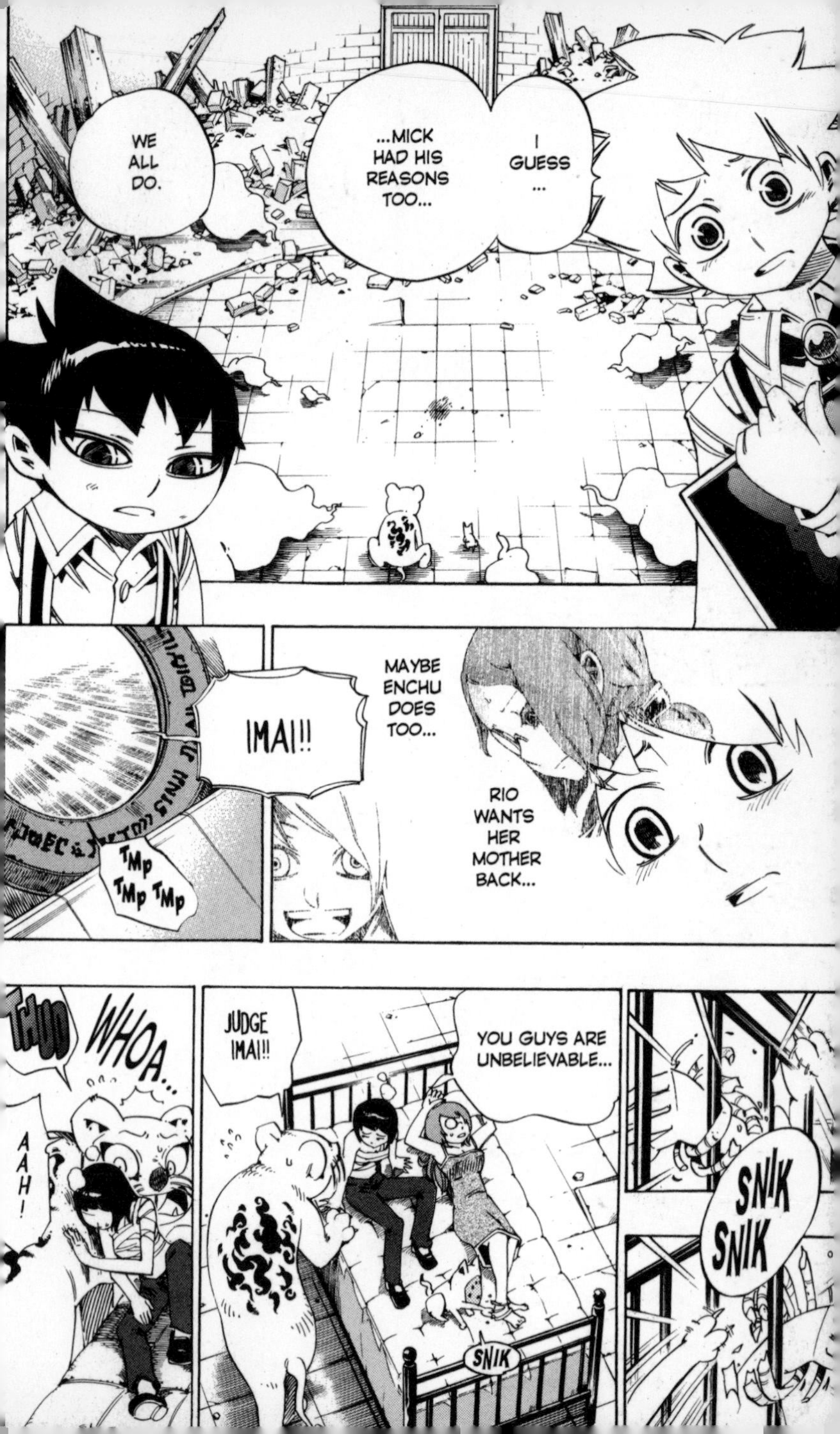
I GUESS ...
...MICK HAD HIS REASONS TOO...
WE ALL DO.
RIO WANTS HER MOTHER BACK...
MAYBE ENCHU DOES TOO...
IMAI!!
TMp TMp TMp
SNIK SNIK
YOU GUYS ARE UNBELIEVABLE...
JUDGE IMAI!!
SNIK
WHOA...
THUD
AAH!

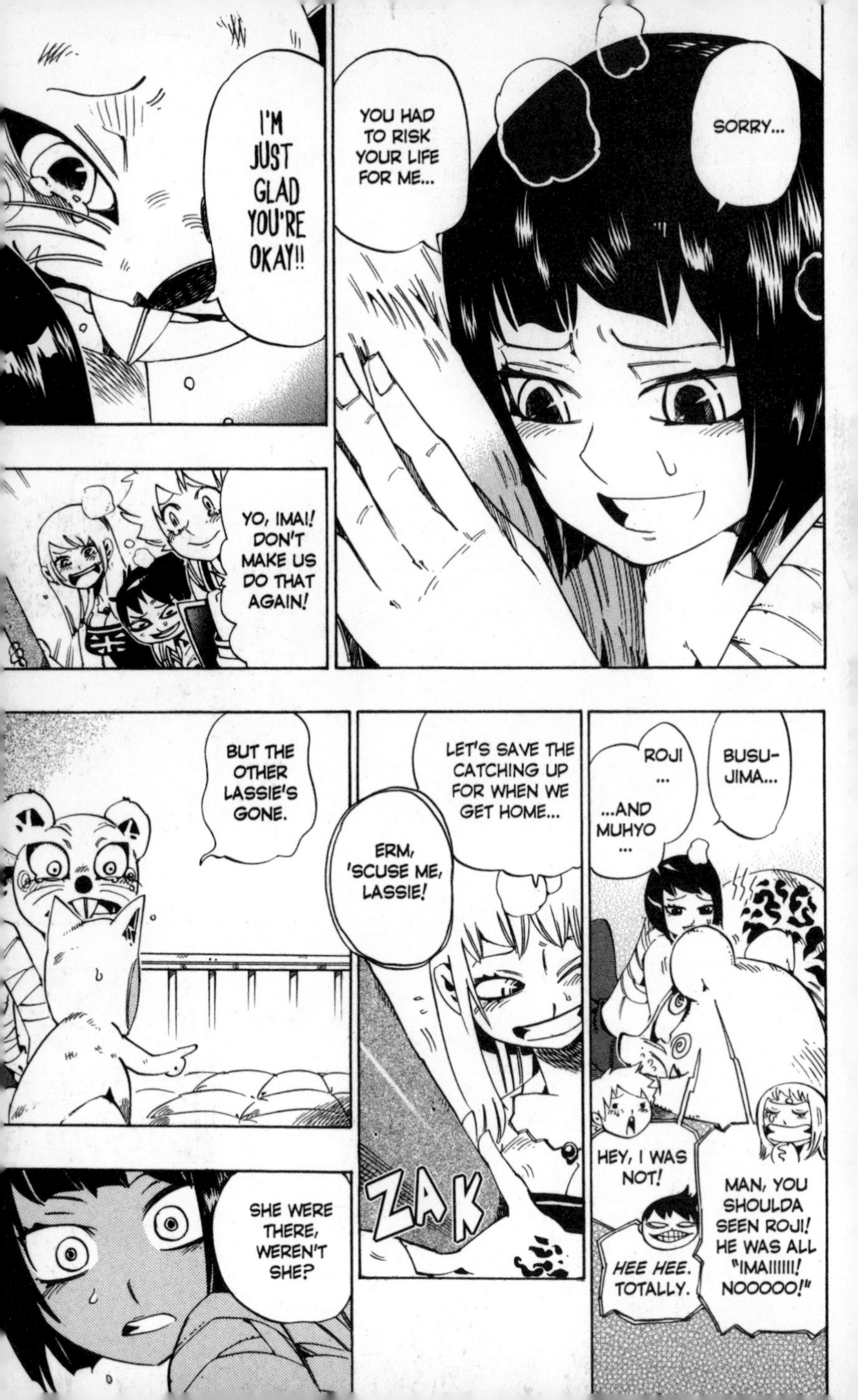
SORRY...
YOU HAD TO RISK YOUR LIFE FOR ME...
I'M JUST GLAD YOU'RE OKAY!!
YO, IMAI! DON'T MAKE US DO THAT AGAIN!
BUSU-JIMA...
ROJI ...
...AND MUHYO ...
MAN, YOU SHOULDA SEEN ROJI! HE WAS ALL "IMAIIIIII! NOOOOO!"
HEY, I WAS NOT!
HEE HEE. TOTALLY.
LET'S SAVE THE CATCHING UP FOR WHEN WE GET HOME...
ERM, 'SCUSE ME, LASSIE!
ZAK
BUT THE OTHER LASSIE'S GONE.
SHE WERE THERE, WEREN'T SHE?

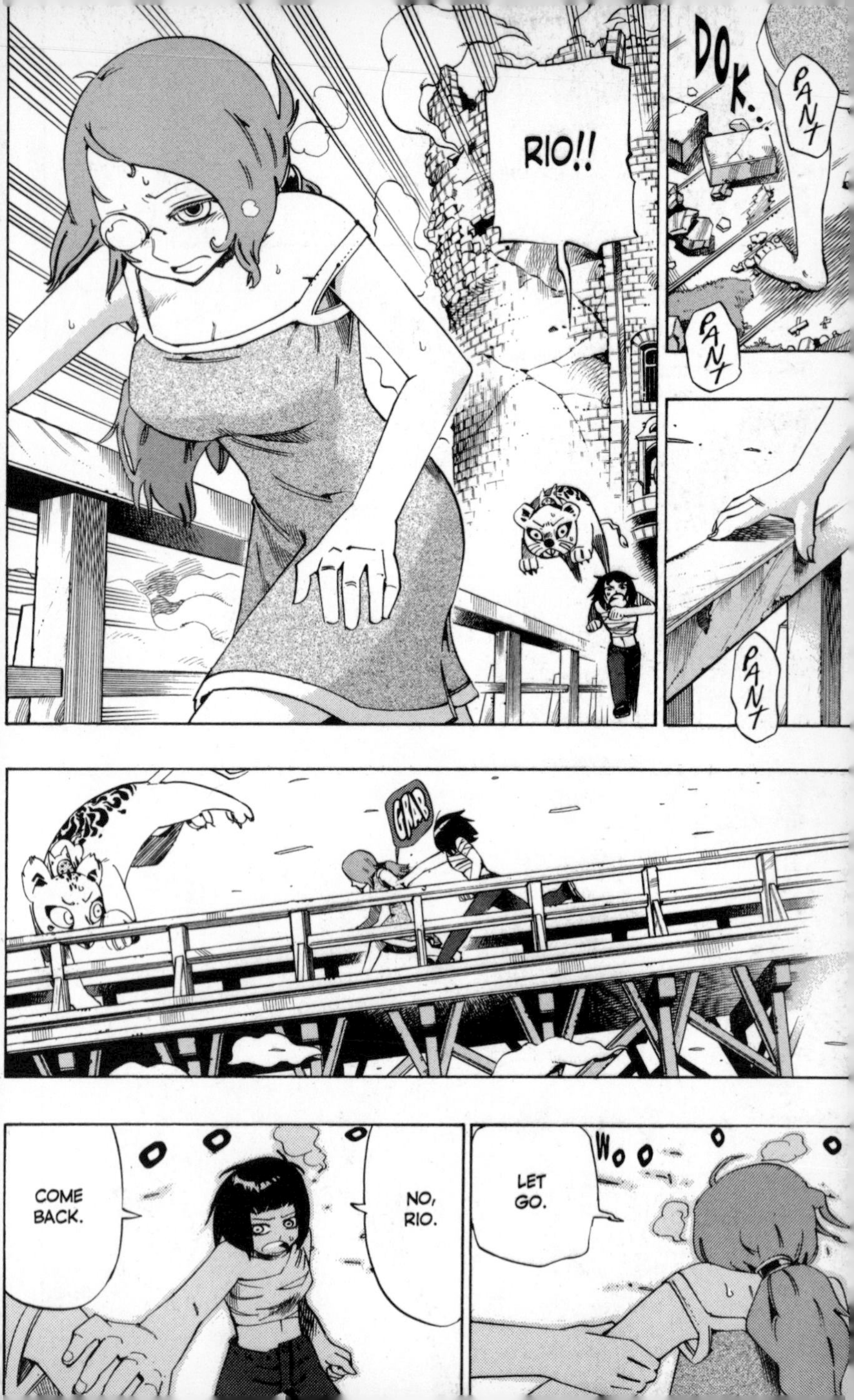
DOK...
PANT
PANT
PANT
RIO!!
GRAB
WOOOOO
LET GO.
NO, RIO.
OOO
COME BACK.

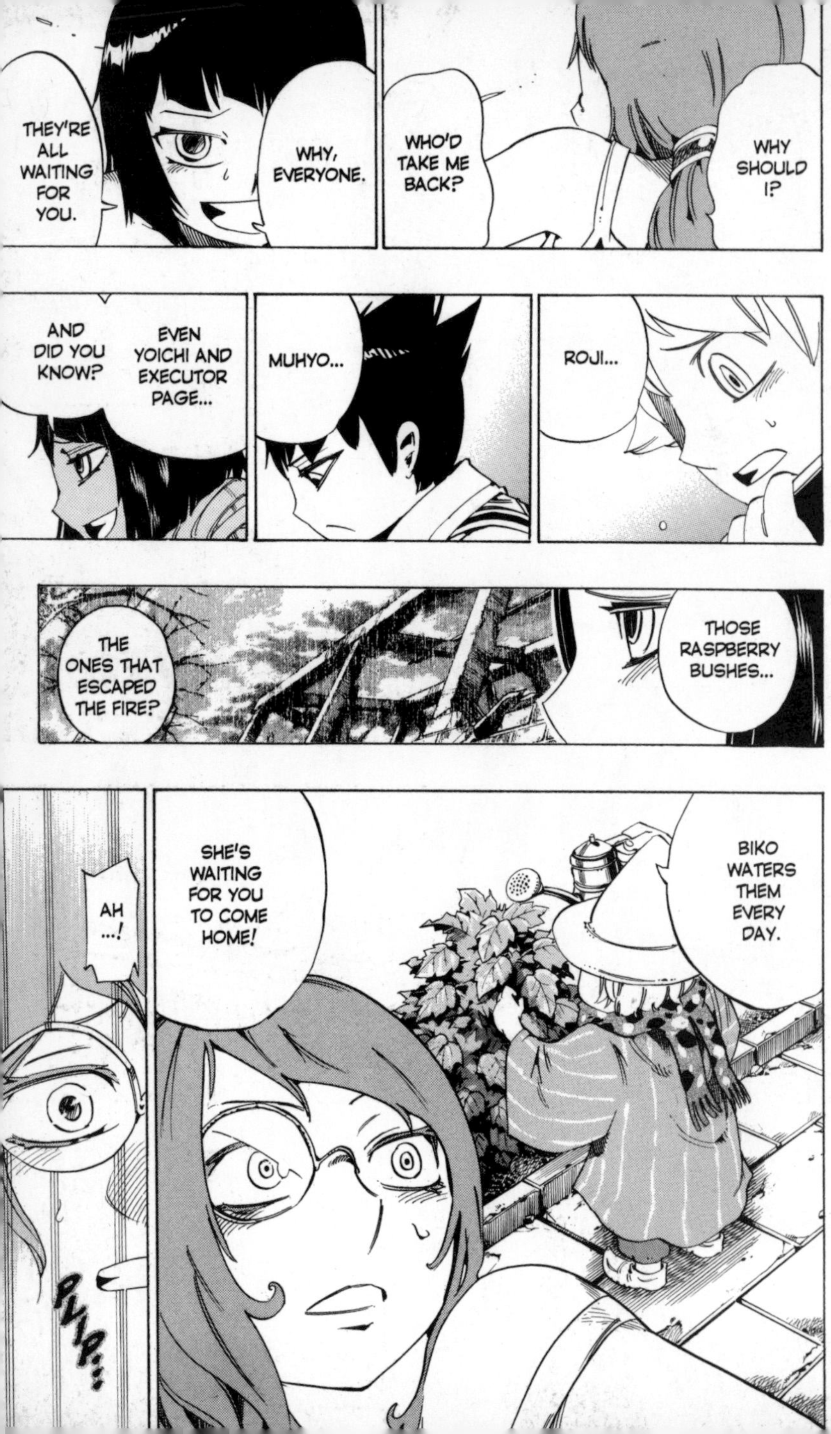
WHY SHOULD I?
WHO'D TAKE ME BACK?
WHY, EVERYONE.
THEY'RE ALL WAITING FOR YOU.
ROJI...
MUHYO...
EVEN YOICHI AND EXECUTOR PAGE...
AND DID YOU KNOW?
THOSE RASPBERRY BUSHES...
THE ONES THAT ESCAPED THE FIRE?
BIKO WATERS THEM EVERY DAY.
SHE'S WAITING FOR YOU TO COME HOME!
AH ...!
PLIP..

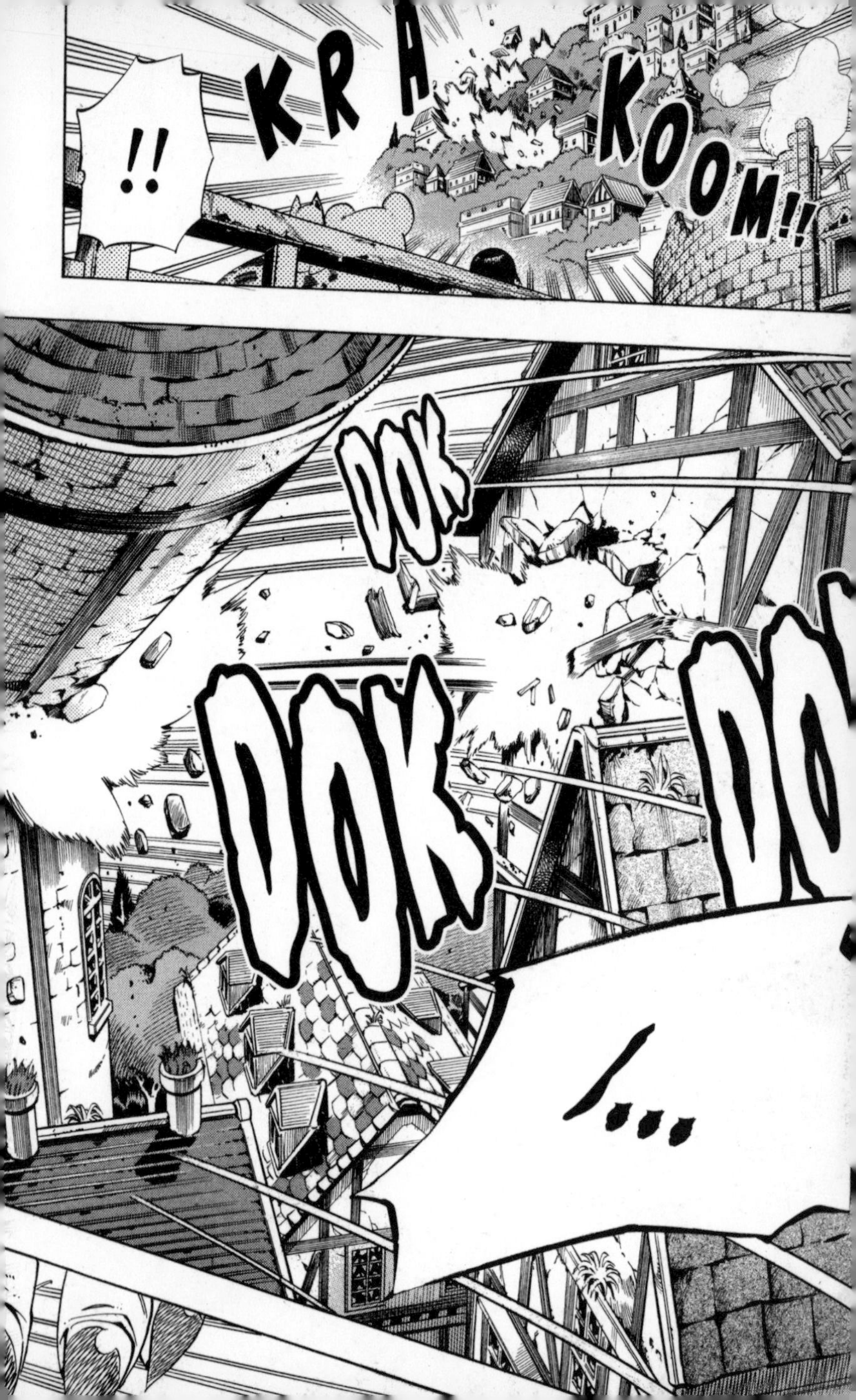
KRA KOOM!!
!!
DOK
DOK
DO
...

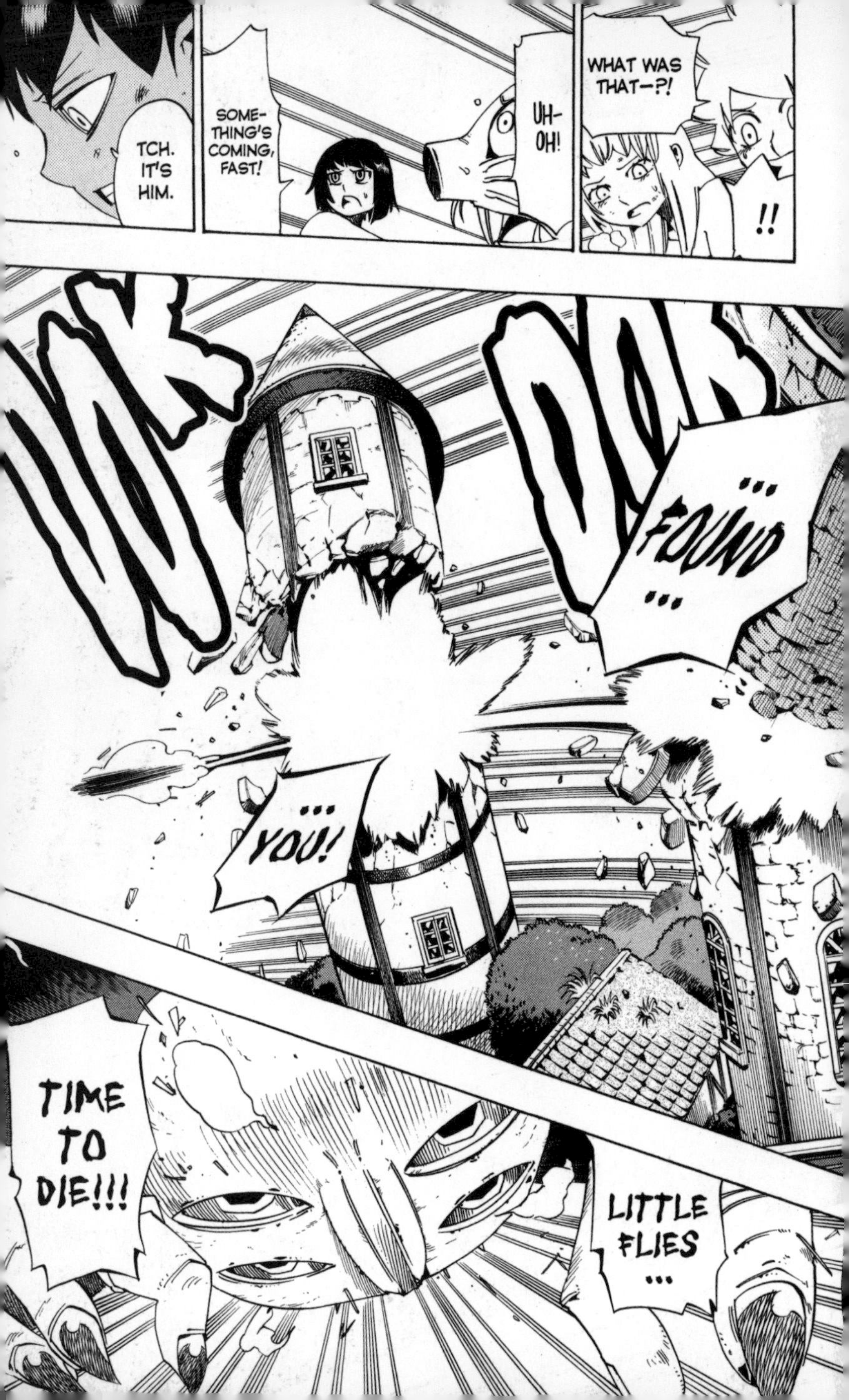
WHAT WAS THAT—?!
!!
UH-OH!
SOME-THING'S COMING, FAST!
TCH. IT'S HIM.
...FOUND...
...YOU!
LITTLE FLIES...
TIME TO DIE!!!

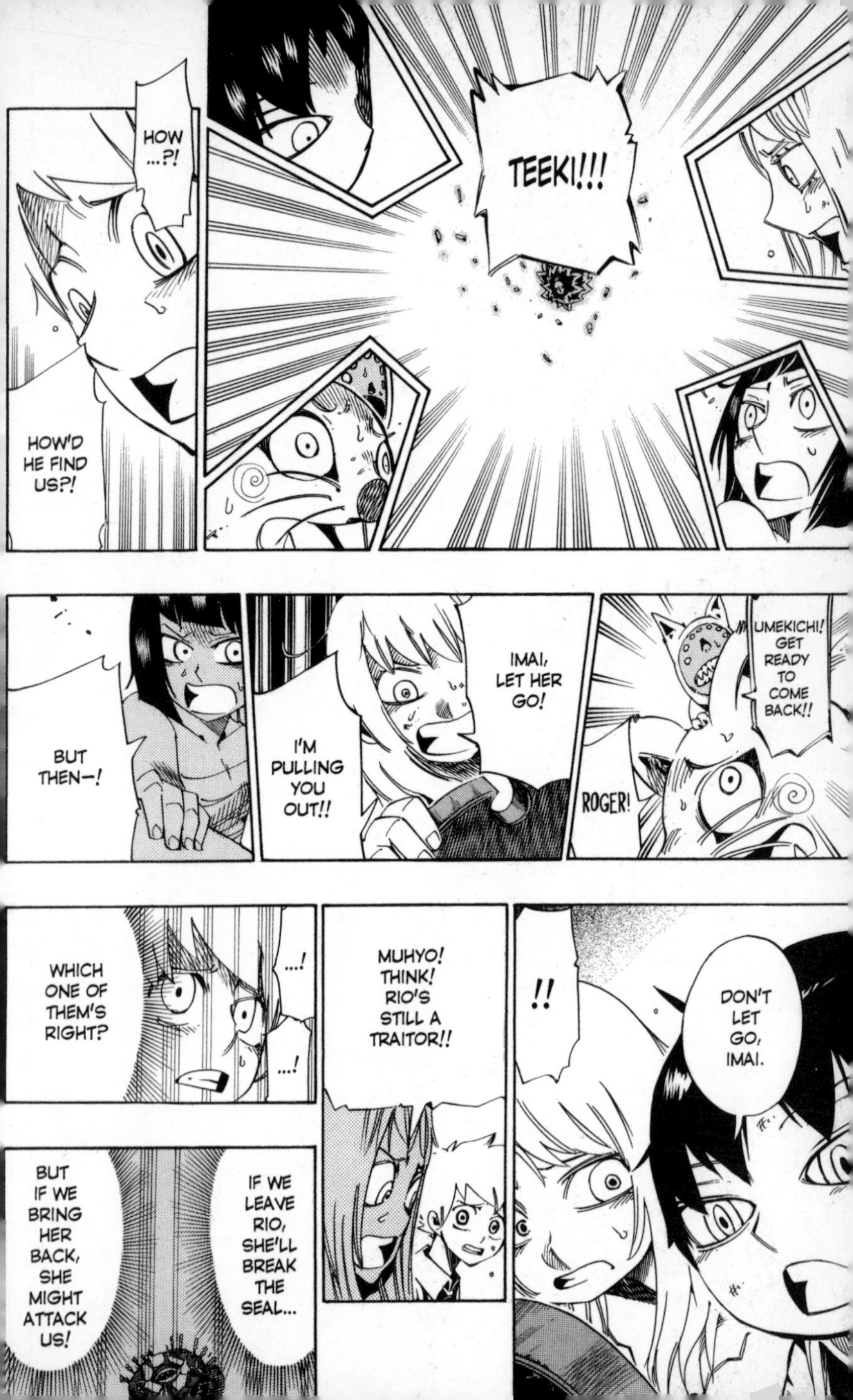
TEEKI!!!
HOW ...?!
HOW'D HE FIND US?!
UMEKICHI! GET READY TO COME BACK!!
ROGER!
IMAI, LET HER GO!
I'M PULLING YOU OUT!!
BUT THEN—!
DON'T LET GO, IMAI.
!!
MUHYO! THINK! RIO'S STILL A TRAITOR!!
...!
...!
WHICH ONE OF THEM'S RIGHT?
IF WE LEAVE RIO, SHE'LL BREAK THE SEAL...
BUT IF WE BRING HER BACK, SHE MIGHT ATTACK US!

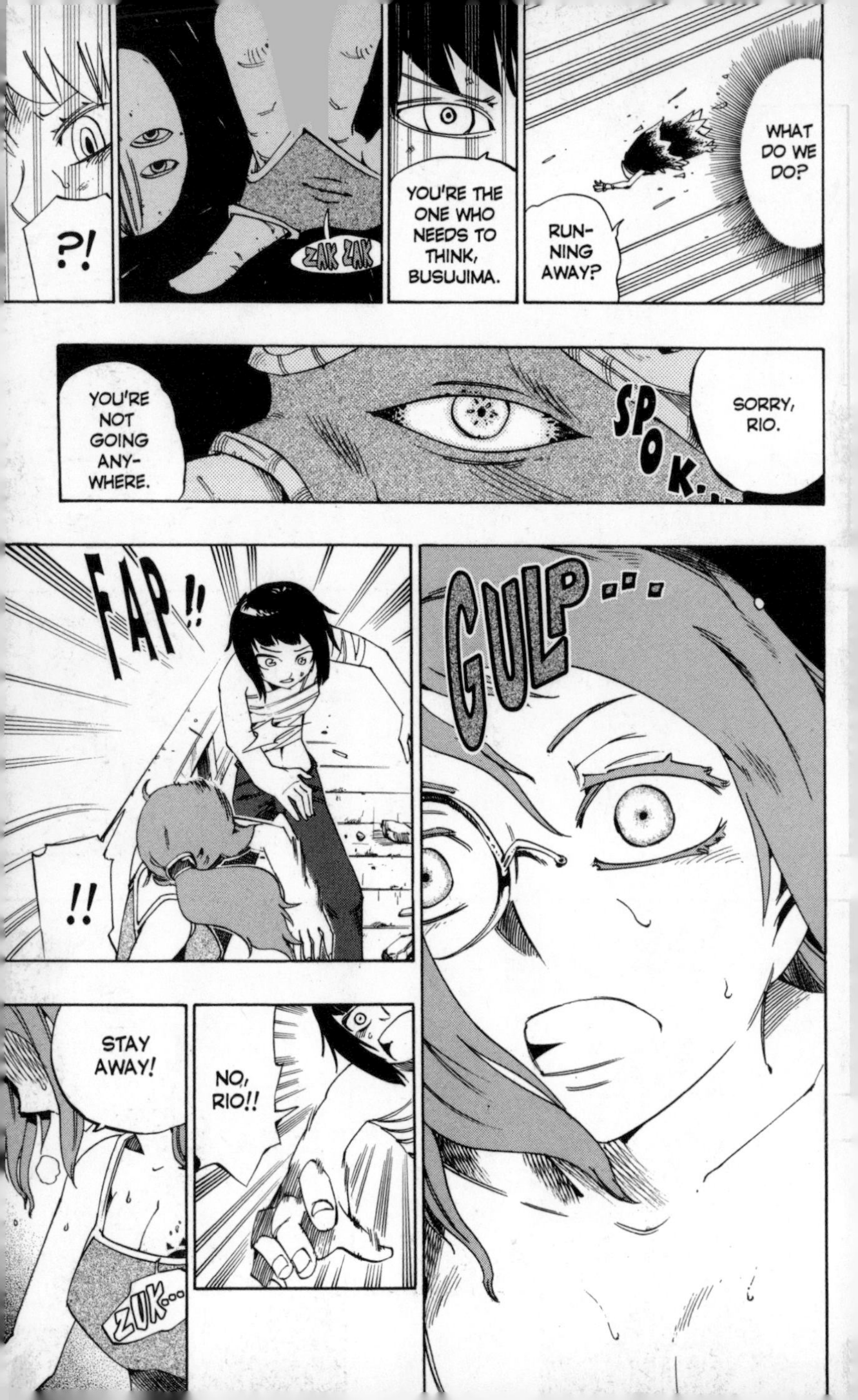
WHAT DO WE DO?
RUN-NING AWAY?
YOU'RE THE ONE WHO NEEDS TO THINK, BUSUJIMA.
ZAK ZAK
?!
SORRY, RIO.
SPOK...
YOU'RE NOT GOING ANY-WHERE.
GULP...
FAP!!
!!
NO, RIO!!
STAY AWAY!
ZUK...

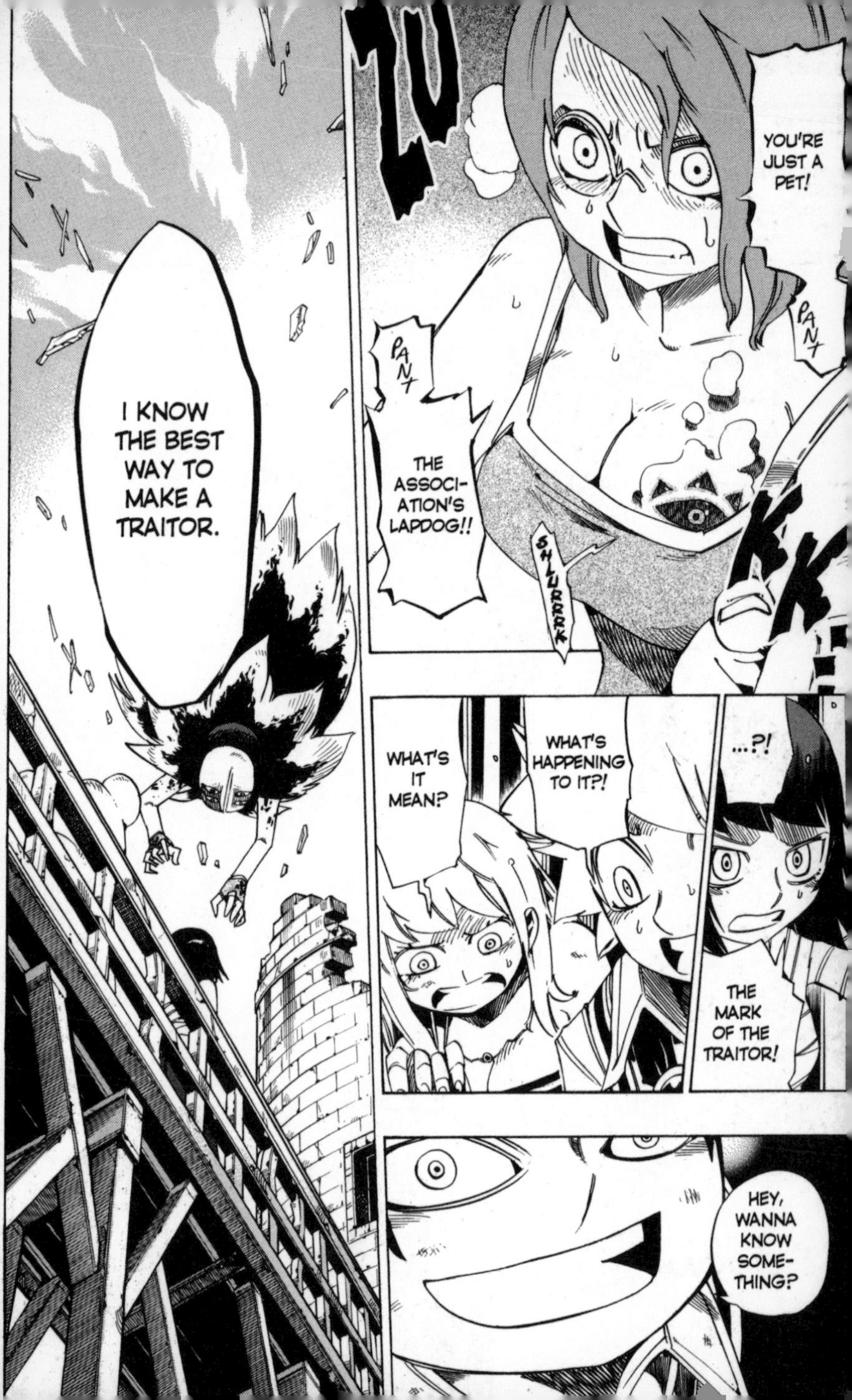
YOU'RE JUST A PET!
PANT
ZU
PANT
THE ASSOCI-ATION'S LAPDOG!!
KK
SHLURRRK
...?!
THE MARK OF THE TRAITOR!
WHAT'S HAPPENING TO IT?!
WHAT'S IT MEAN?
HEY, WANNA KNOW SOME-THING?
I KNOW THE BEST WAY TO MAKE A TRAITOR.

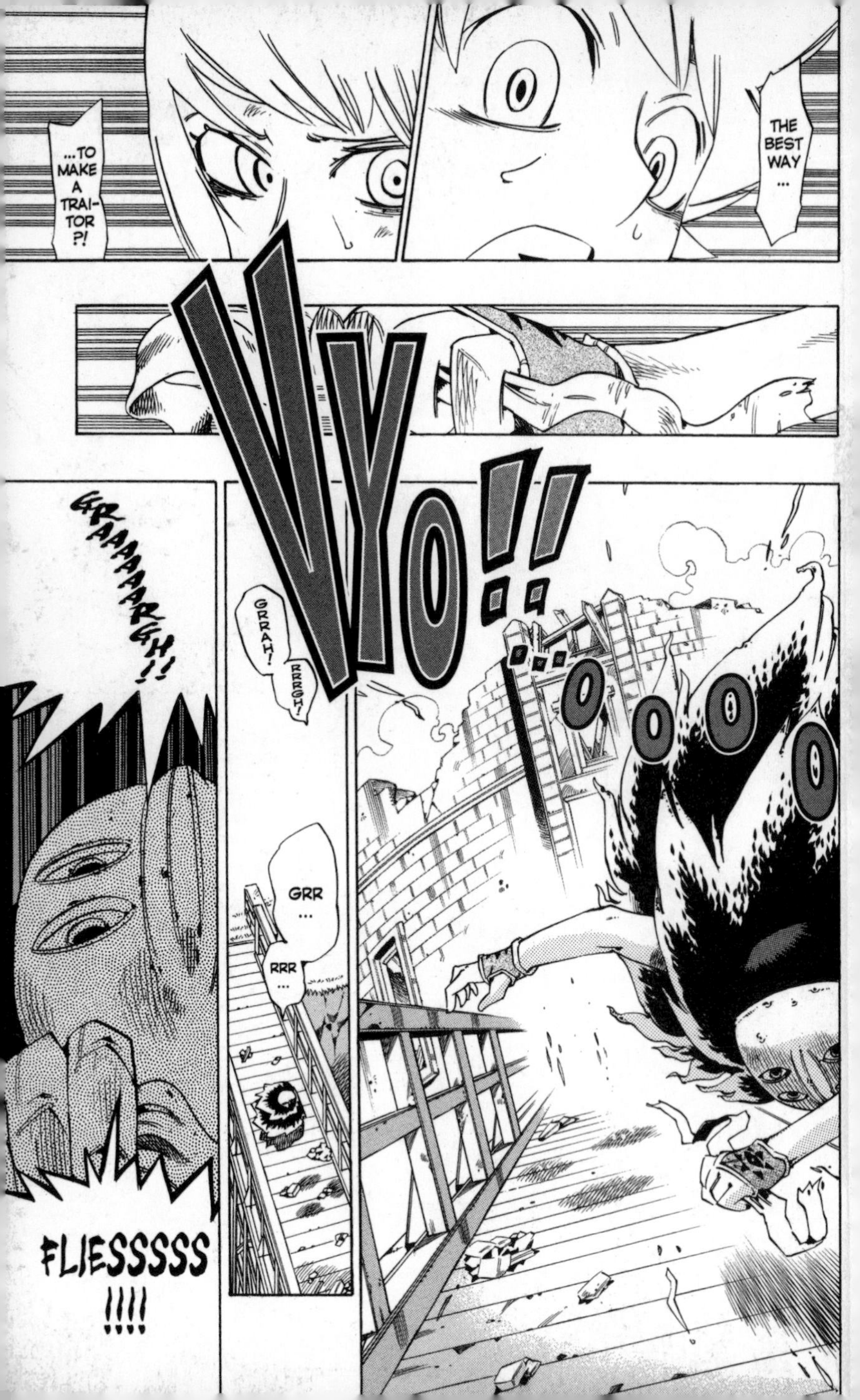
THE BEST WAY ...
...TO MAKE A TRAITOR?!
VVYO!!
...OOOO
GRRAH!
RRRGH!
GRR ...
RRR ...
GRAAAAAARGH!!
FLIESSSSS !!!!

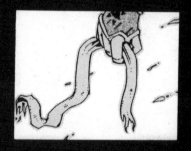

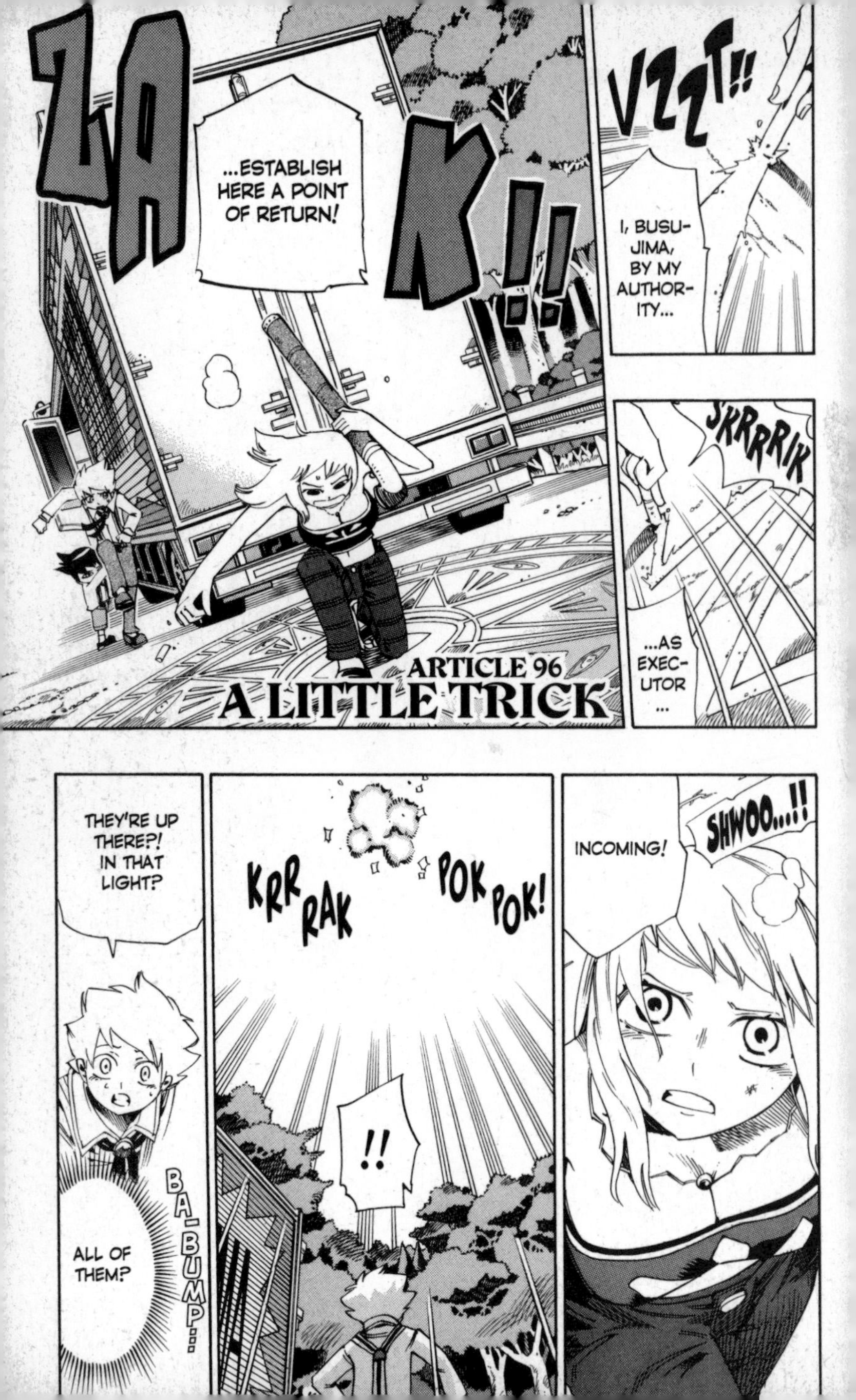
VZZT!!
I, BUSUJIMA, BY MY AUTHORITY...
SKRRRRIK
...AS EXECUTOR...
ZAK!!
...ESTABLISH HERE A POINT OF RETURN!
ARTICLE 96
A LITTLE TRICK
SHWOO...!!
INCOMING!
KRR RAK
POK POK!
!!
THEY'RE UP THERE?! IN THAT LIGHT?
BA-BUMP!!
ALL OF THEM?

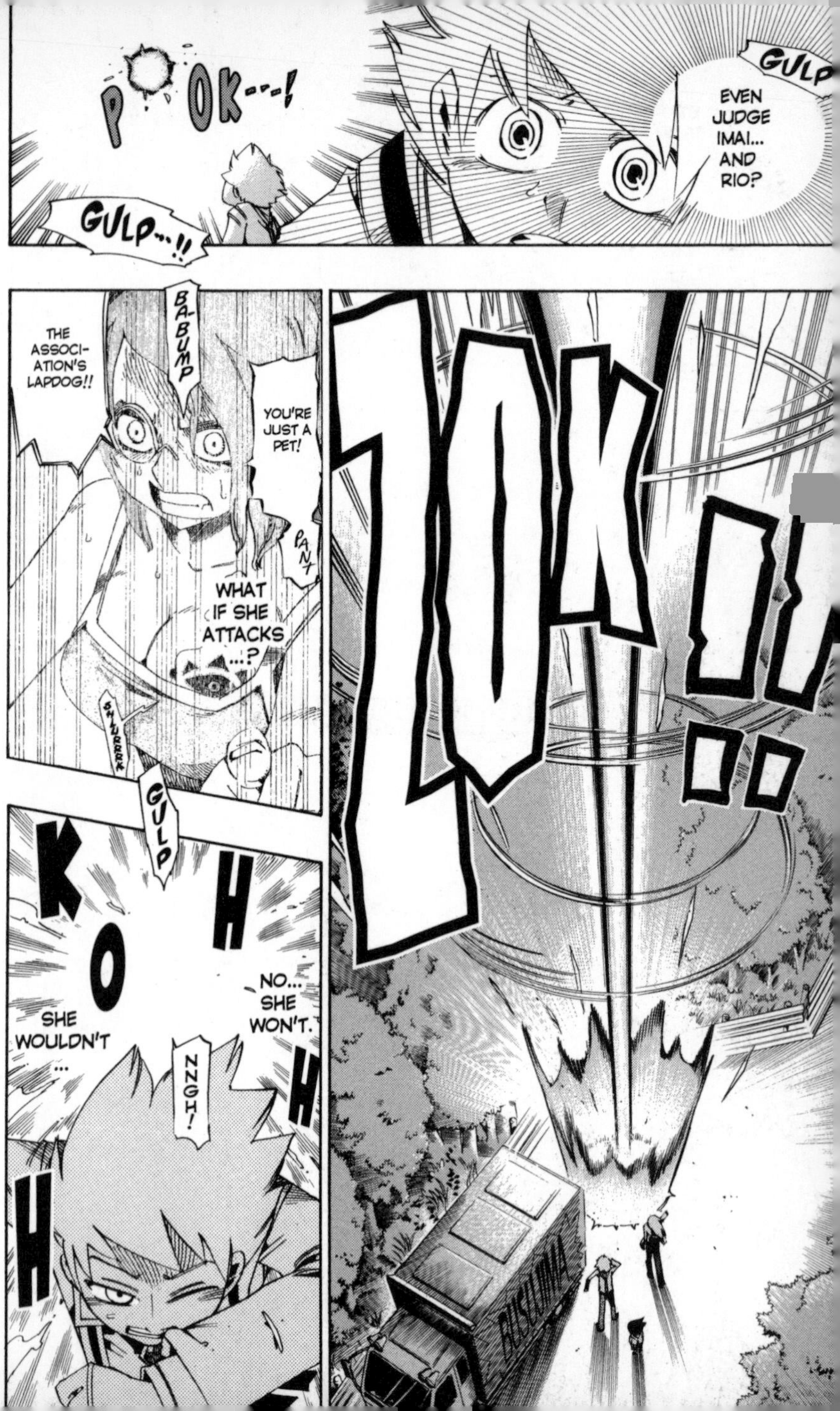
GULP
EVEN JUDGE IMAI... AND RIO?
POOK---!
GULP---!!
ZOKOO!!
BA-BUMP
YOU'RE JUST A PET!
THE ASSOCIATION'S LAPDOG!!
PANT
WHAT IF SHE ATTACKS ...?
SHWURRRK
GULP
KOHHHH
NO... SHE WON'T.
NNGH!
SHE WOULDN'T ...

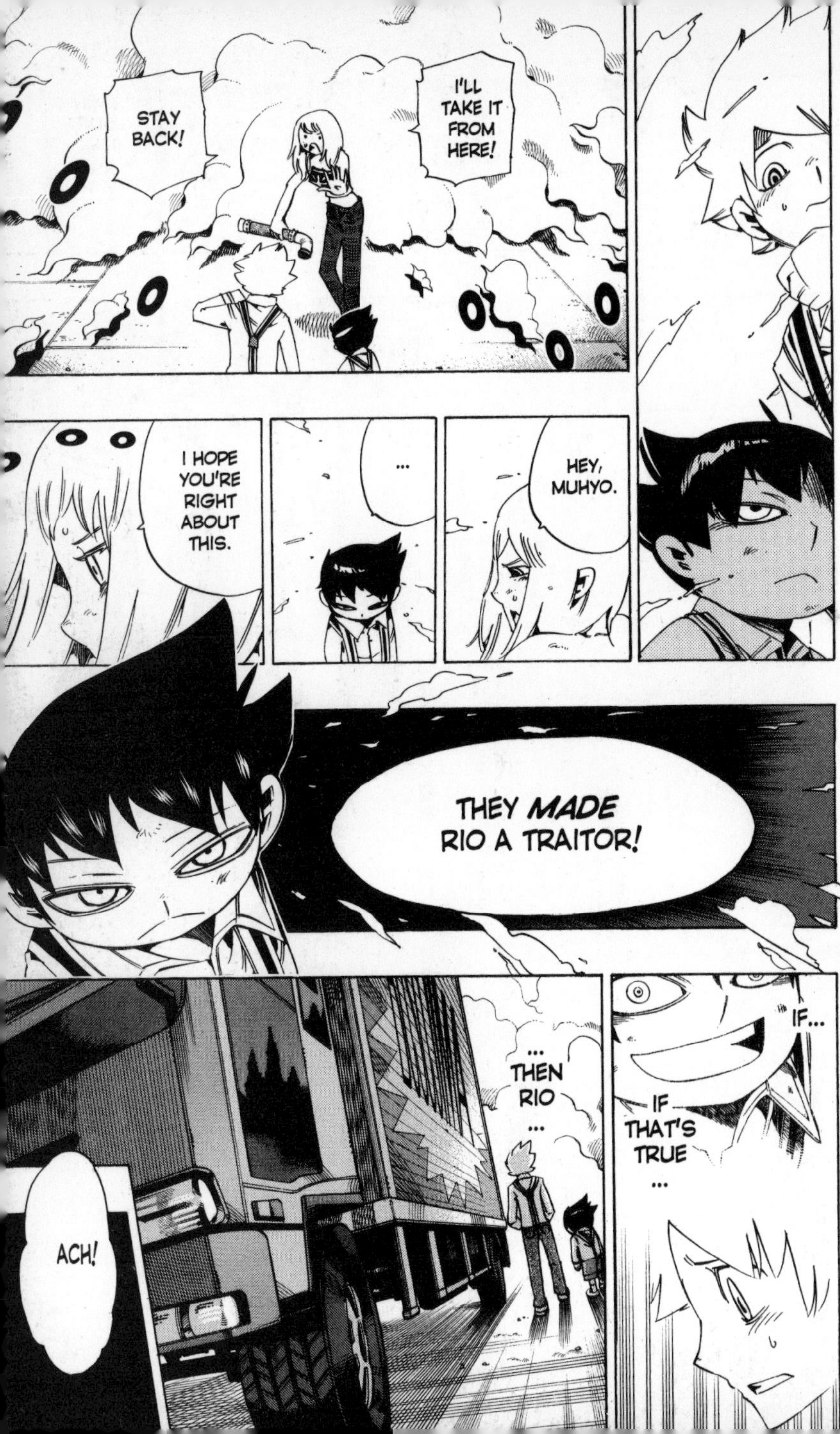
I'LL TAKE IT FROM HERE!
STAY BACK!
HEY, MUHYO.
...
I HOPE YOU'RE RIGHT ABOUT THIS.
THEY *MADE* RIO A TRAITOR!
IF...
IF THAT'S TRUE ...
... THEN RIO ...
ACH!

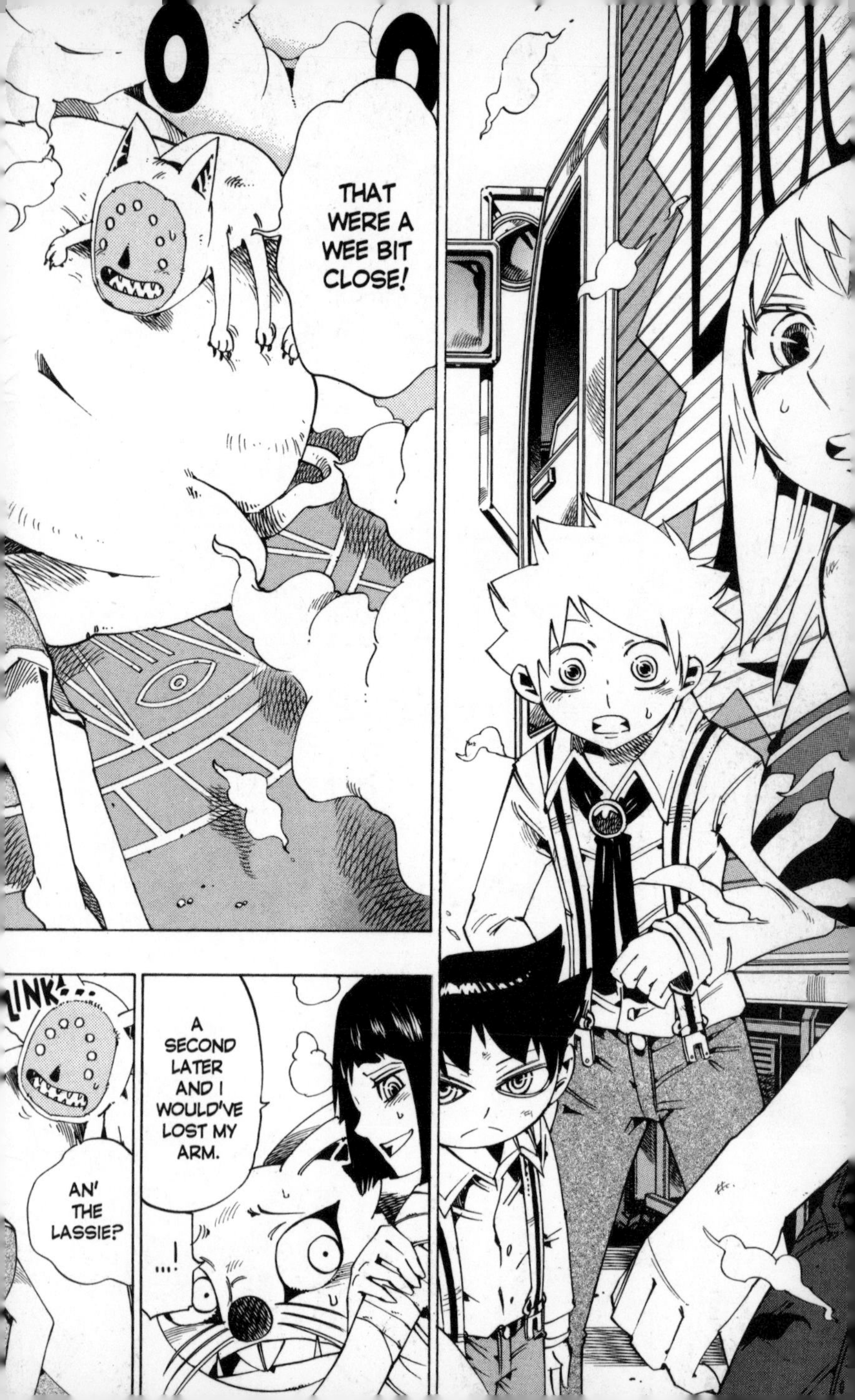
THAT WERE A WEE BIT CLOSE!
A SECOND LATER AND I WOULD'VE LOST MY ARM.
...!
LINK...
AN' THE LASSIE?

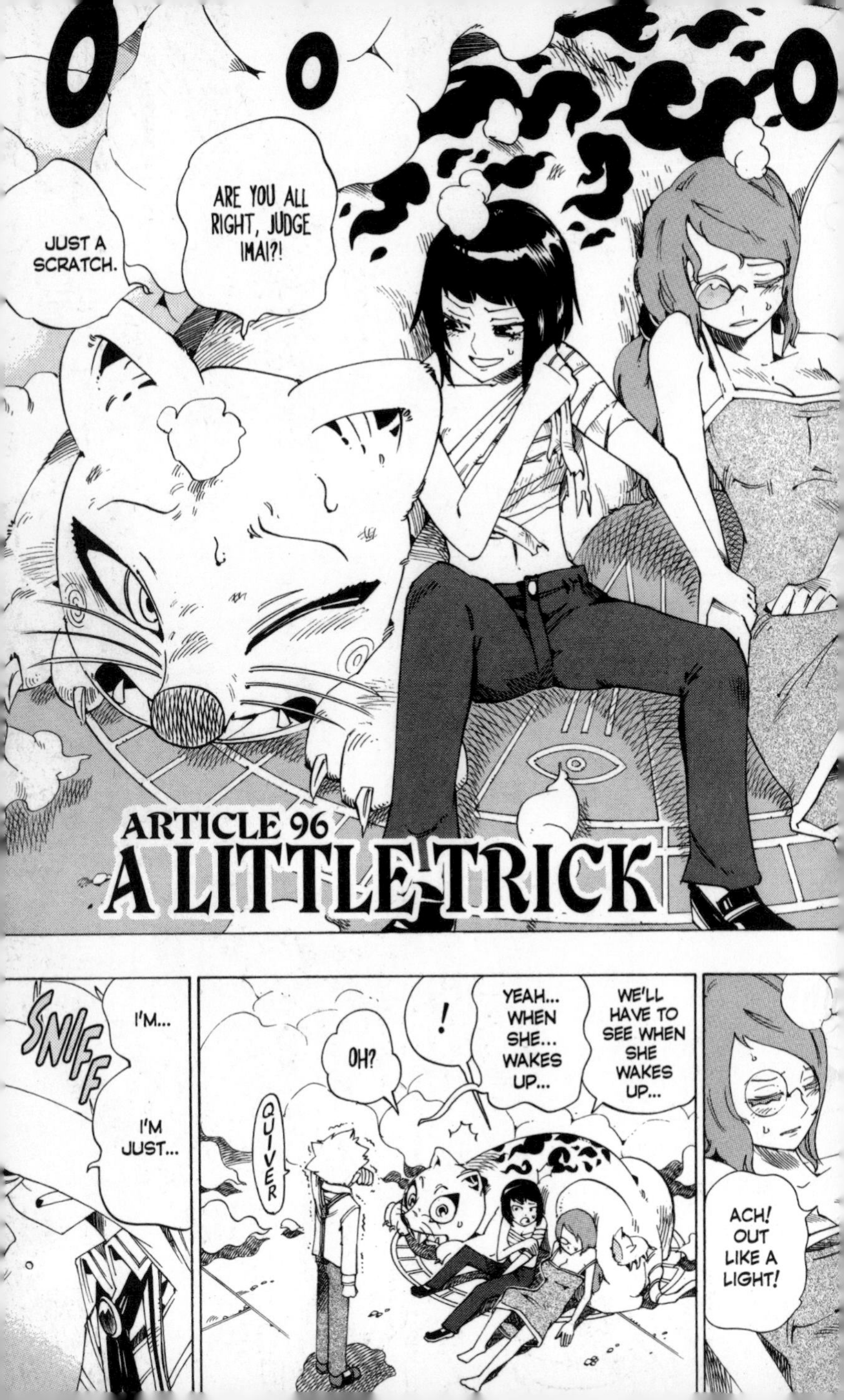
ARE YOU ALL RIGHT, JUDGE IMAI?!
JUST A SCRATCH.
ARTICLE 96
A LITTLE TRICK
ACH! OUT LIKE A LIGHT!
WE'LL HAVE TO SEE WHEN SHE WAKES UP...
YEAH... WHEN SHE... WAKES UP...
!
OH?
QUIVER
I'M...
SNIFF
I'M JUST...

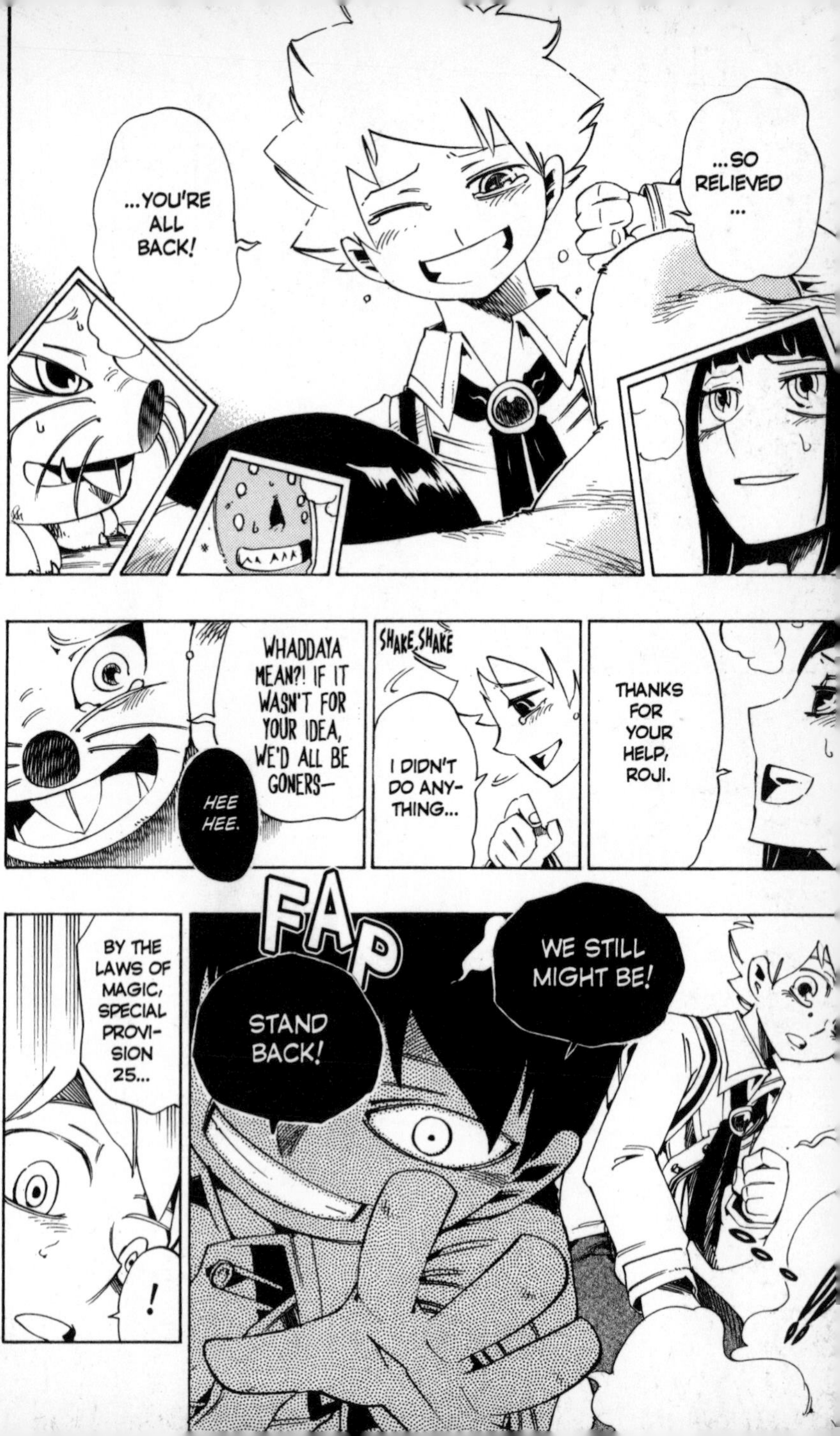
...SO RELIEVED ...
...YOU'RE ALL BACK!
THANKS FOR YOUR HELP, ROJI.
SHAKE, SHAKE
I DIDN'T DO ANYTHING...
WHADDAYA MEAN?! IF IT WASN'T FOR YOUR IDEA, WE'D ALL BE GONERS—
HEE HEE.
FAP
WE STILL MIGHT BE!
STAND BACK!
BY THE LAWS OF MAGIC, SPECIAL PROVISION 25...
!

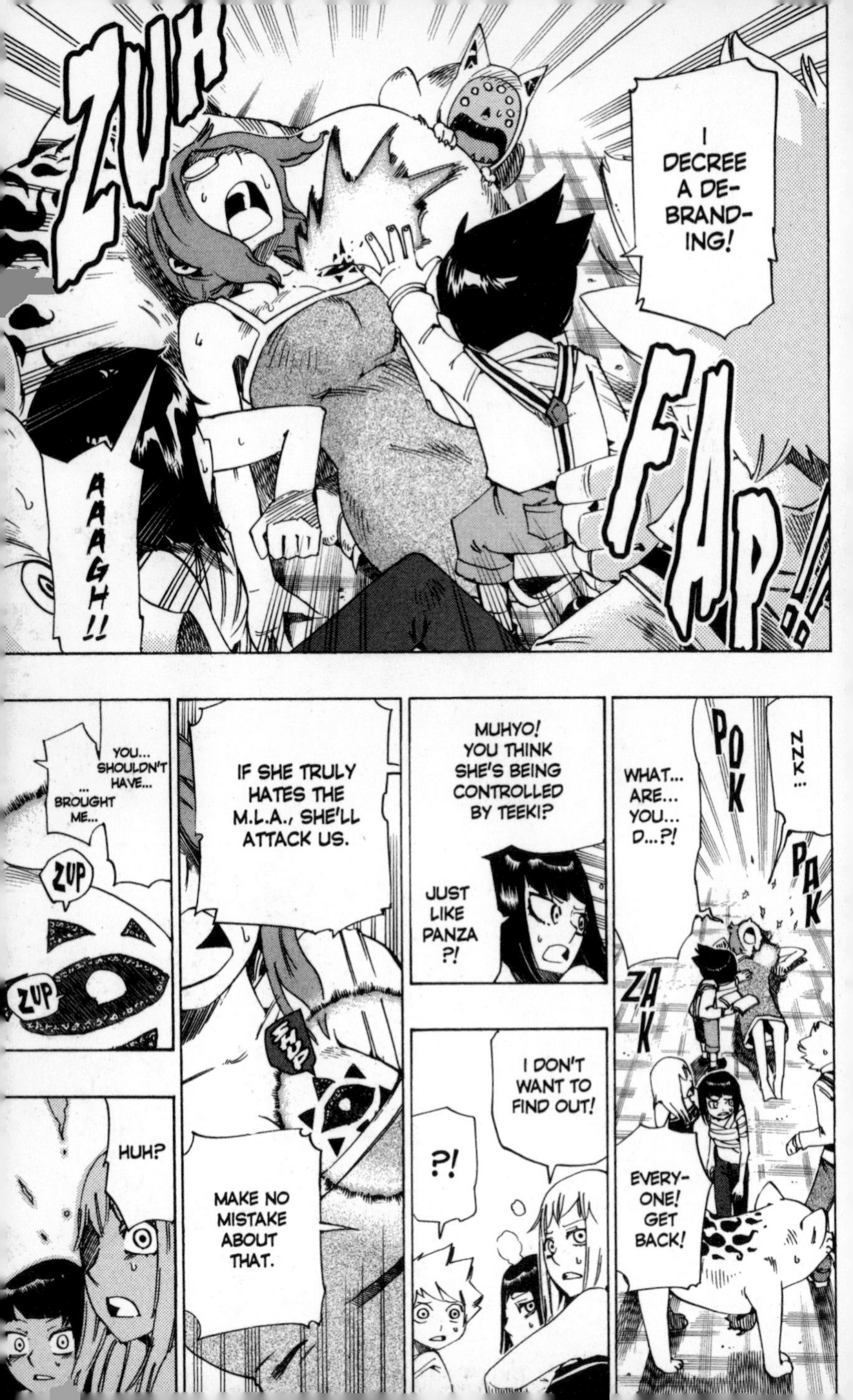
I DECREE A DE-BRANDING!
ZUH
FAP!!
AAAAGH!!
NNK...
POK
WHAT... ARE... YOU... D...?!
PAK
ZAK
EVERY-ONE! GET BACK!
MUHYO! YOU THINK SHE'S BEING CONTROLLED BY TEEKI?
JUST LIKE PANZA?!
I DON'T WANT TO FIND OUT!
?!
IF SHE TRULY HATES THE M.L.A., SHE'LL ATTACK US.
MAKE NO MISTAKE ABOUT THAT.
YOU... SHOULDN'T HAVE... ...BROUGHT ME...
ZUP
ZUP
HUH?

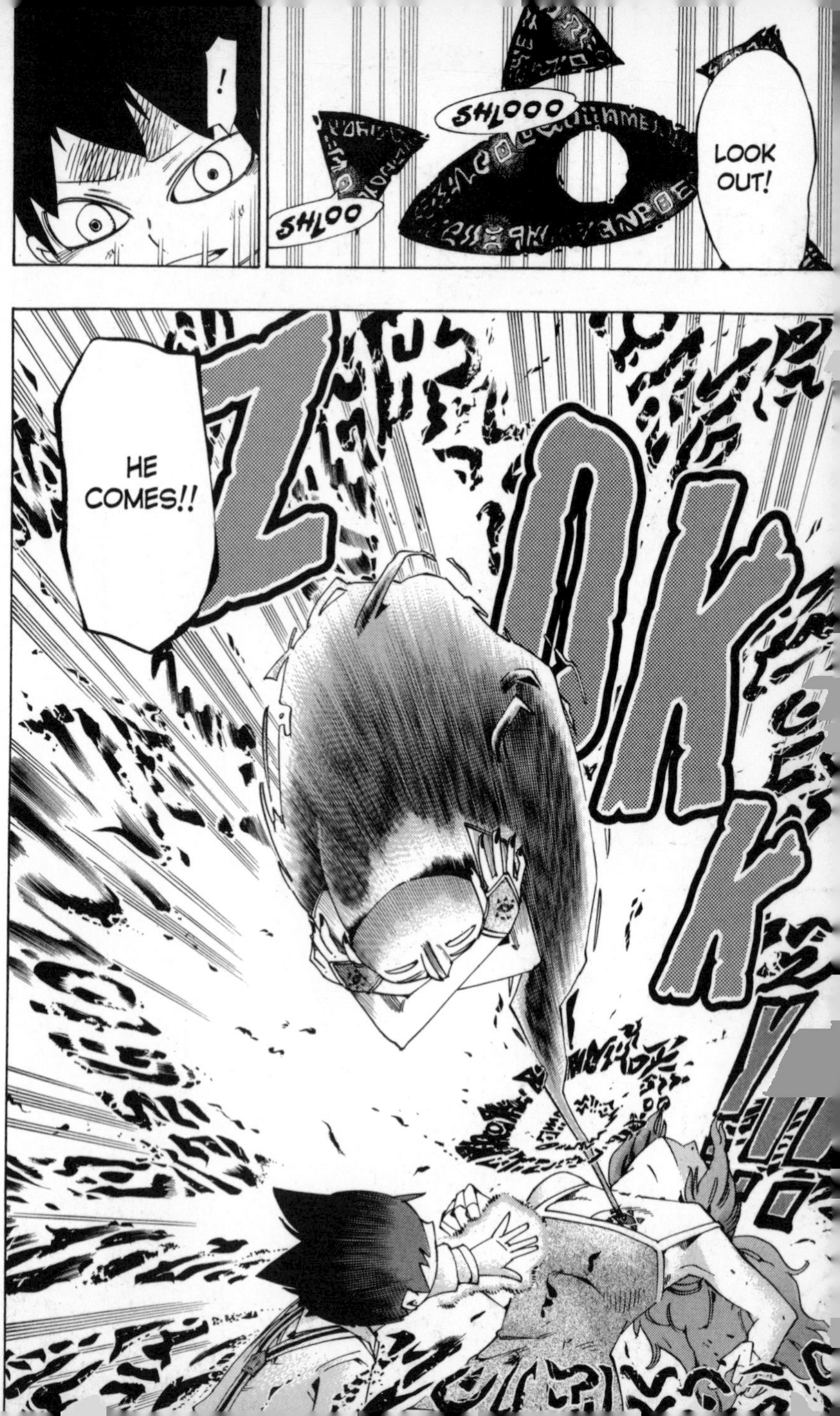
LOOK OUT!
SHLOOO
SHLOO
!
HE COMES!!

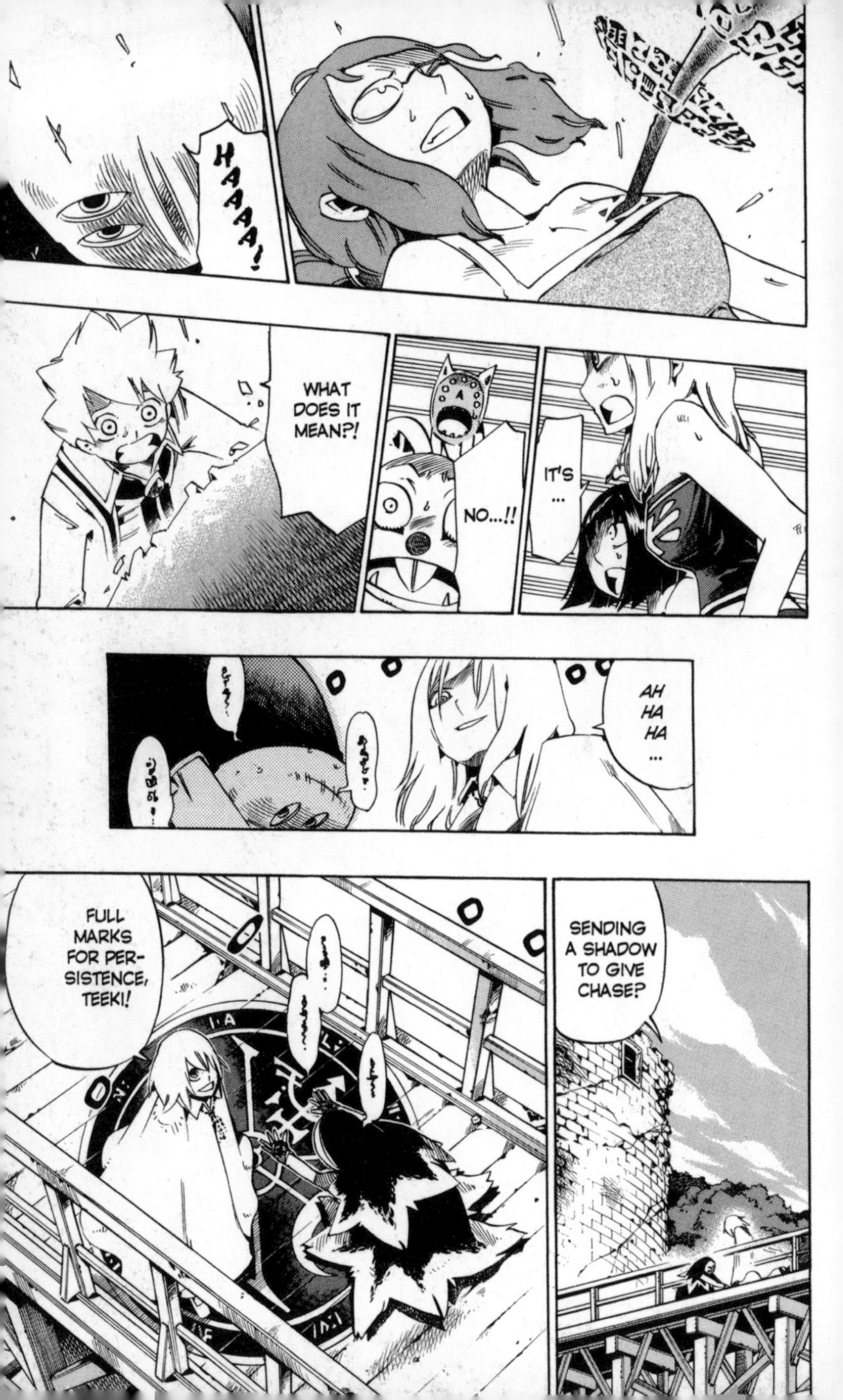
HAAAA!
IT'S ...
NO...!!
WHAT DOES IT MEAN?!
AH HA HA ...
SENDING A SHADOW TO GIVE CHASE?
FULL MARKS FOR PER-SISTENCE, TEEKI!

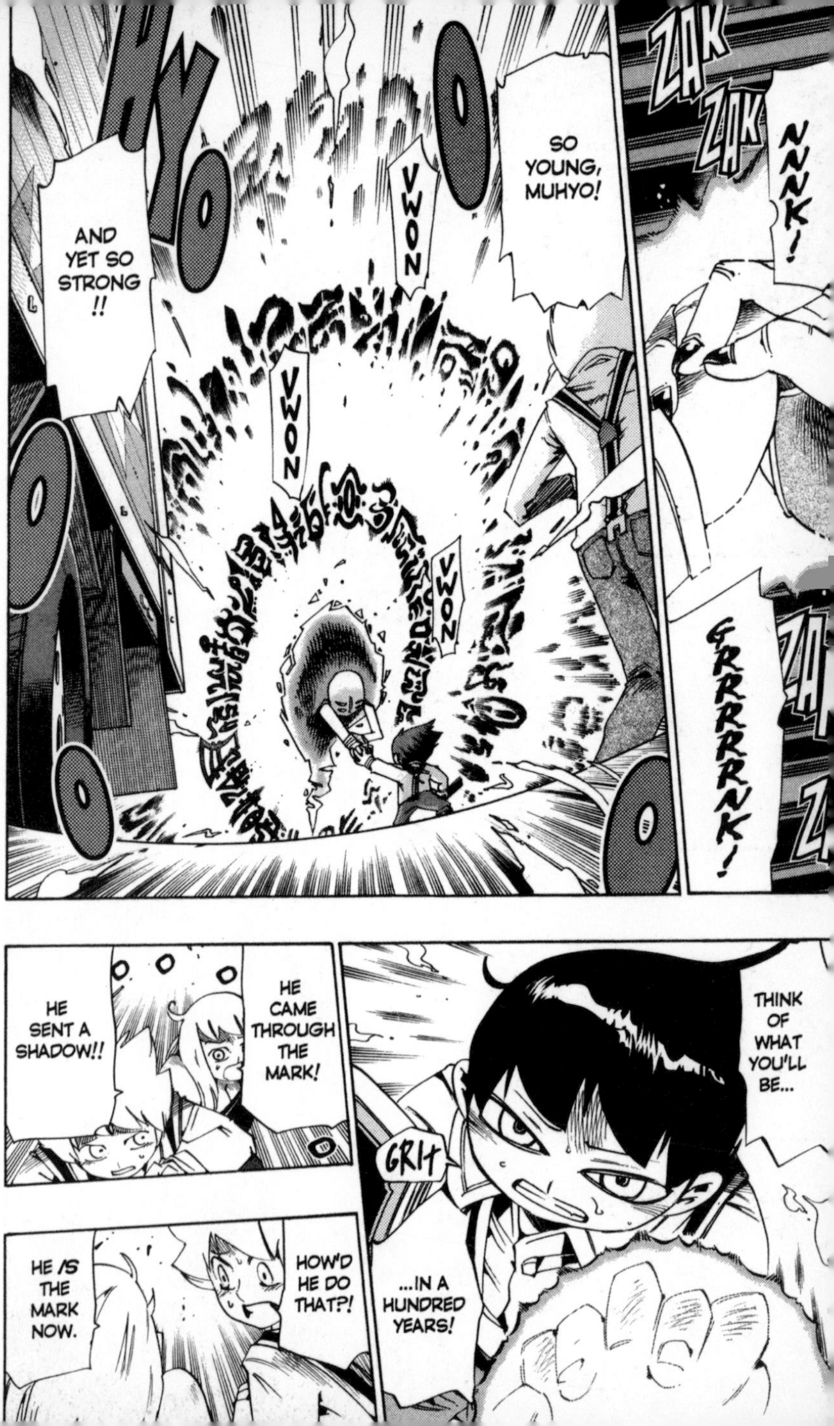
ZAK
ZAK
NNNK!
GRRRRRNK!
SO YOUNG, MUHYO!
VWON
HYO
AND YET SO STRONG!!
VWON
VWON
THINK OF WHAT YOU'LL BE...
GRIT
...IN A HUNDRED YEARS!
HE CAME THROUGH THE MARK!
HE SENT A SHADOW!!
HOW'D HE DO THAT?!
HE IS THE MARK NOW.

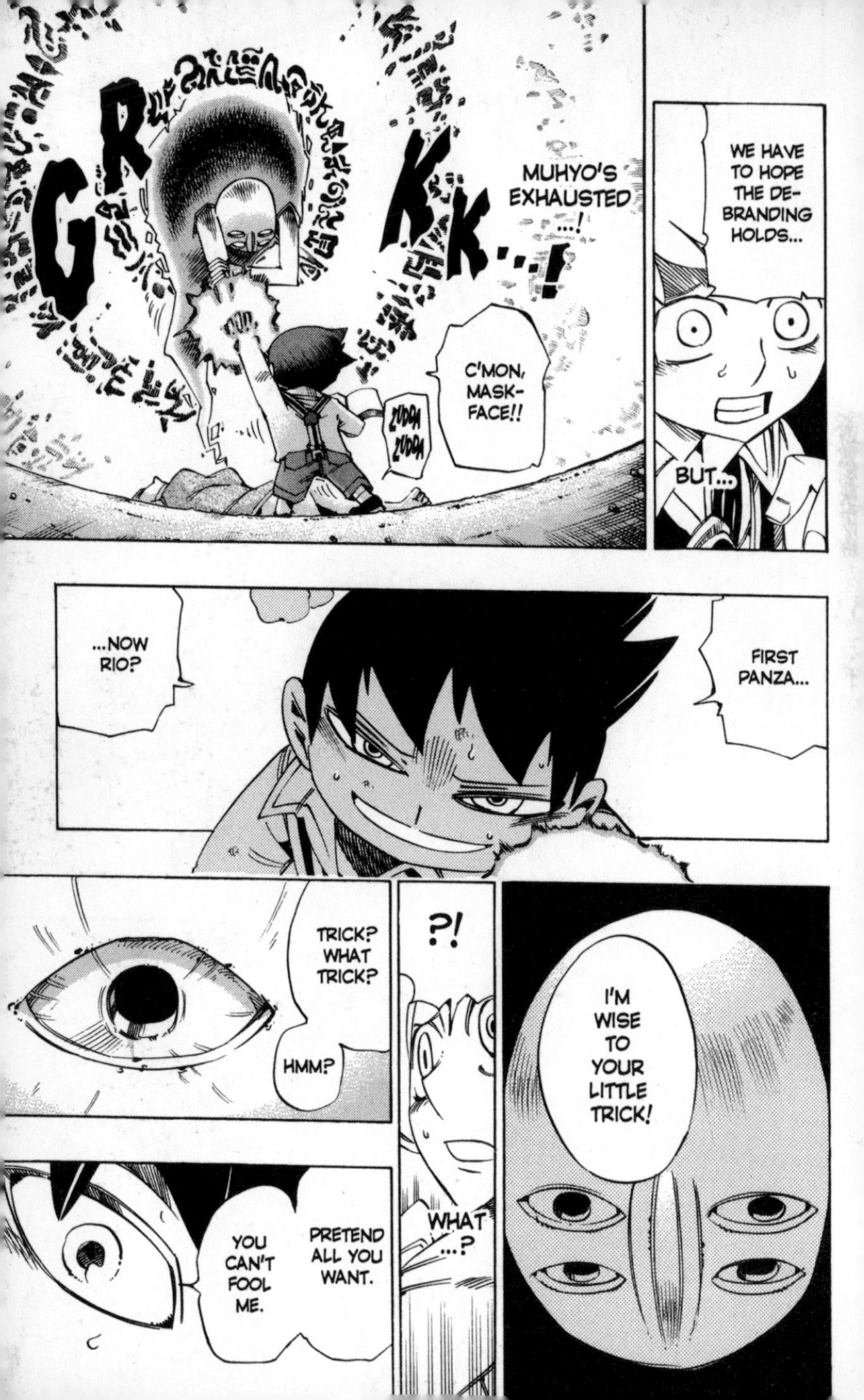
WE HAVE TO HOPE THE DE-BRANDING HOLDS...
BUT...
MUHYO'S EXHAUSTED ...!
GRKK...!
C'MON, MASK-FACE!!
ZUDDA ZUDDA
FIRST PANZA...
...NOW RIO?
I'M WISE TO YOUR LITTLE TRICK!
?!
WHAT ...?
TRICK? WHAT TRICK?
HMM?
PRETEND ALL YOU WANT.
YOU CAN'T FOOL ME.

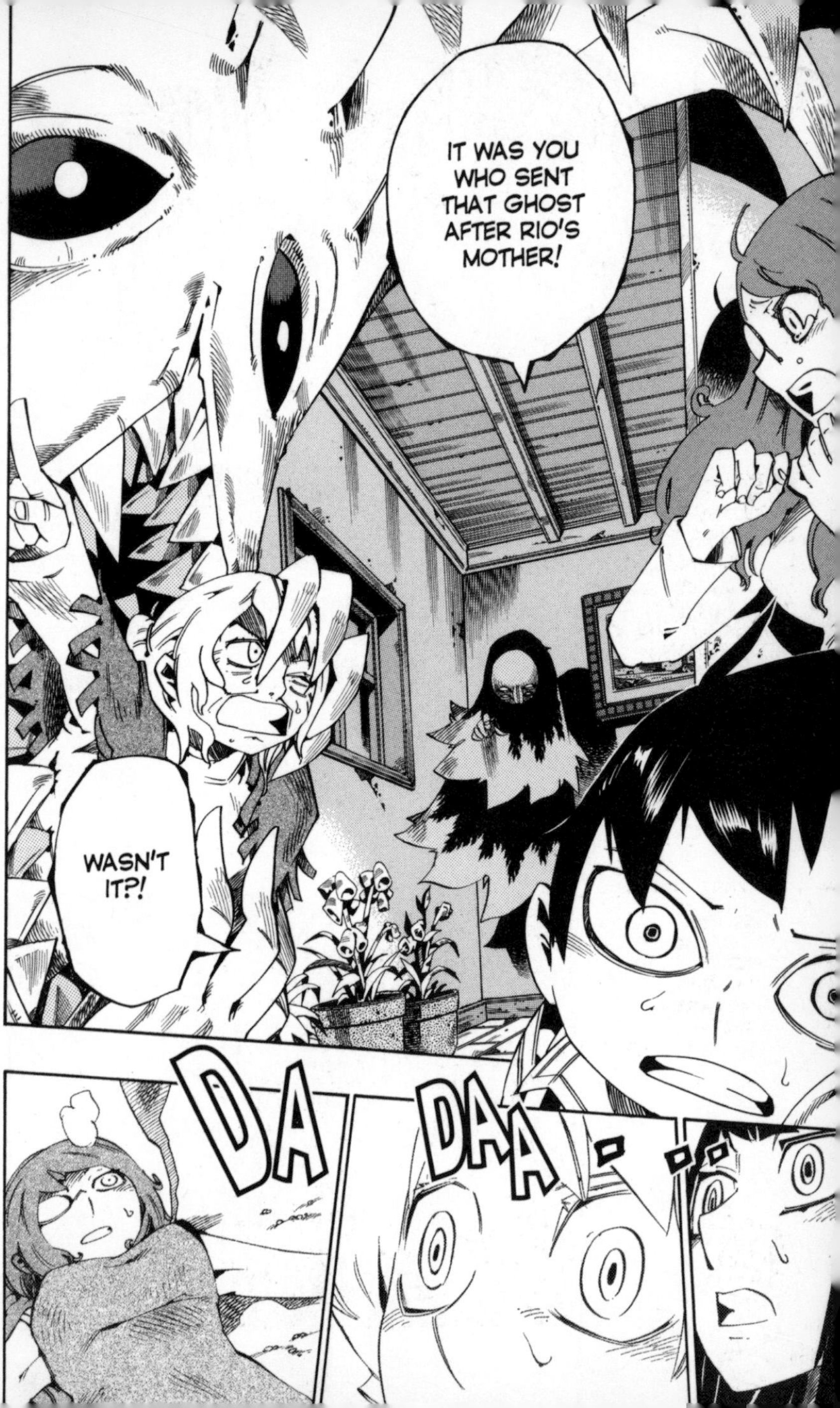
IT WAS YOU WHO SENT THAT GHOST AFTER RIO'S MOTHER!
WASN'T IT?!
DA
DAA...

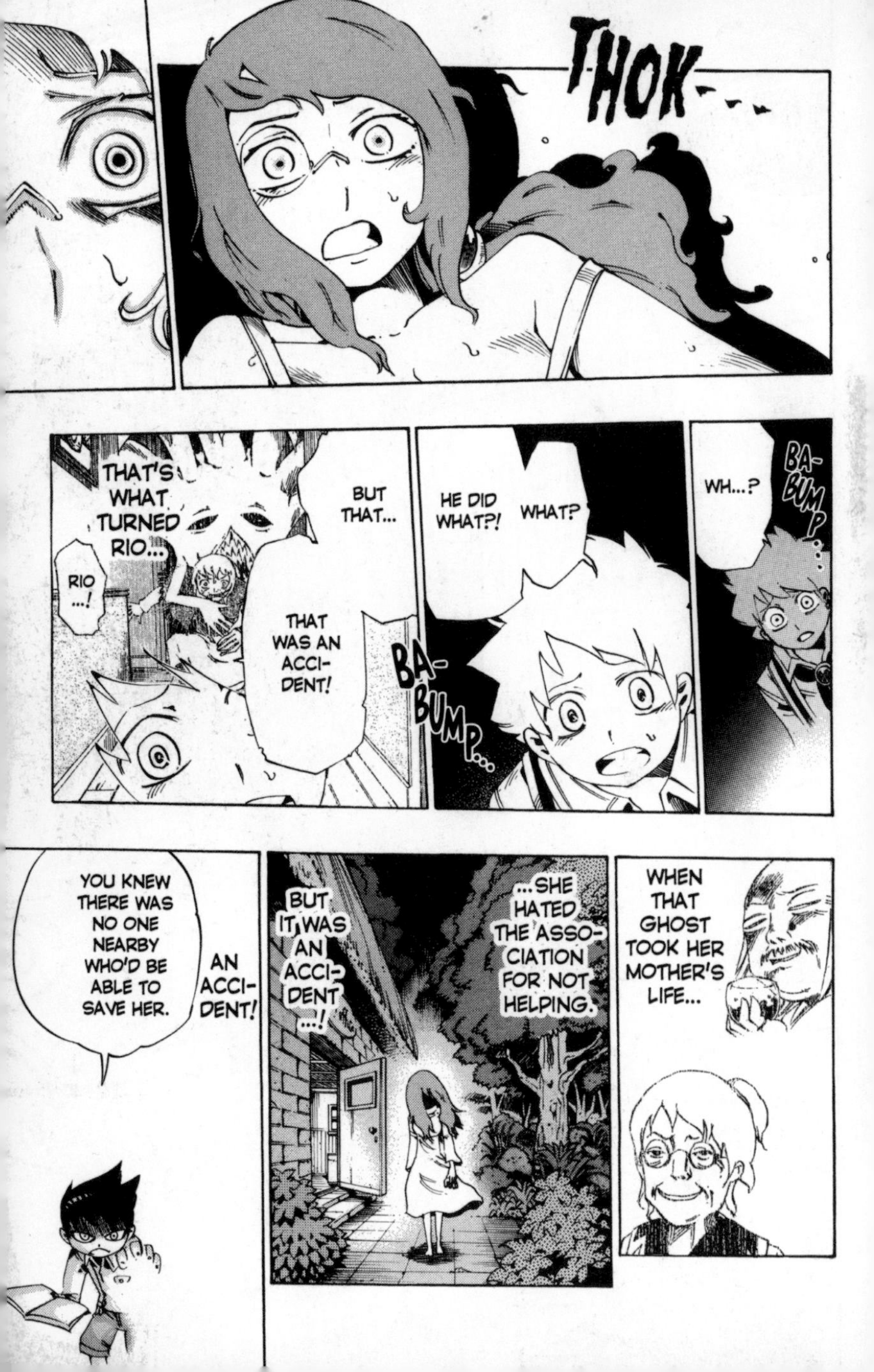
THOK...
BA-BUMP...
WH...?
WHAT?
HE DID WHAT?!
BA-BUMP...
BUT THAT...
THAT WAS AN ACCI-DENT!
THAT'S WHAT TURNED RIO...
RIO...!
WHEN THAT GHOST TOOK HER MOTHER'S LIFE...
...SHE HATED THE ASSO-CIATION FOR NOT HELPING.
BUT IT WAS AN ACCI-DENT...!
AN ACCI-DENT!
YOU KNEW THERE WAS NO ONE NEARBY WHO'D BE ABLE TO SAVE HER.

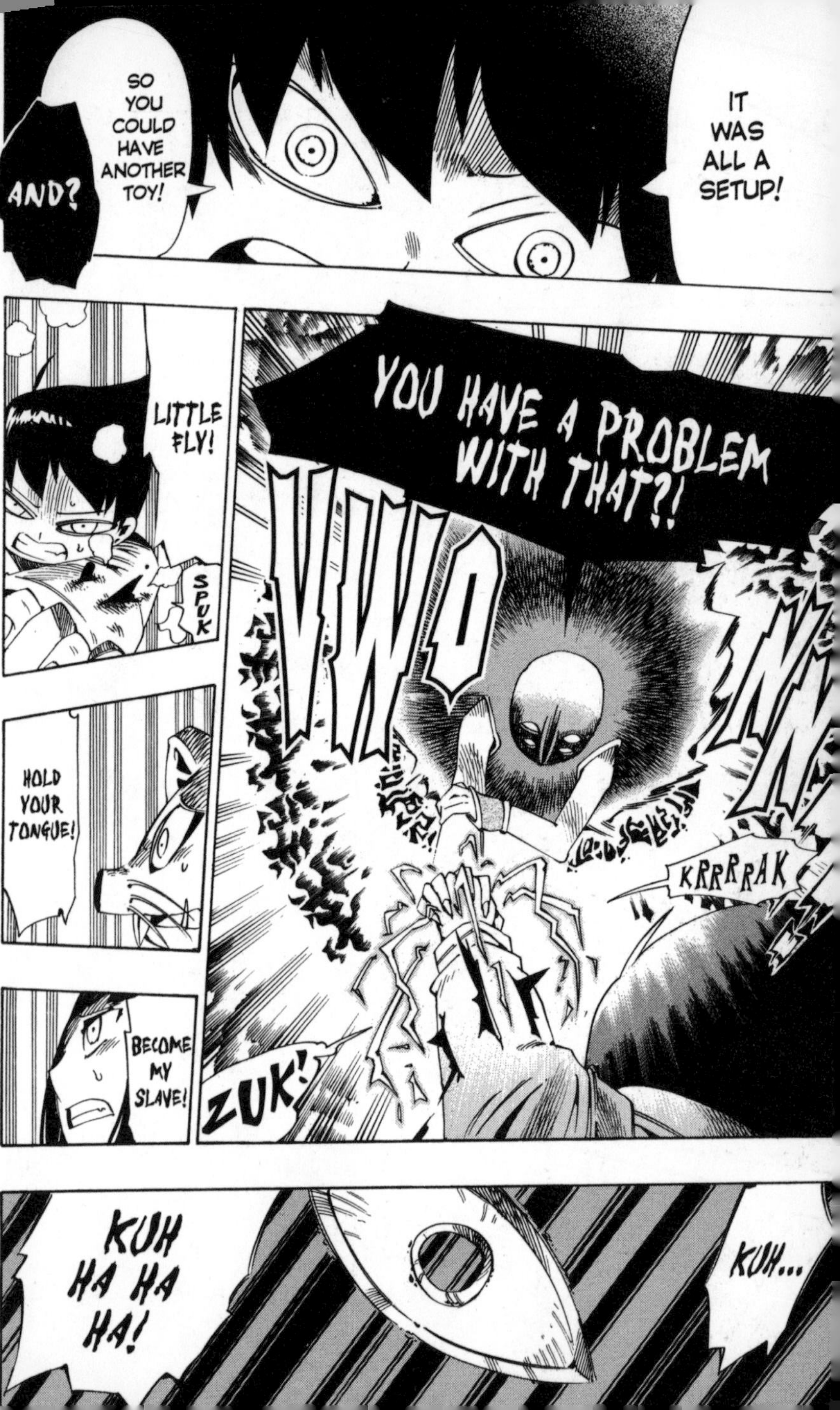
IT WAS ALL A SETUP!
SO YOU COULD HAVE ANOTHER TOY!
AND?
YOU HAVE A PROBLEM WITH THAT?!
VWO
KRRRRAK
ZUK!
LITTLE FLY!
SPUK
HOLD YOUR TONGUE!
BECOME MY SLAVE!
KUH...
KUH HA HA HA!

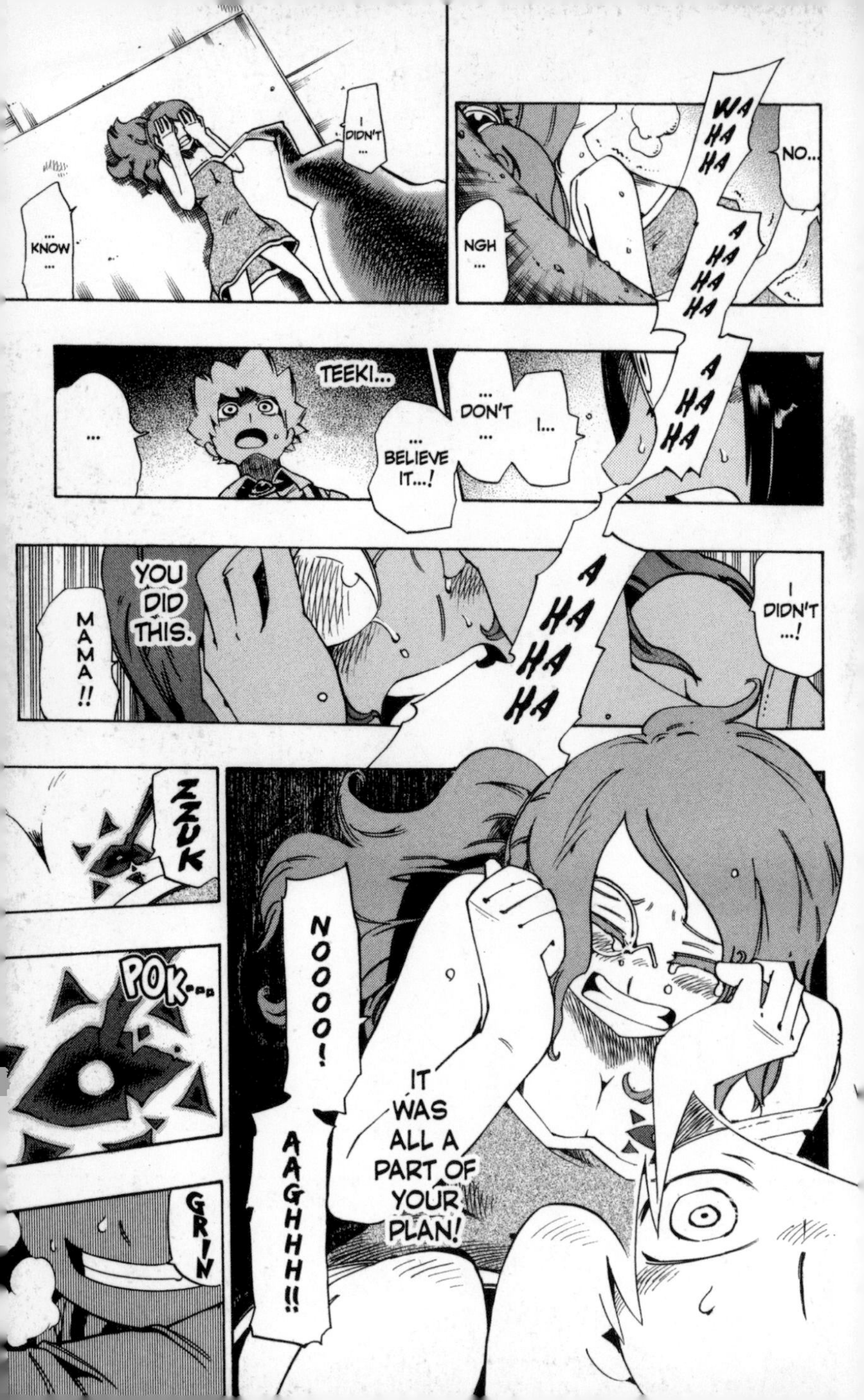

WA HA HA A HA HA HA HA A HA HA HA A HA HA HA HA
NO...
NGH ...
I DIDN'T ...
... KNOW ...
... DON'T I...
... BELIEVE IT...!
TEEKI...
...
I DIDN'T ...!
YOU DID THIS.
MAMA!!
NOOOOO! AAGHHHH!!
IT WAS ALL A PART OF YOUR PLAN!
ZZUK
POK...
GRIN

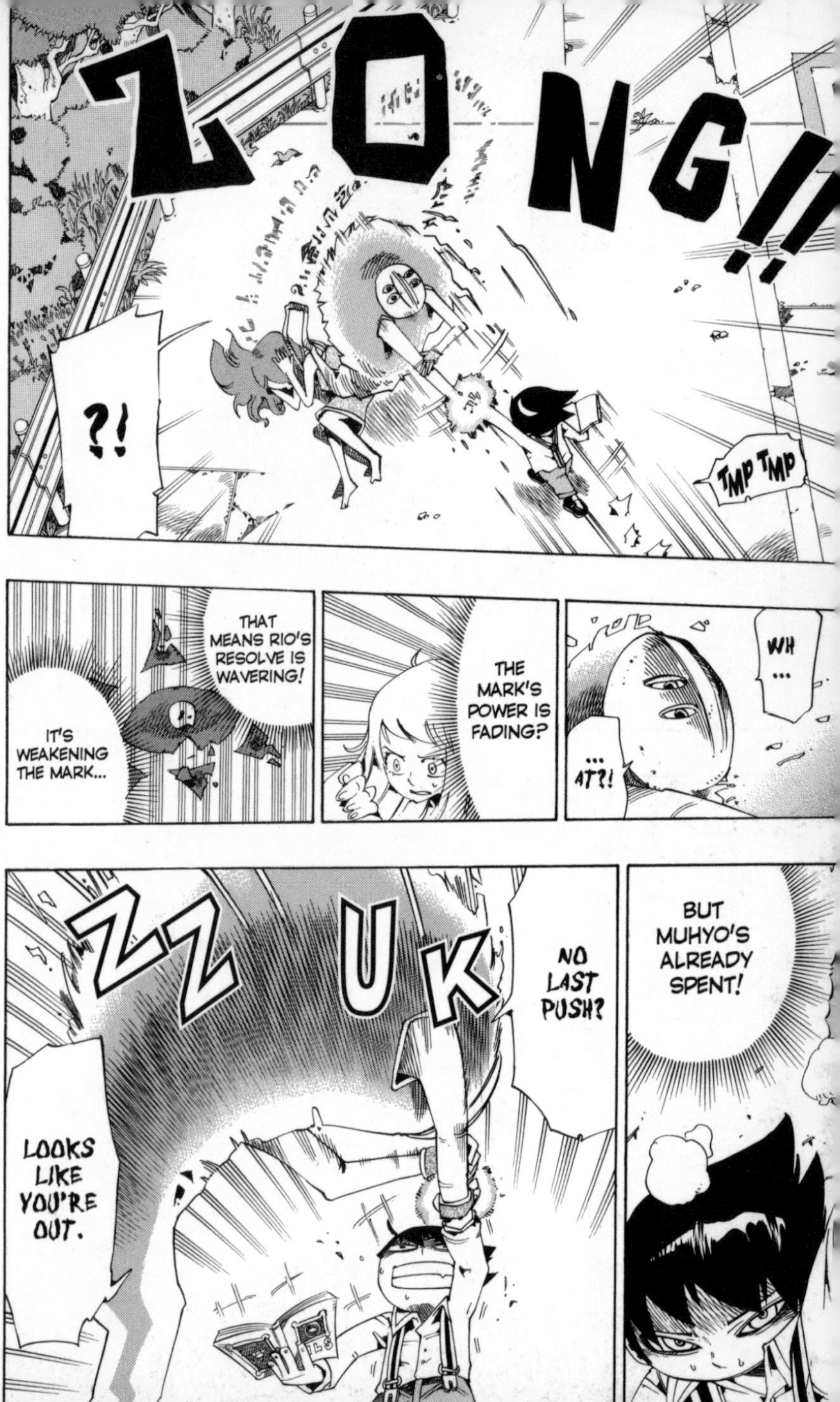
ZONG!!
TMP TMP
?!
WH...
...AT?!
THE MARK'S POWER IS FADING?
THAT MEANS RIO'S RESOLVE IS WAVERING!
IT'S WEAKENING THE MARK...
BUT MUHYO'S ALREADY SPENT!
NO LAST PUSH?
ZZUK
LOOKS LIKE YOU'RE OUT.

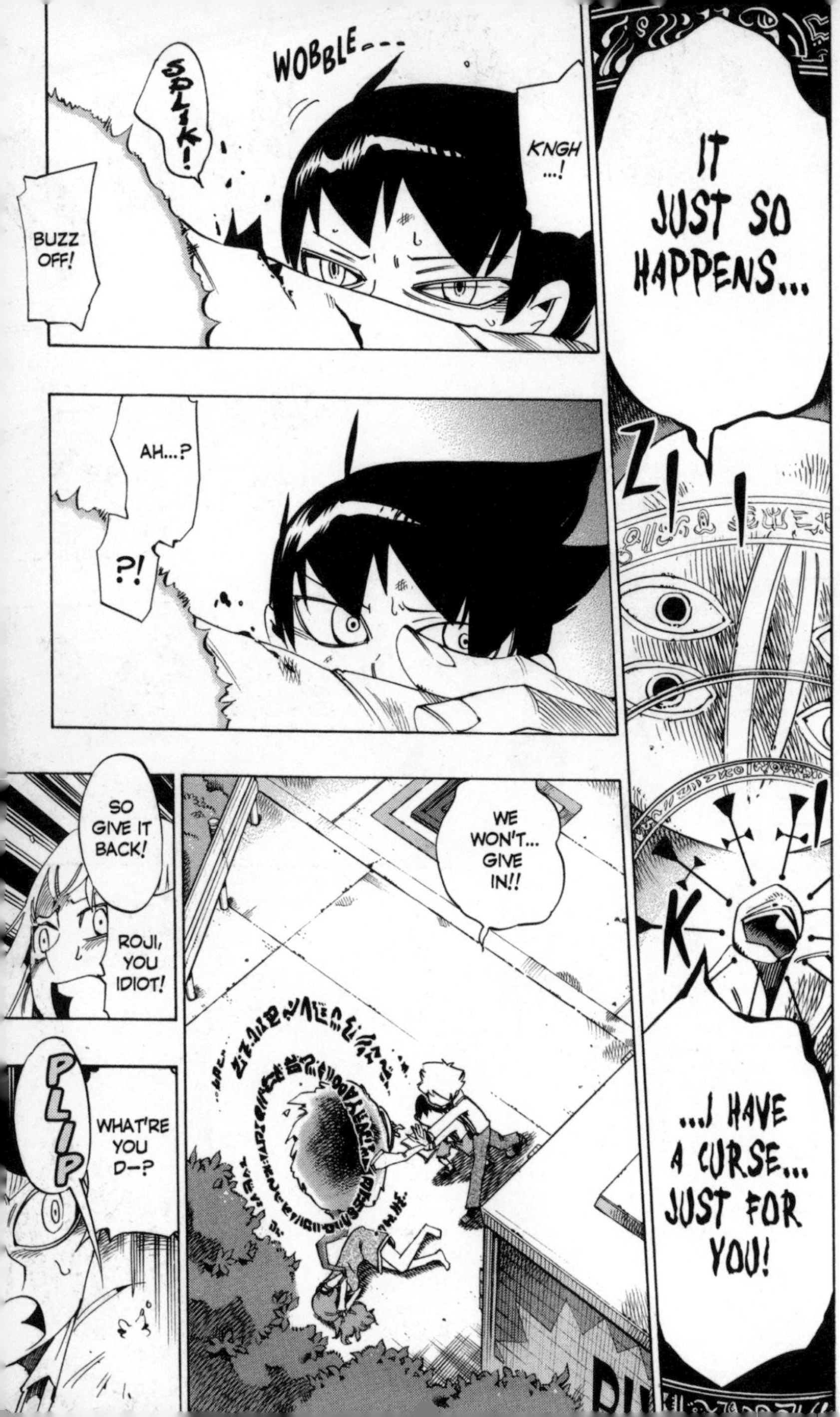
IT JUST SO HAPPENS...
...I HAVE A CURSE... JUST FOR YOU!
KNGH ...!
WOBBLE...
SPLIK!
BUZZ OFF!
AH...?
?!
WE WON'T... GIVE IN!!
SO GIVE IT BACK!
ROJI, YOU IDIOT!
PLIP
WHAT'RE YOU D—?

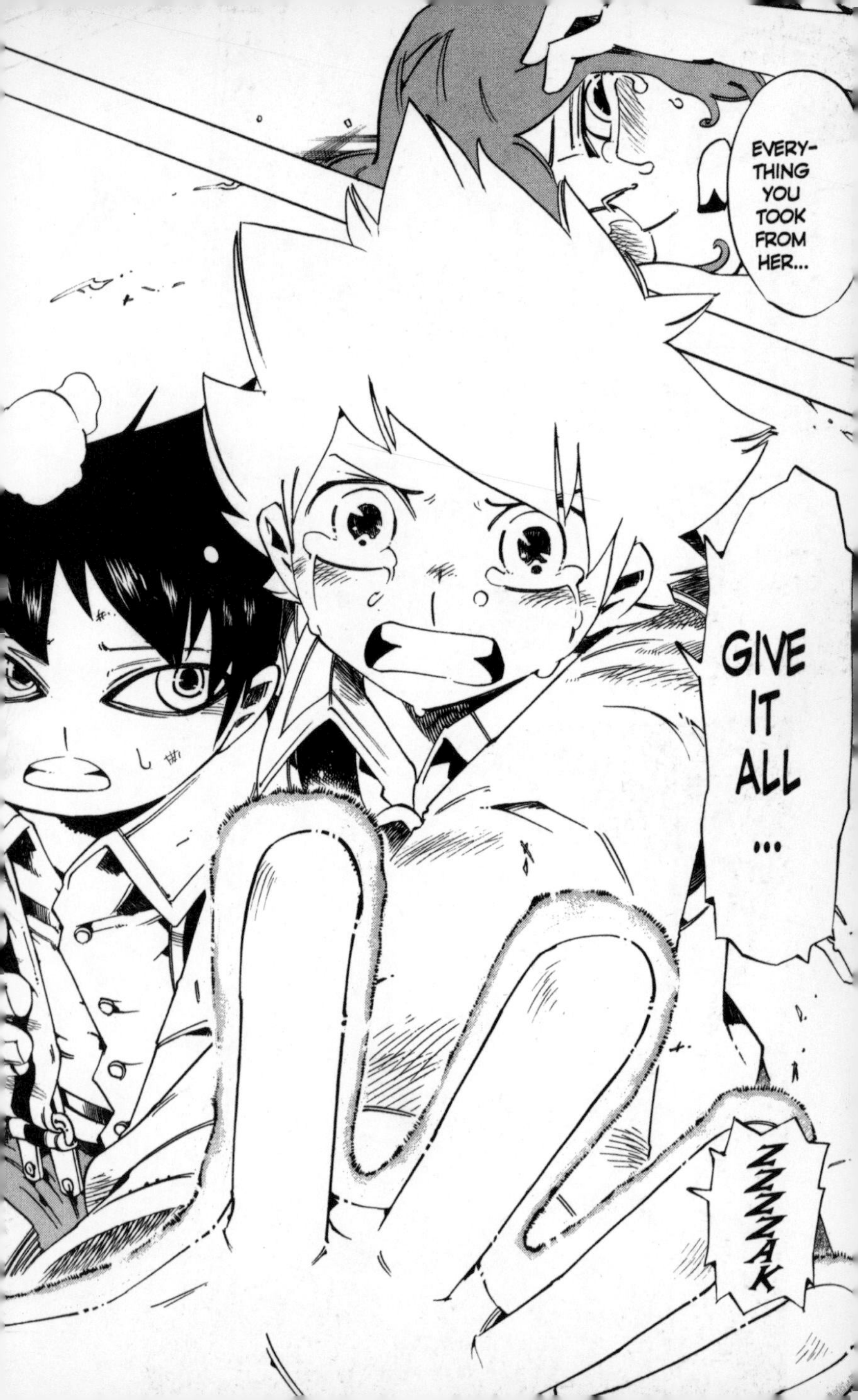
EVERY-THING YOU TOOK FROM HER...
GIVE IT ALL ...
ZZZZAK

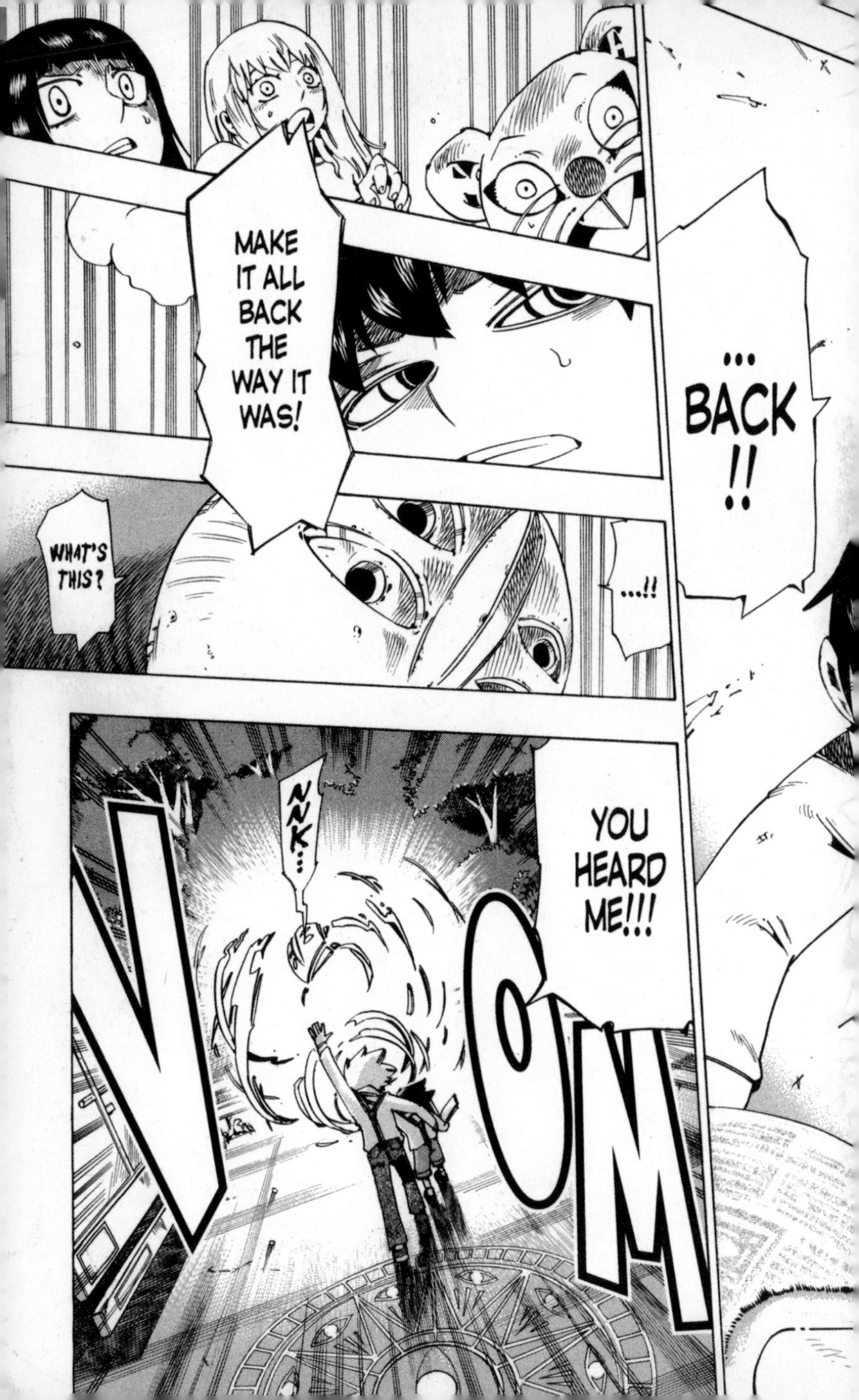
MAKE IT ALL BACK THE WAY IT WAS!
...BACK!!
...!!
WHAT'S THIS?
YOU HEARD ME!!!
NNK...

IT'S ANOTHER Q & A SESSION!
LET'S SEE WHAT THEY WANT THIS TIME!

Q1: IS MUHYO IN ELEMENTARY SCHOOL?
Q2: DOES MUHYO HAVE SOMETHING AGAINST MILK?
Q3: WHY IS MUHYO SO SHORT?

-K.H., AICHI PREFECTURE

A1: HE'S NOT IN ELEMENTARY SCHOOL.
HE'S AT LEAST IN JUNIOR HIGH. AT LEAST.

A2:

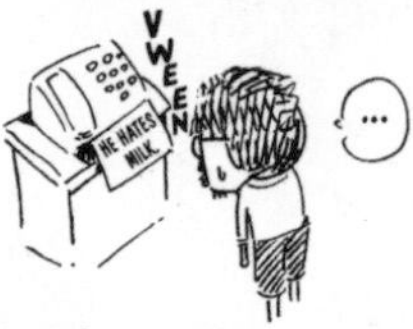
...
VWEEN
HE HATES MILK.

ACCORDING TO ROJI, HE DOESN'T LIKE MILK.

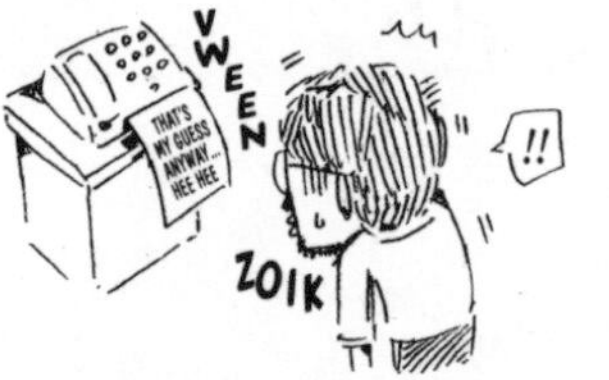
!!
VWEEN
THAT'S MY GUESS ANYWAY... HEE HEE
ZOIK

A3:
LET'S NOT ASK THAT, SHALL WE? (*EEEEP!*) I MEAN, SOME PEOPLE CAN DRINK ALL THE MILK THEY WANT AND STILL NOT GET TALL. LIKE ME AND A BUNCH OF OTHER PEOPLE I KNOW! I'M SURE IT'S JUST A COINCIDENCE HE DOESN'T LIKE...

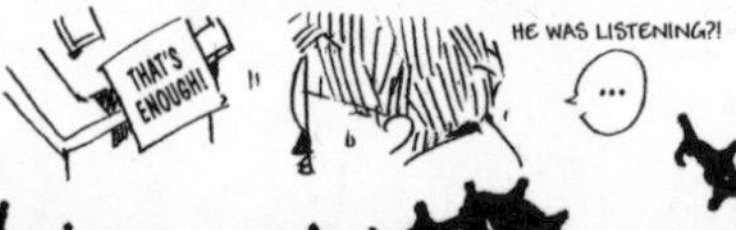
HE WAS LISTENING?!
...
THAT'S ENOUGH!

ARTICLE 97
AROROPATHY

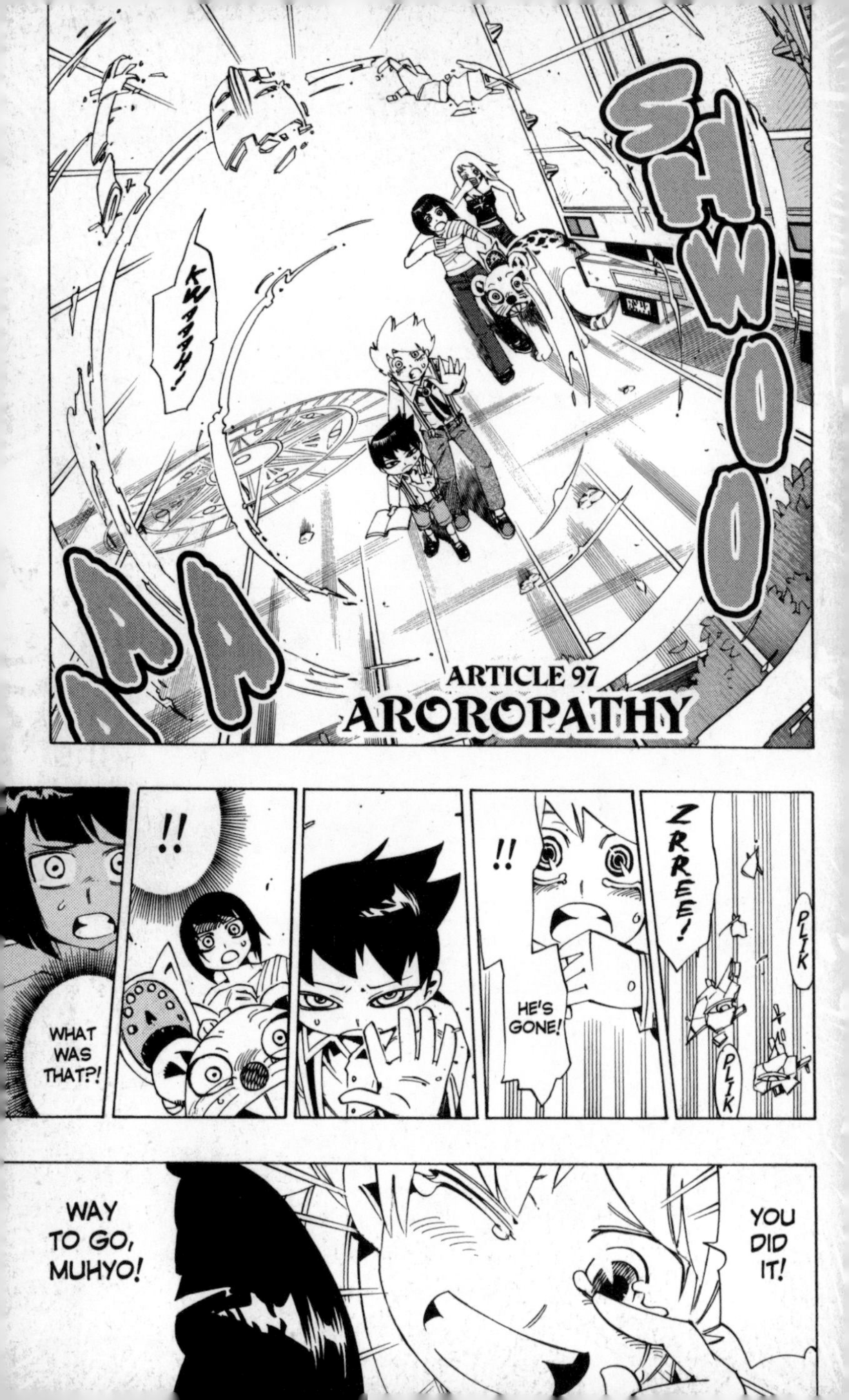
SHWOOO
KWAPPH!
AAA
ZRREE!
PLIK
PLIK
HE'S GONE!
!!
!!
WHAT WAS THAT?!
YOU DID IT!
WAY TO GO, MUHYO!

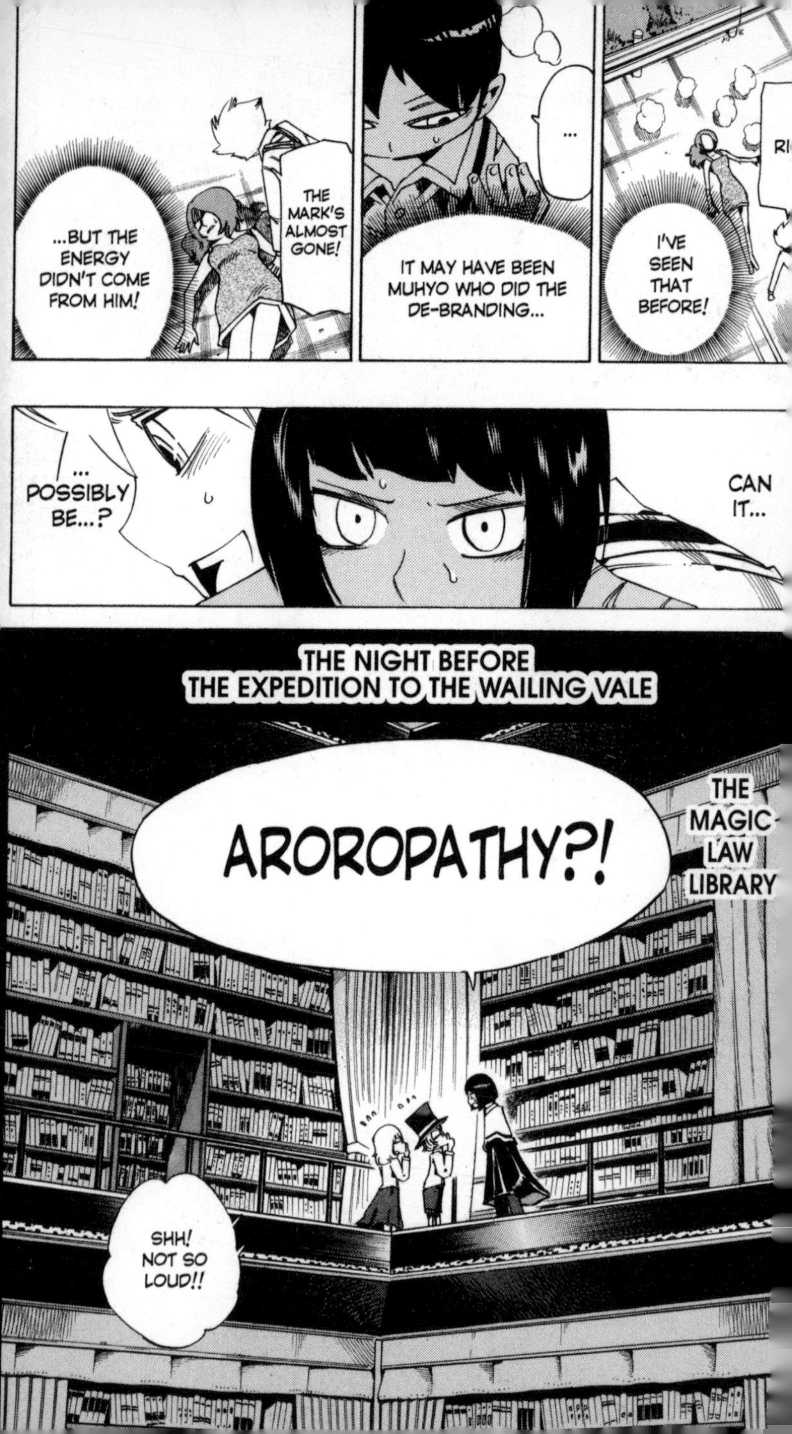
RI
I'VE SEEN THAT BEFORE!
...
IT MAY HAVE BEEN MUHYO WHO DID THE DE-BRANDING...
THE MARK'S ALMOST GONE!
...BUT THE ENERGY DIDN'T COME FROM HIM!
CAN IT...
... POSSIBLY BE...?
THE NIGHT BEFORE THE EXPEDITION TO THE WAILING VALE
THE MAGIC LAW LIBRARY
ARAROPATHY?!
SHH! NOT SO LOUD!!

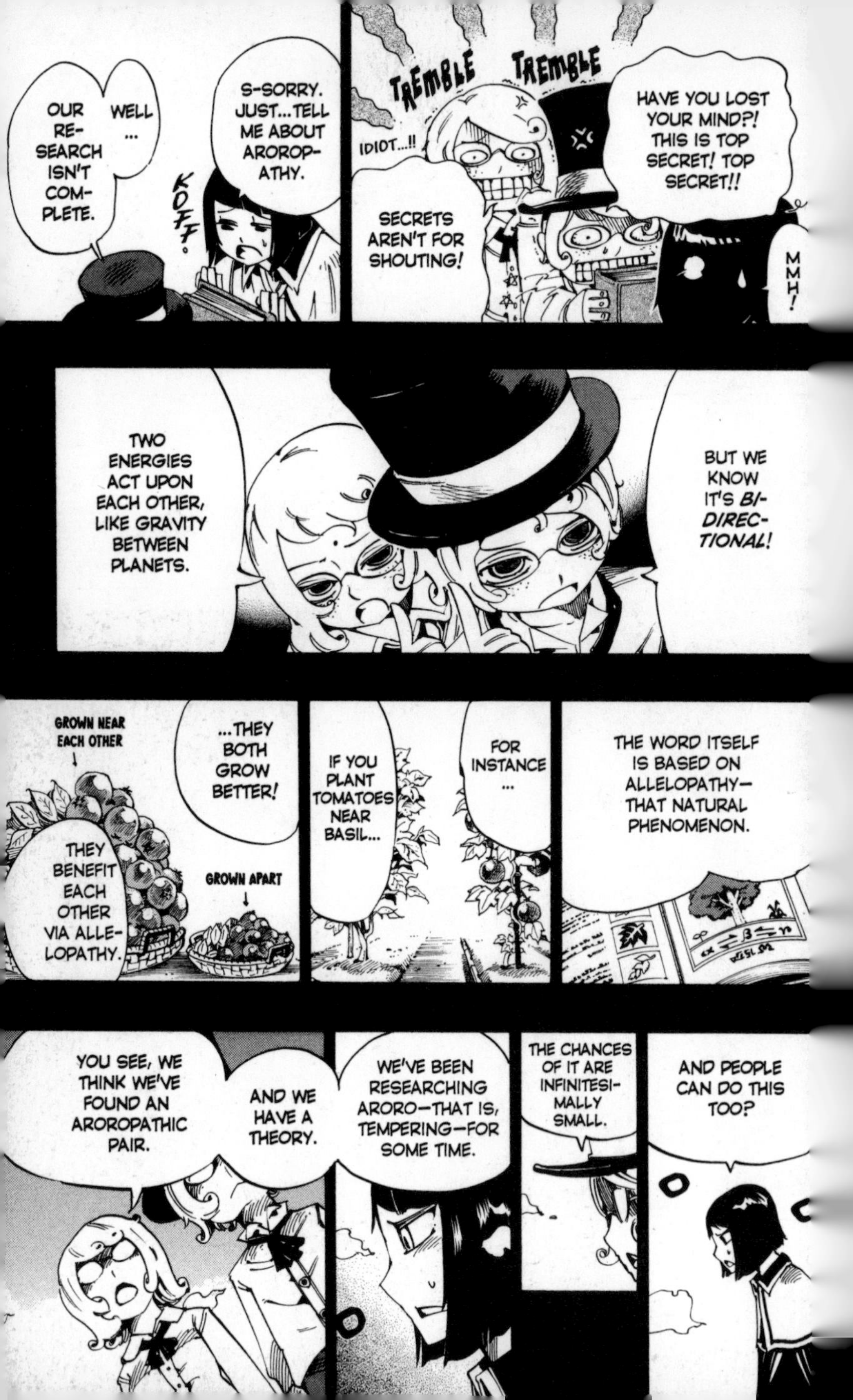
TREMBLE TREMBLE
HAVE YOU LOST YOUR MIND?! THIS IS TOP SECRET! TOP SECRET!!
MMH!
IDIOT...!!
SECRETS AREN'T FOR SHOUTING!
S-SORRY. JUST...TELL ME ABOUT AROROPATHY.
KOFF
WELL...
OUR RESEARCH ISN'T COMPLETE.
BUT WE KNOW IT'S *BI-DIRECTIONAL*!
TWO ENERGIES ACT UPON EACH OTHER, LIKE GRAVITY BETWEEN PLANETS.
THE WORD ITSELF IS BASED ON ALLELOPATHY— THAT NATURAL PHENOMENON.
FOR INSTANCE...
IF YOU PLANT TOMATOES NEAR BASIL...
...THEY BOTH GROW BETTER!
GROWN NEAR EACH OTHER
THEY BENEFIT EACH OTHER VIA ALLELOPATHY.
GROWN APART
AND PEOPLE CAN DO THIS TOO?
THE CHANCES OF IT ARE INFINITESIMALLY SMALL.
WE'VE BEEN RESEARCHING ARORO—THAT IS, TEMPERING—FOR SOME TIME.
AND WE HAVE A THEORY.
YOU SEE, WE THINK WE'VE FOUND AN AROROPATHIC PAIR.

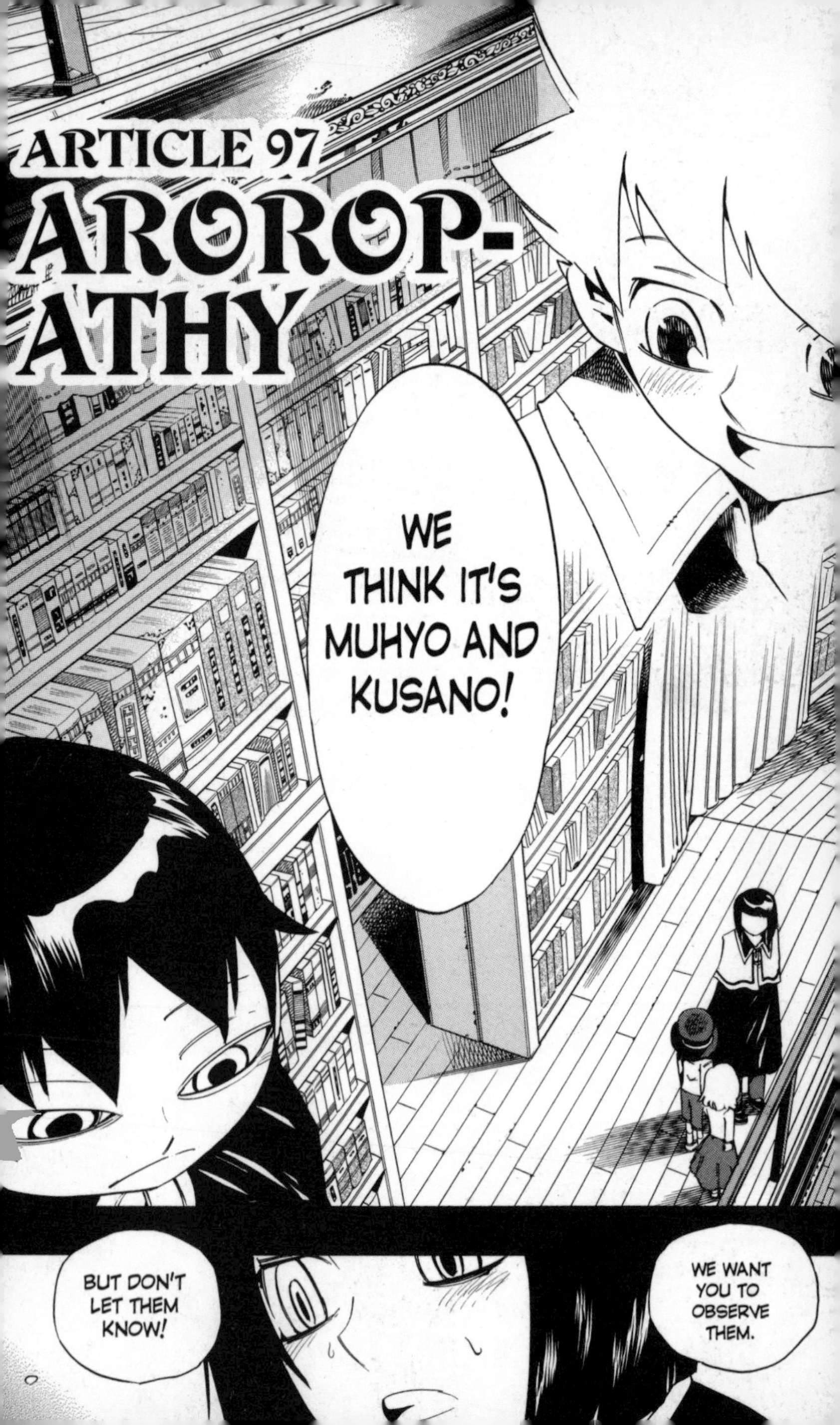
ARTICLE 97
AROROP-ATHY
WE THINK IT'S MUHYO AND KUSANO!
WE WANT YOU TO OBSERVE THEM.
BUT DON'T LET THEM KNOW!

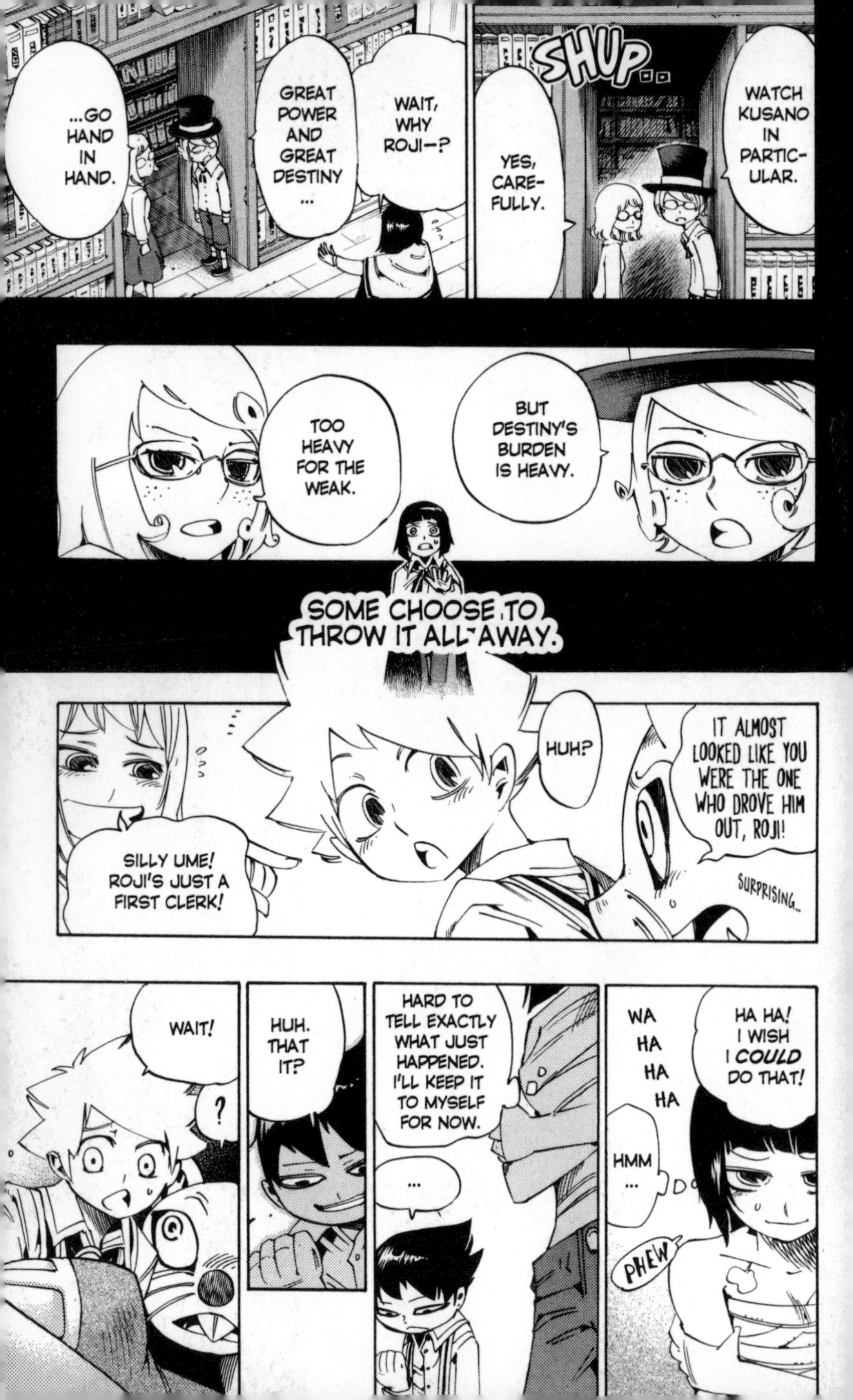
WATCH KUSANO IN PARTICULAR.
SHUP..
YES, CAREFULLY.
WAIT, WHY ROJI—?
GREAT POWER AND GREAT DESTINY ...
...GO HAND IN HAND.
BUT DESTINY'S BURDEN IS HEAVY.
TOO HEAVY FOR THE WEAK.
SOME CHOOSE TO THROW IT ALL AWAY.
IT ALMOST LOOKED LIKE YOU WERE THE ONE WHO DROVE HIM OUT, ROJI!
SURPRISING...
HUH?
SILLY UME! ROJI'S JUST A FIRST CLERK!
HA HA! I WISH I *COULD* DO THAT!
WA HA HA HA
HMM ...
PHEW
HARD TO TELL EXACTLY WHAT JUST HAPPENED. I'LL KEEP IT TO MYSELF FOR NOW.
...
HUH. THAT IT?
WAIT!
?

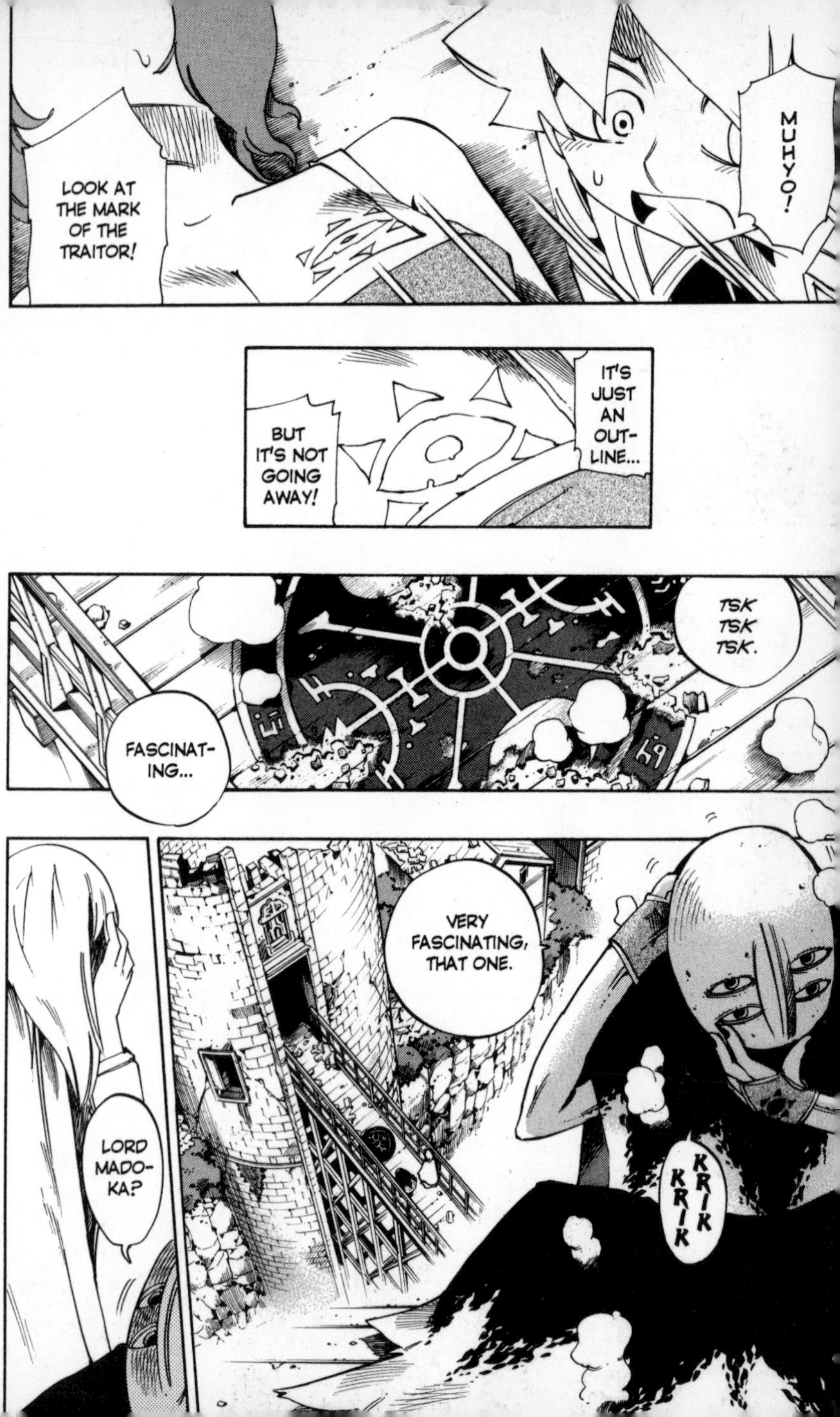
MUHYO!
LOOK AT THE MARK OF THE TRAITOR!
IT'S JUST AN OUTLINE...
BUT IT'S NOT GOING AWAY!
TSK TSK TSK.
FASCINATING...
VERY FASCINATING, THAT ONE.
KRIK KRIK
LORD MADOKA?

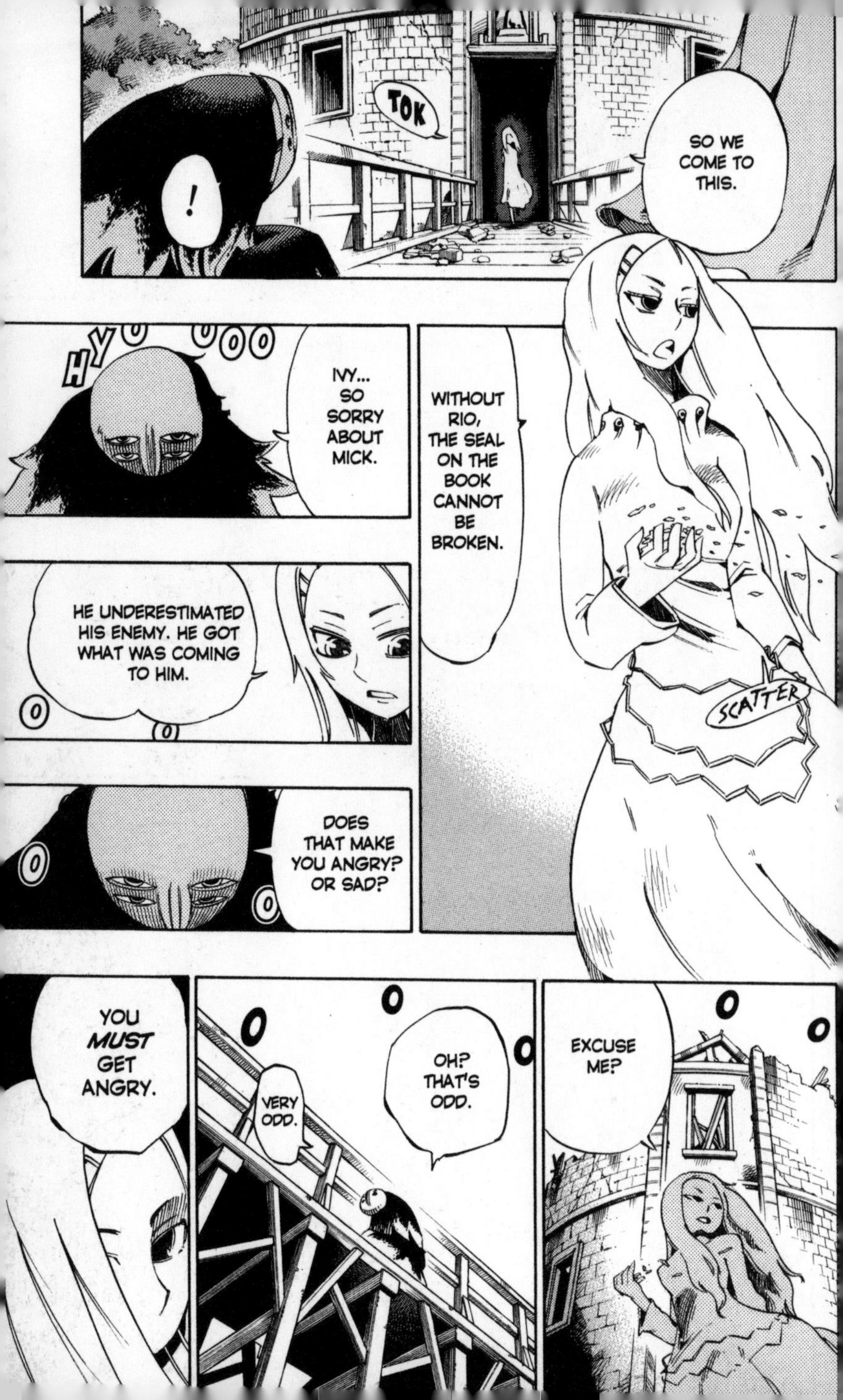
TOK
!
SO WE COME TO THIS.
WITHOUT RIO, THE SEAL ON THE BOOK CANNOT BE BROKEN.
SCATTER
HYUOOO
IVY... SO SORRY ABOUT MICK.
HE UNDERESTIMATED HIS ENEMY. HE GOT WHAT WAS COMING TO HIM.
DOES THAT MAKE YOU ANGRY? OR SAD?
EXCUSE ME?
OH? THAT'S ODD.
VERY ODD.
YOU *MUST* GET ANGRY.

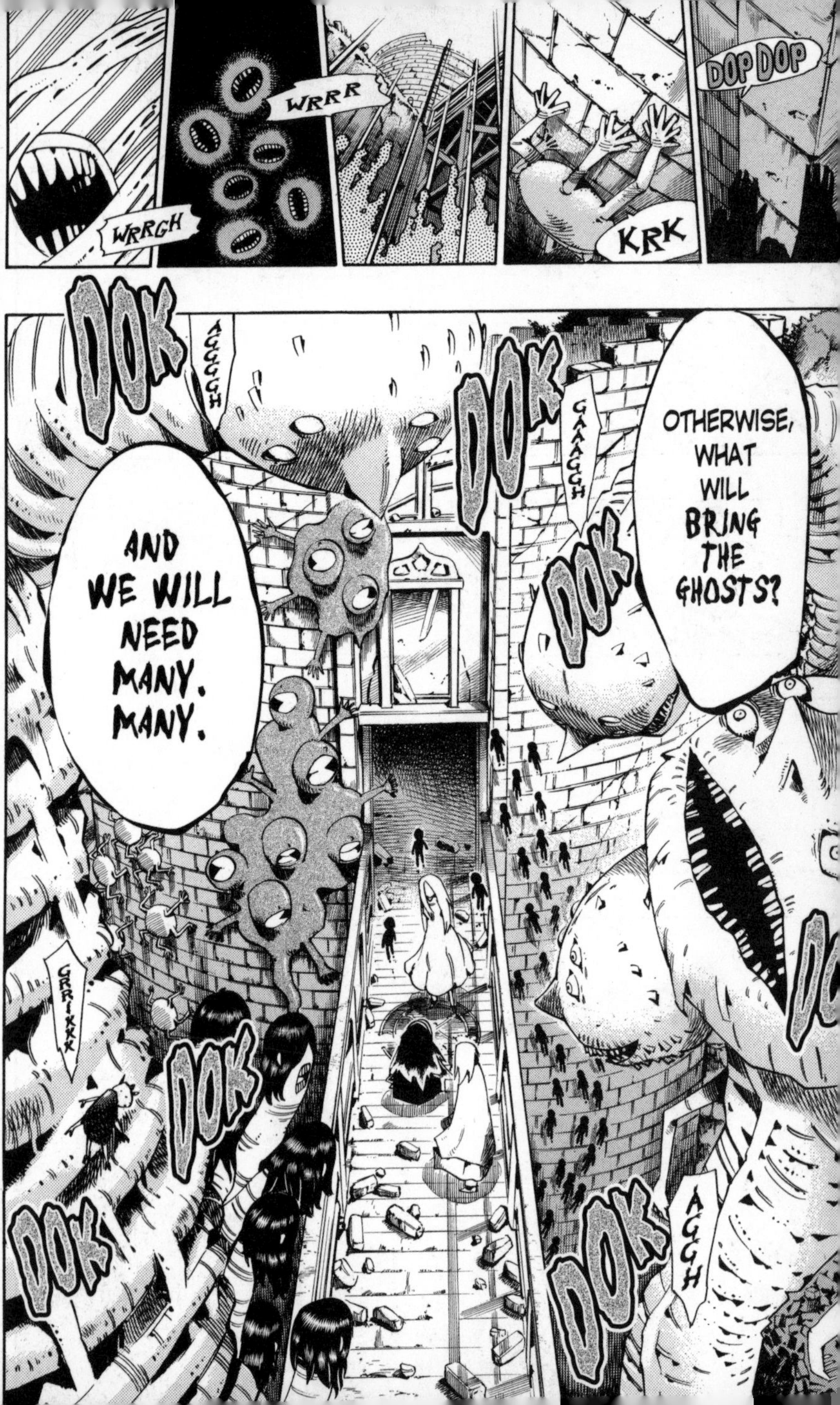
DOP DOP
KRK
WRRR
WRRGH
OTHERWISE, WHAT WILL BRING THE GHOSTS?
DOK
GAAAGGH
DOK
DOK
AGGGGH
AND WE WILL NEED MANY. MANY.
AGGH
DOK
DOK
GRRIKKK
DOK

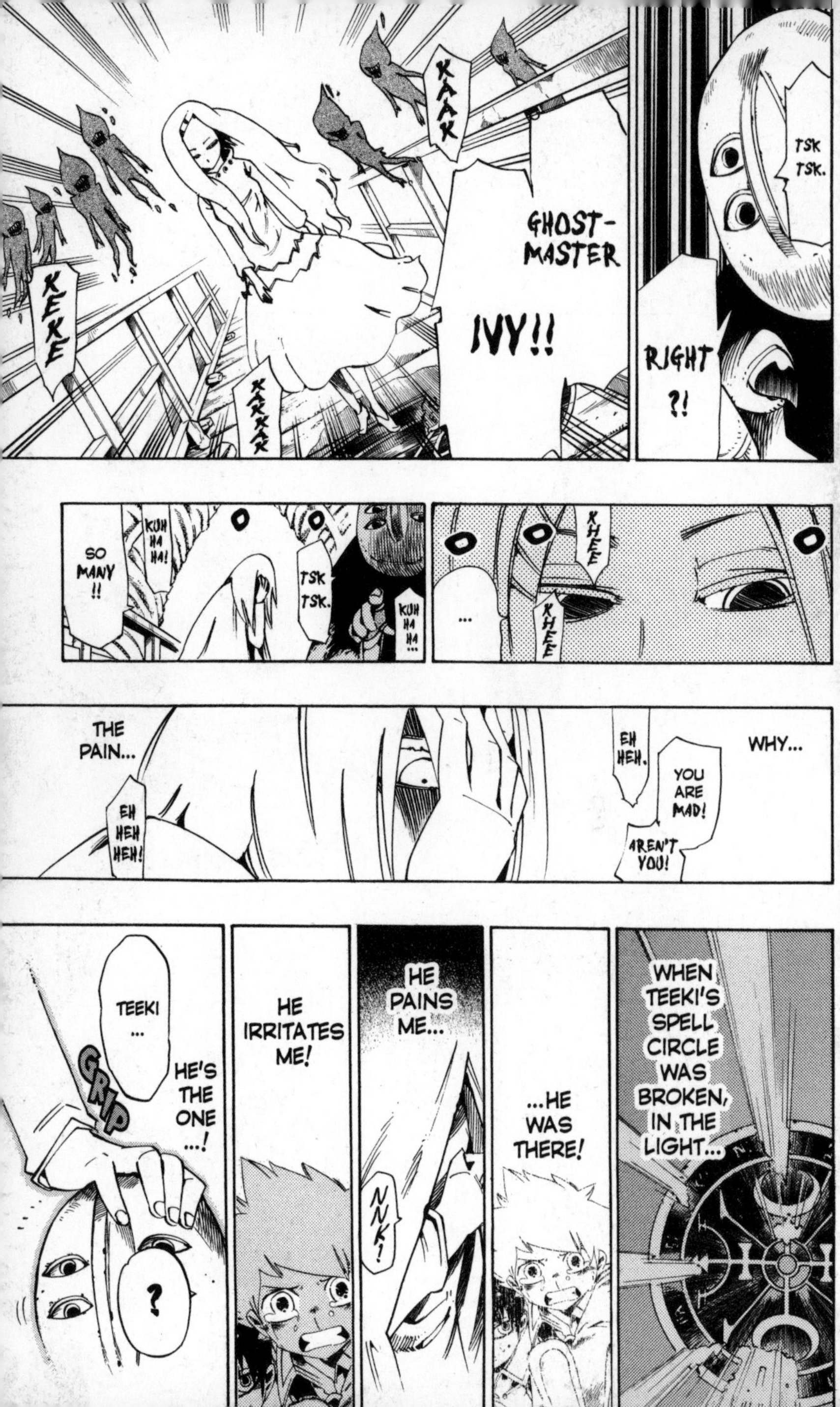
TSK TSK.
RIGHT ?!
KAAK
GHOST-MASTER
IVY!!
KAKKAK
KEKE
KHEE
KHEE
...
TSK TSK.
KUH HA HA...
KUH HA HA!
SO MANY !!
WHY...
EH HEH.
YOU ARE MAD!
AREN'T YOU!
THE PAIN...
EH HEH HEH!
WHEN TEEKI'S SPELL CIRCLE WAS BROKEN, IN THE LIGHT...
...HE WAS THERE!
HE PAINS ME...
NNK!
HE IRRITATES ME!
TEEKI ...
HE'S THE ONE ...!
GRIP
?

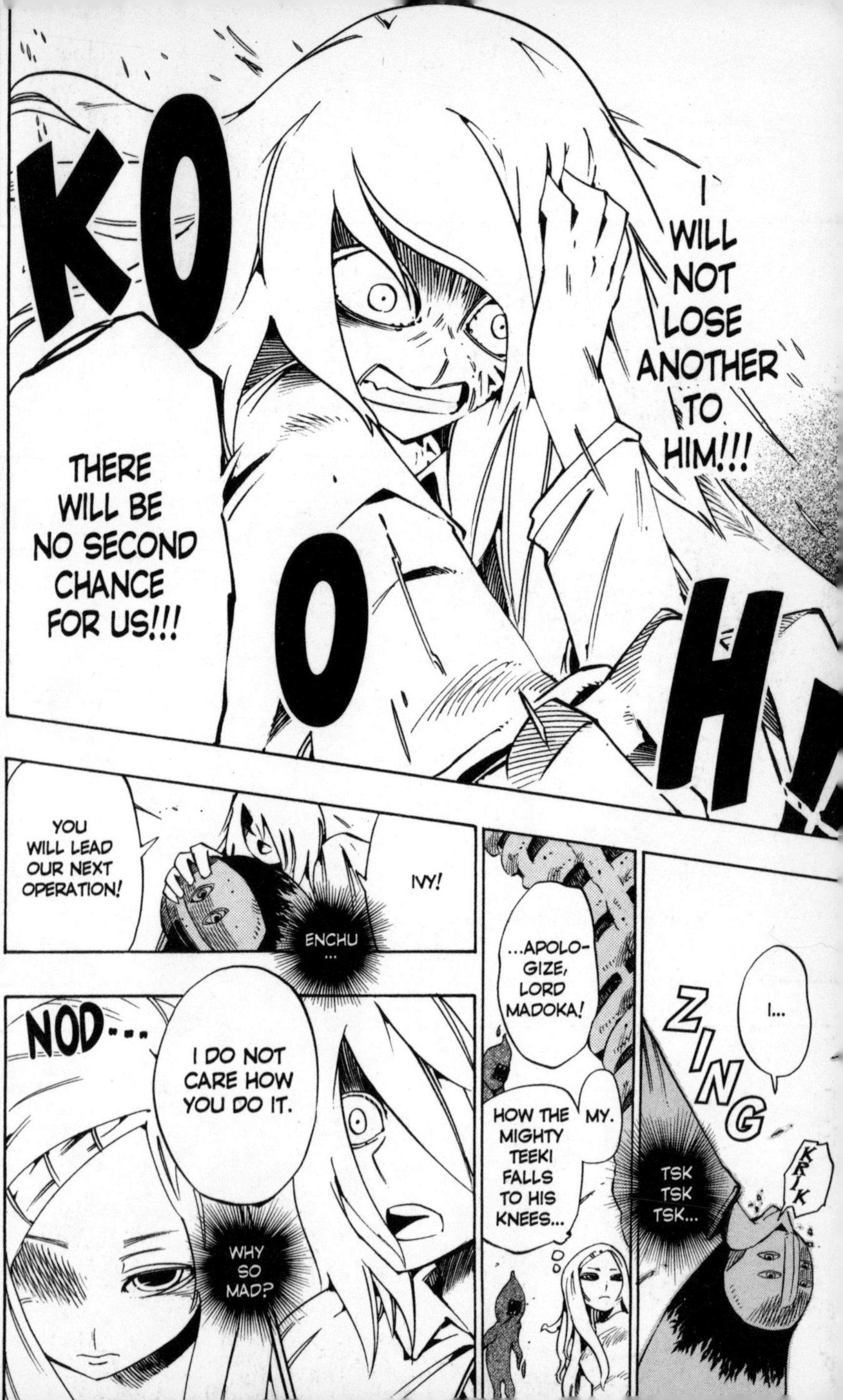
I WILL NOT LOSE ANOTHER TO HIM!!!
THERE WILL BE NO SECOND CHANCE FOR US!!!
KO O H!!
I...
ZING
KRIK
TSK TSK TSK...
...APOLO-GIZE, LORD MADOKA!
MY.
HOW THE MIGHTY TEEKI FALLS TO HIS KNEES...
IVY!
YOU WILL LEAD OUR NEXT OPERATION!
ENCHU...
I DO NOT CARE HOW YOU DO IT.
NOD...
WHY SO MAD?

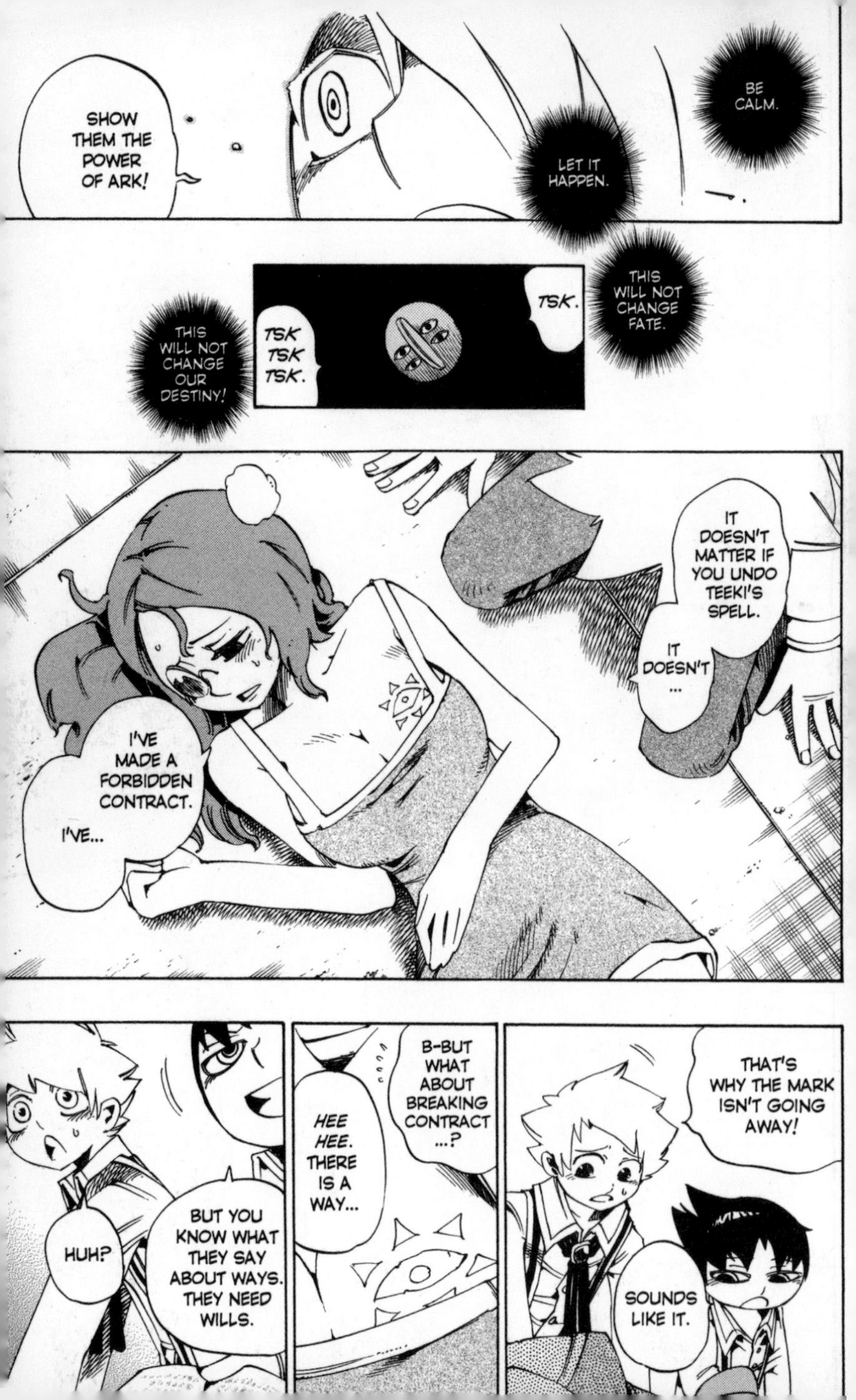
BE CALM.
LET IT HAPPEN.
SHOW THEM THE POWER OF ARK!
THIS WILL NOT CHANGE FATE.
TSK.
TSK TSK TSK.
THIS WILL NOT CHANGE OUR DESTINY!
IT DOESN'T MATTER IF YOU UNDO TEEKI'S SPELL.
IT DOESN'T ...
I'VE MADE A FORBIDDEN CONTRACT.
I'VE...
THAT'S WHY THE MARK ISN'T GOING AWAY!
SOUNDS LIKE IT.
B-BUT WHAT ABOUT BREAKING CONTRACT ...?
HEE HEE. THERE IS A WAY...
BUT YOU KNOW WHAT THEY SAY ABOUT WAYS. THEY NEED WILLS.
HUH?

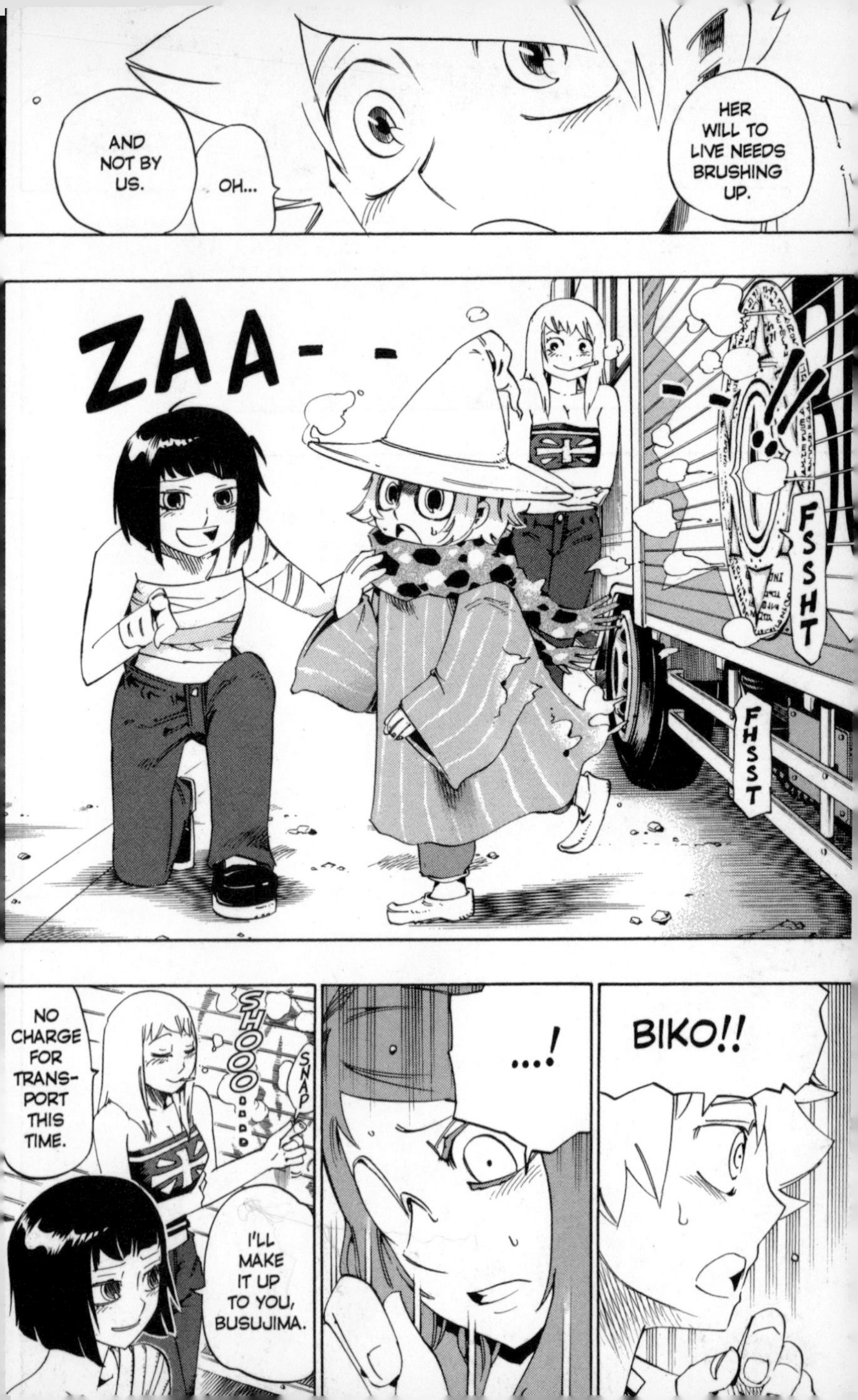
HER WILL TO LIVE NEEDS BRUSHING UP.
OH...
AND NOT BY US.
FSSHT
FHSST
ZAA- -
BIKO!!
...!
SNAP
SHOOOO
NO CHARGE FOR TRANS-PORT THIS TIME.
I'LL MAKE IT UP TO YOU, BUSUJIMA.

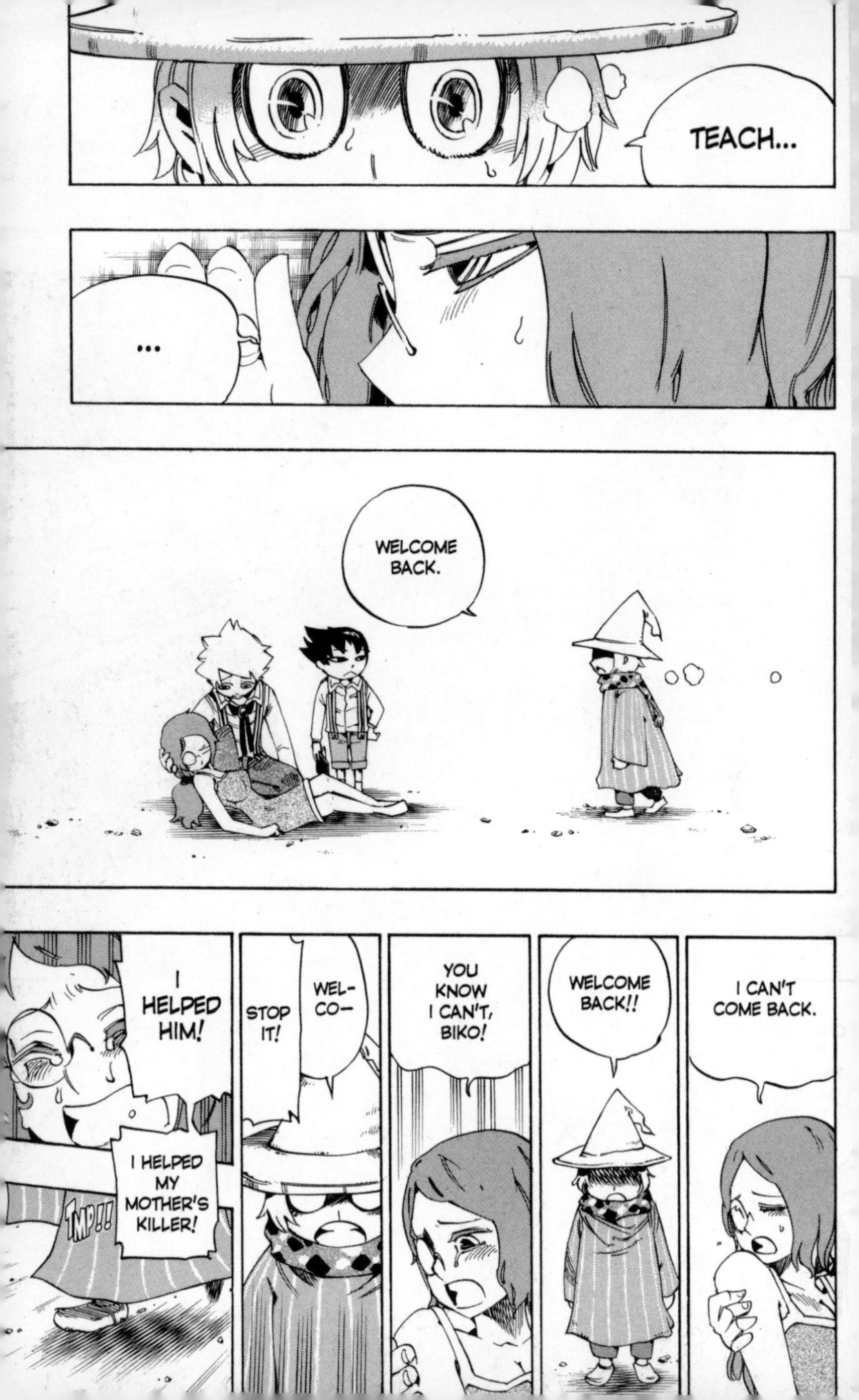
TEACH...
...
WELCOME BACK.
I CAN'T COME BACK.
WELCOME BACK!!
YOU KNOW I CAN'T, BIKO!
WEL- CO—
STOP IT!
I HELPED HIM!
I HELPED MY MOTHER'S KILLER!
TMP!!

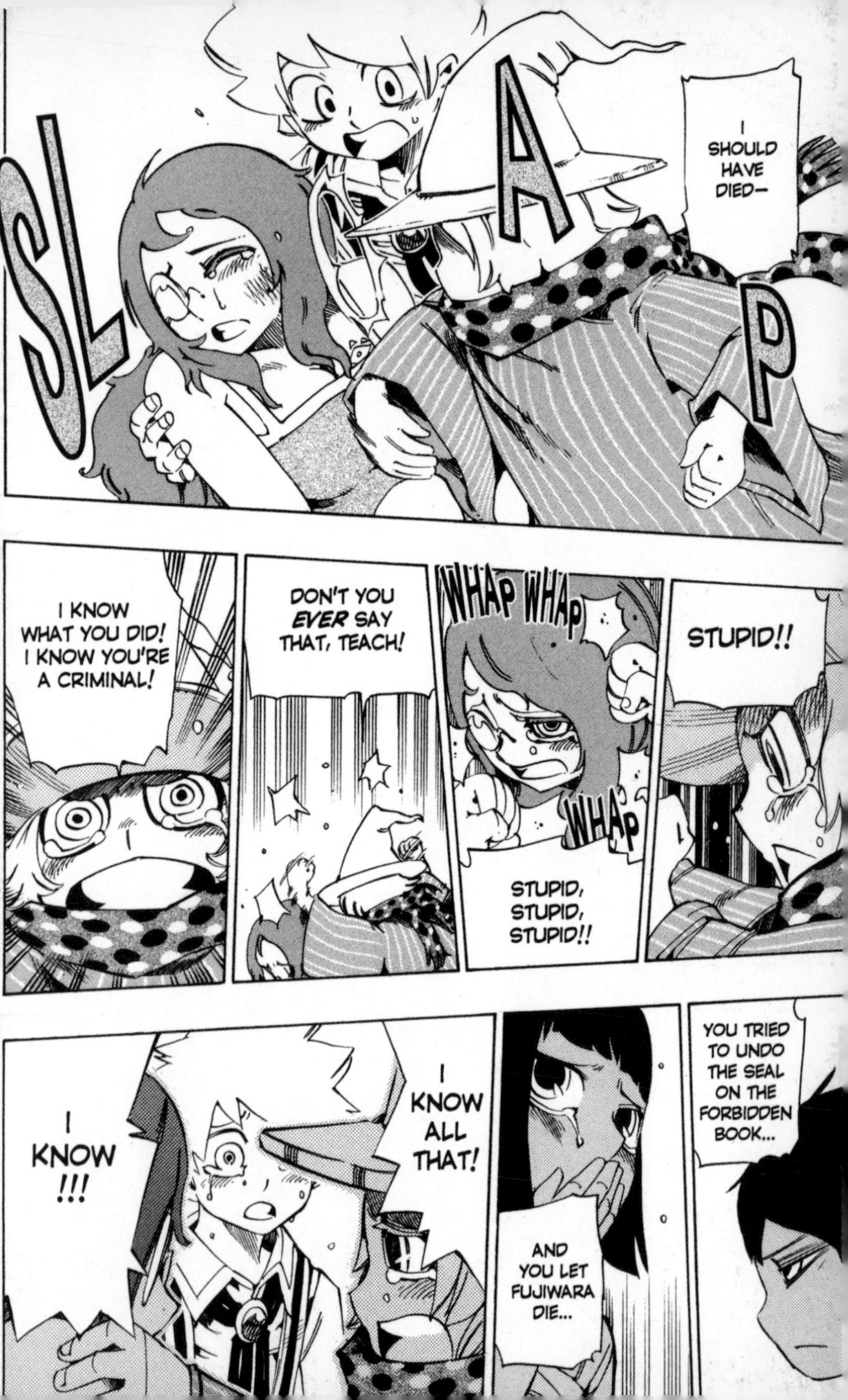
I SHOULD HAVE DIED—
SLAP
STUPID!!
WHAP WHAP
WHAP
STUPID, STUPID, STUPID!!
DON'T YOU *EVER* SAY THAT, TEACH!
I KNOW WHAT YOU DID! I KNOW YOU'RE A CRIMINAL!
YOU TRIED TO UNDO THE SEAL ON THE FORBIDDEN BOOK...
AND YOU LET FUJIWARA DIE...
I KNOW ALL THAT!
I KNOW!!!

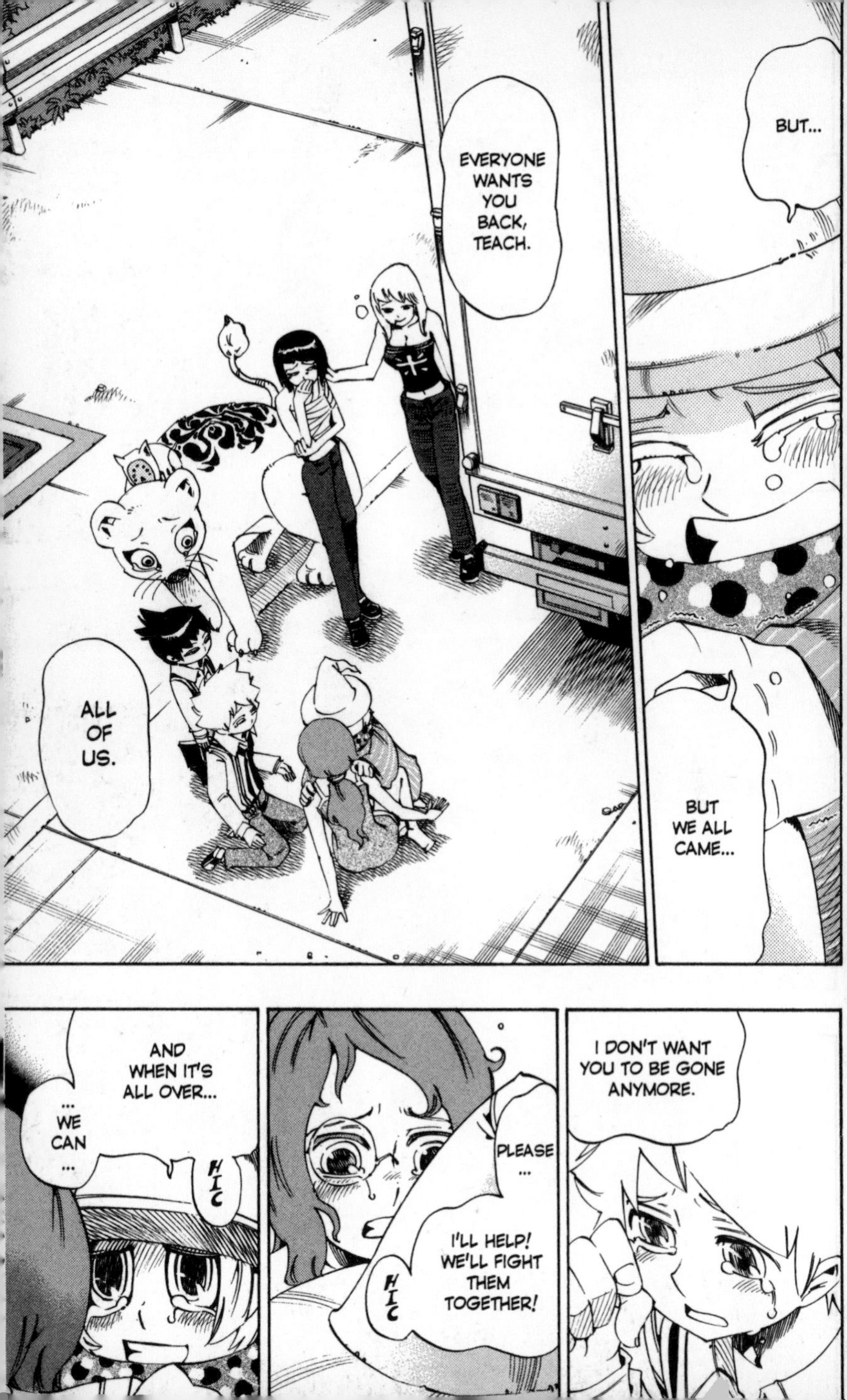
BUT...
BUT WE ALL CAME...
EVERYONE WANTS YOU BACK, TEACH.
ALL OF US.
I DON'T WANT YOU TO BE GONE ANYMORE.
PLEASE...
HIC
I'LL HELP! WE'LL FIGHT THEM TOGETHER!
AND WHEN IT'S ALL OVER...
...WE CAN...
HIC

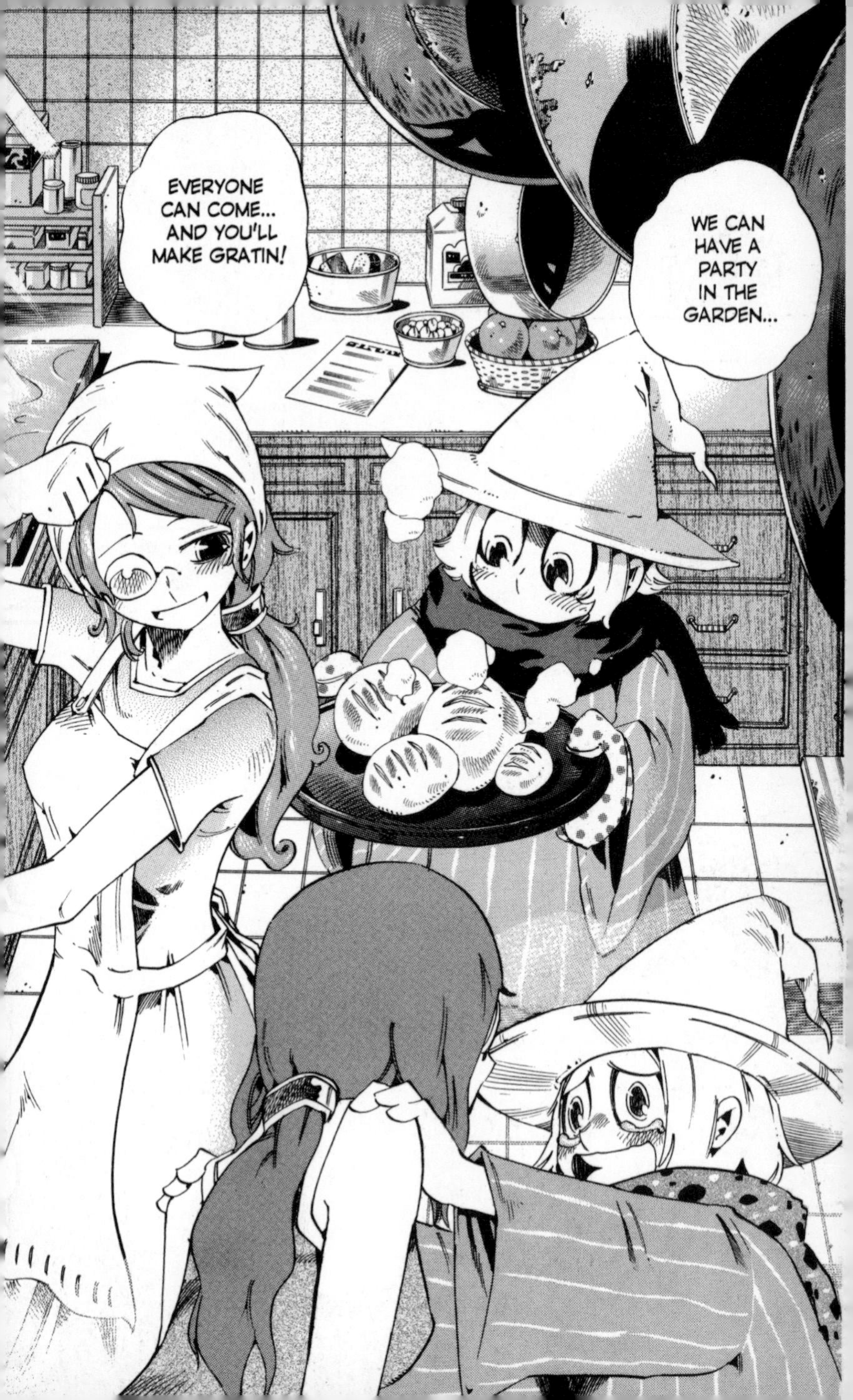
WE CAN HAVE A PARTY IN THE GARDEN...
EVERYONE CAN COME... AND YOU'LL MAKE GRATIN!

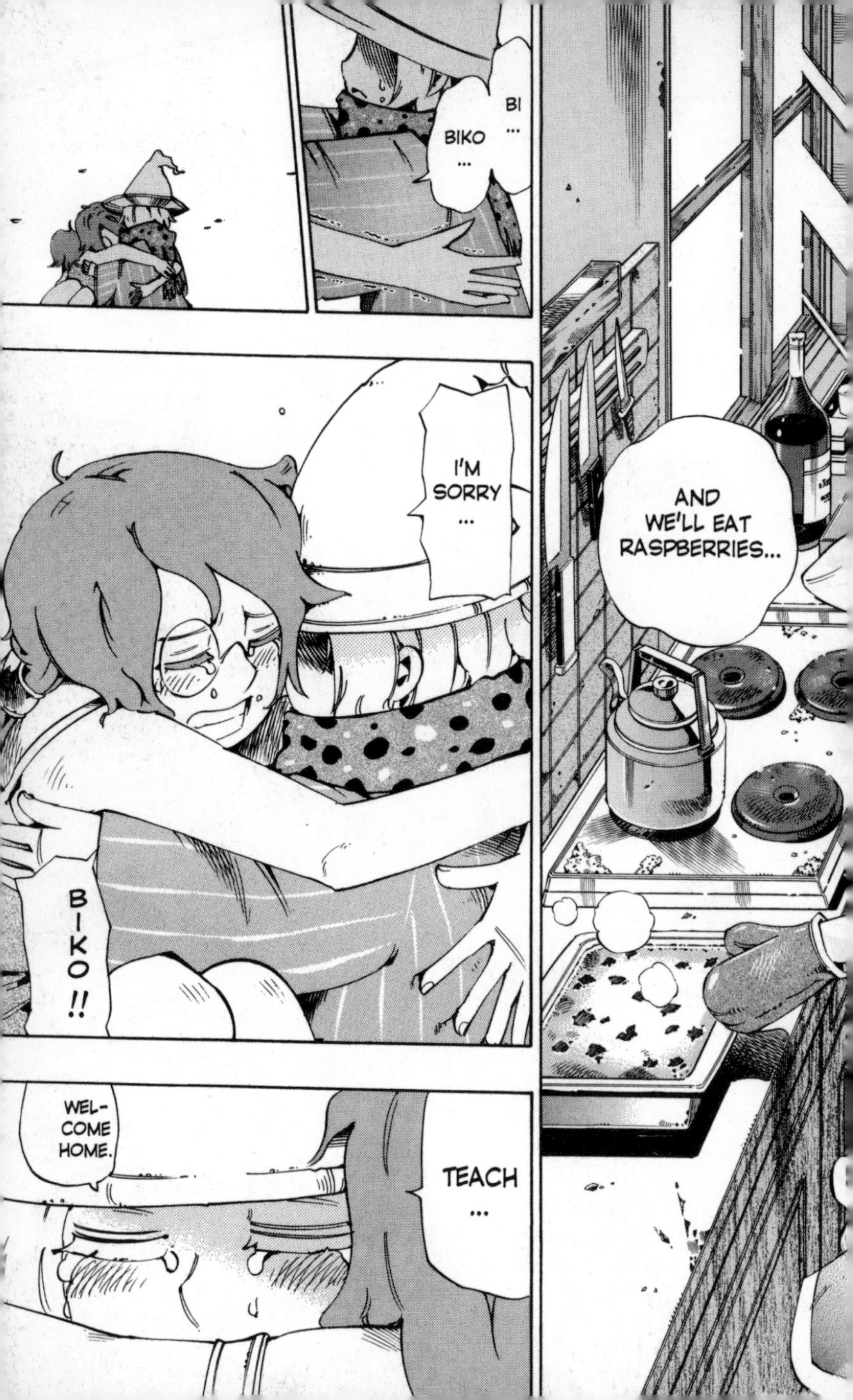
AND WE'LL EAT RASPBERRIES...
BI... BIKO...
I'M SORRY...
BIKO!!
TEACH...
WEL-COME HOME.

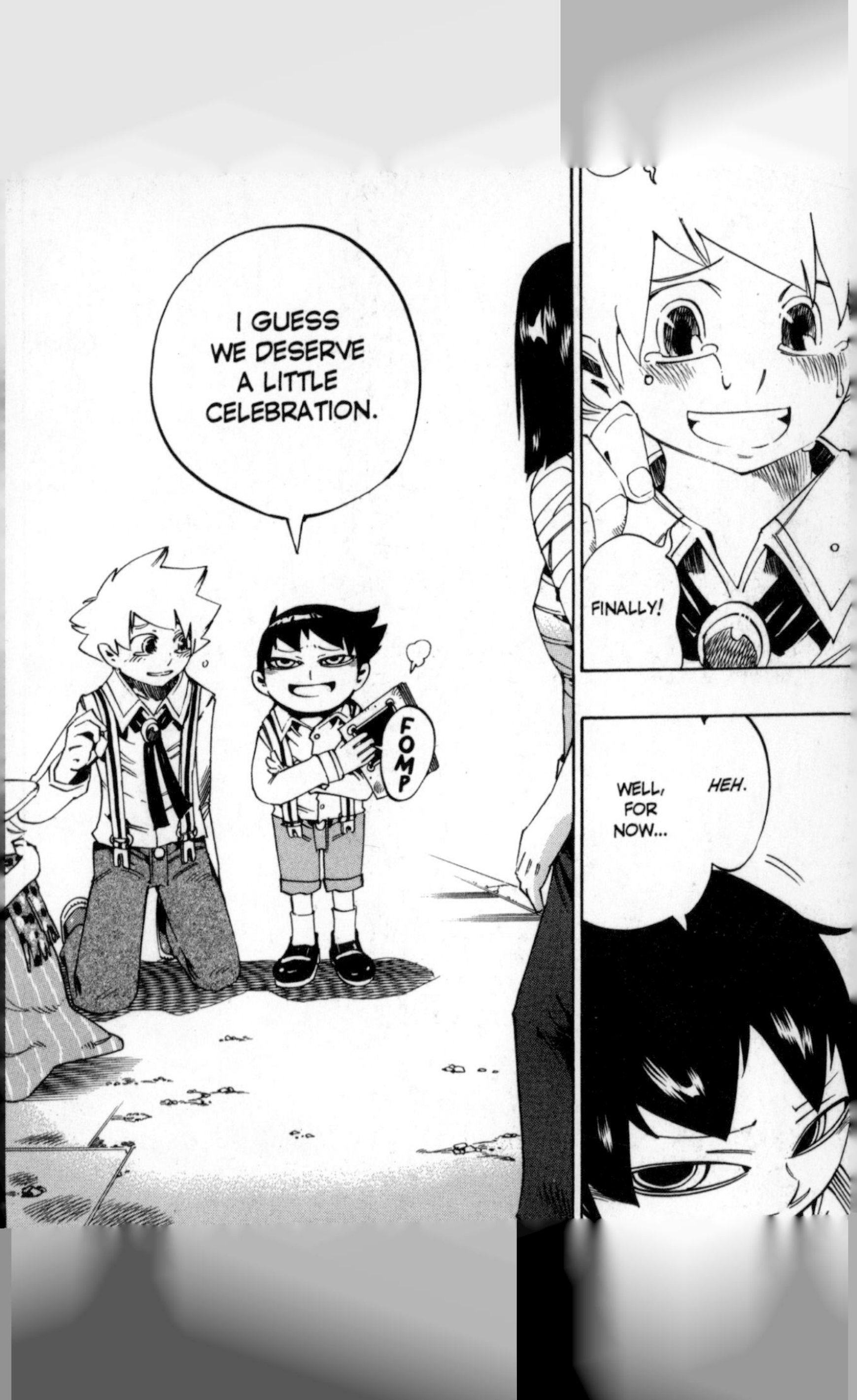
FINALLY!
HEH.
WELL, FOR NOW...
I GUESS WE DESERVE A LITTLE CELEBRATION.
FOMP

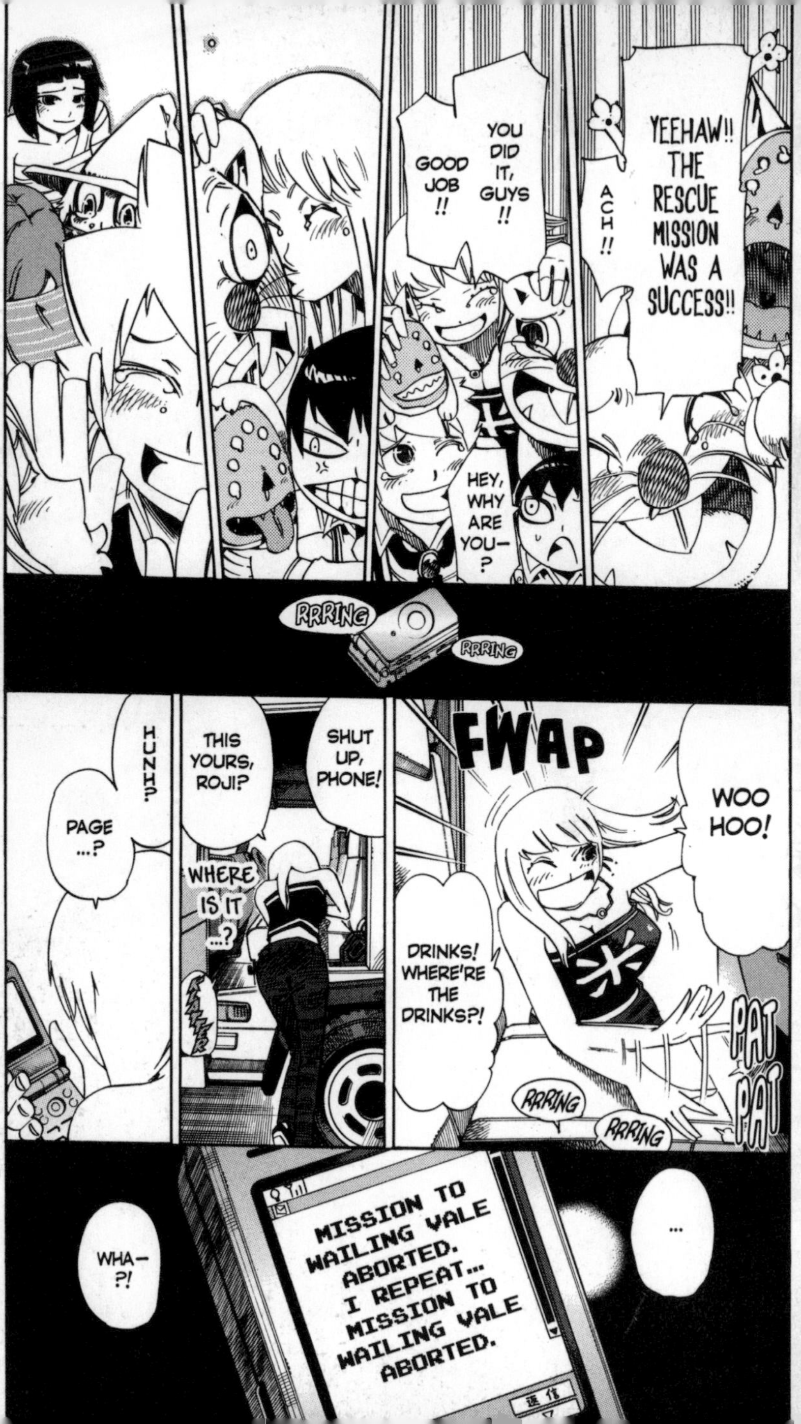
YEEHAW!! THE RESCUE MISSION WAS A SUCCESS!!
ACH!!
YOU DID IT, GUYS!!
GOOD JOB!!
HEY, WHY ARE YOU—?
RRRING
RRRING
WOO HOO!
FWAP
PAT PAT
DRINKS! WHERE'RE THE DRINKS?!
RRRING
RRRING
SHUT UP, PHONE!
THIS YOURS, ROJI?
WHERE IS IT ...?
HUNH?
PAGE ...?
...
MISSION TO WAILING VALE ABORTED. I REPEAT... MISSION TO WAILING VALE ABORTED.
WHA—?!

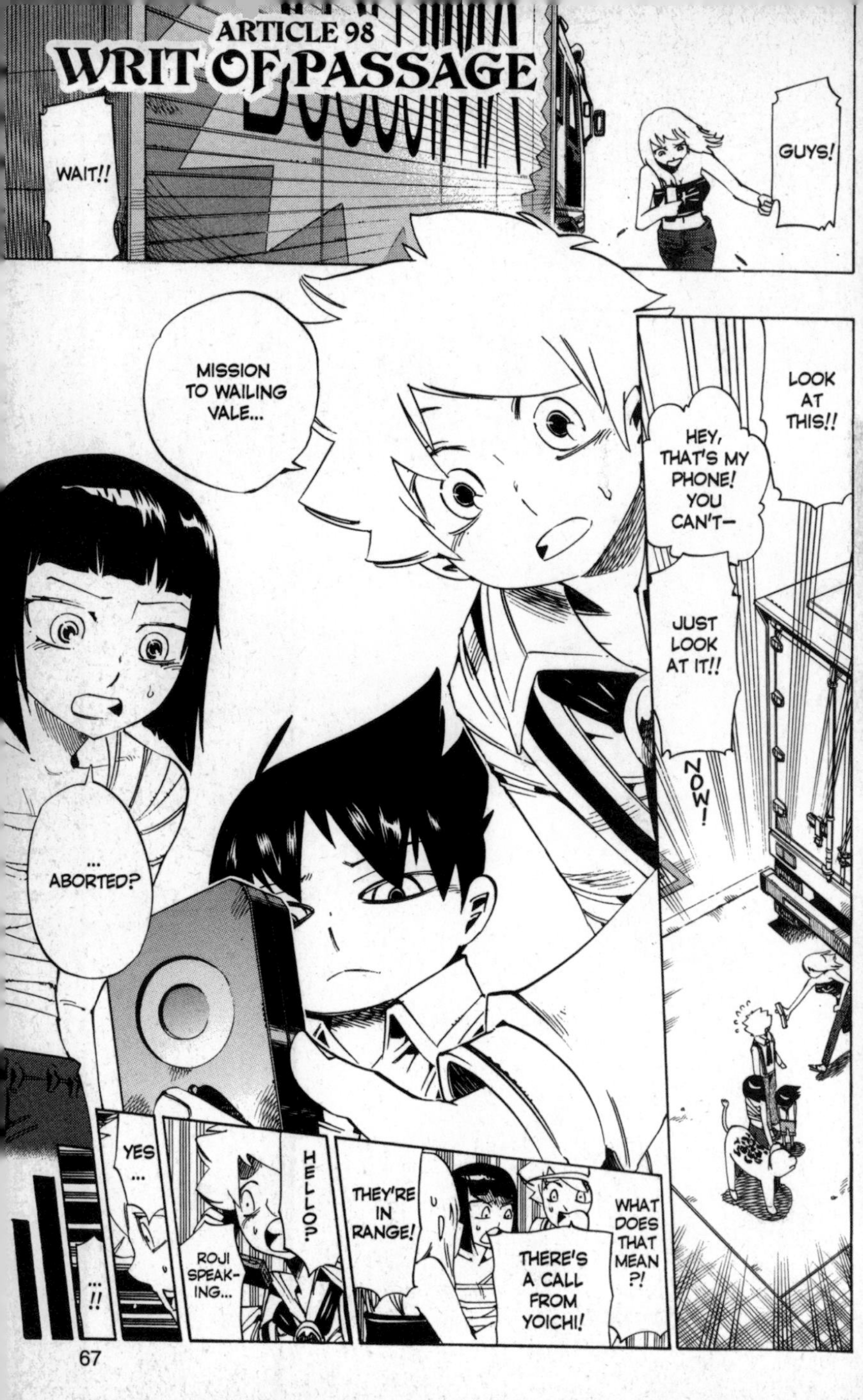
ARTICLE 98
WRIT OF PASSAGE
GUYS!
WAIT!!
LOOK AT THIS!!
HEY, THAT'S MY PHONE! YOU CAN'T—
JUST LOOK AT IT!!
NOW!
MISSION TO WAILING VALE...
...ABORTED?
WHAT DOES THAT MEAN?!
THERE'S A CALL FROM YOICHI!
THEY'RE IN RANGE!
HELLO?
ROJI SPEAK-ING...
YES...
...!!

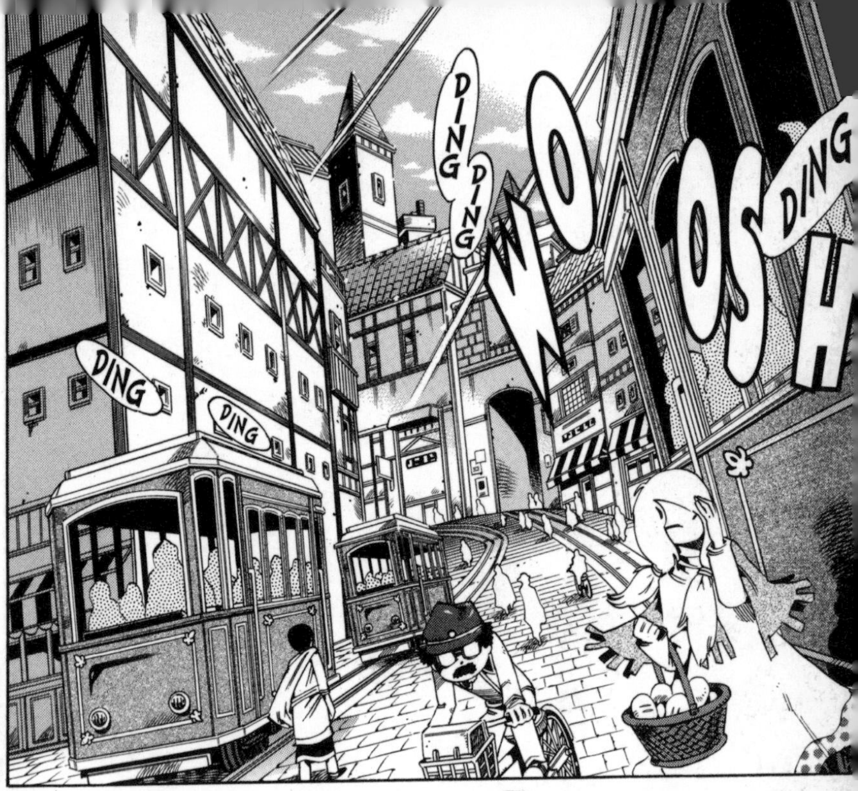
DING
WOOSH
DING DING
DING
DING

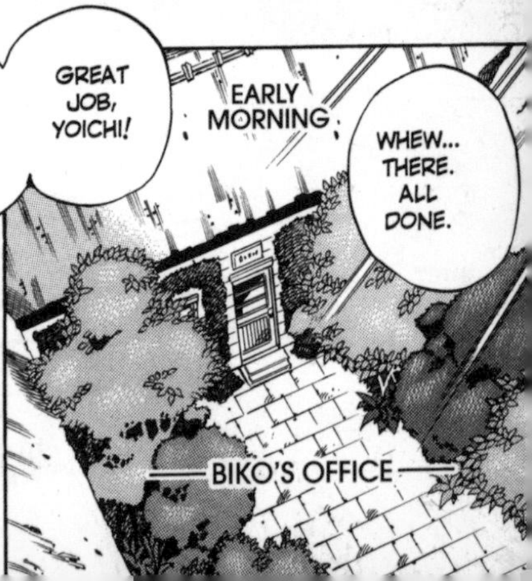
EARLY MORNING
BIKO'S OFFICE
WHEW... THERE. ALL DONE.

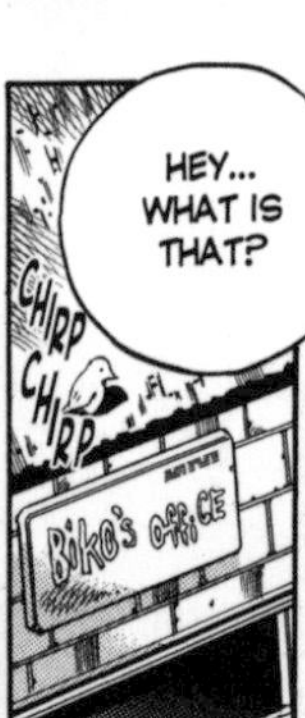
GREAT JOB, YOICHI!
HEY... WHAT IS THAT?
CHIRP CHIRP CHIRP
BIKO'S OFFICE

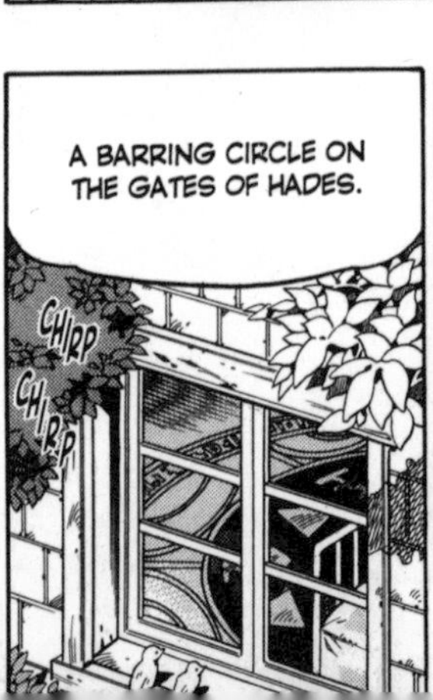
A BARRING CIRCLE ON THE GATES OF HADES.
CHIRP CHIRP

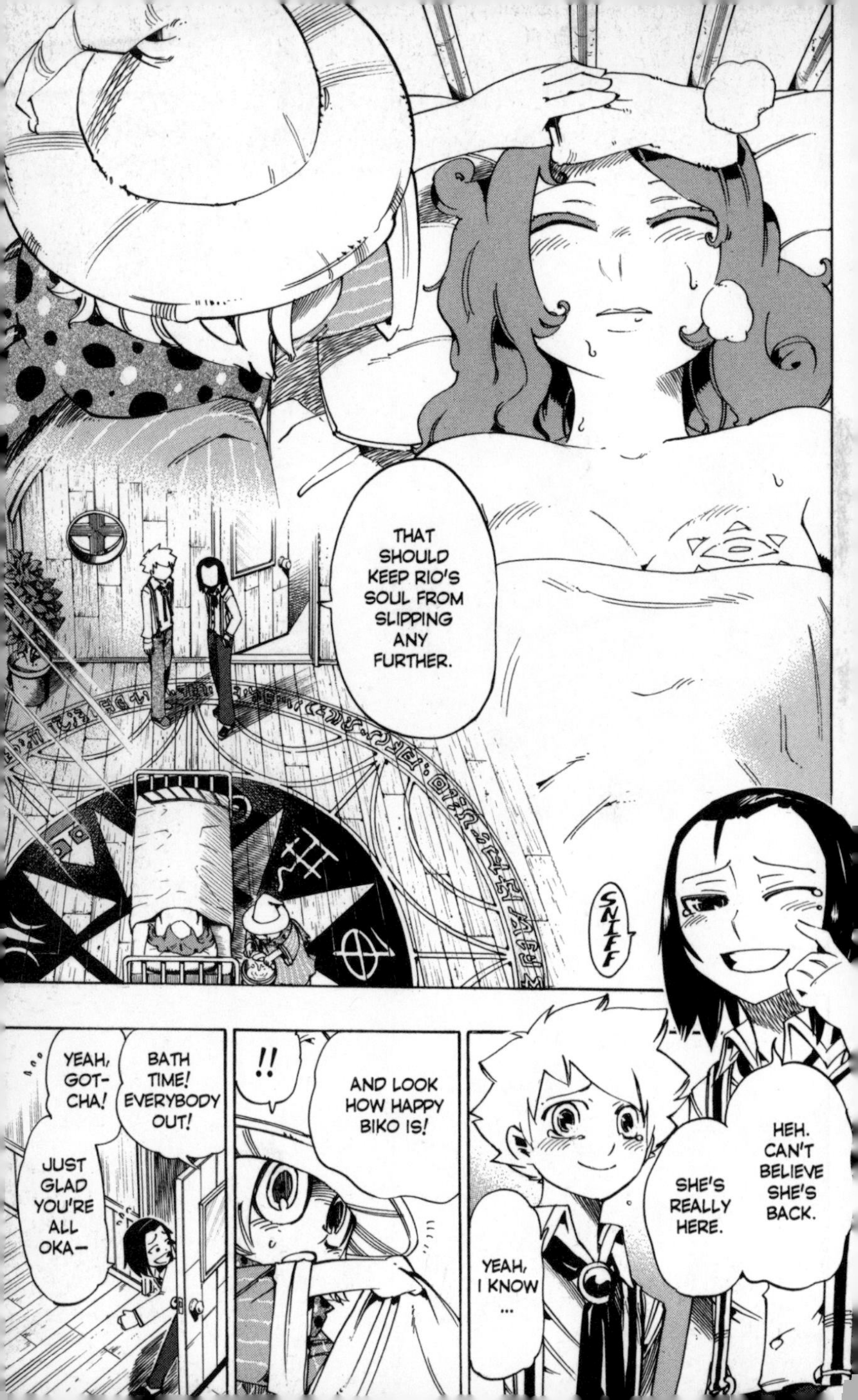
THAT SHOULD KEEP RIO'S SOUL FROM SLIPPING ANY FURTHER.
SNIFF
HEH. CAN'T BELIEVE SHE'S BACK.
SHE'S REALLY HERE.
YEAH, I KNOW ...
!!
AND LOOK HOW HAPPY BIKO IS!
BATH TIME! EVERYBODY OUT!
YEAH, GOT-CHA!
JUST GLAD YOU'RE ALL OKA—

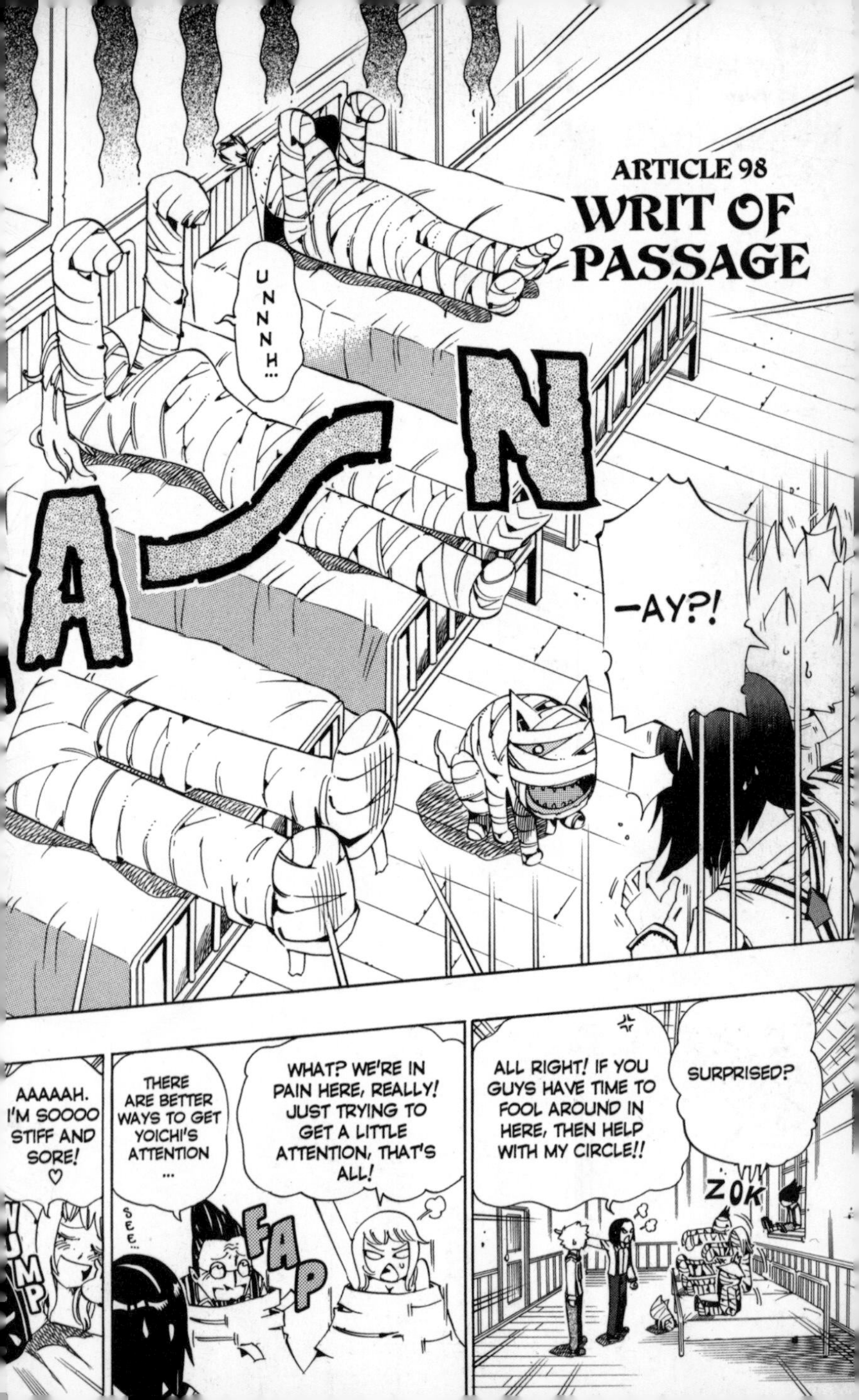
ARTICLE 98
WRIT OF PASSAGE
UNNNH...
A~N
-AY?!
SURPRISED?
ZOK
ALL RIGHT! IF YOU GUYS HAVE TIME TO FOOL AROUND IN HERE, THEN HELP WITH MY CIRCLE!!
WHAT? WE'RE IN PAIN HERE, REALLY! JUST TRYING TO GET A LITTLE ATTENTION, THAT'S ALL!
FAP
THERE ARE BETTER WAYS TO GET YOICHI'S ATTENTION ...
SEE...
AAAAAH. I'M SOOOO STIFF AND SORE! ♡
WUMP

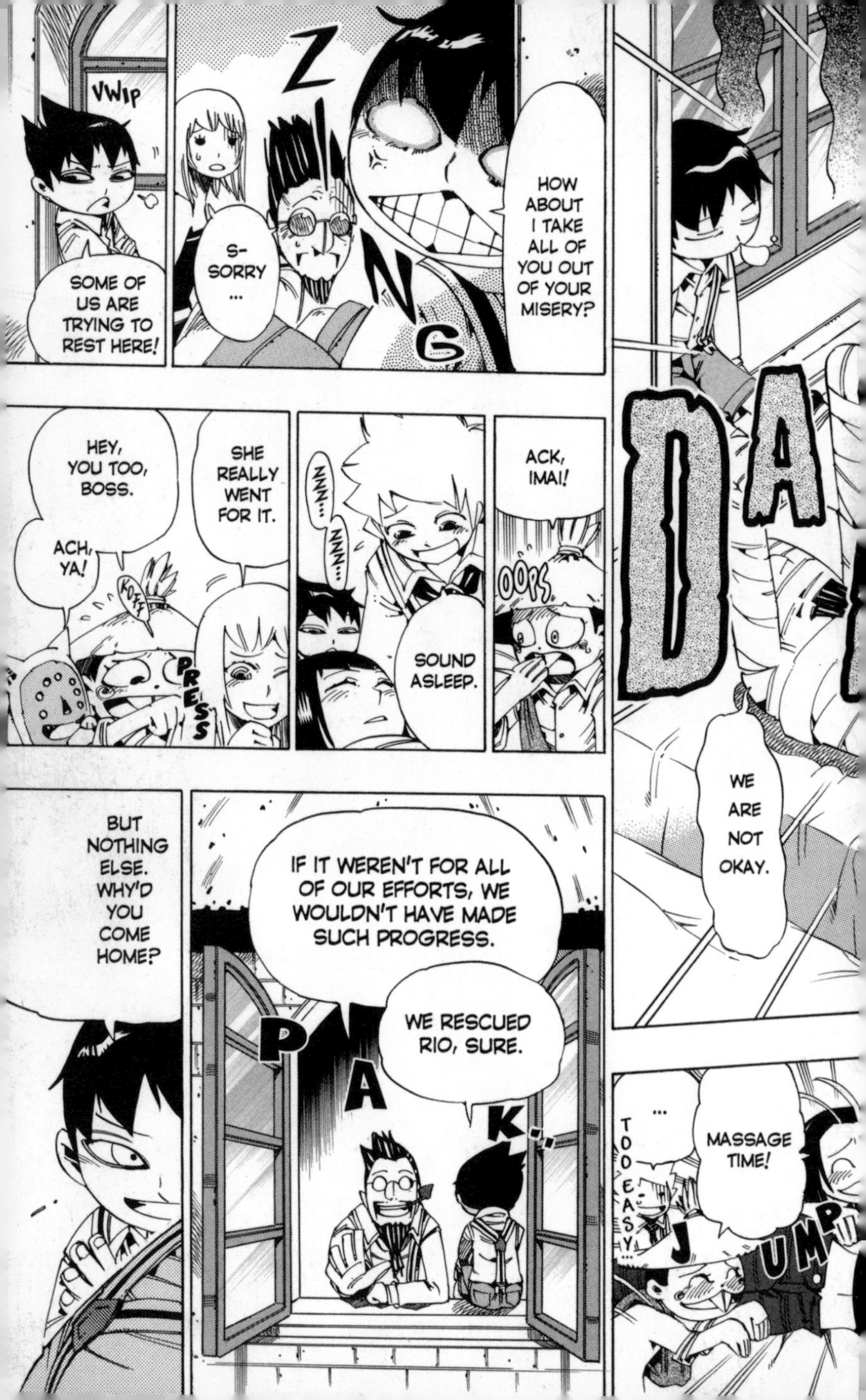
DA
WE ARE NOT OKAY.
HOW ABOUT I TAKE ALL OF YOU OUT OF YOUR MISERY?
ZING
S-SORRY...
VWIP
SOME OF US ARE TRYING TO REST HERE!
ACK, IMAI!
OOPS
SOUND ASLEEP.
ZZZ...
ZZZ...
SHE REALLY WENT FOR IT.
HEY, YOU TOO, BOSS.
ACH, YA!
KOFF
PRESS
...
MASSAGE TIME!
TOO EASY...
JUMP
IF IT WEREN'T FOR ALL OF OUR EFFORTS, WE WOULDN'T HAVE MADE SUCH PROGRESS.
WE RESCUED RIO, SURE.
PAK
BUT NOTHING ELSE. WHY'D YOU COME HOME?

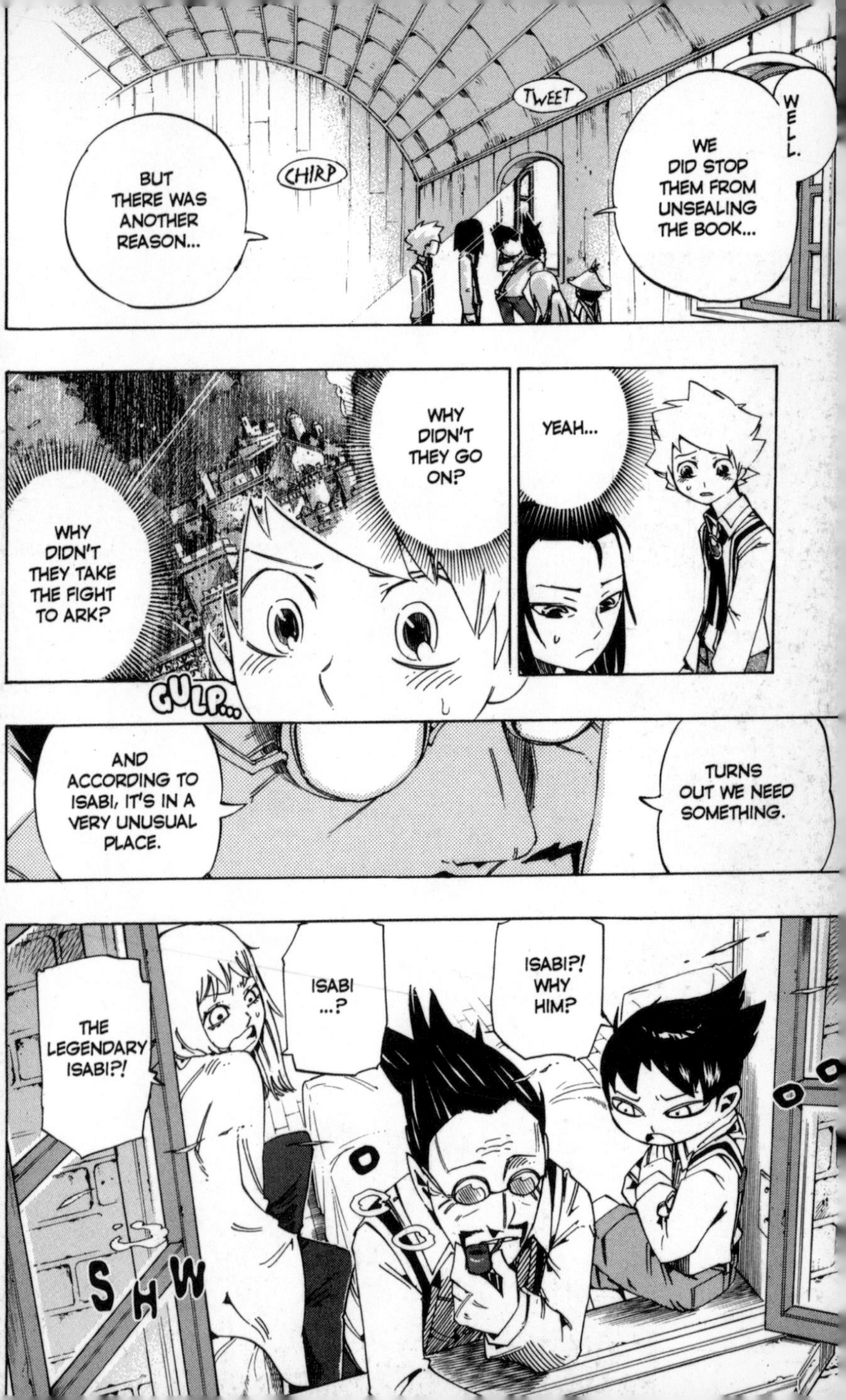
WELL.
WE DID STOP THEM FROM UNSEALING THE BOOK...
TWEET
CHIRP
BUT THERE WAS ANOTHER REASON...
YEAH...
WHY DIDN'T THEY GO ON?
WHY DIDN'T THEY TAKE THE FIGHT TO ARK?
GULP...
TURNS OUT WE NEED SOMETHING.
AND ACCORDING TO ISABI, IT'S IN A VERY UNUSUAL PLACE.
ISABI?! WHY HIM?
ISABI ...?
THE LEGENDARY ISABI?!
SHW

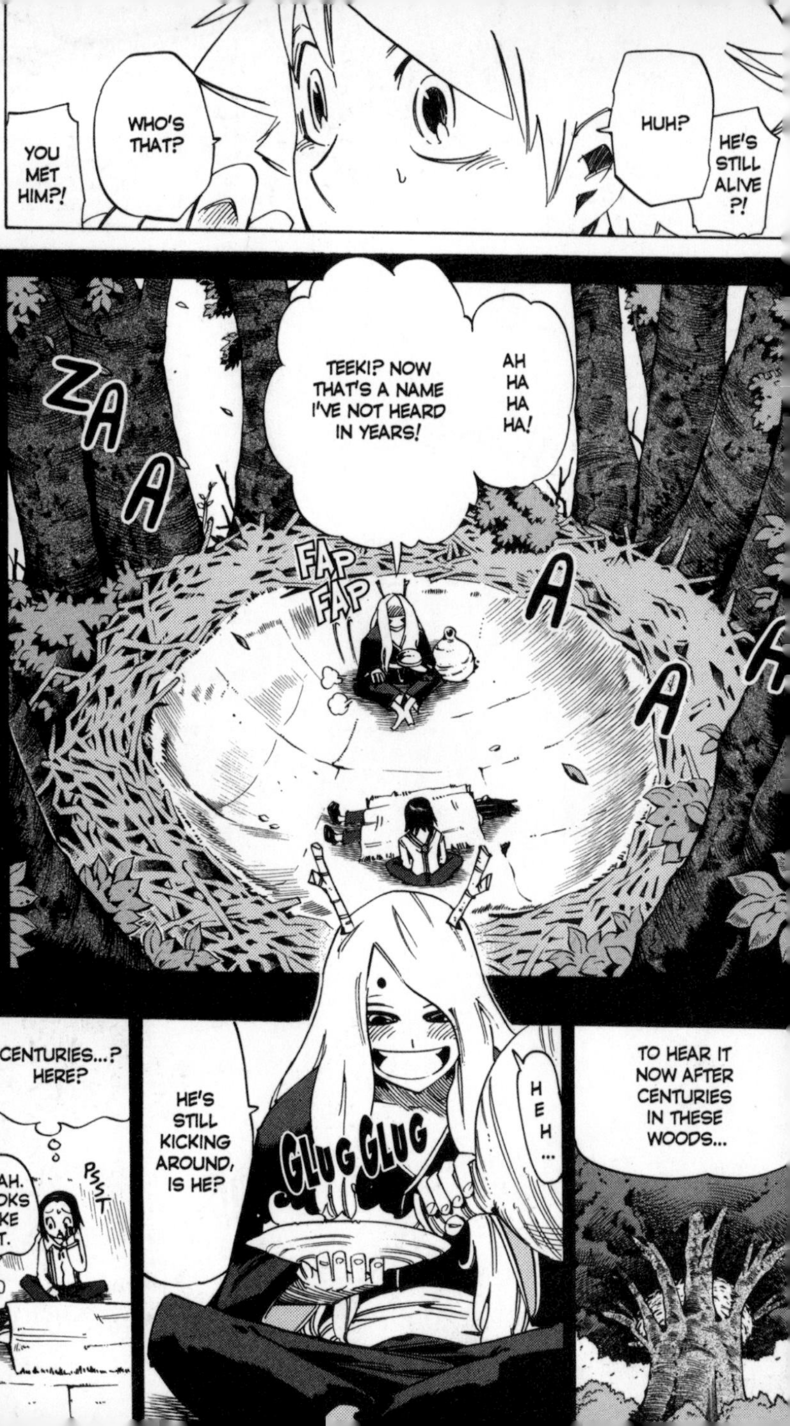
HUH?
HE'S STILL ALIVE?!
WHO'S THAT?
YOU MET HIM?!
AH HA HA HA!
TEEKI? NOW THAT'S A NAME I'VE NOT HEARD IN YEARS!
ZAAAAA
FAP FAP
TO HEAR IT NOW AFTER CENTURIES IN THESE WOODS...
HEH...
HE'S STILL KICKING AROUND, IS HE?
GLUG GLUG
CENTURIES...? HERE?
PSST
YEAH. LOOKS LIKE IT.

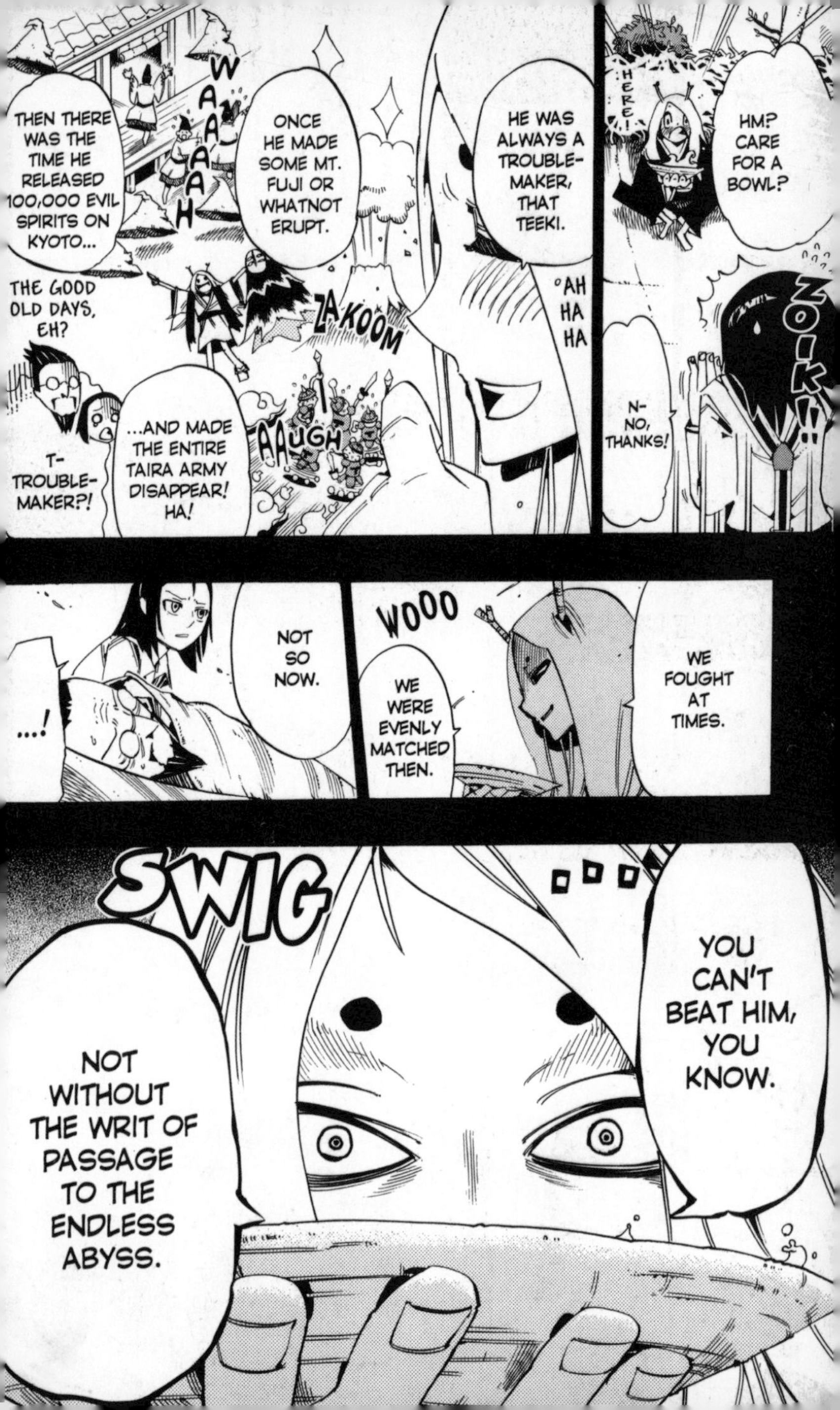
HM? CARE FOR A BOWL?
HERE!
ZOIK!!
N- NO, THANKS!
HE WAS ALWAYS A TROUBLE-MAKER, THAT TEEKI.
AH HA HA
ONCE HE MADE SOME MT. FUJI OR WHATNOT ERUPT.
WAAAAAH
THEN THERE WAS THE TIME HE RELEASED 100,000 EVIL SPIRITS ON KYOTO...
ZAKOOM
AAUGH
...AND MADE THE ENTIRE TAIRA ARMY DISAPPEAR! HA!
THE GOOD OLD DAYS, EH?
T-TROUBLE-MAKER?!
WE FOUGHT AT TIMES.
WOOO
WE WERE EVENLY MATCHED THEN.
NOT SO NOW.
...!
YOU CAN'T BEAT HIM, YOU KNOW.
SWIG
NOT WITHOUT THE WRIT OF PASSAGE TO THE ENDLESS ABYSS.

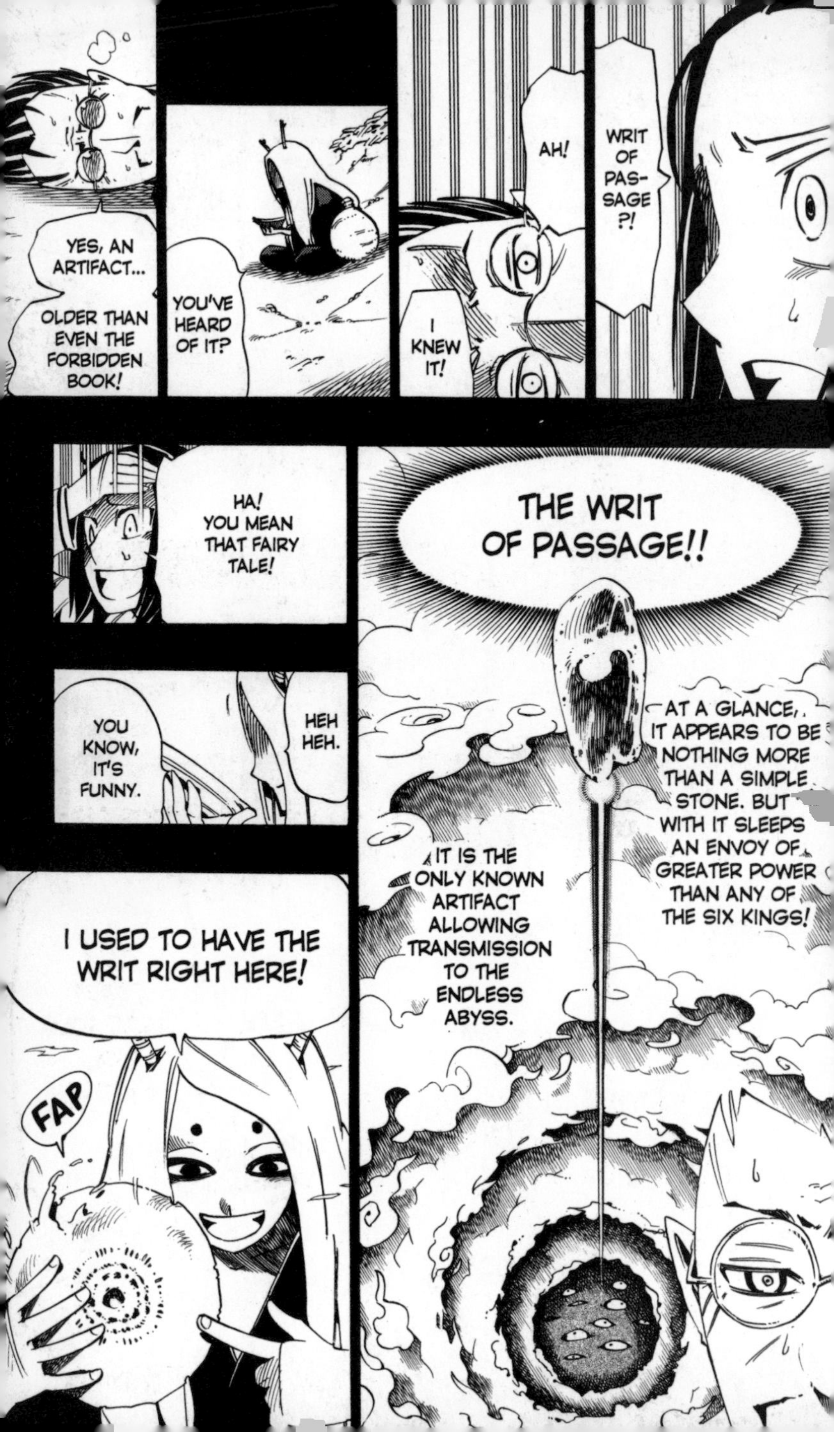
WRIT OF PAS-SAGE?!
AH!
I KNEW IT!
YOU'VE HEARD OF IT?
YES, AN ARTIFACT...
OLDER THAN EVEN THE FORBIDDEN BOOK!
THE WRIT OF PASSAGE!!
AT A GLANCE, IT APPEARS TO BE NOTHING MORE THAN A SIMPLE STONE. BUT WITH IT SLEEPS AN ENVOY OF GREATER POWER THAN ANY OF THE SIX KINGS!
IT IS THE ONLY KNOWN ARTIFACT ALLOWING TRANSMISSION TO THE ENDLESS ABYSS.
HA! YOU MEAN THAT FAIRY TALE!
HEH HEH.
YOU KNOW, IT'S FUNNY.
I USED TO HAVE THE WRIT RIGHT HERE!
FAP

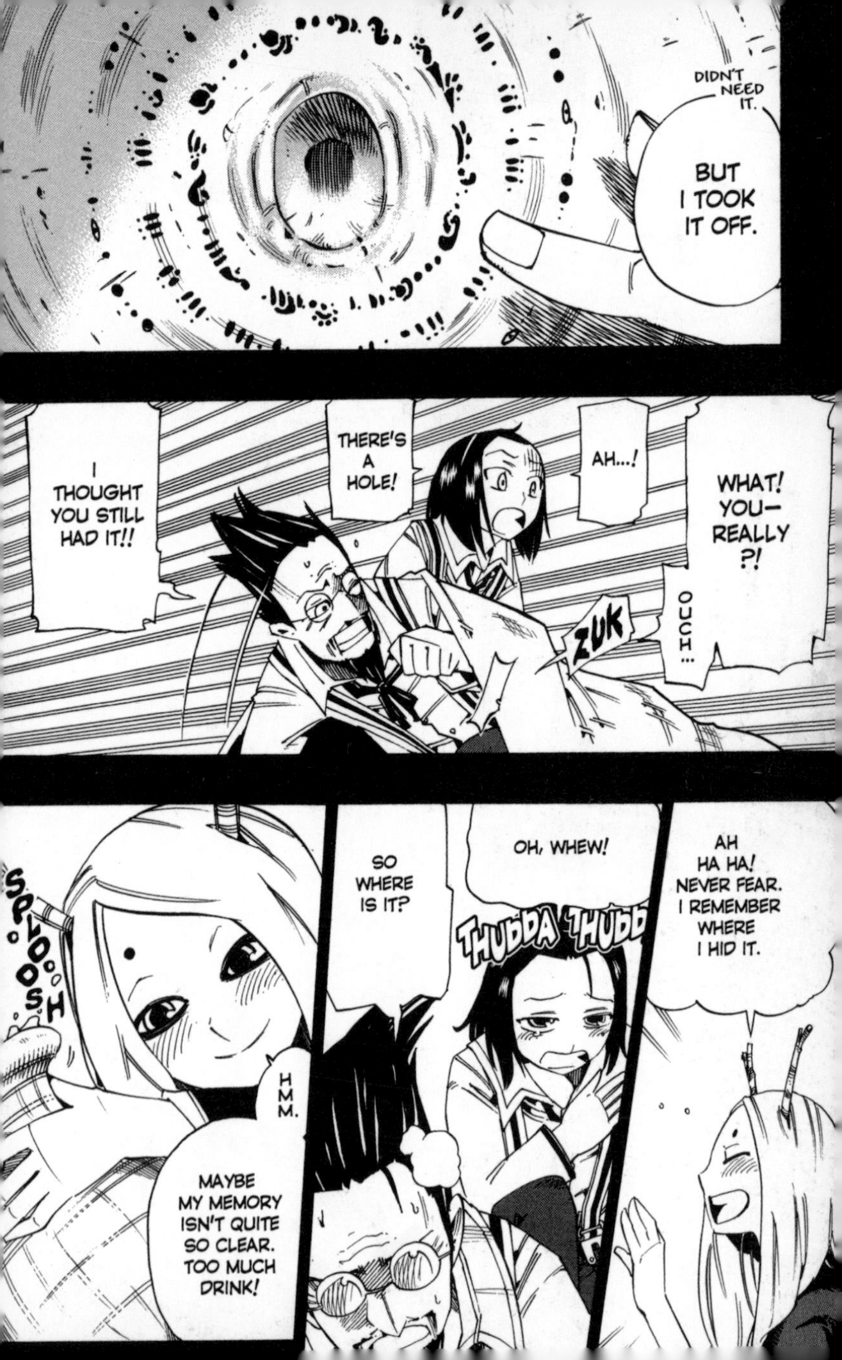
DIDN'T NEED IT.
BUT I TOOK IT OFF.
WHAT! YOU— REALLY ?!
OUCH...
AH...!
ZUK
THERE'S A HOLE!
I THOUGHT YOU STILL HAD IT!!
AH HA HA! NEVER FEAR. I REMEMBER WHERE I HID IT.
OH, WHEW!
THUDDA THUDD
SO WHERE IS IT?
HMM.
SPLOOOSH
MAYBE MY MEMORY ISN'T QUITE SO CLEAR. TOO MUCH DRINK!

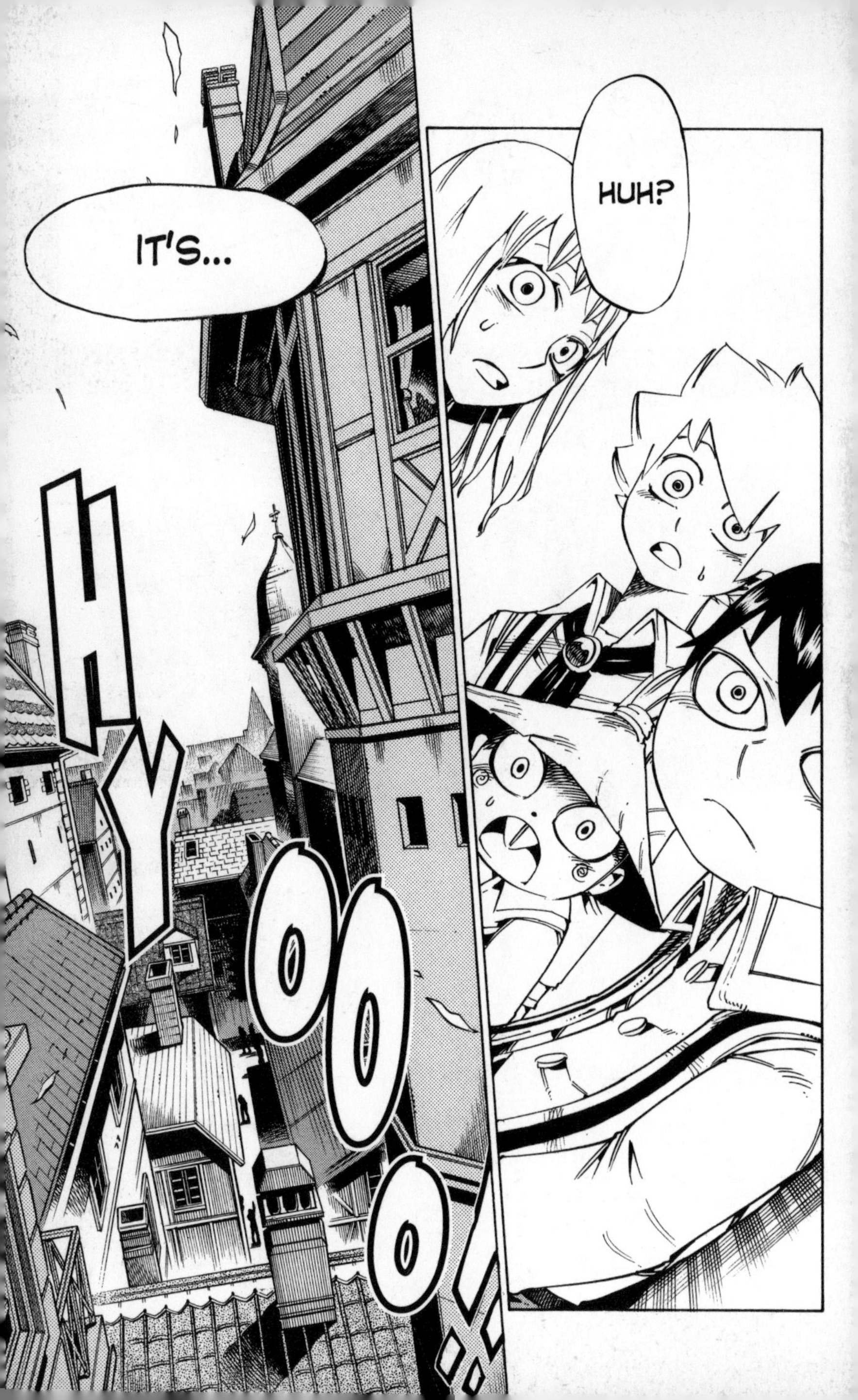
HUH?
IT'S...
HYOOO

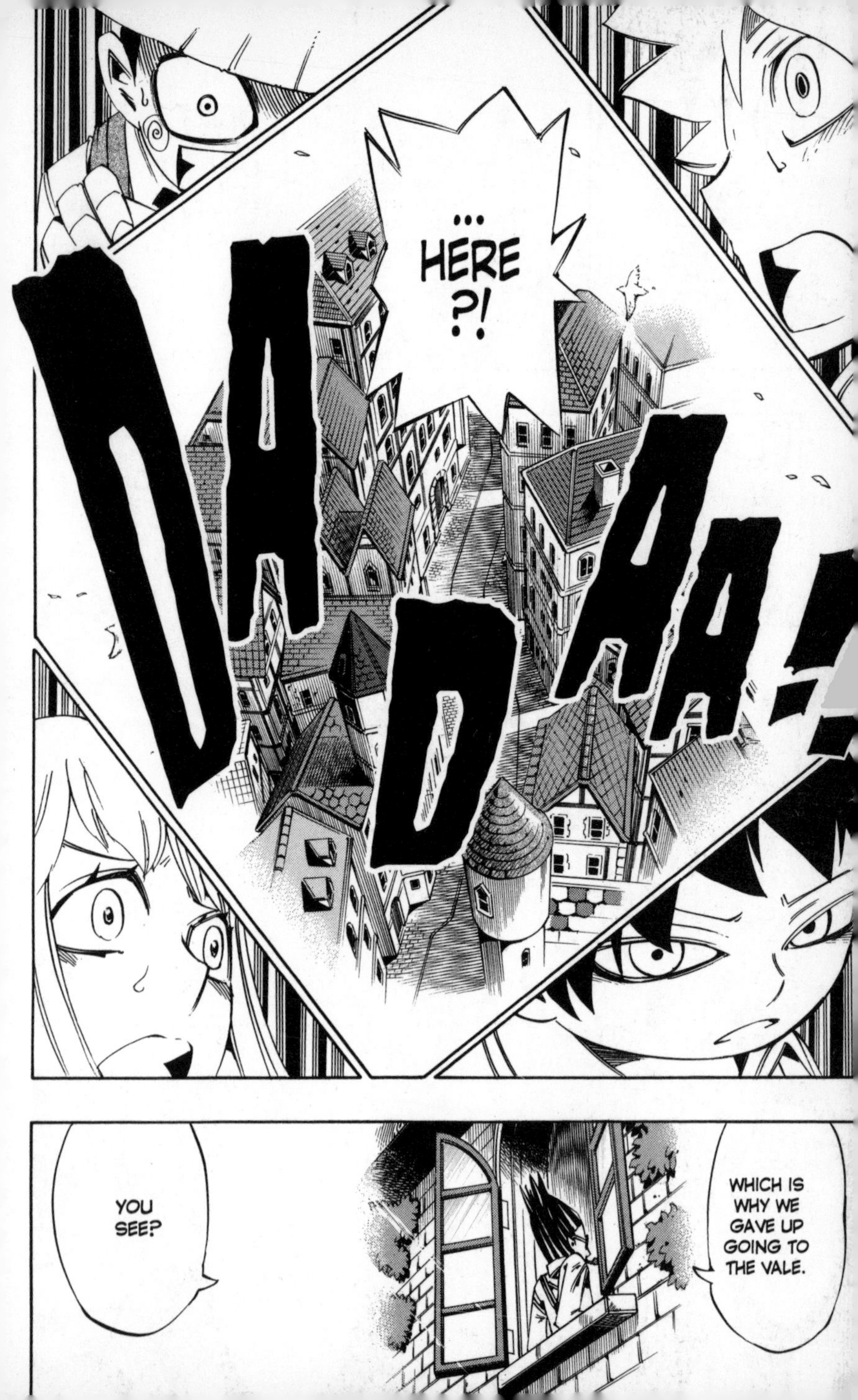
... HERE ?!
DADAA!
WHICH IS WHY WE GAVE UP GOING TO THE VALE.
YOU SEE?

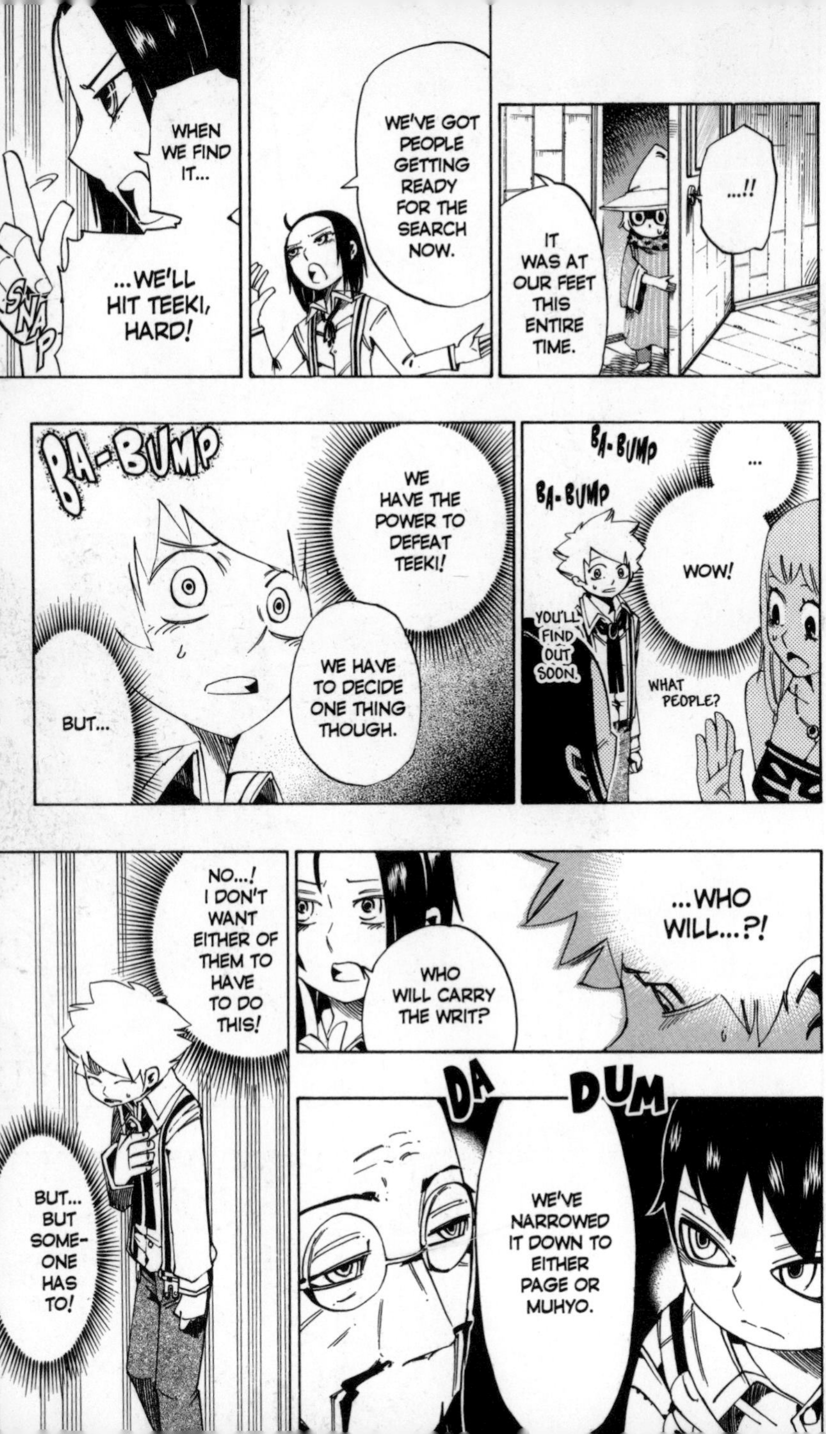
...!!
IT WAS AT OUR FEET THIS ENTIRE TIME.
WE'VE GOT PEOPLE GETTING READY FOR THE SEARCH NOW.
WHEN WE FIND IT...
SNAP
...WE'LL HIT TEEKI, HARD!
BA-BUMP
...
BA-BUMP
WOW!
WHAT PEOPLE?
YOU'LL FIND OUT SOON.
BA-BUMP
WE HAVE THE POWER TO DEFEAT TEEKI!
WE HAVE TO DECIDE ONE THING THOUGH.
BUT...
...WHO WILL...?!
WHO WILL CARRY THE WRIT?
DA DUM
WE'VE NARROWED IT DOWN TO EITHER PAGE OR MUHYO.
NO...! I DON'T WANT EITHER OF THEM TO HAVE TO DO THIS!
BUT... BUT SOME-ONE HAS TO!

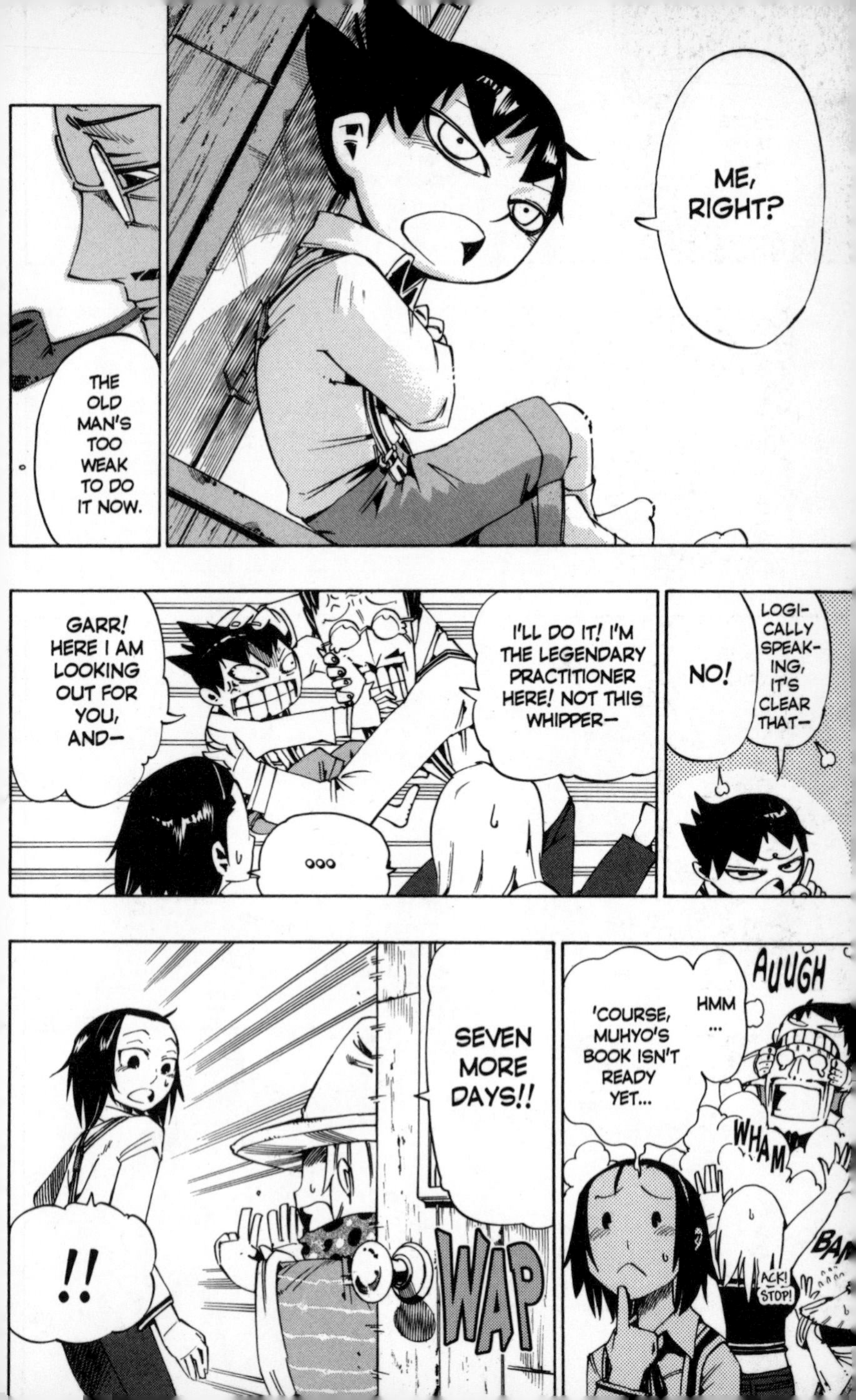
ME, RIGHT?
THE OLD MAN'S TOO WEAK TO DO IT NOW.
LOGI-CALLY SPEAK-ING, IT'S CLEAR THAT—
NO!
I'LL DO IT! I'M THE LEGENDARY PRACTITIONER HERE! NOT THIS WHIPPER—
GARR! HERE I AM LOOKING OUT FOR YOU, AND—
...
AUUGH
HMM ...
'COURSE, MUHYO'S BOOK ISN'T READY YET...
WHAM
BAM
ACK! STOP!
SEVEN MORE DAYS!!
WAP
!!

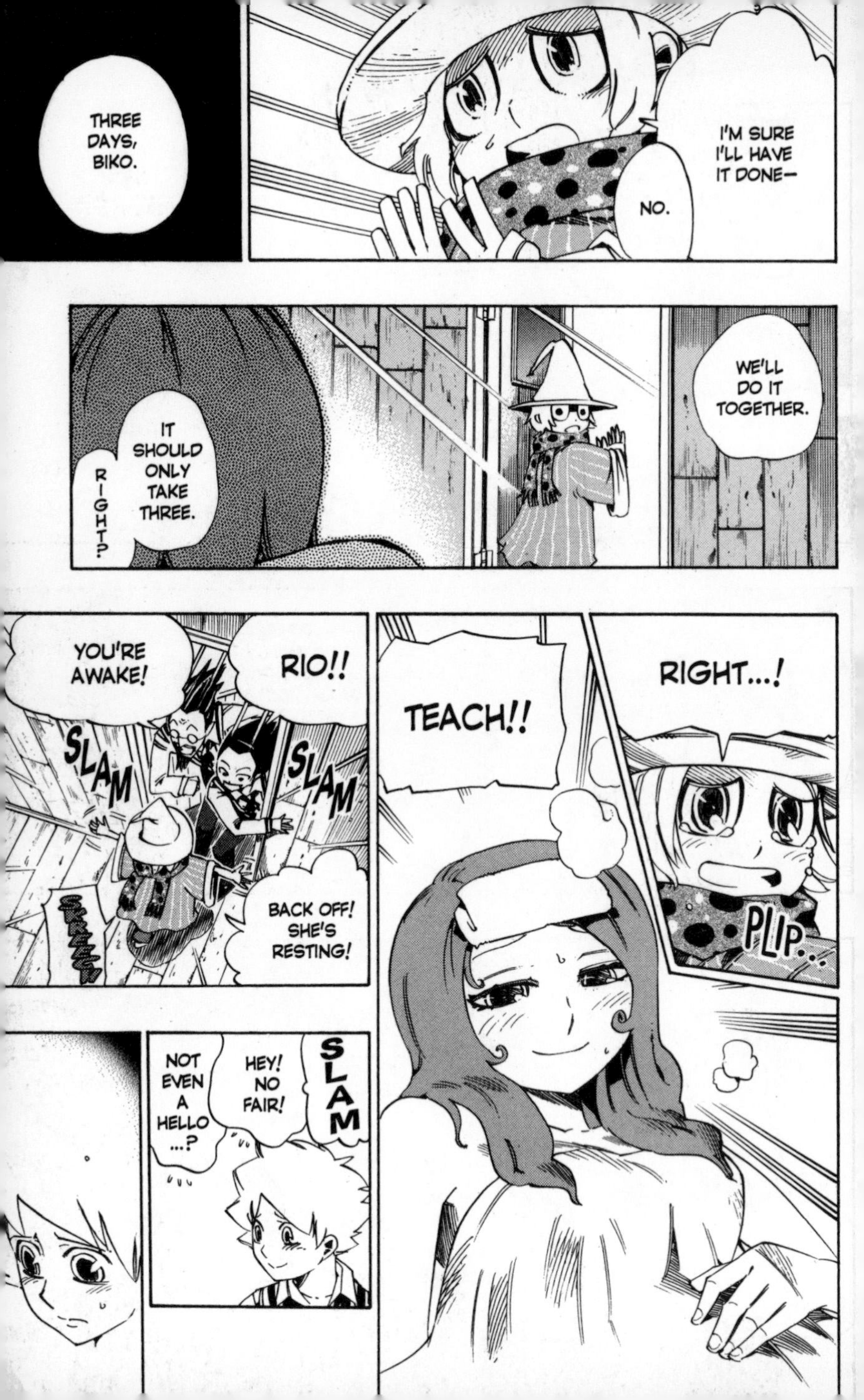
I'M SURE I'LL HAVE IT DONE—
NO.
THREE DAYS, BIKO.
WE'LL DO IT TOGETHER.
IT SHOULD ONLY TAKE THREE.
RIGHT?
RIGHT...!
PLIP...
TEACH!!
RIO!!
YOU'RE AWAKE!
SLAM
SLAM
BACK OFF! SHE'S RESTING!
SLAM
HEY! NO FAIR!
NOT EVEN A HELLO ...?

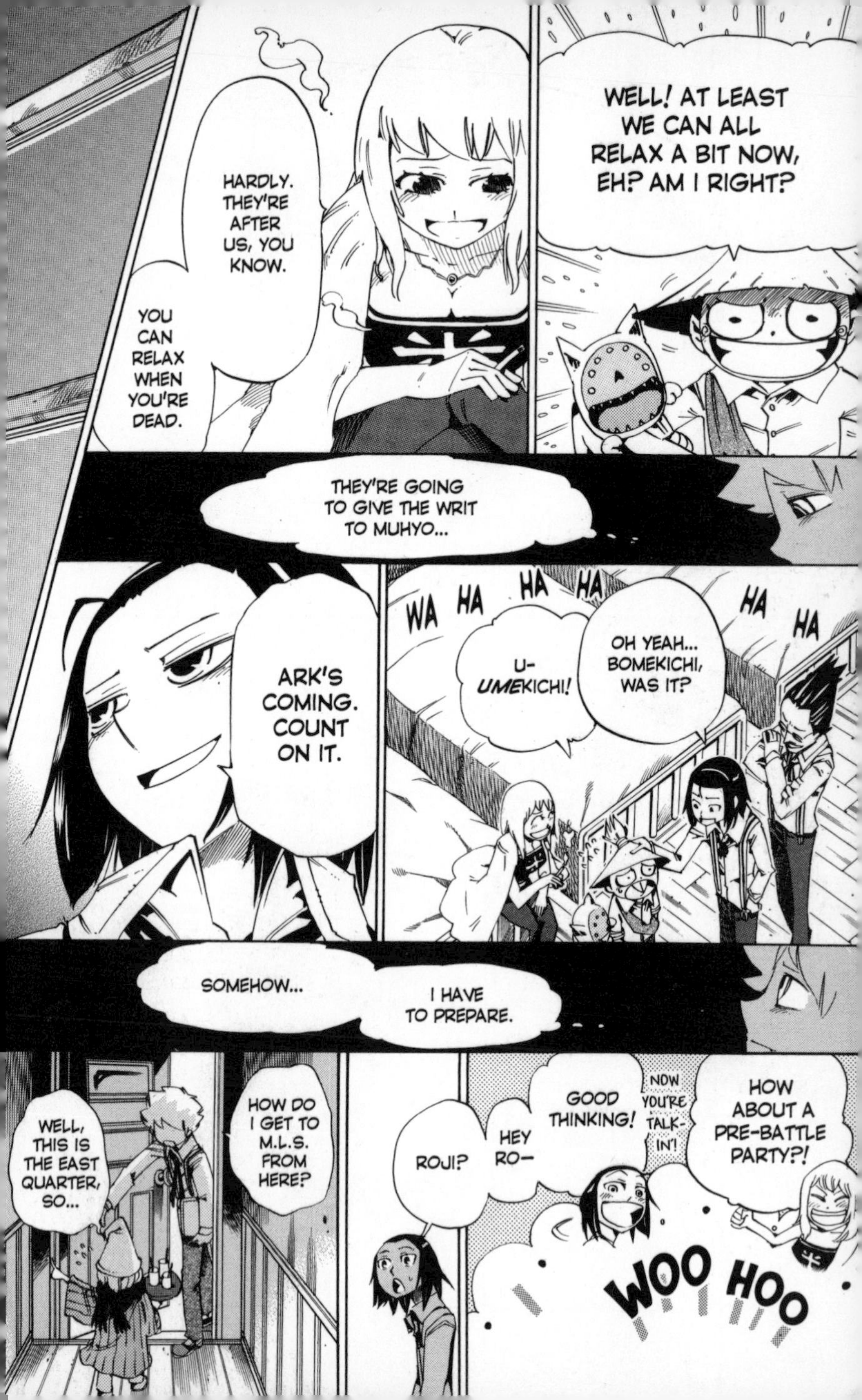
WELL! AT LEAST WE CAN ALL RELAX A BIT NOW, EH? AM I RIGHT?
HARDLY. THEY'RE AFTER US, YOU KNOW.
YOU CAN RELAX WHEN YOU'RE DEAD.
THEY'RE GOING TO GIVE THE WRIT TO MUHYO...
HA HA
OH YEAH... BOMEKICHI, WAS IT?
HA HA
U-UMEKICHI!
HA
WA
ARK'S COMING. COUNT ON IT.
SOMEHOW...
I HAVE TO PREPARE.
HOW ABOUT A PRE-BATTLE PARTY?!
NOW YOU'RE TALK-IN'!
GOOD THINKING!
HEY RO—
ROJI?
WOO HOO
HOW DO I GET TO M.L.S. FROM HERE?
WELL, THIS IS THE EAST QUARTER, SO...

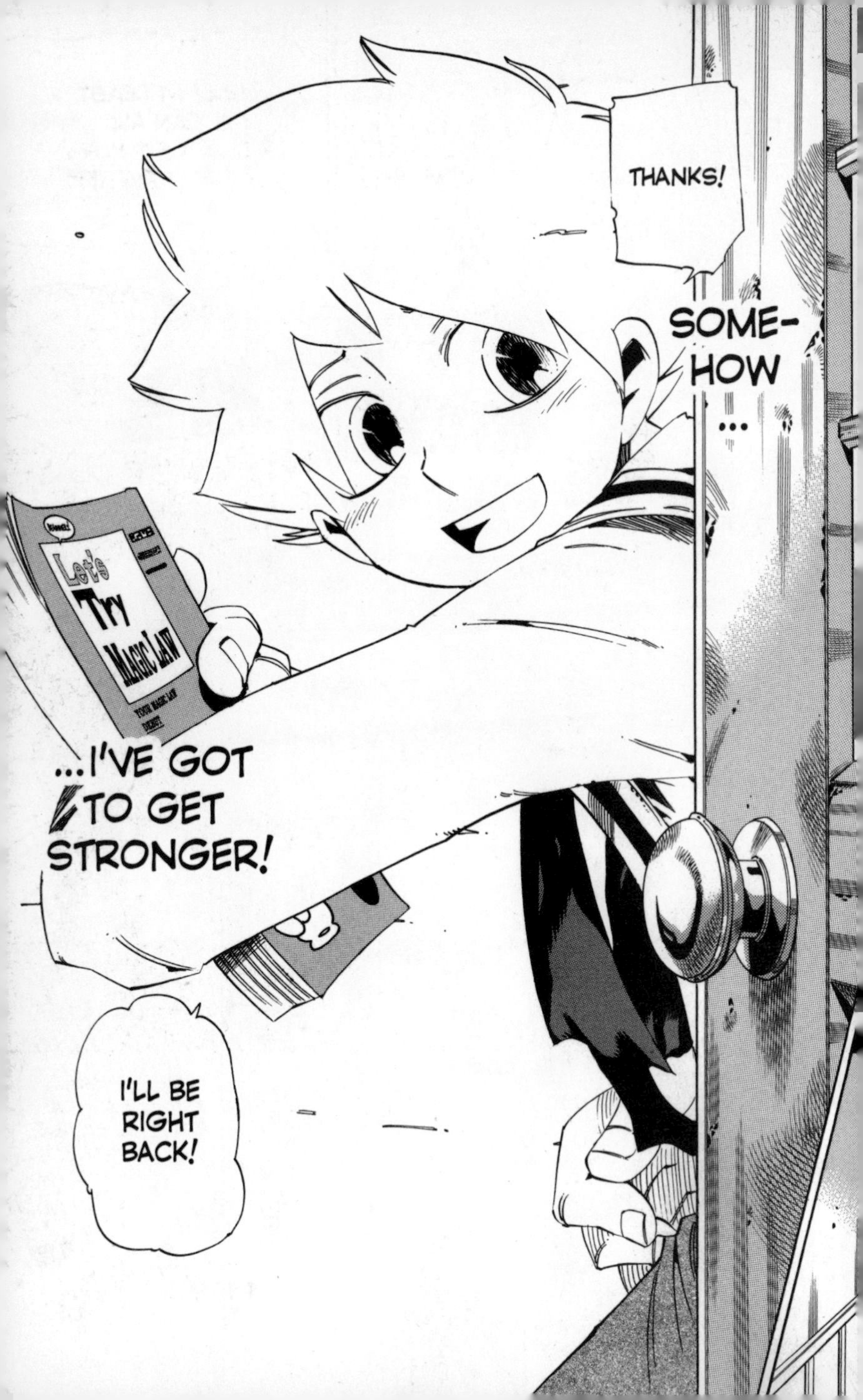
THANKS!
SOME-HOW...
...I'VE GOT TO GET STRONGER!
Let's Try MAGIC LAW
I'LL BE RIGHT BACK!

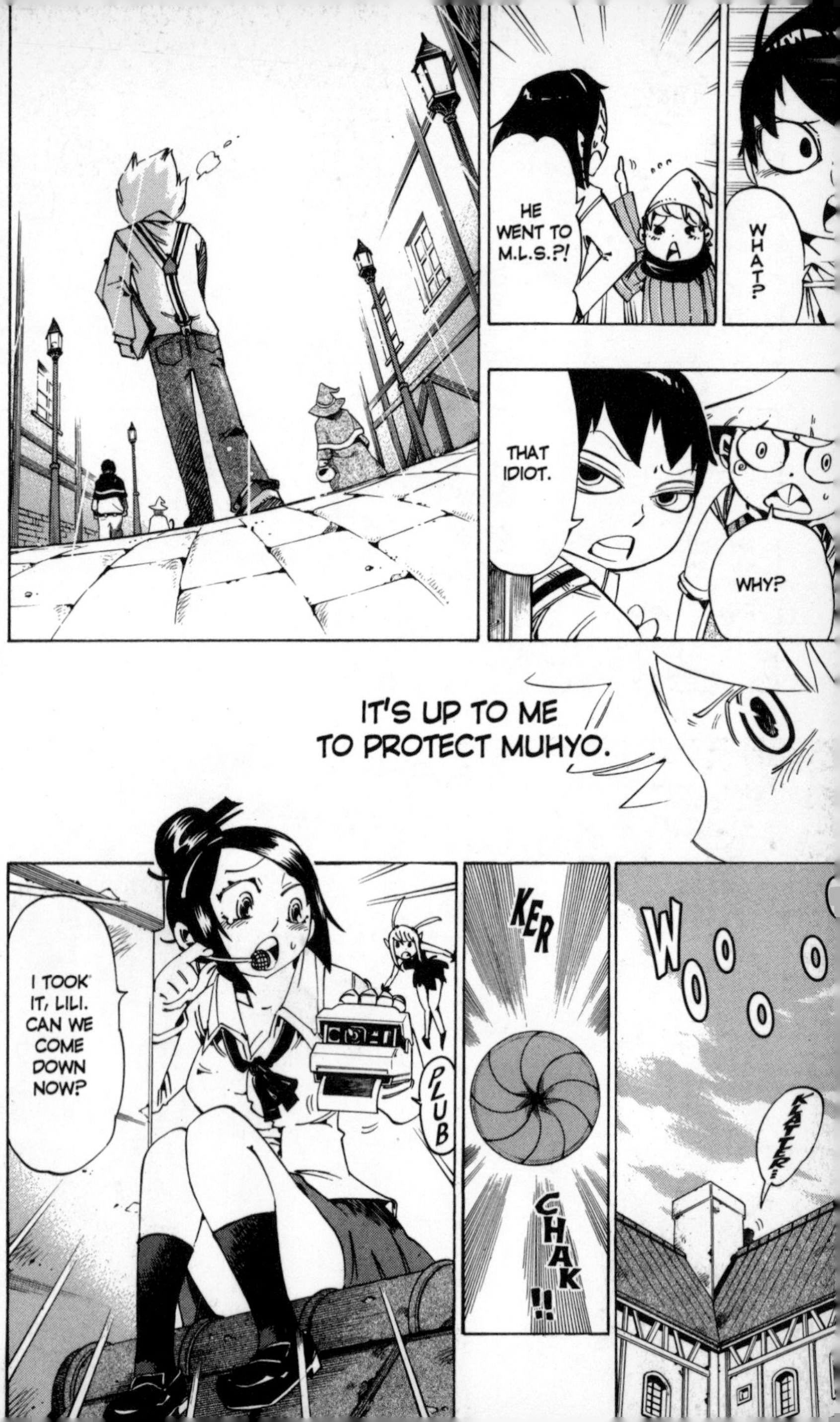
WHAT?
HE WENT TO M.L.S.?!
WHY?
THAT IDIOT.
IT'S UP TO ME TO PROTECT MUHYO.
WOOOOO
KATTER...
KER
CHAK!!
PLUB
I TOOK IT, LILI. CAN WE COME DOWN NOW?

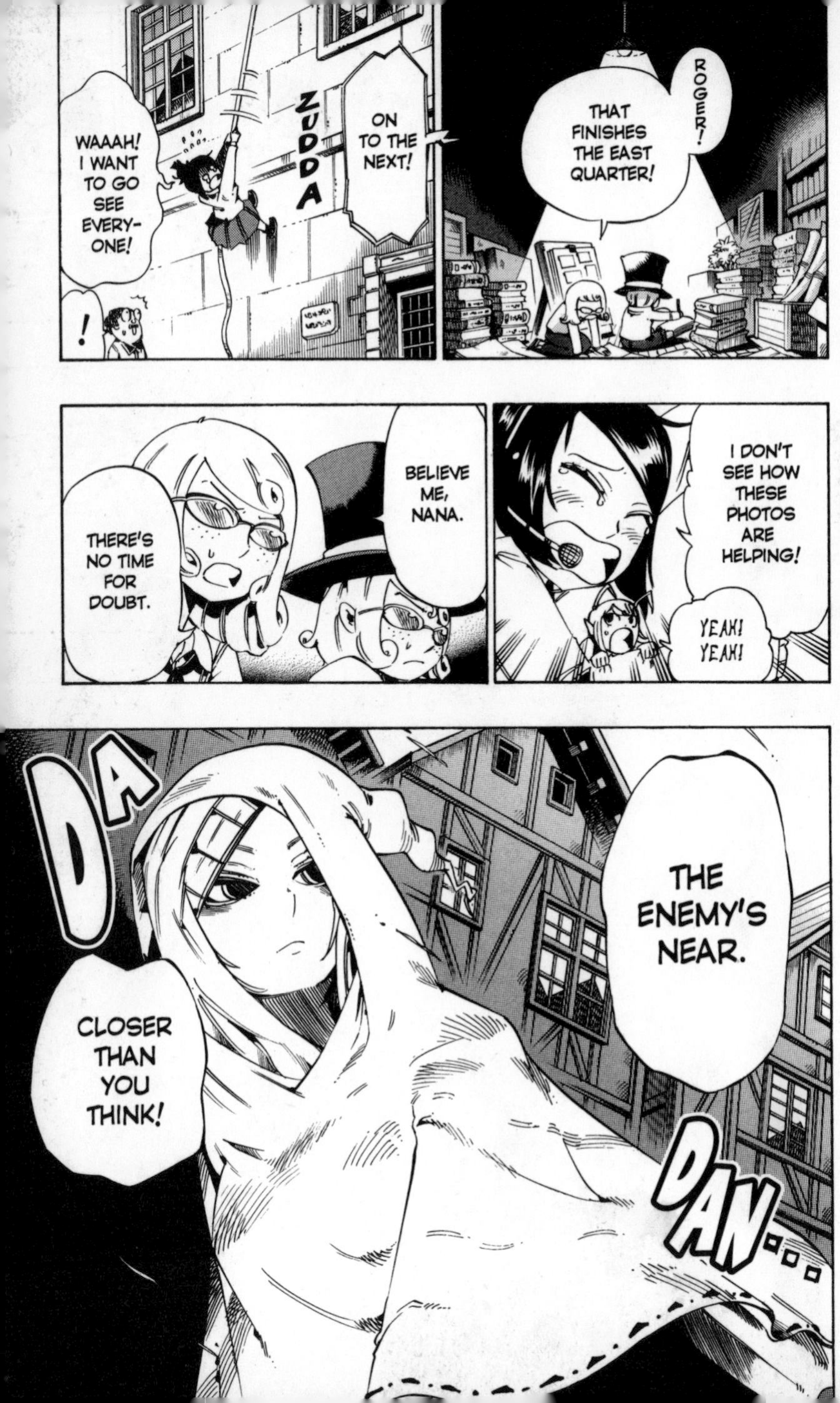
THAT FINISHES THE EAST QUARTER!
ROGER!
ON TO THE NEXT!
ZUDDA
WAAAH! I WANT TO GO SEE EVERY-ONE!
!
I DON'T SEE HOW THESE PHOTOS ARE HELPING!
YEAH! YEAH!
BELIEVE ME, NANA.
THERE'S NO TIME FOR DOUBT.
DA
THE ENEMY'S NEAR.
CLOSER THAN YOU THINK!
DAN...

Q:
I KNOW THAT THE HIGHEST-RANKING ENVOYS, LIKE LUALALIE, ARE CALLED THE SIX KINGS, BUT WHAT RANK WAS THE ENVOY THAT PAGE'S TEACHER ANTONIO SUMMONED TO FIGHT TEEKI?

-M.T., KANAGAWA PREFECTURE

A:
WELL, THIS →

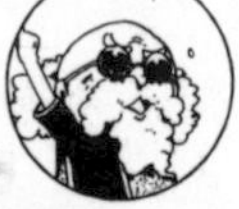

IS ANTONIO SAKUMARU.

AND THIS →

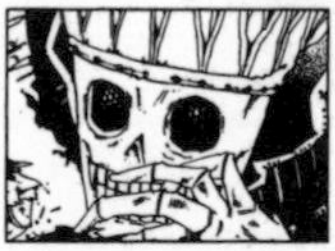

IS THE ENVOY.

WOW, YOU'RE REALLY FINDING THE UNUSUAL ONES TO ASK ABOUT. THEY USED SEVERAL PEOPLE TO SUMMON THIS ENVOY, SO IT'S DEFINITELY HIGH-LEVEL MAGIC LAW. I DON'T HAVE A RANK TO GIVE YOU, PER SE, BUT I DO KNOW THAT THE NAME OF THE MAGIC LAW THEY USED IS THE "ADVENT OF THE COMMANDER OF THE MAGIC REALM."

Q: JUST WHO IS ASSISTANT JUDGE OHKI? IS SHE IMAI'S NEW PARTNER?

-K.H., AICHI PREFECTURE

A: ASSISTANT JUDGE OHKI IS →

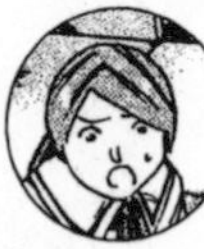

YET ANOTHER MINOR CHARACTER QUESTION! ASSISTANT JUDGE OHKI IS NOT IMAI'S PARTNER. SHE WAS ON NIGHT DUTY AND GOT INVOLVED BY CHANCE. BUT MAYBE SHE'LL MAKE ANOTHER APPEARANCE SOMEDAY...?

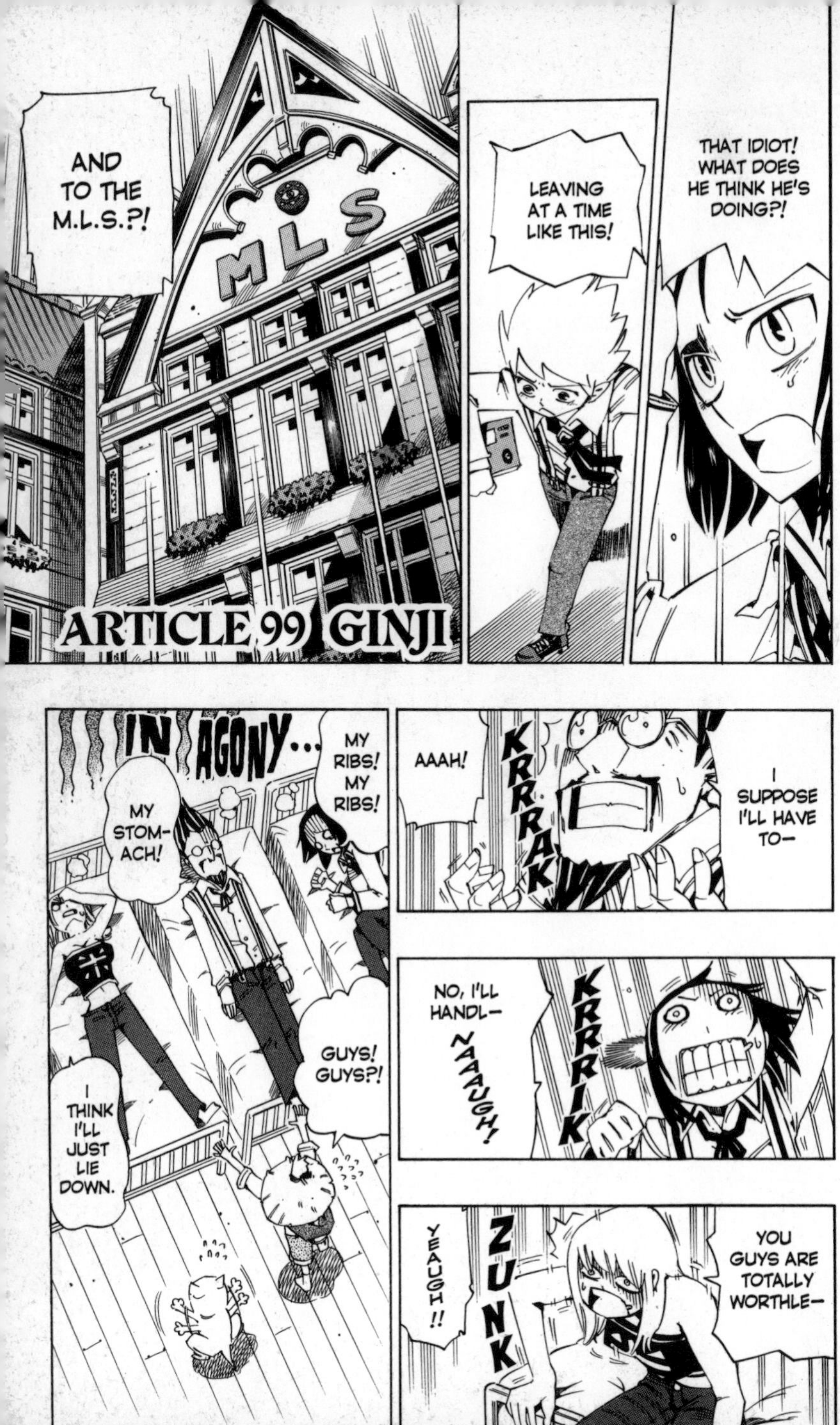
THAT IDIOT! WHAT DOES HE THINK HE'S DOING?!
LEAVING AT A TIME LIKE THIS!
AND TO THE M.L.S.?!
MLS
ARTICLE 99 GINJI
I SUPPOSE I'LL HAVE TO—
KRRRAK
AAAH!
KRRRIK
NO, I'LL HANDL—
NAAAUGH!
YOU GUYS ARE TOTALLY WORTHLE—
ZUNK
YEAUGH!!
MY RIBS! MY RIBS!
IN AGONY...
MY STOMACH!
GUYS! GUYS?!
I THINK I'LL JUST LIE DOWN.

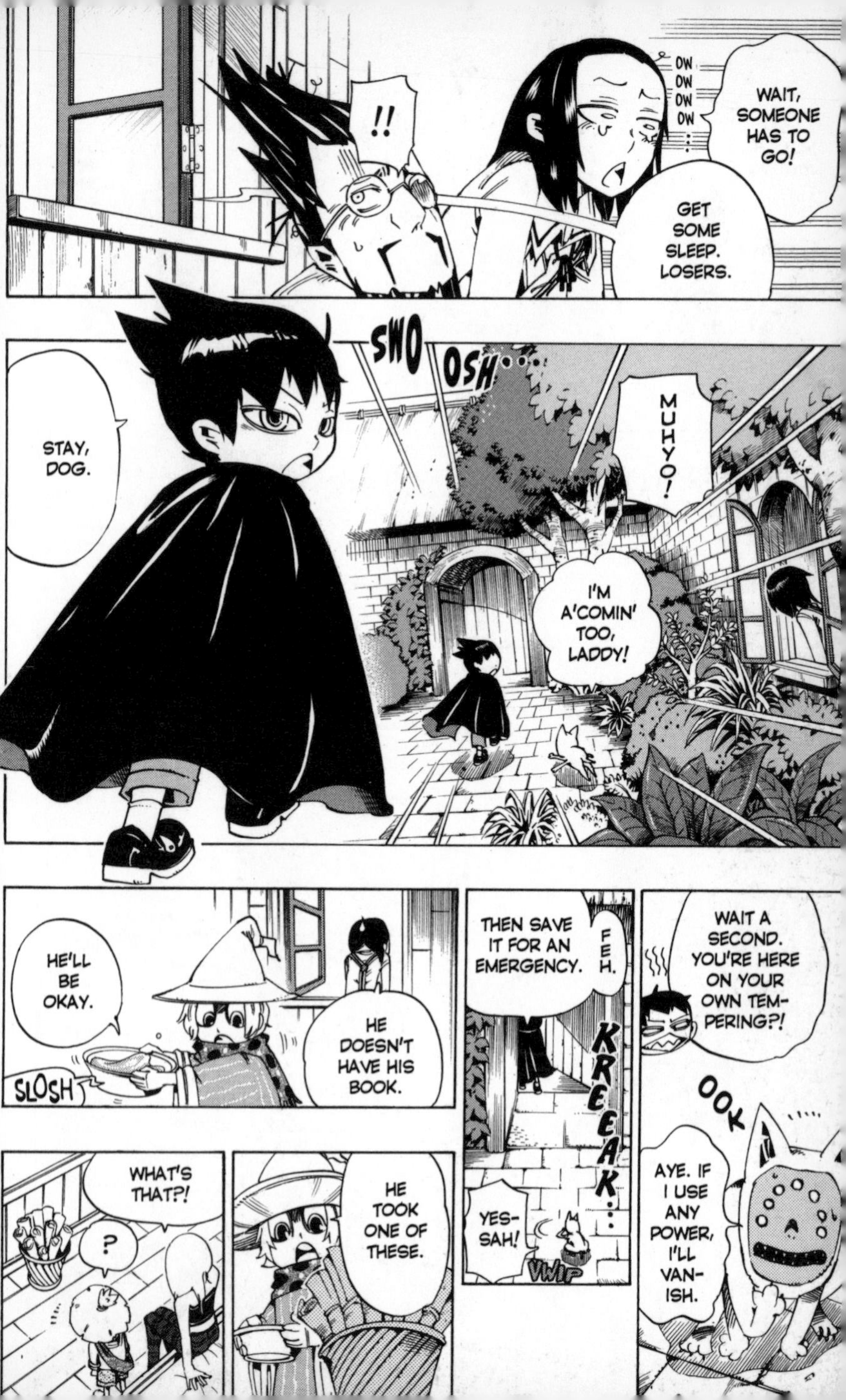
WAIT, SOMEONE HAS TO GO!
OW OW OW OW ...
!!
GET SOME SLEEP. LOSERS.
MUHYO!
SWO OSH...
I'M A'COMIN' TOO, LADDY!
STAY, DOG.
WAIT A SECOND. YOU'RE HERE ON YOUR OWN TEM-PERING?!
OOK
AYE. IF I USE ANY POWER, I'LL VAN-ISH.
FEH.
THEN SAVE IT FOR AN EMERGENCY.
KREEAK...
YES-SAH!
VWIP
HE'LL BE OKAY.
HE DOESN'T HAVE HIS BOOK.
SLOSH
HE TOOK ONE OF THESE.
WHAT'S THAT?!
?

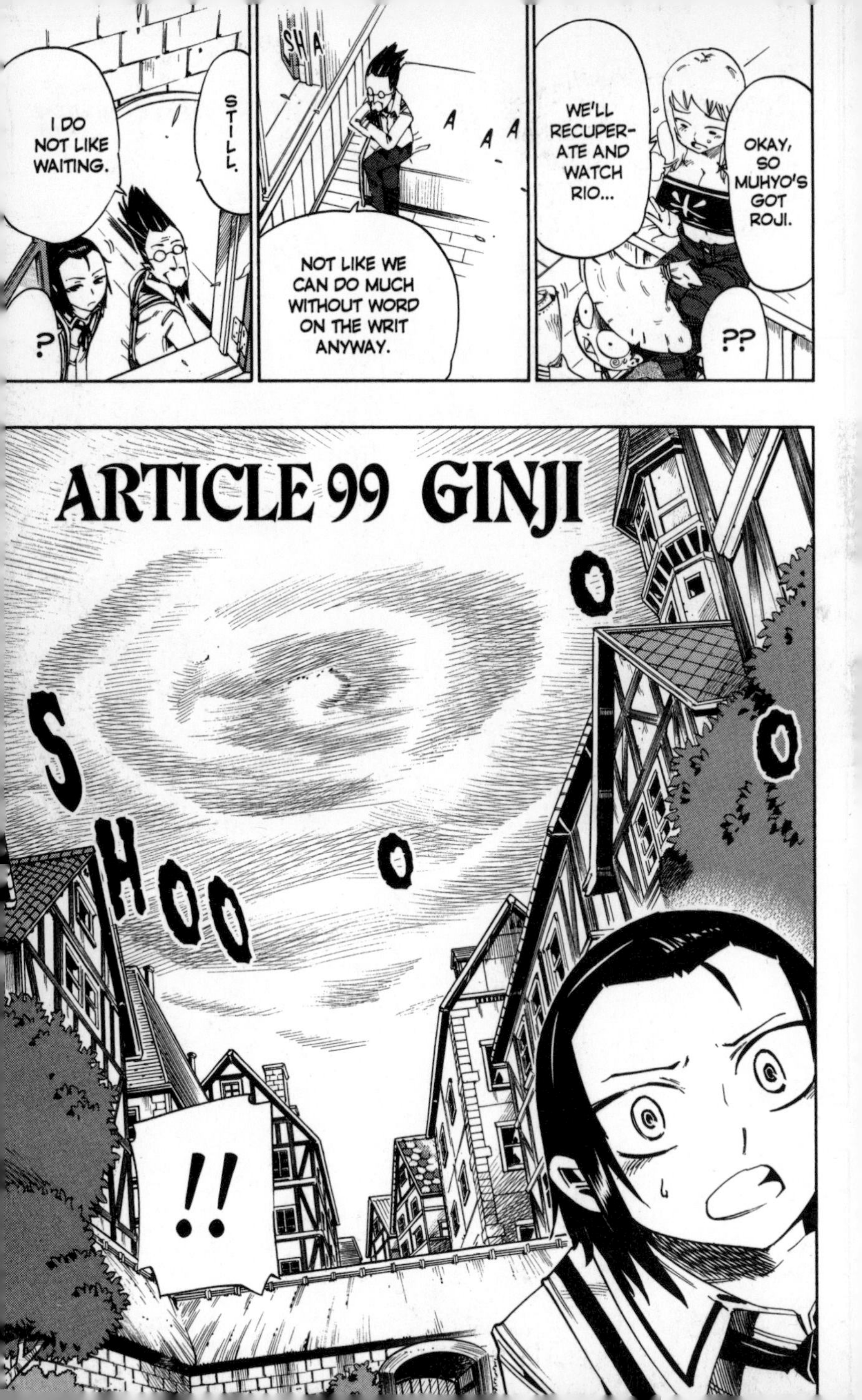
OKAY, SO MUHYO'S GOT ROJI.
WE'LL RECUPERATE AND WATCH RIO...
??
SHA
A A A A
NOT LIKE WE CAN DO MUCH WITHOUT WORD ON THE WRIT ANYWAY.
STILL.
I DO NOT LIKE WAITING.
?
ARTICLE 99 GINJI
SHOOOOO
!!

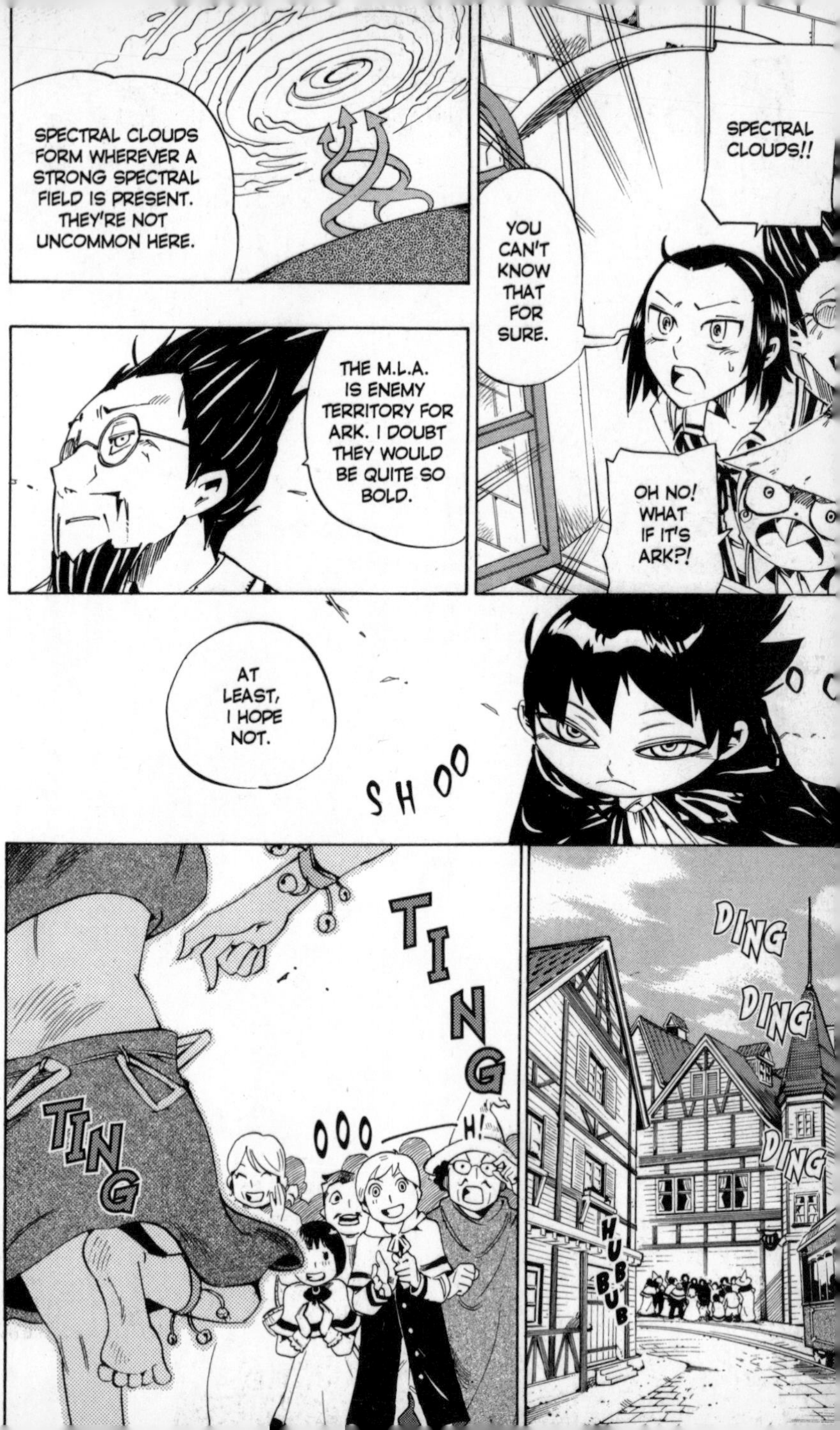
SPECTRAL CLOUDS!!
YOU CAN'T KNOW THAT FOR SURE.
OH NO! WHAT IF IT'S ARK?!
SPECTRAL CLOUDS FORM WHEREVER A STRONG SPECTRAL FIELD IS PRESENT. THEY'RE NOT UNCOMMON HERE.
THE M.L.A. IS ENEMY TERRITORY FOR ARK. I DOUBT THEY WOULD BE QUITE SO BOLD.
AT LEAST, I HOPE NOT.
SHOO
DING
DING
DING
HUBBUB
TING
OOOH!
TING

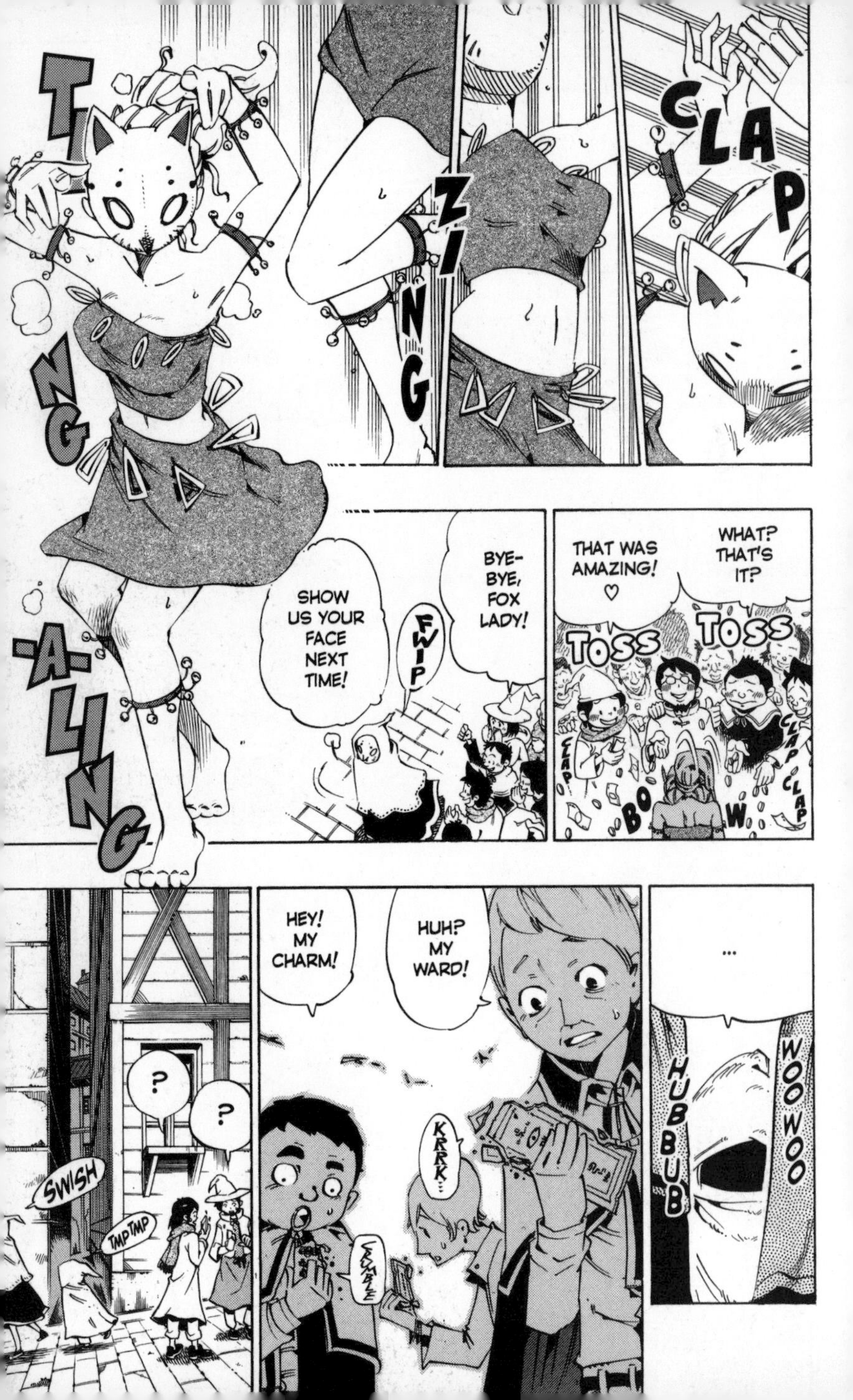
CLAP
ZING
WHAT? THAT'S IT?
THAT WAS AMAZING! ♡
TOSS TOSS
CLAP CLAP
BOW
CLAP
BYE-BYE, FOX LADY!
SHOW US YOUR FACE NEXT TIME!
FWIP
TING-A-LING
...
WOOWOO
HUBBUB
HUH? MY WARD!
HEY! MY CHARM!
KRRK...
FUMBLE
?
?
SWISH
TMP TMP

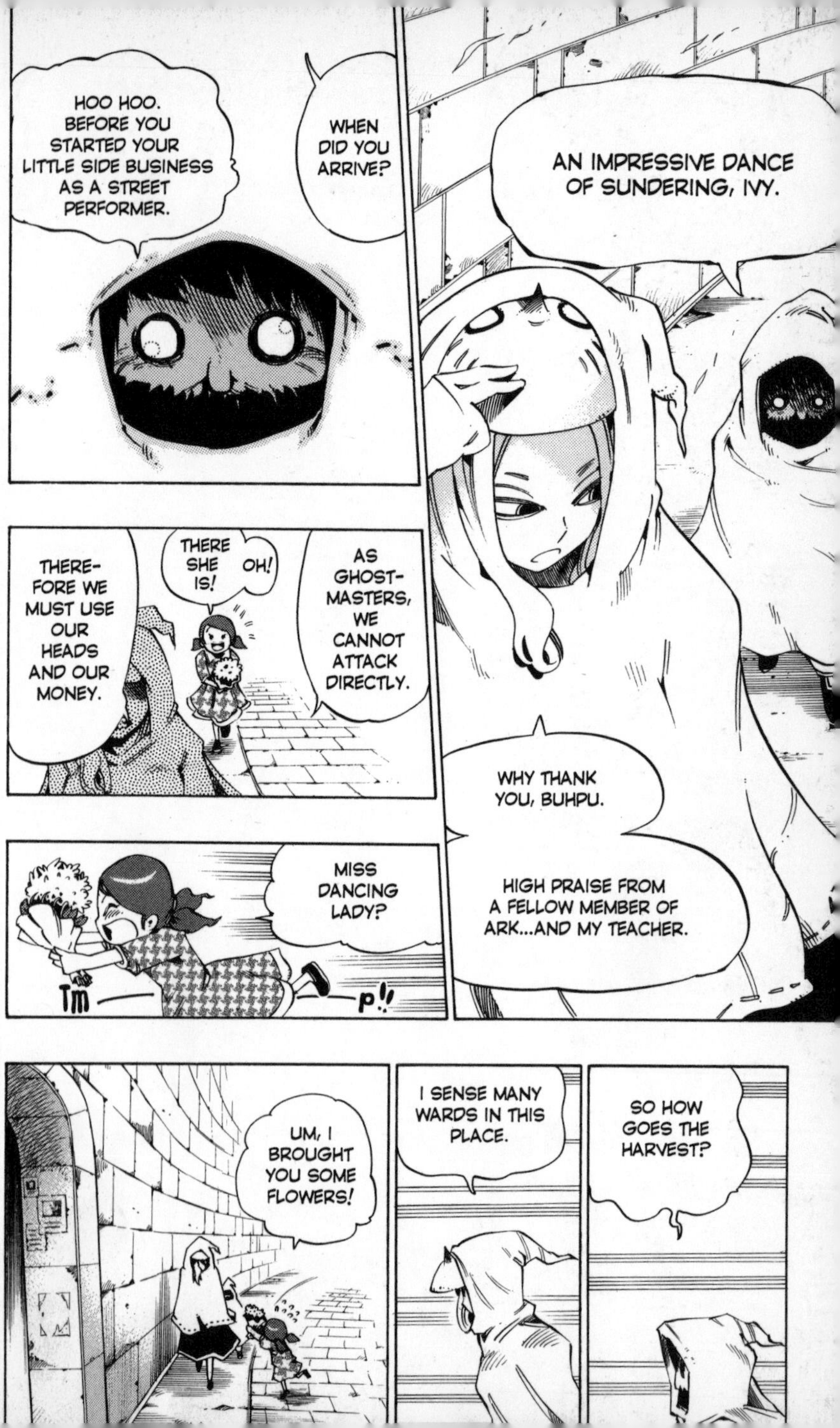
AN IMPRESSIVE DANCE OF SUNDERING, IVY.
WHY THANK YOU, BUHPU.
HIGH PRAISE FROM A FELLOW MEMBER OF ARK...AND MY TEACHER.
WHEN DID YOU ARRIVE?
HOO HOO. BEFORE YOU STARTED YOUR LITTLE SIDE BUSINESS AS A STREET PERFORMER.
AS GHOST-MASTERS, WE CANNOT ATTACK DIRECTLY.
OH!
THERE SHE IS!
THERE-FORE WE MUST USE OUR HEADS AND OUR MONEY.
MISS DANCING LADY?
Tm——p!!
SO HOW GOES THE HARVEST?
I SENSE MANY WARDS IN THIS PLACE.
UM, I BROUGHT YOU SOME FLOWERS!

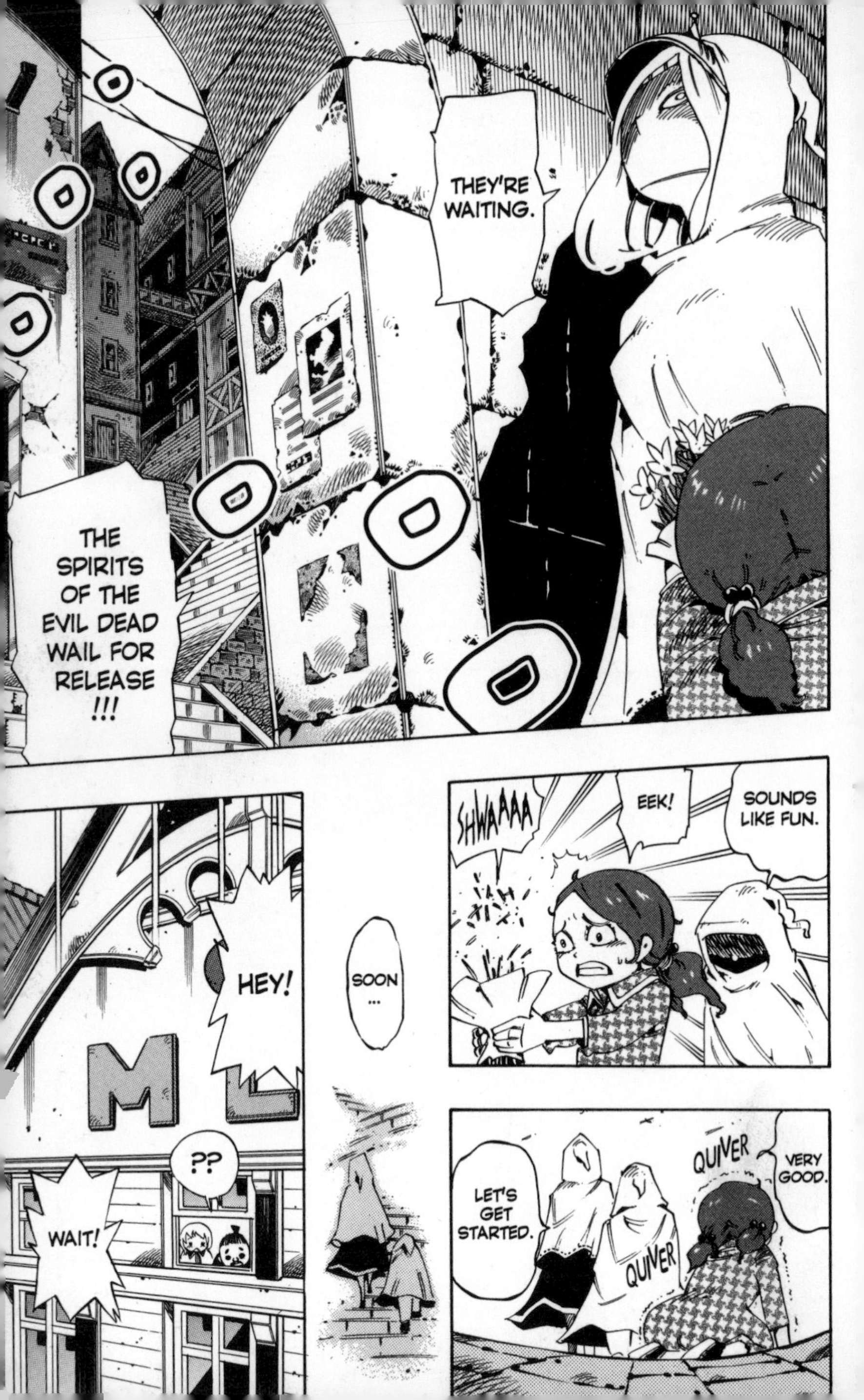
THEY'RE WAITING.
THE SPIRITS OF THE EVIL DEAD WAIL FOR RELEASE!!!
SOUNDS LIKE FUN.
EEK!
SHWAAAA
VERY GOOD.
QUIVER
QUIVER
LET'S GET STARTED.
SOON...
HEY!
??
WAIT!

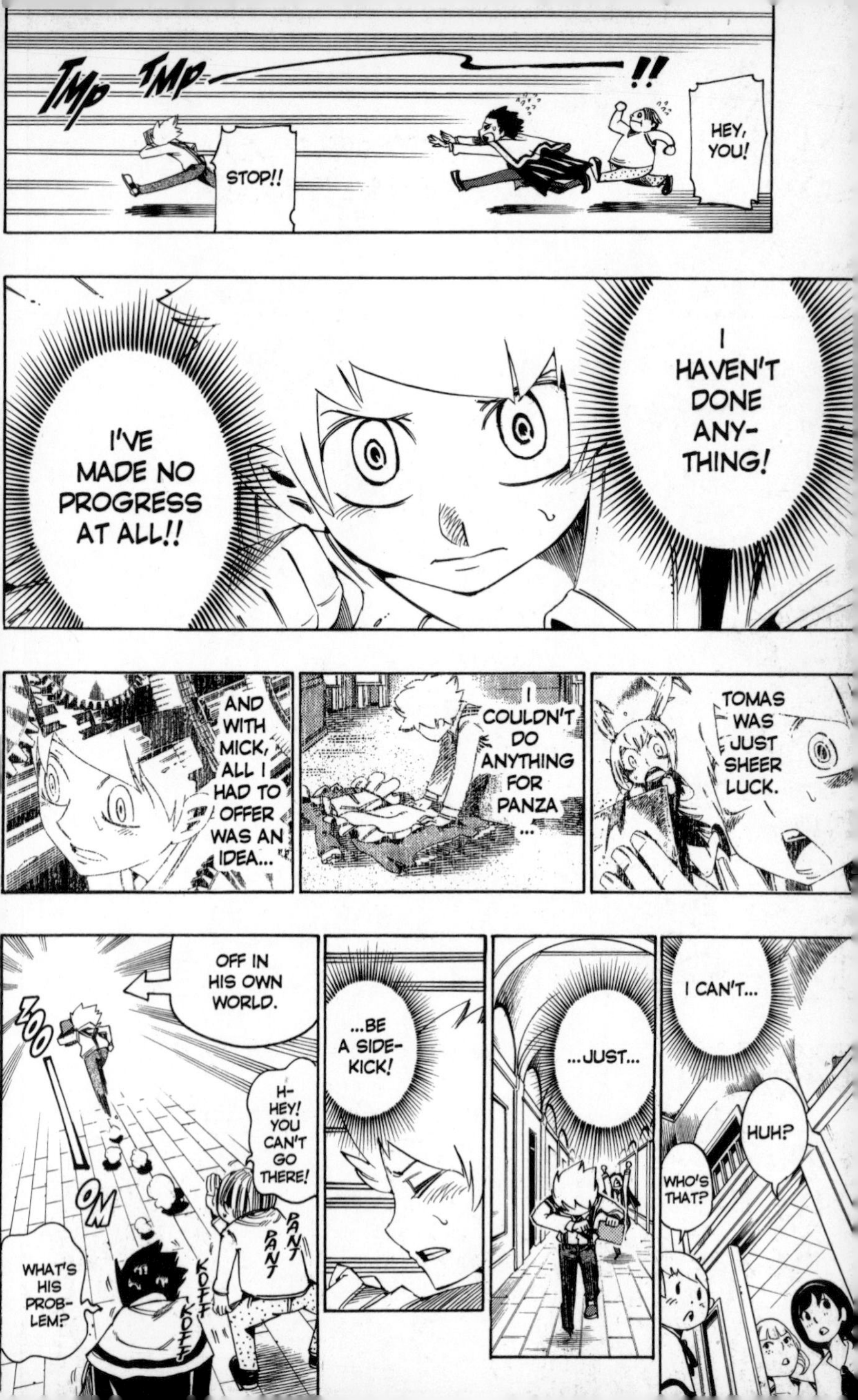
HEY, YOU!
!!
TMP TMP
STOP!!
I HAVEN'T DONE ANY-THING!
I'VE MADE NO PROGRESS AT ALL!!
TOMAS WAS JUST SHEER LUCK.
I COULDN'T DO ANYTHING FOR PANZA...
AND WITH MICK, ALL I HAD TO OFFER WAS AN IDEA...
I CAN'T...
HUH?
WHO'S THAT?
...JUST...
...BE A SIDE-KICK!
OFF IN HIS OWN WORLD.
H-HEY! YOU CAN'T GO THERE!
ZOOM
PANT PANT
WHAT'S HIS PROB-LEM?
KOFF KOFF

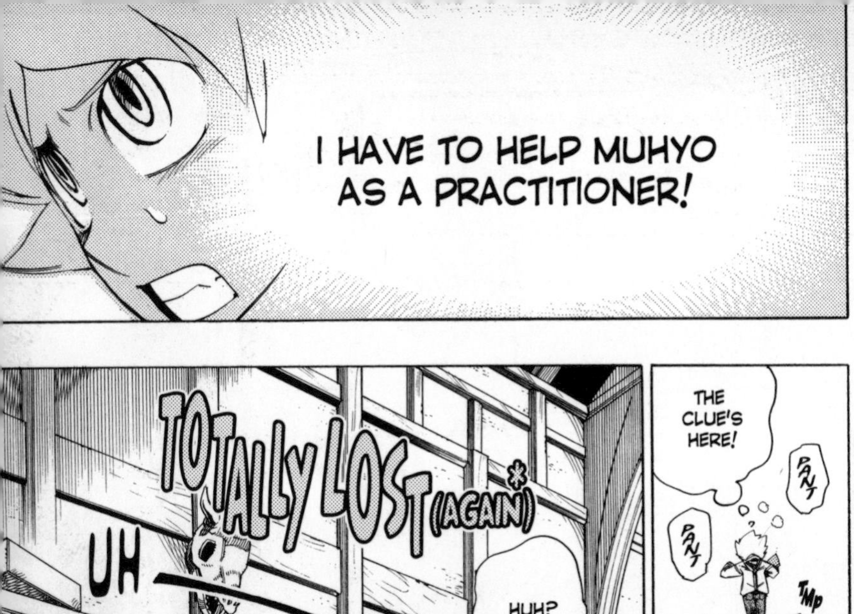
I HAVE TO HELP MUHYO AS A PRACTITIONER!
THE CLUE'S HERE!
PANT
PANT
TMP
TMP
TMP
AT M.L.S.!
PANT
PANT
TOTALLY LOST (AGAIN)*
HUH?
UH—OH...
UM...
WHERE AM I?

*SEE ARTICLE 46

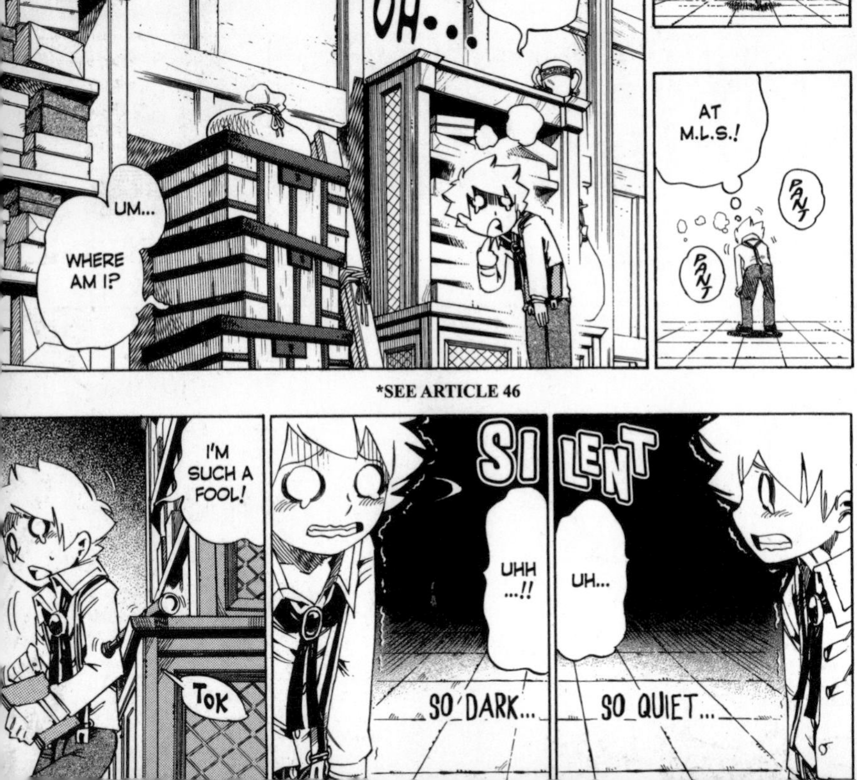
SILENT
UH...
SO QUIET...
UHH ...!!
SO DARK...
I'M SUCH A FOOL!
TOK

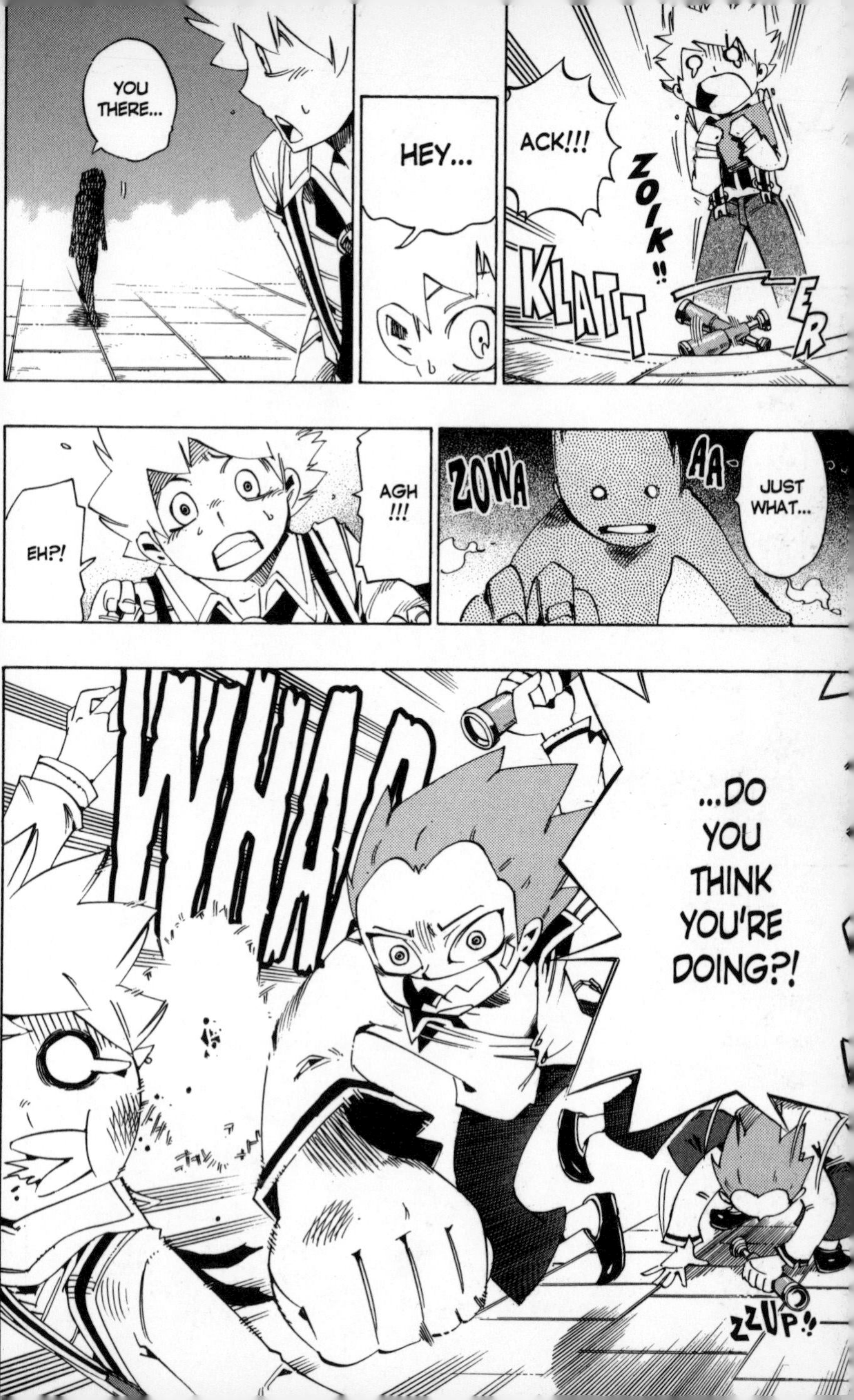
ACK!!!
ZOIK!!
KLATTER
HEY...
YOU THERE...
JUST WHAT...
ZOWA
AA
AGH !!!
EH?!
...DO YOU THINK YOU'RE DOING?!
ZZUP!!

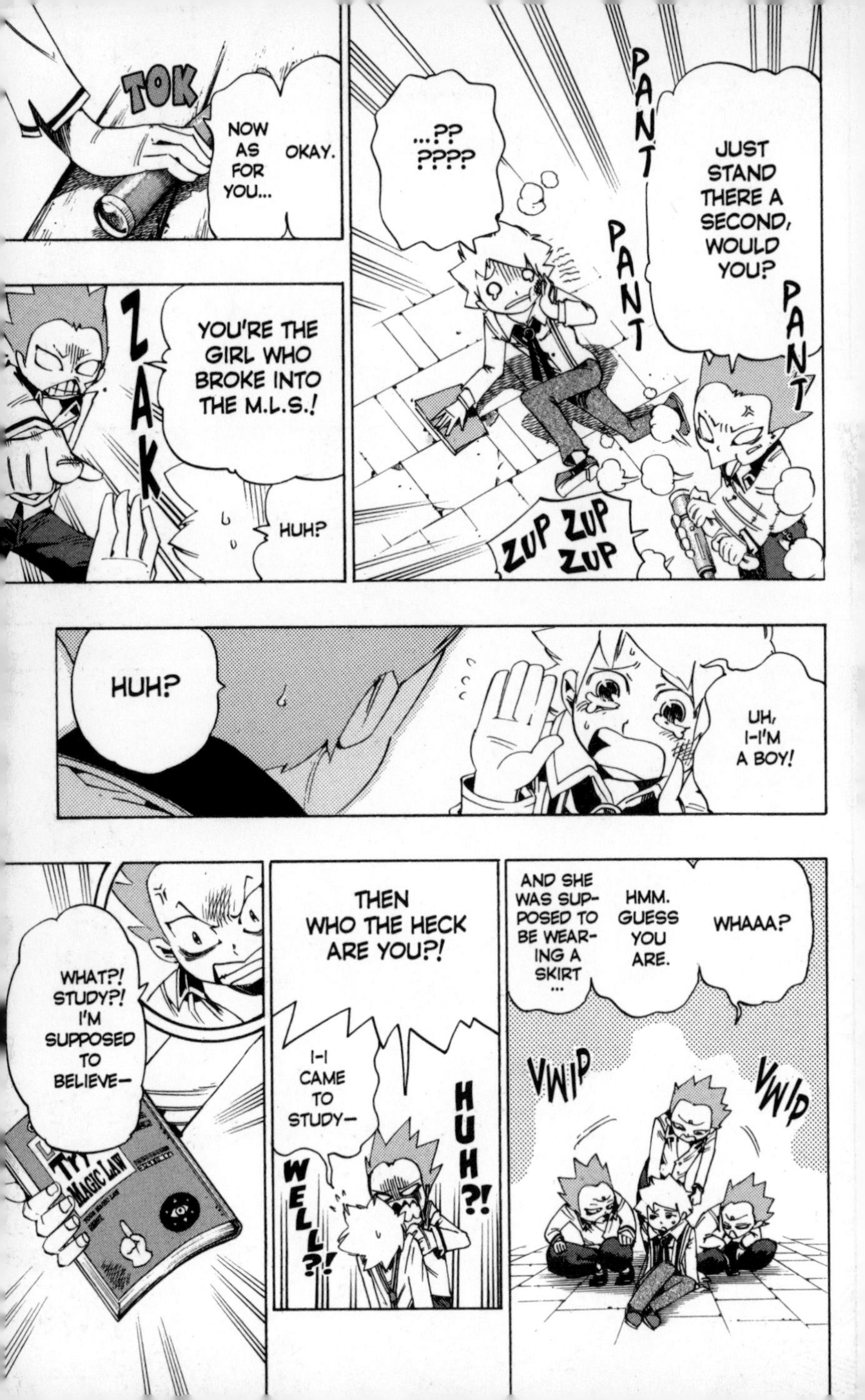
PANT
PANT
JUST STAND THERE A SECOND, WOULD YOU?
PANT
...?? ????
ZUP ZUP ZUP
OKAY.
NOW AS FOR YOU...
TOK
YOU'RE THE GIRL WHO BROKE INTO THE M.L.S.!
ZAK
HUH?
UH, I-I'M A BOY!
HUH?
WHAAA?
HMM. GUESS YOU ARE.
AND SHE WAS SUP-POSED TO BE WEAR-ING A SKIRT ...
VWIP
VWIP
THEN WHO THE HECK ARE YOU?!
HUH?!
I-I CAME TO STUDY—
WELL?!
WHAT?! STUDY?! I'M SUPPOSED TO BELIEVE—
MAGIC LAW

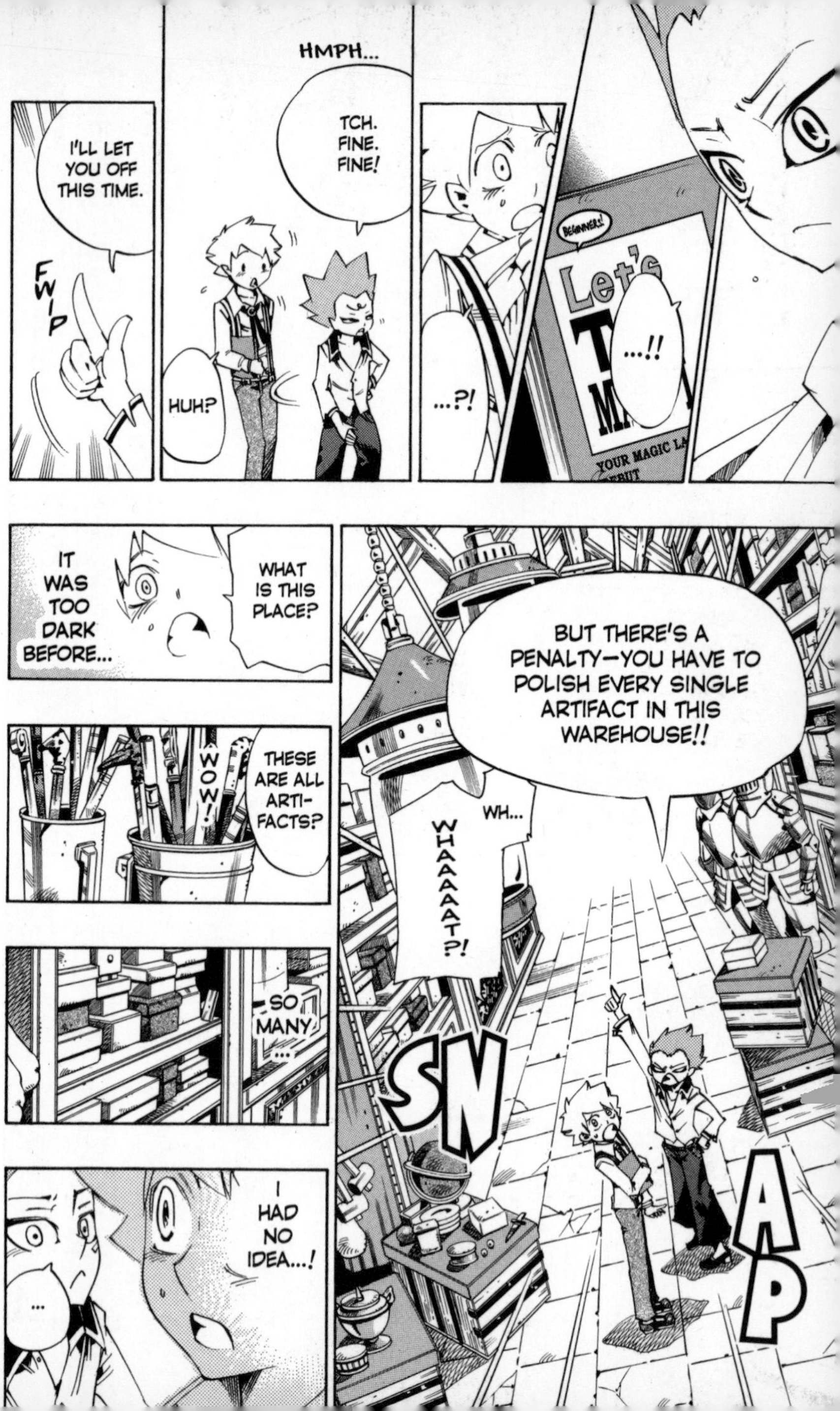
BEGINNERS!
Let's
...!!
...?!
HMPH...
TCH. FINE. FINE!
HUH?
I'LL LET YOU OFF THIS TIME.
FWIP
BUT THERE'S A PENALTY—YOU HAVE TO POLISH EVERY SINGLE ARTIFACT IN THIS WAREHOUSE!!
WH...
WHAAAAAAT?!
SNAP
WHAT IS THIS PLACE?
IT WAS TOO DARK BEFORE...
THESE ARE ALL ARTI-FACTS?
WOW!
SO MANY...
I HAD NO IDEA...!
...

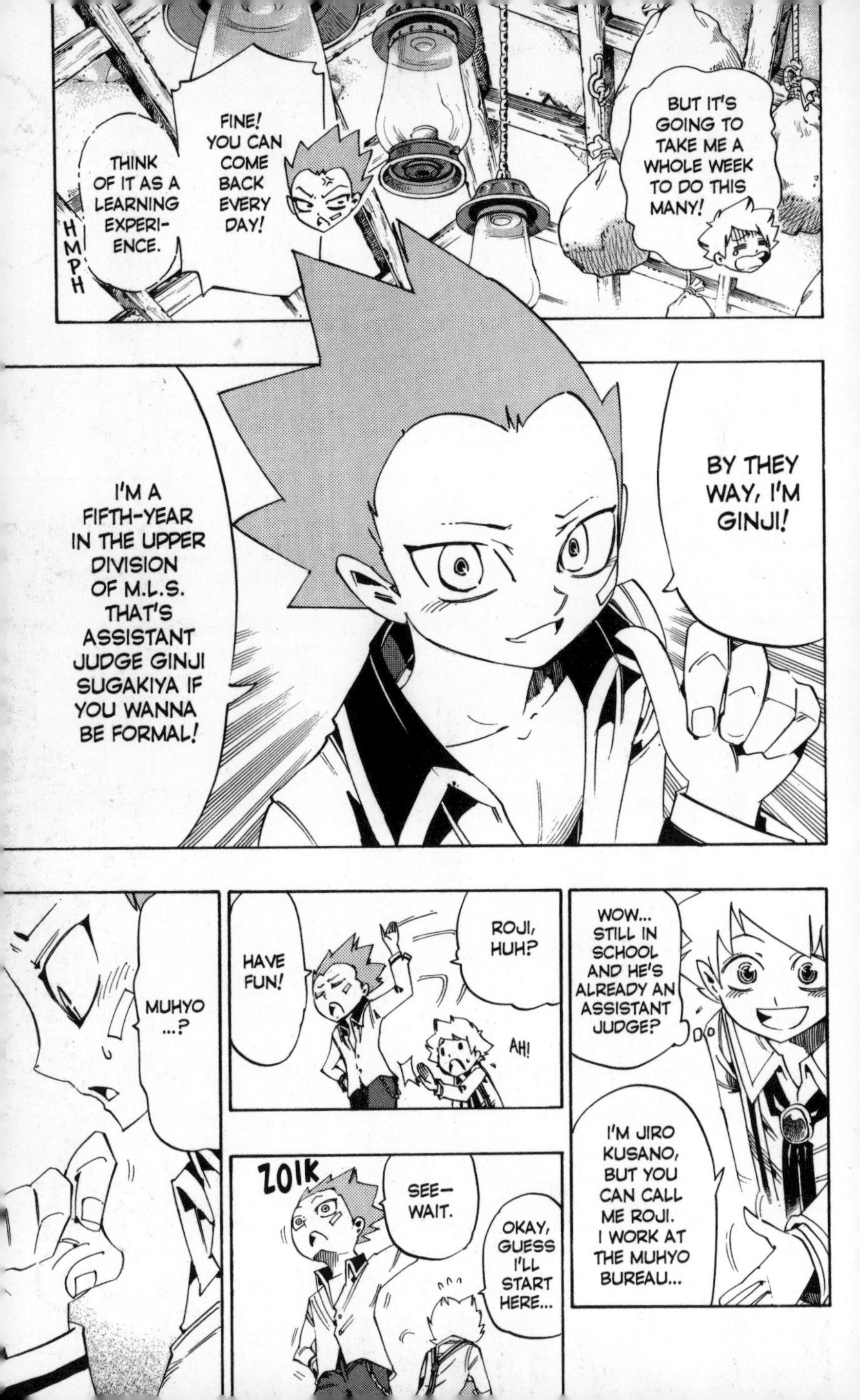

BUT IT'S GOING TO TAKE ME A WHOLE WEEK TO DO THIS MANY!
FINE! YOU CAN COME BACK EVERY DAY!
THINK OF IT AS A LEARNING EXPERI- ENCE.
HMPH
BY THEY WAY, I'M GINJI!
I'M A FIFTH-YEAR IN THE UPPER DIVISION OF M.L.S. THAT'S ASSISTANT JUDGE GINJI SUGAKIYA IF YOU WANNA BE FORMAL!
WOW... STILL IN SCHOOL AND HE'S ALREADY AN ASSISTANT JUDGE?
I'M JIRO KUSANO, BUT YOU CAN CALL ME ROJI. I WORK AT THE MUHYO BUREAU...
ROJI, HUH?
AH!
HAVE FUN!
ZOIK
SEE— WAIT.
OKAY, GUESS I'LL START HERE...
MUHYO ...?

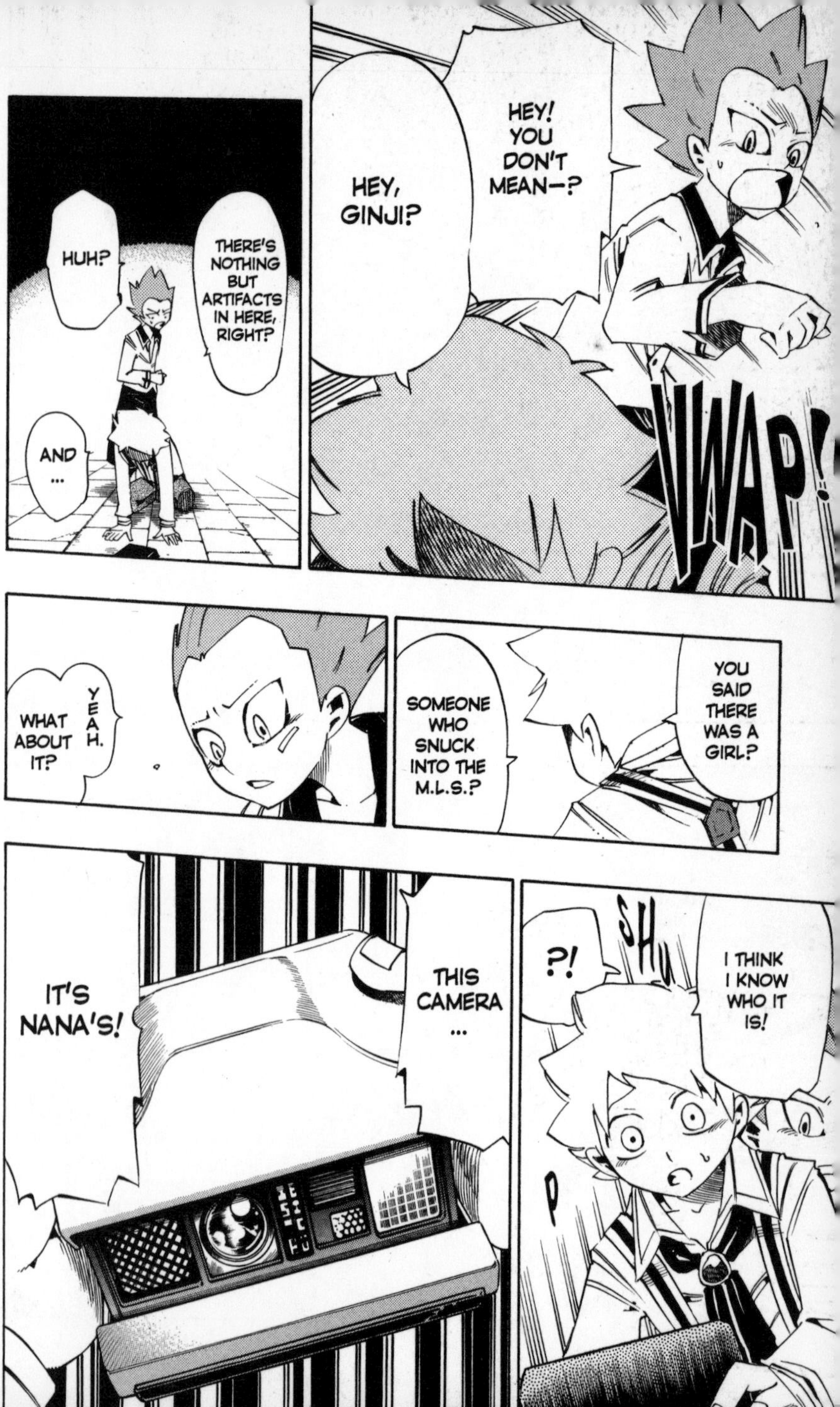
HEY! YOU DON'T MEAN—?
HEY, GINJI?
WAP!
THERE'S NOTHING BUT ARTIFACTS IN HERE, RIGHT?
HUH?
AND ...
YOU SAID THERE WAS A GIRL?
SOMEONE WHO SNUCK INTO THE M.L.S.?
YEAH.
WHAT ABOUT IT?
I THINK I KNOW WHO IT IS!
SHU
?!
THIS CAMERA ...
IT'S NANA'S!

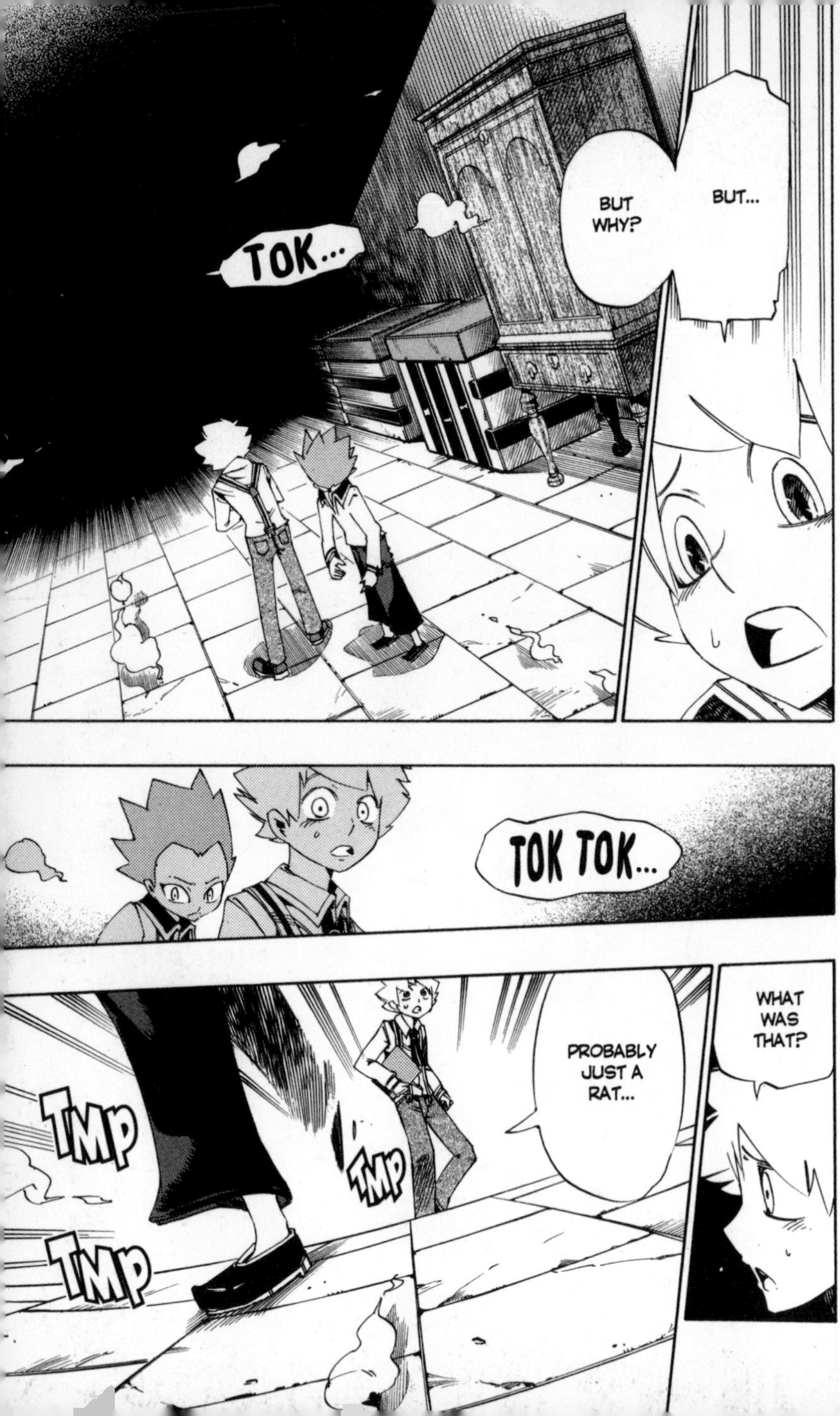
BUT...
BUT WHY?
TOK...
TOK TOK...
WHAT WAS THAT?
PROBABLY JUST A RAT...
TMP
TMP
TMP

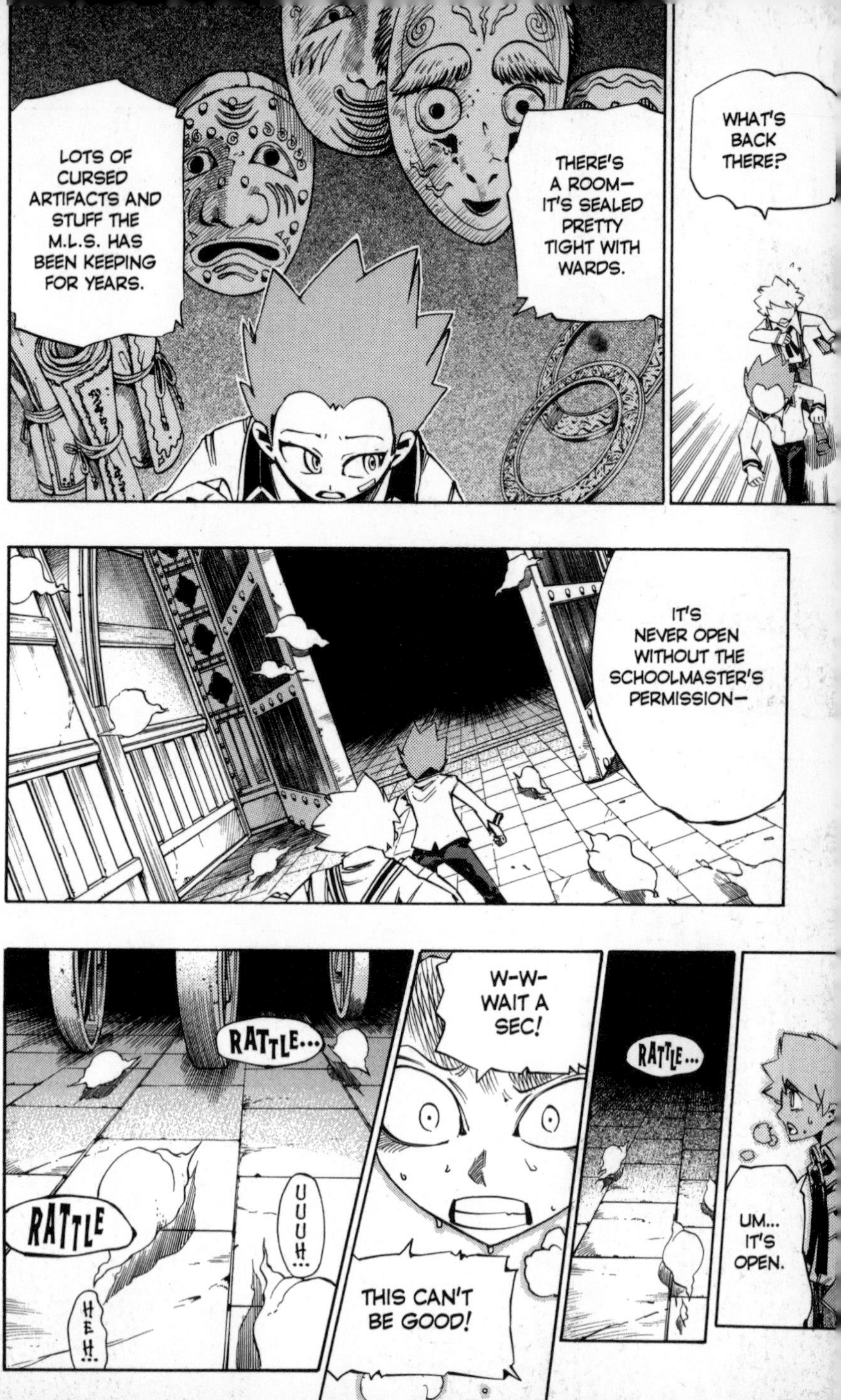
WHAT'S BACK THERE?
THERE'S A ROOM—IT'S SEALED PRETTY TIGHT WITH WARDS.
LOTS OF CURSED ARTIFACTS AND STUFF THE M.L.S. HAS BEEN KEEPING FOR YEARS.
IT'S NEVER OPEN WITHOUT THE SCHOOLMASTER'S PERMISSION—
UM... IT'S OPEN.
RATTLE...
W-W-WAIT A SEC!
THIS CAN'T BE GOOD!
RATTLE...
UUUH...
RATTLE
HEH...

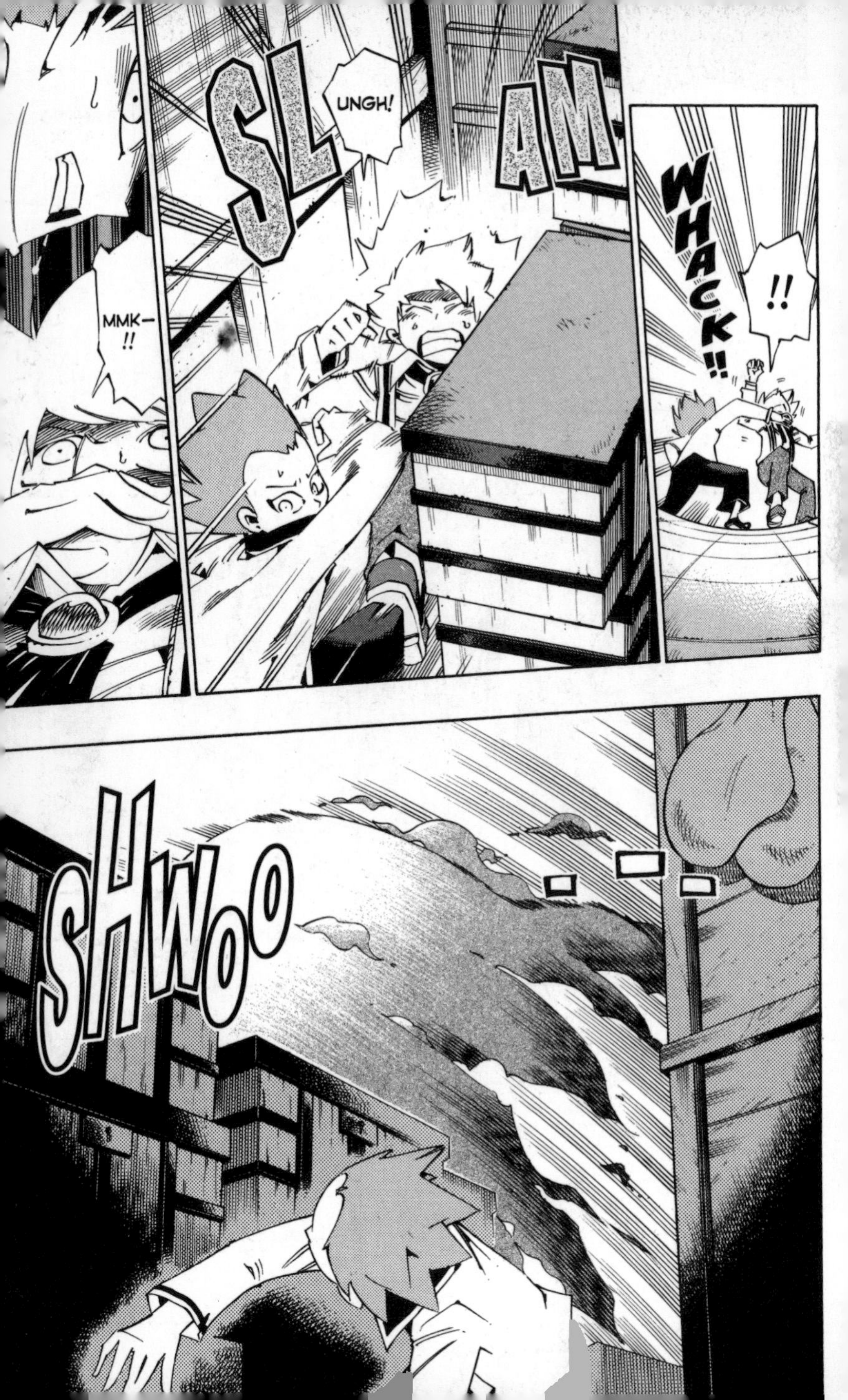
WHACK!!
!!
SLAM
UNGH!
MMK—!!
. . .
SHWOOO

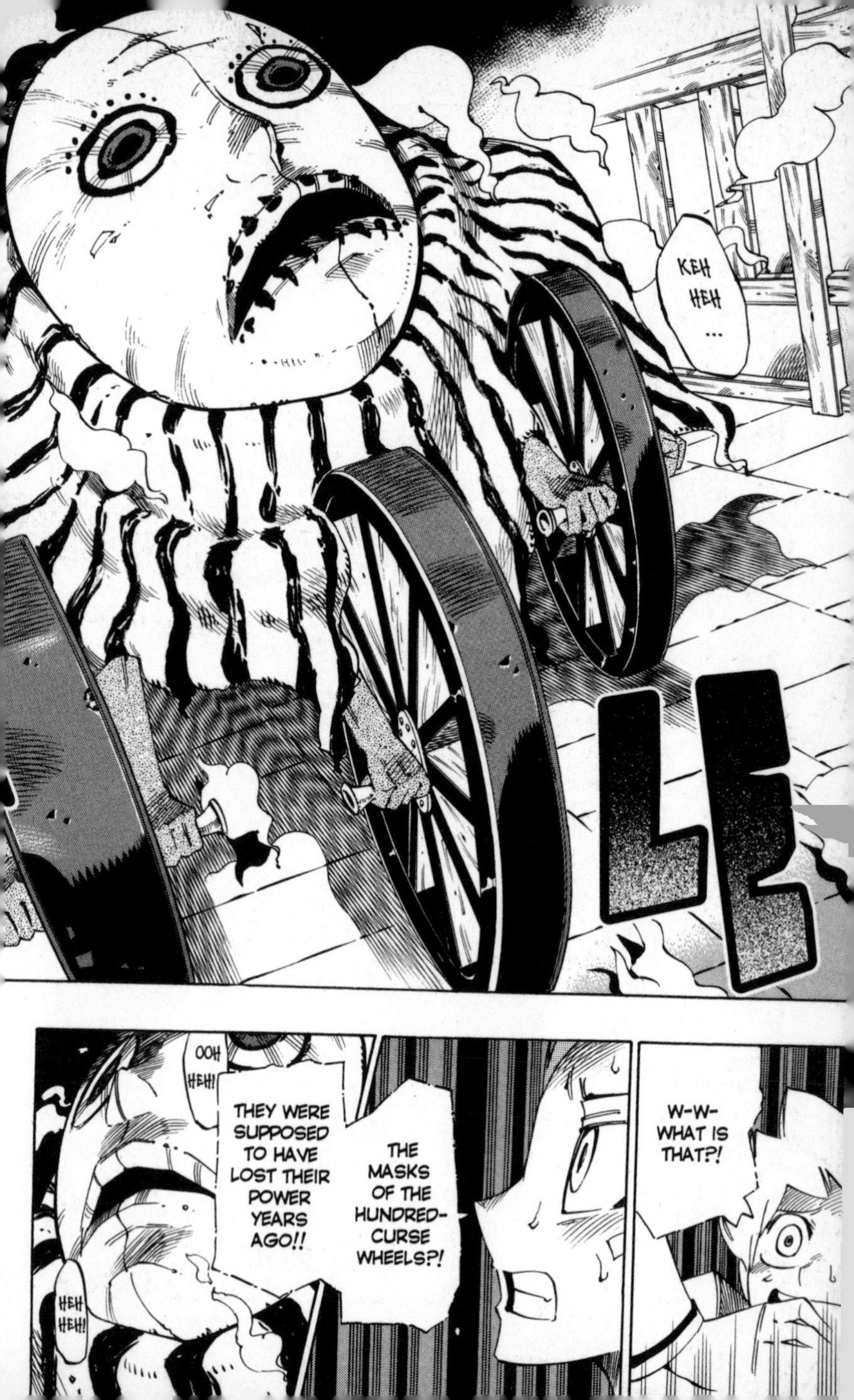
KEH HEH ...
LE
W-W-WHAT IS THAT?!
THE MASKS OF THE HUNDRED-CURSE WHEELS?!
THEY WERE SUPPOSED TO HAVE LOST THEIR POWER YEARS AGO!!
OOH HEH!
HEH HEH!

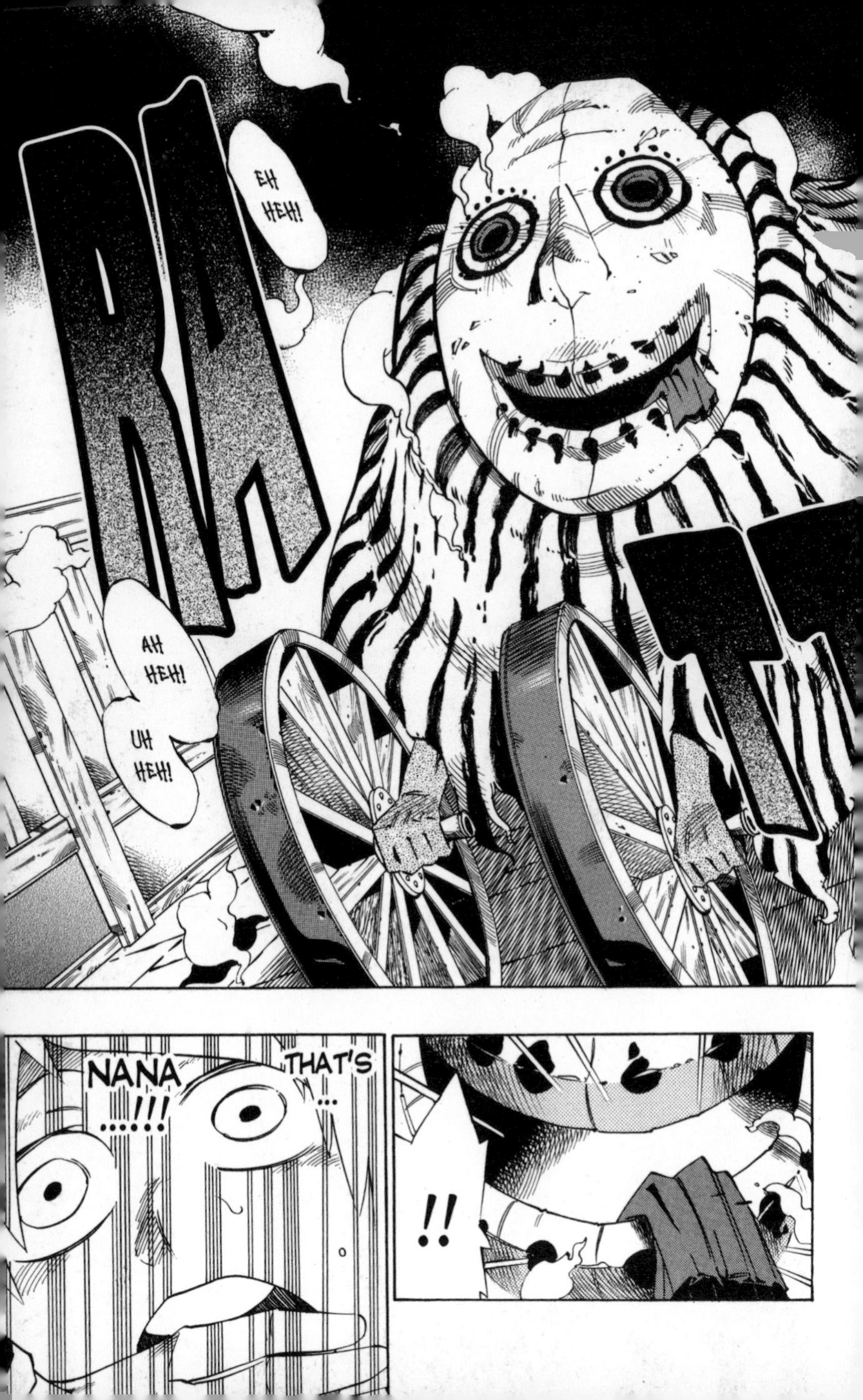
EH HEH!
AH HEH!
UH HEH!
!!
THAT'S...
NANA...!!!

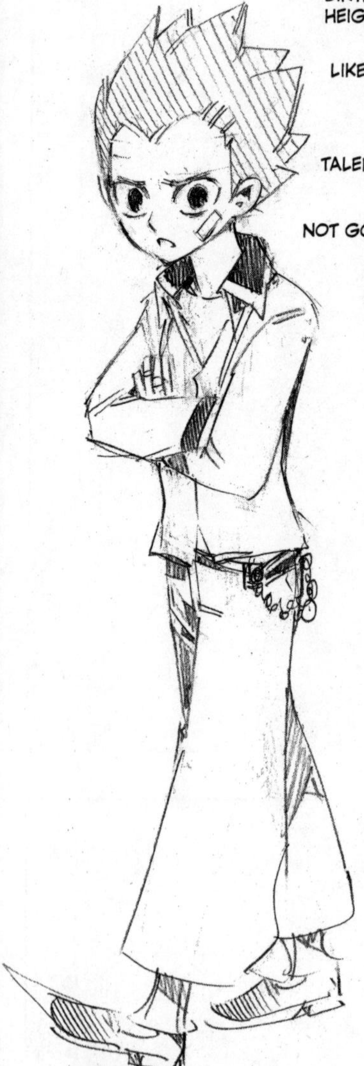

GINJI SUGAKIYA
BIRTHDAY: AUGUST 11
HEIGHT: 163 CM

LIKES: RAMEN
MANGA (MOSTLY SPORTS RELATED)
ARTIFACT TRAINING

TALENTS: POLISHING AND CURATING ARTIFACTS
ALL TRACK EVENTS

NOT GOOD WITH:
GIRLS (CAN'T LOOK THEM IN THE EYE)
LINING UP (UNLESS IT'S AT A RAMEN SHOP)
FREE TIME (ONLY CALM WHEN HE'S BUSY)

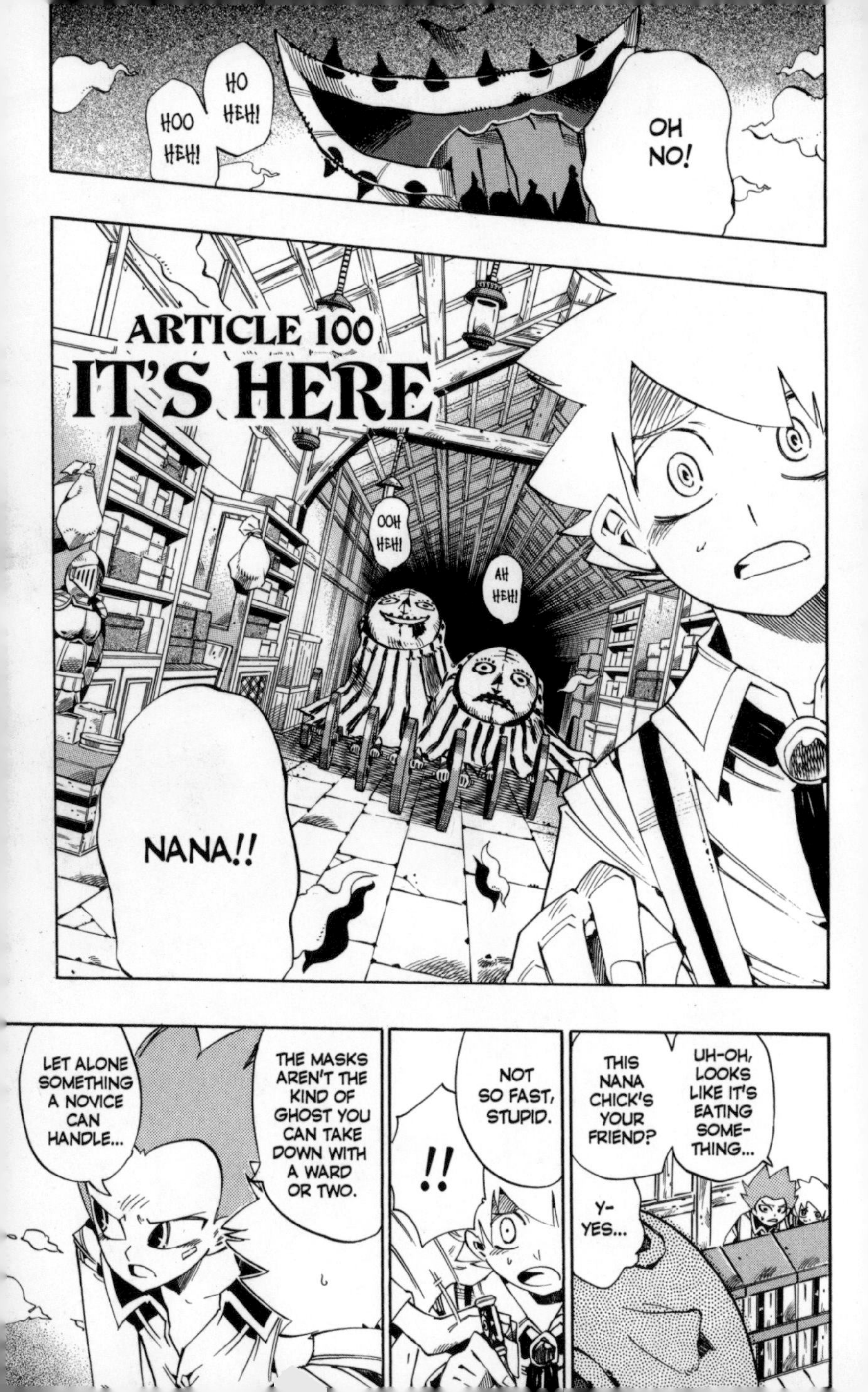
OH NO!
HO HEH!
HOO HEH!
ARTICLE 100
IT'S HERE
OOH HEH!
AH HEH!
NANA!!
UH-OH, LOOKS LIKE IT'S EATING SOME-THING...
THIS NANA CHICK'S YOUR FRIEND?
Y-YES...
NOT SO FAST, STUPID.
!!
THE MASKS AREN'T THE KIND OF GHOST YOU CAN TAKE DOWN WITH A WARD OR TWO.
LET ALONE SOMETHING A NOVICE CAN HANDLE...

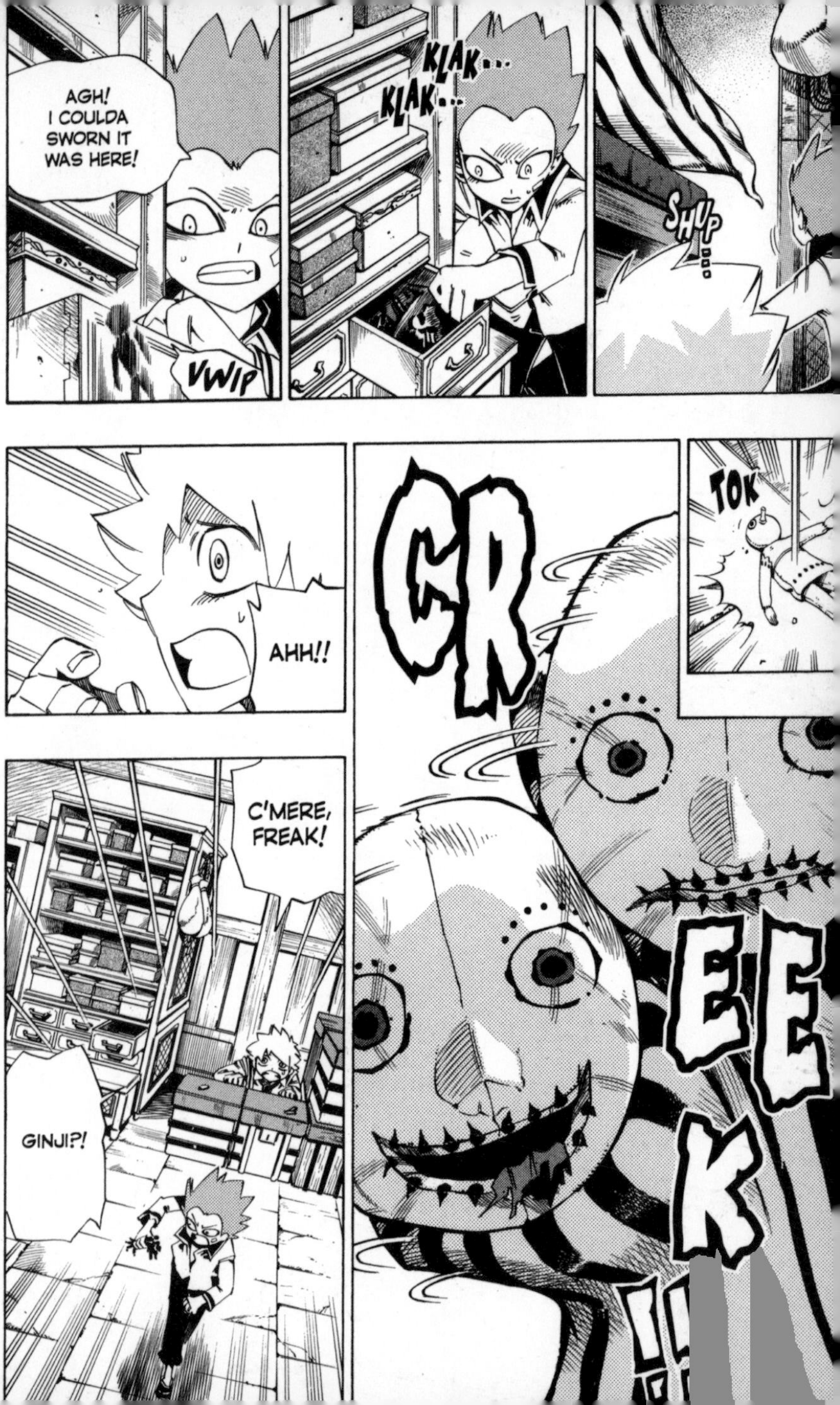
SHUP...
KLAK...
KLAK...
AGH! I COULDA SWORN IT WAS HERE!
VWIP
TOK
CREEK!!
AHH!!
C'MERE, FREAK!
GINJI?!

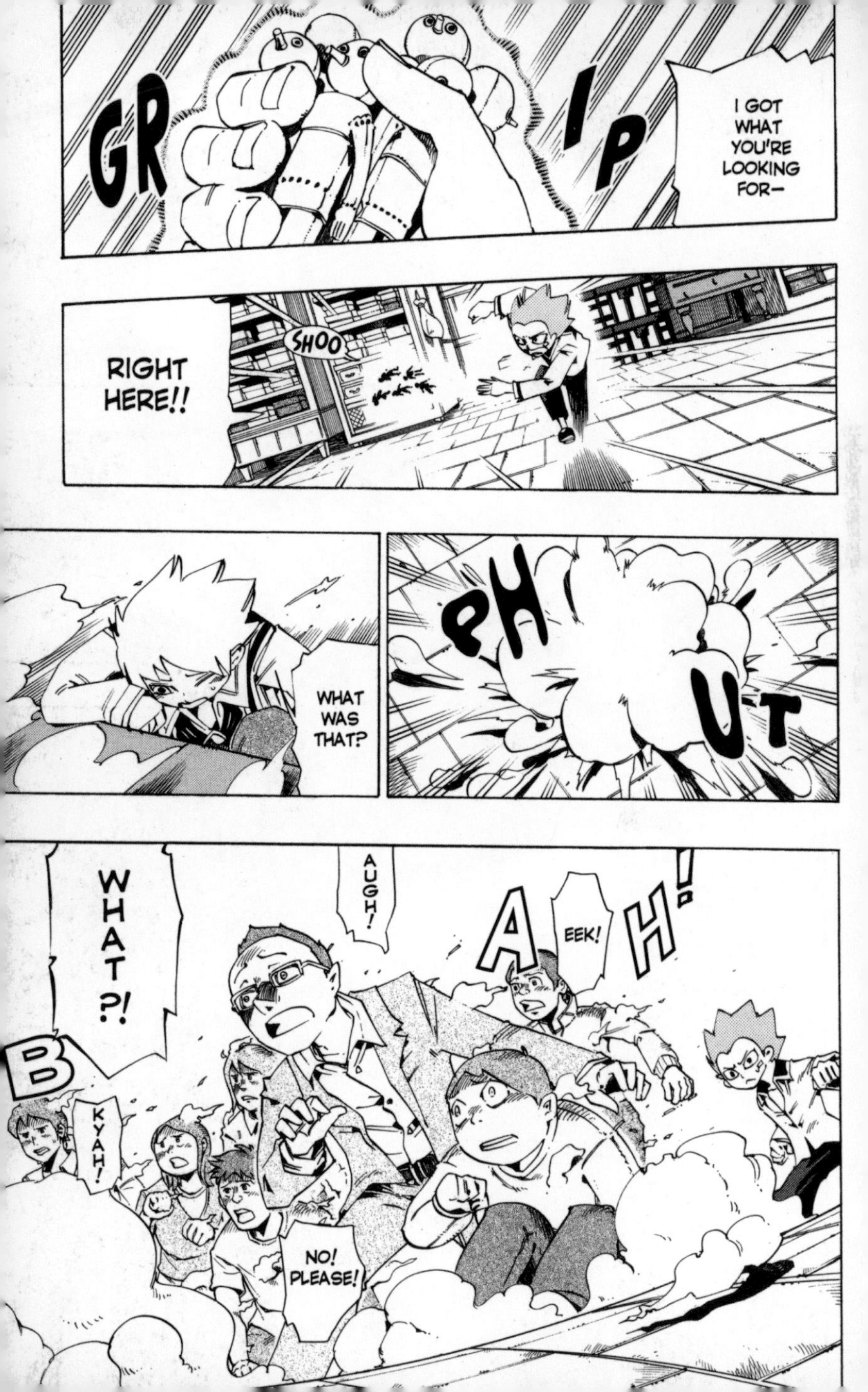
I GOT WHAT YOU'RE LOOKING FOR—
GRIP
SHOO
RIGHT HERE!!
PHUT
WHAT WAS THAT?
AH!
EEK!
AUGH!
WHAT?!
B
KYAH!
NO! PLEASE!

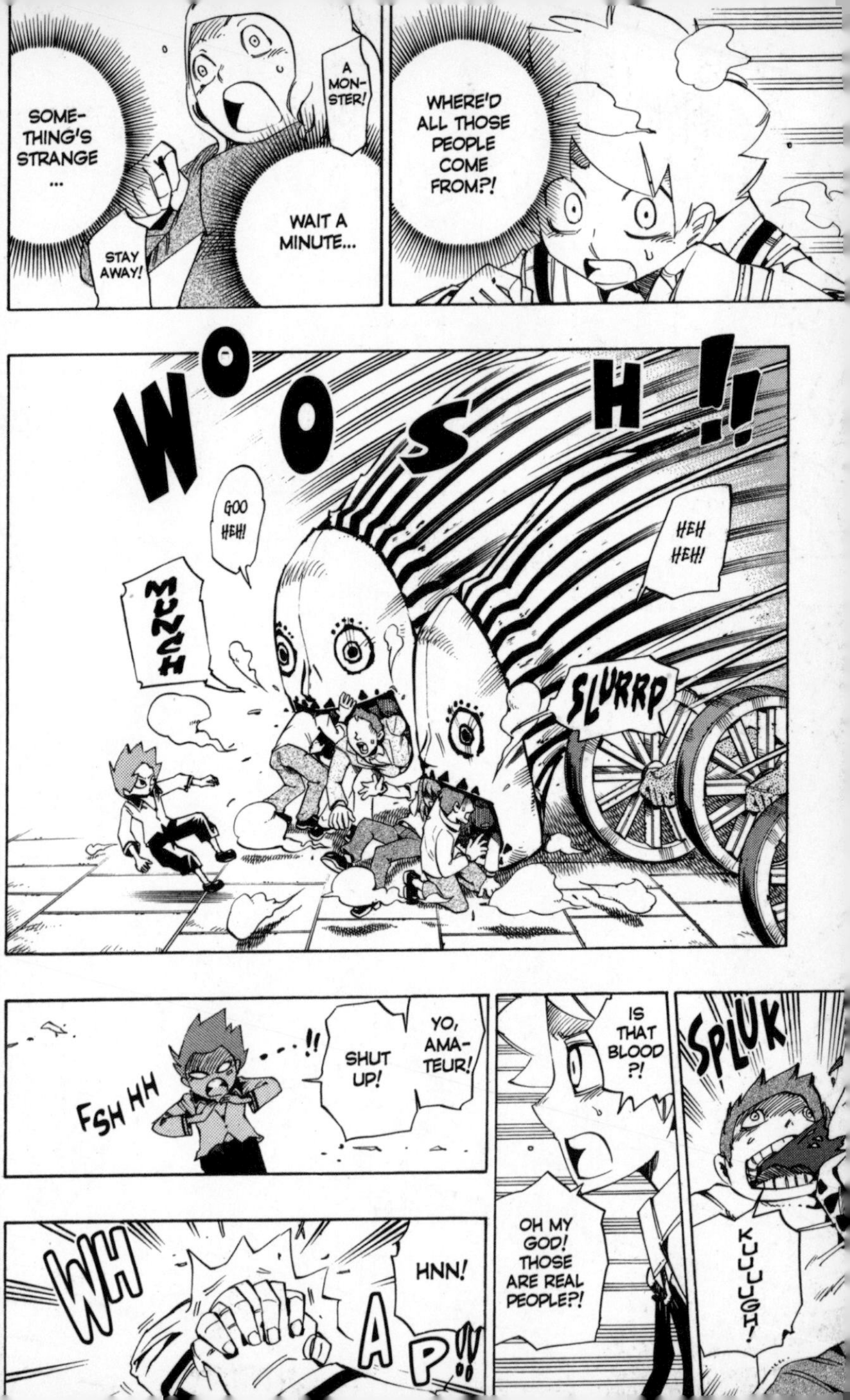
WHERE'D ALL THOSE PEOPLE COME FROM?!
A MONSTER!
SOME-THING'S STRANGE ...
WAIT A MINUTE...
STAY AWAY!
WOOSH!!
HEH HEH!
GOO HEH!
MUNCH
SLURRP
SPLUK
KUUUGH!
IS THAT BLOOD?!
OH MY GOD! THOSE ARE REAL PEOPLE?!
YO, AMA-TEUR!
SHUT UP!
...!!
FSHHH
HNN!
WHAP!!

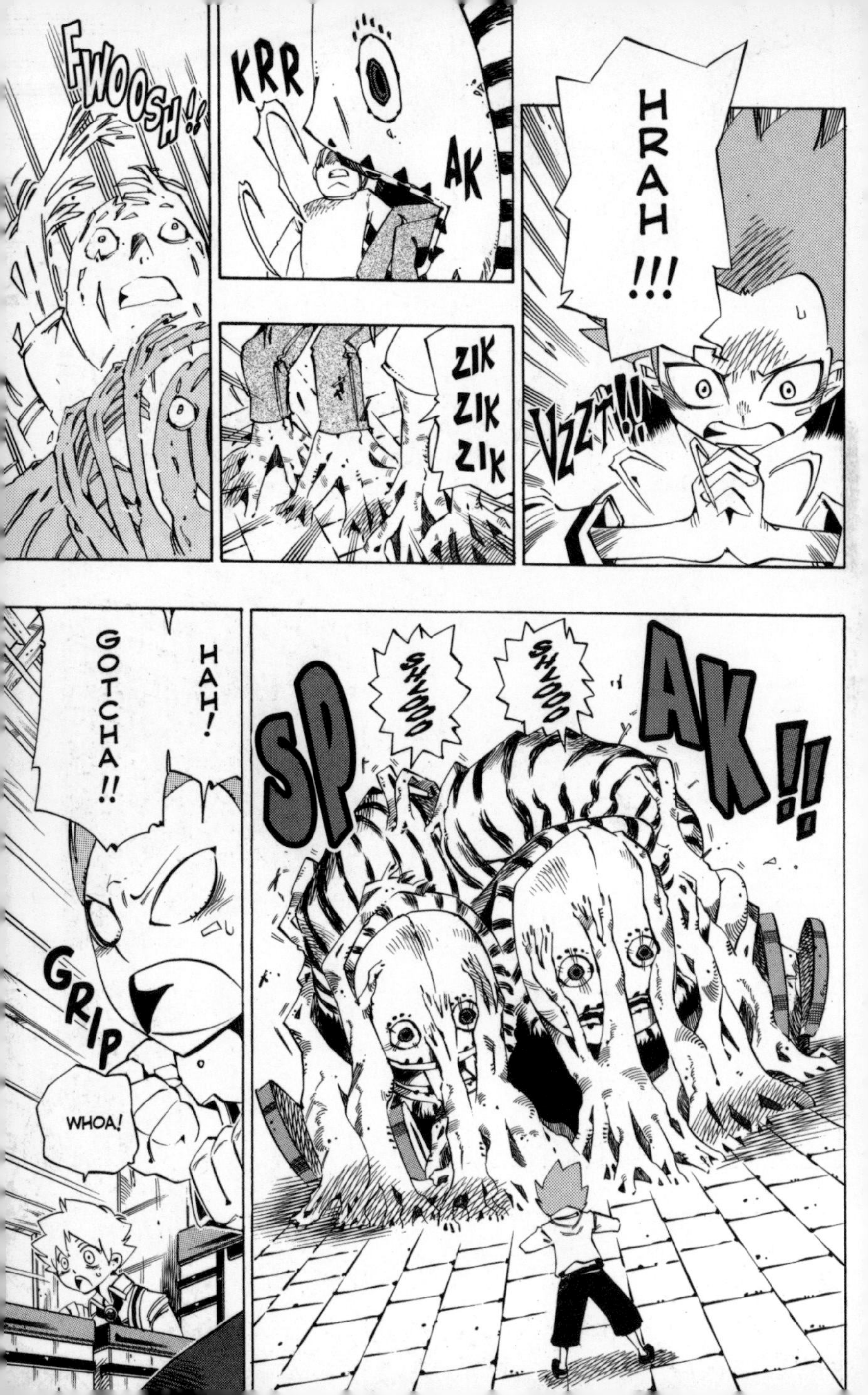
HRAH!!!
VZZT!!
KRR
AK
ZIK ZIK ZIK
FWOOSH!!
SHVOOO
SHVOOO
SP
AK!!
HAH!
GOTCHA!!
GRIP
WHOA!

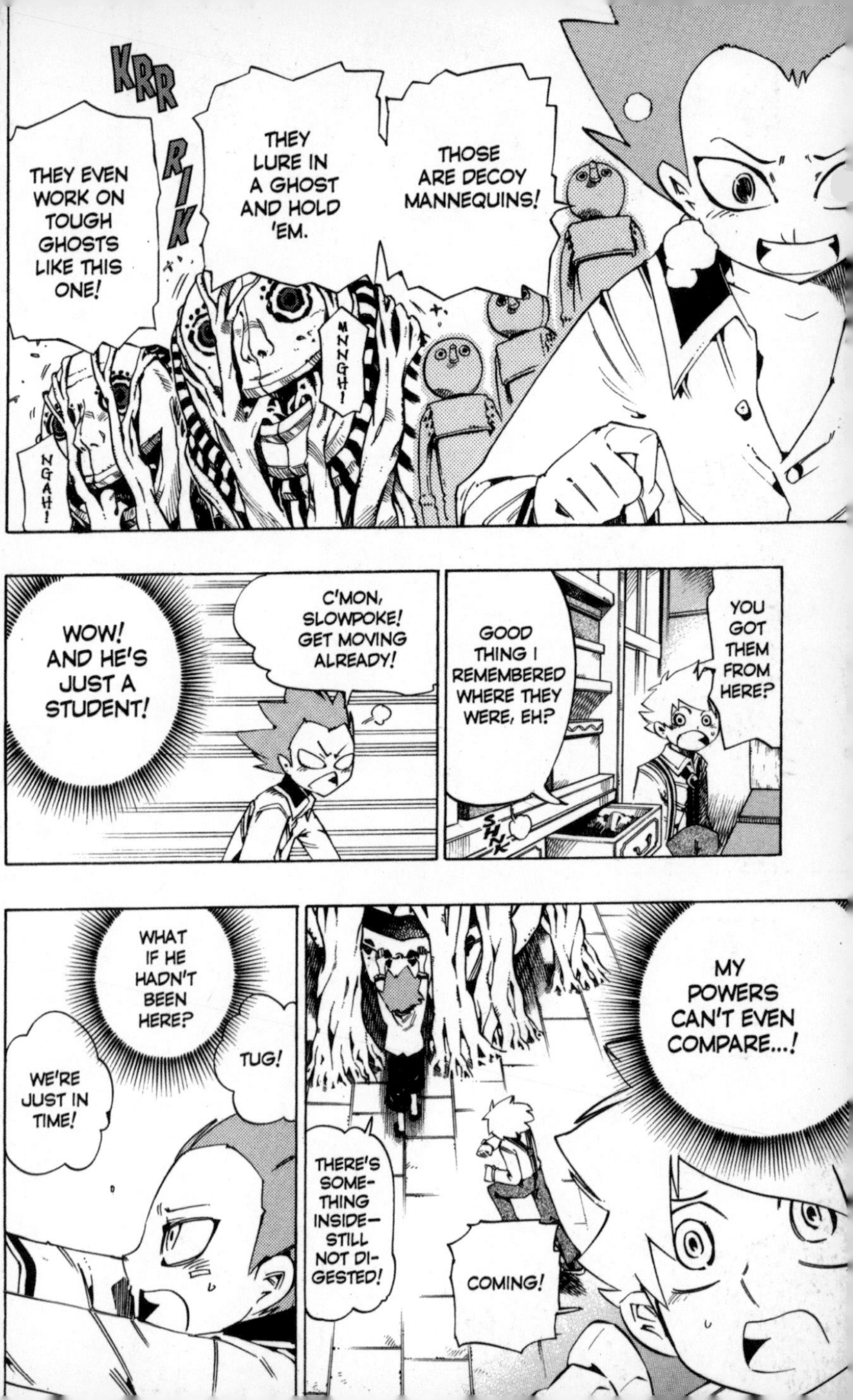
THOSE ARE DECOY MANNEQUINS!
THEY LURE IN A GHOST AND HOLD 'EM.
KRRRIK
THEY EVEN WORK ON TOUGH GHOSTS LIKE THIS ONE!
MNNGH!
NGAH!
YOU GOT THEM FROM HERE?
GOOD THING I REMEMBERED WHERE THEY WERE, EH?
SHNK
C'MON, SLOWPOKE! GET MOVING ALREADY!
WOW! AND HE'S JUST A STUDENT!
MY POWERS CAN'T EVEN COMPARE...!
COMING!
THERE'S SOME-THING INSIDE—STILL NOT DI-GESTED!
WHAT IF HE HADN'T BEEN HERE?
TUG!
WE'RE JUST IN TIME!

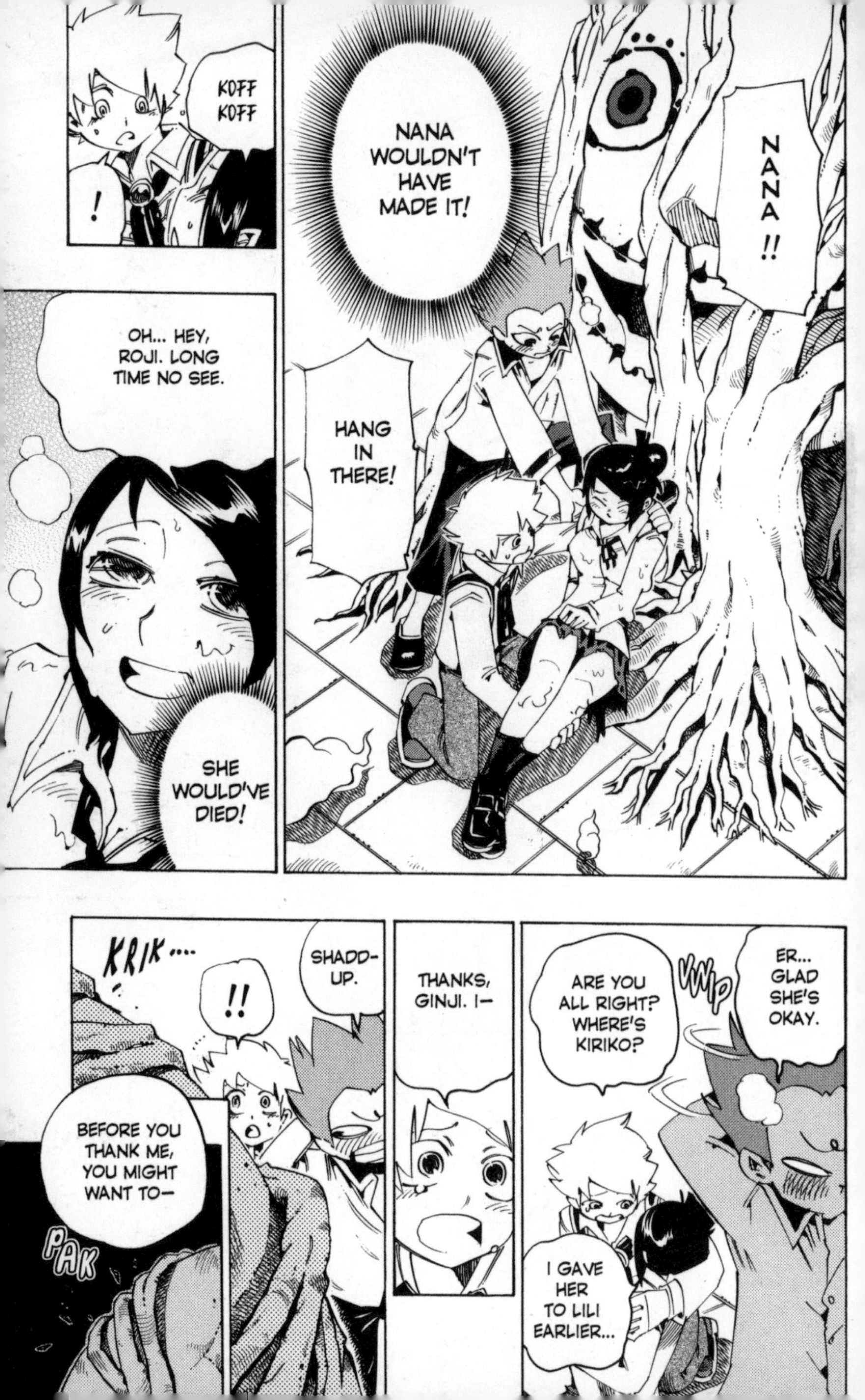
NANA!!
NANA WOULDN'T HAVE MADE IT!
HANG IN THERE!
KOFF KOFF
!
OH... HEY, ROJI. LONG TIME NO SEE.
SHE WOULD'VE DIED!
ER... GLAD SHE'S OKAY.
VWIP
ARE YOU ALL RIGHT? WHERE'S KIRIKO?
I GAVE HER TO LILI EARLIER...
THANKS, GINJI. I—
SHADD-UP.
KRIK....
!!
BEFORE YOU THANK ME, YOU MIGHT WANT TO—
PAK

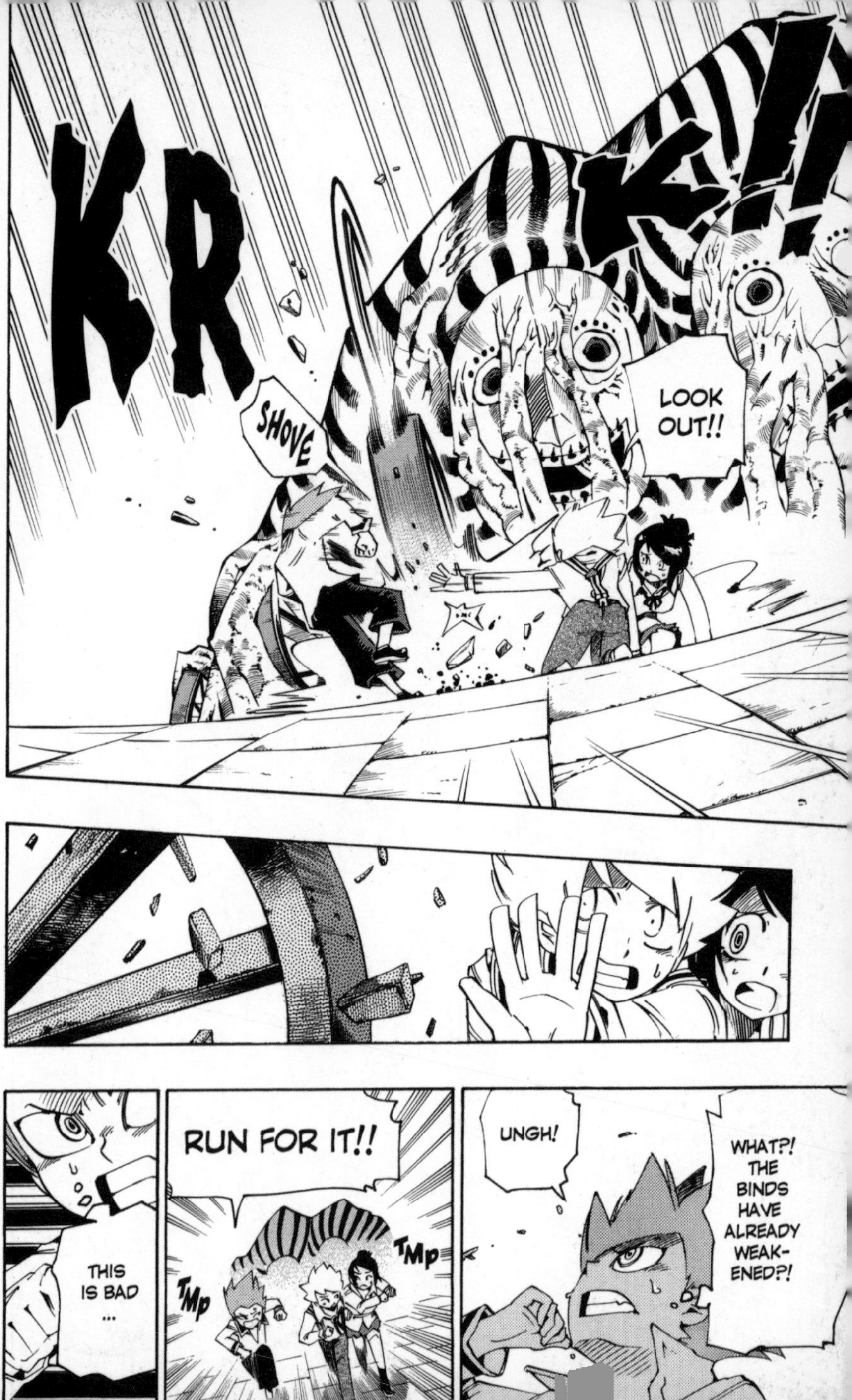

KR
K!!
LOOK OUT!!
SHOVE
WHAT?! THE BINDS HAVE ALREADY WEAK-ENED?!
UNGH!
RUN FOR IT!!
TMp
TMp
THIS IS BAD ...

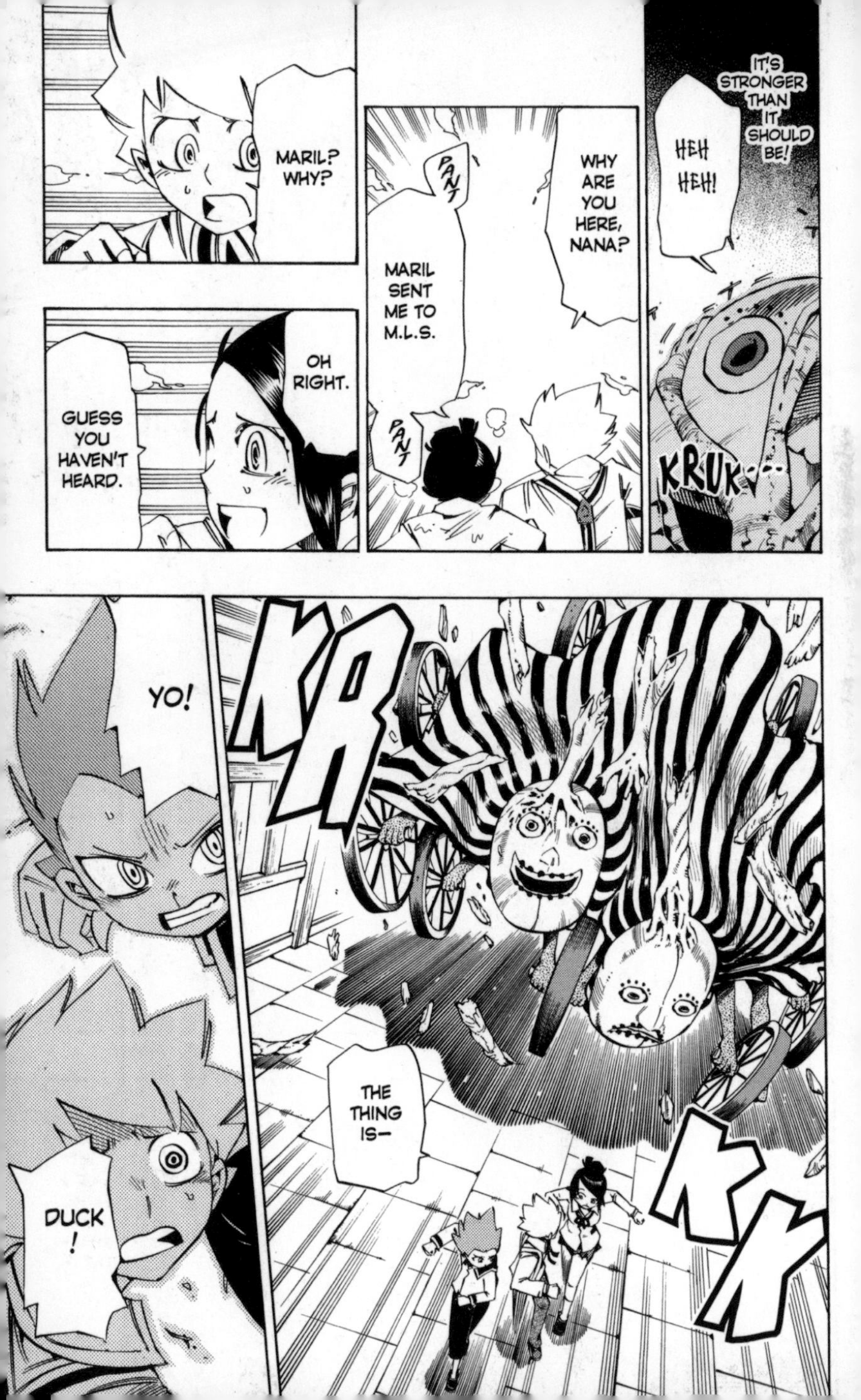
IT'S STRONGER THAN IT SHOULD BE!
HEH HEH!
KRUK...
WHY ARE YOU HERE, NANA?
PANT
MARIL SENT ME TO M.L.S.
PANT
MARIL? WHY?
OH RIGHT.
GUESS YOU HAVEN'T HEARD.
KA
THE THING IS—
YO!
DUCK!

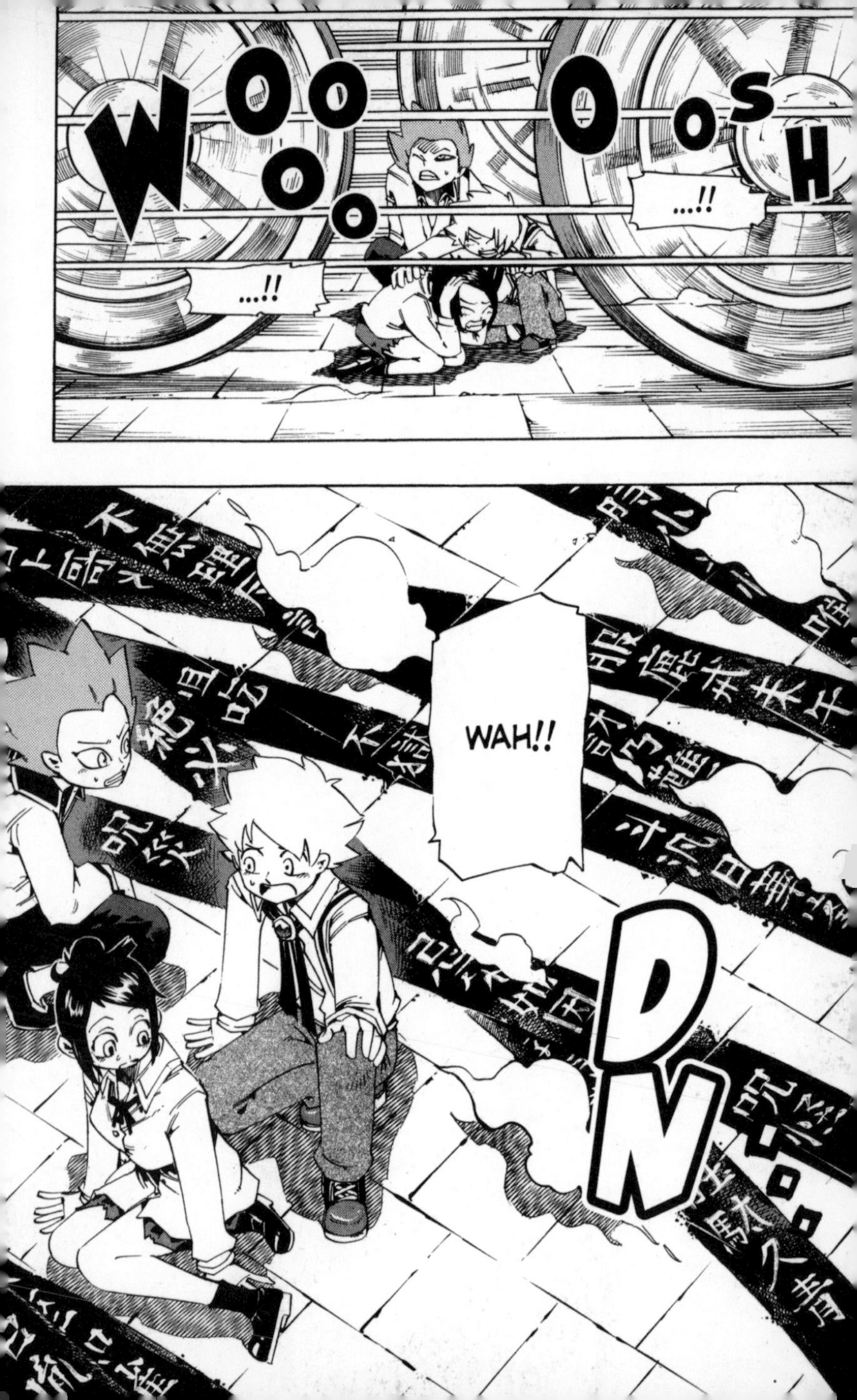
WOOOOOOSH
...!!
...!!
WAH!!
DN..

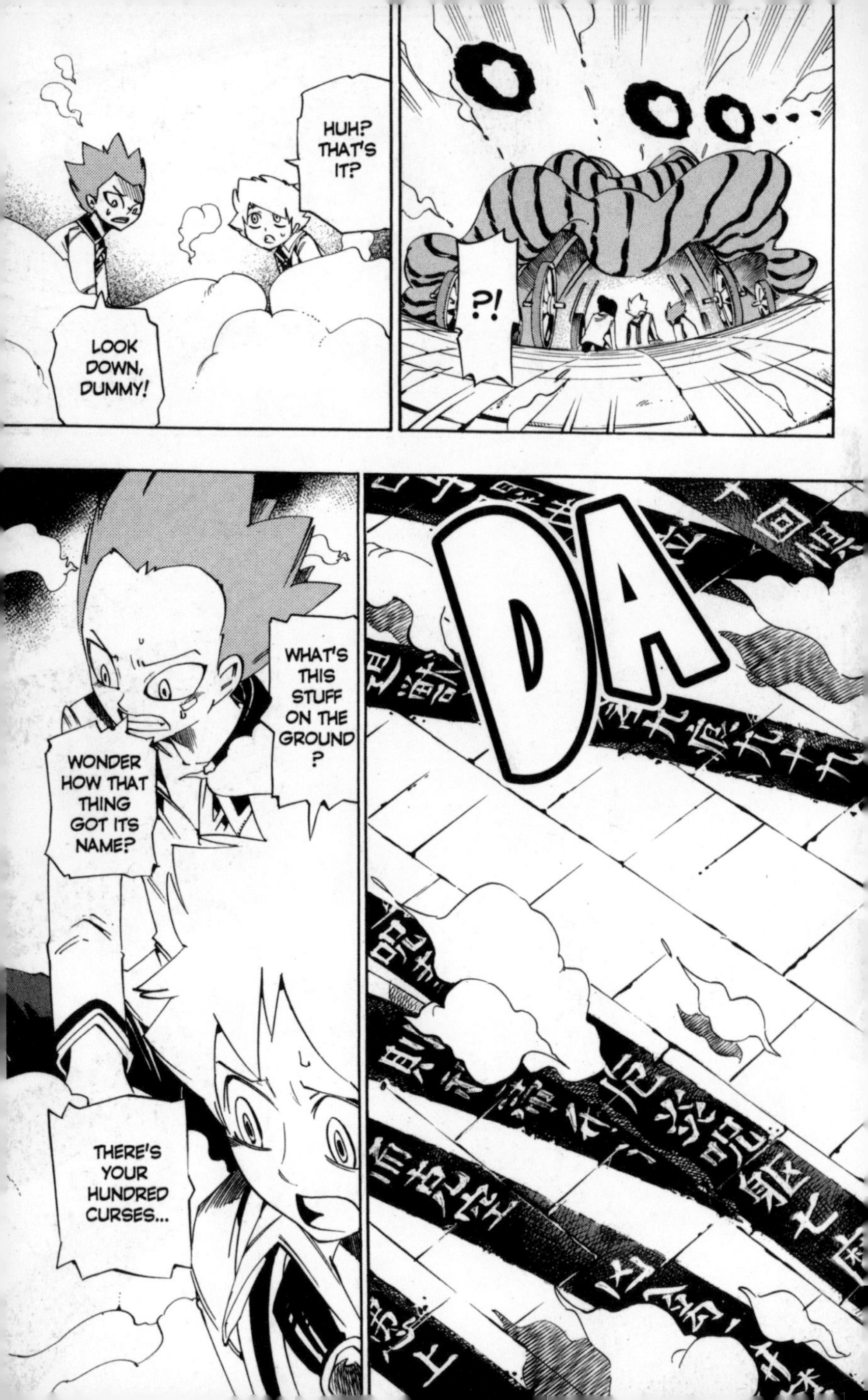
OOO...
?!
HUH? THAT'S IT?
LOOK DOWN, DUMMY!
DA
WHAT'S THIS STUFF ON THE GROUND?
WONDER HOW THAT THING GOT ITS NAME?
THERE'S YOUR HUNDRED CURSES...

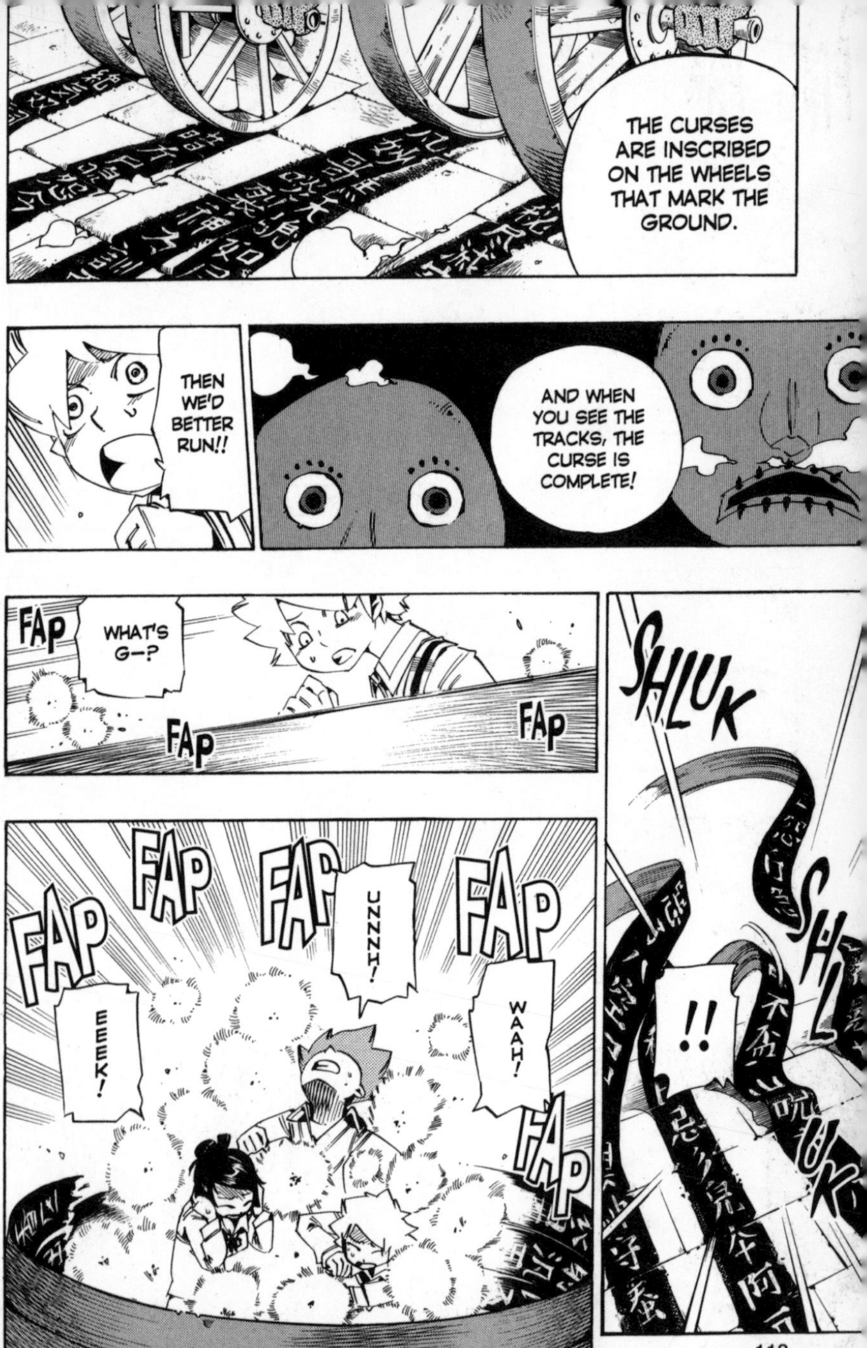
THE CURSES ARE INSCRIBED ON THE WHEELS THAT MARK THE GROUND.
AND WHEN YOU SEE THE TRACKS, THE CURSE IS COMPLETE!
THEN WE'D BETTER RUN!!
SHLUK
!!
SHLUK
FAP
FAP
WHAT'S G--?
FAP
FAP
WAAH!
UNNNH!
FAP
FAP
FAP
EEEK!
FAP

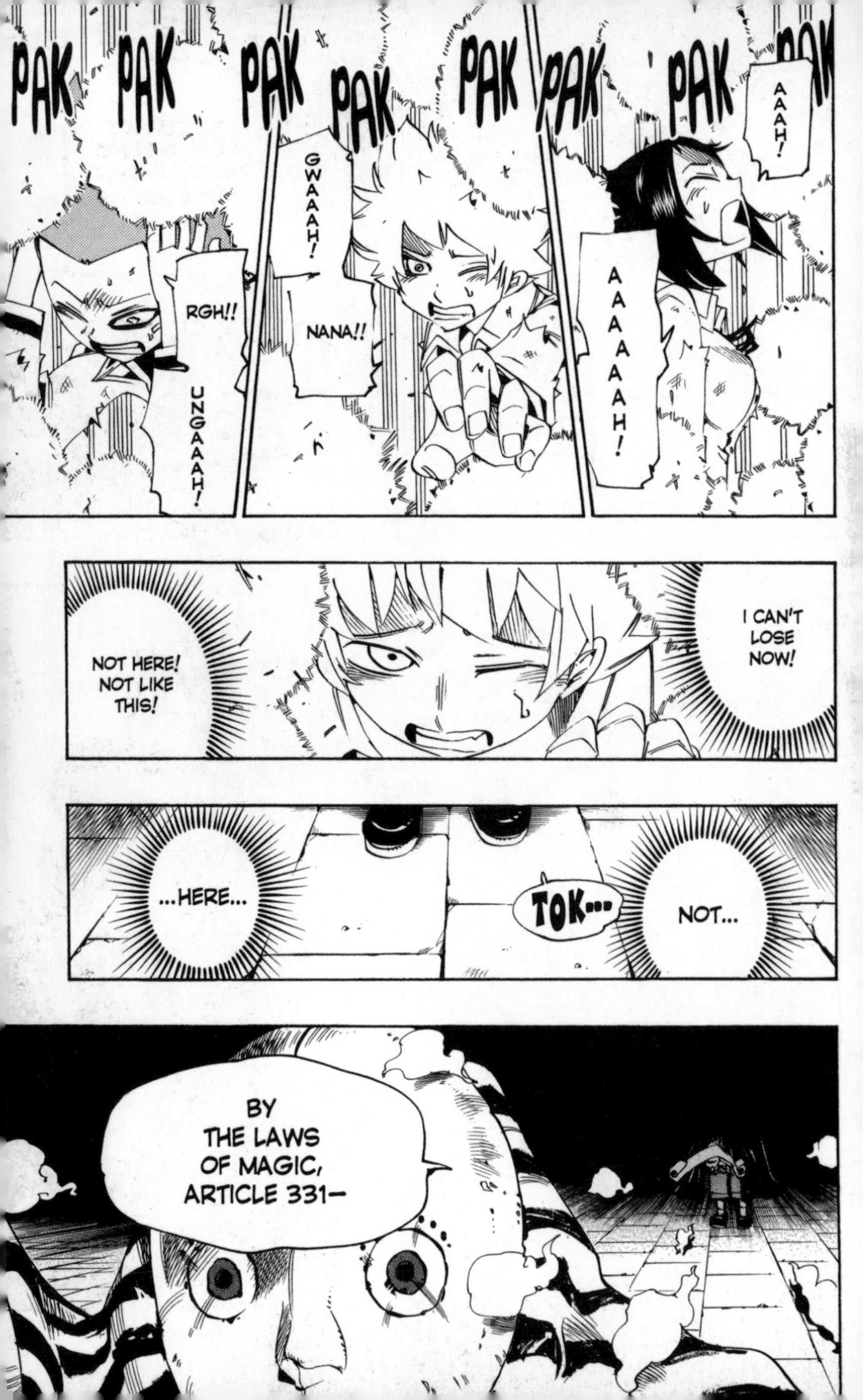
PAK PAK
AAAH!
AAAAAAAH!
PAK PAK PAK
GWAAAAH!
NANA!!
PAK PAK PAK
RGH!!
UNGAAAH!
I CAN'T LOSE NOW!
NOT HERE! NOT LIKE THIS!
NOT...
TOK...
...HERE...
BY THE LAWS OF MAGIC, ARTICLE 331–

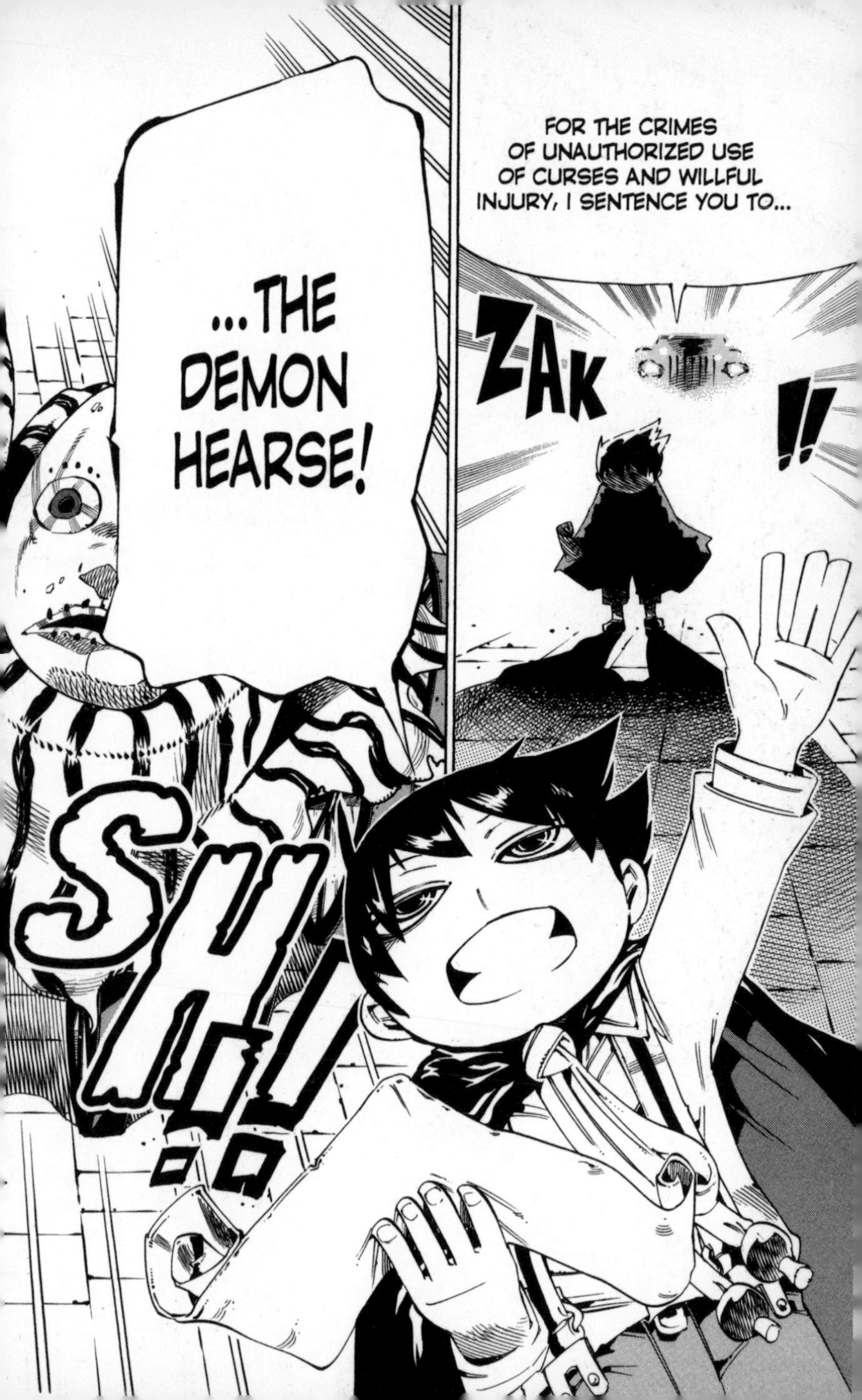
FOR THE CRIMES OF UNAUTHORIZED USE OF CURSES AND WILLFUL INJURY, I SENTENCE YOU TO...
ZAK
!!
...THE DEMON HEARSE!
SHU

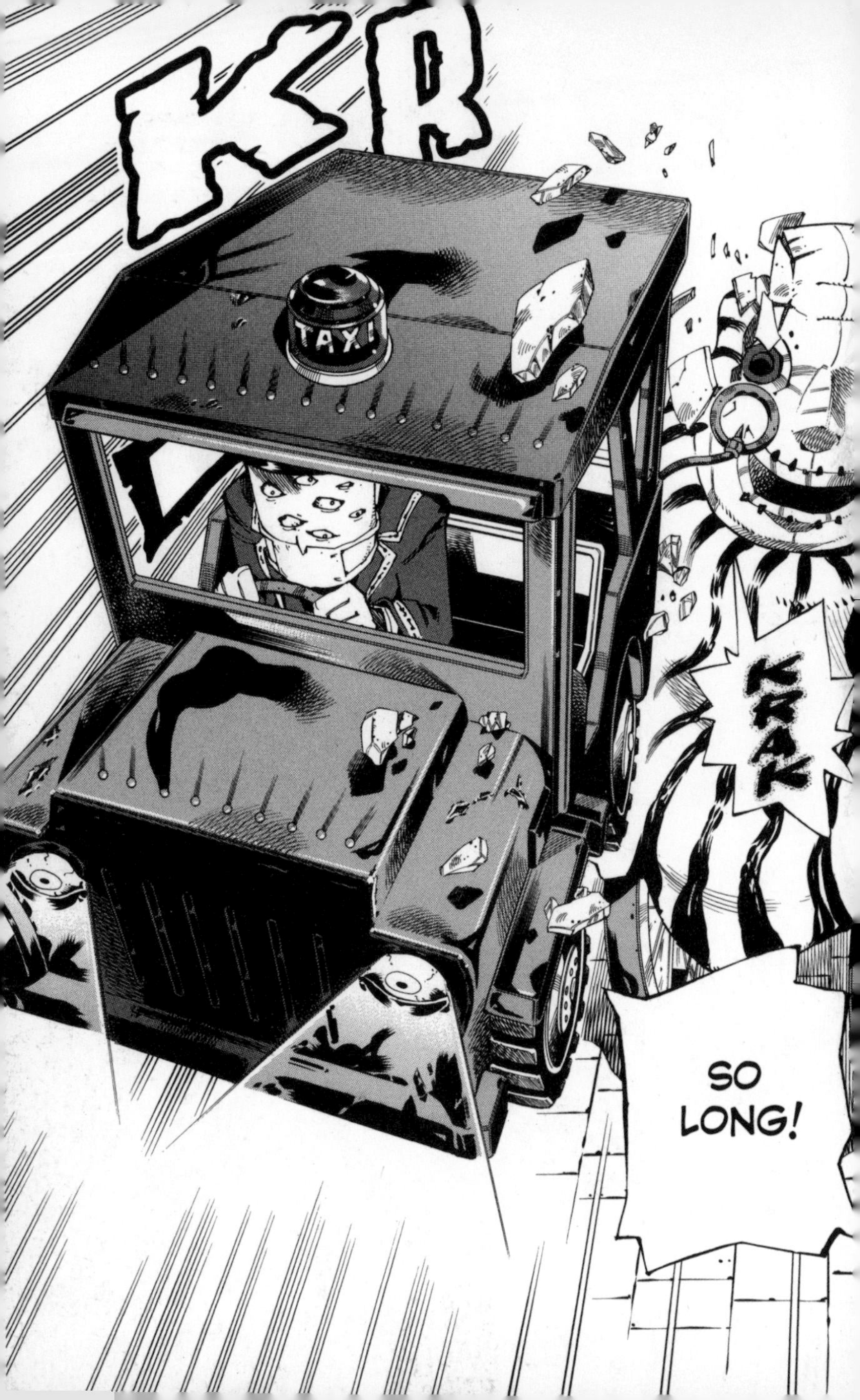
KR
TAXI
KRAK
SO LONG!

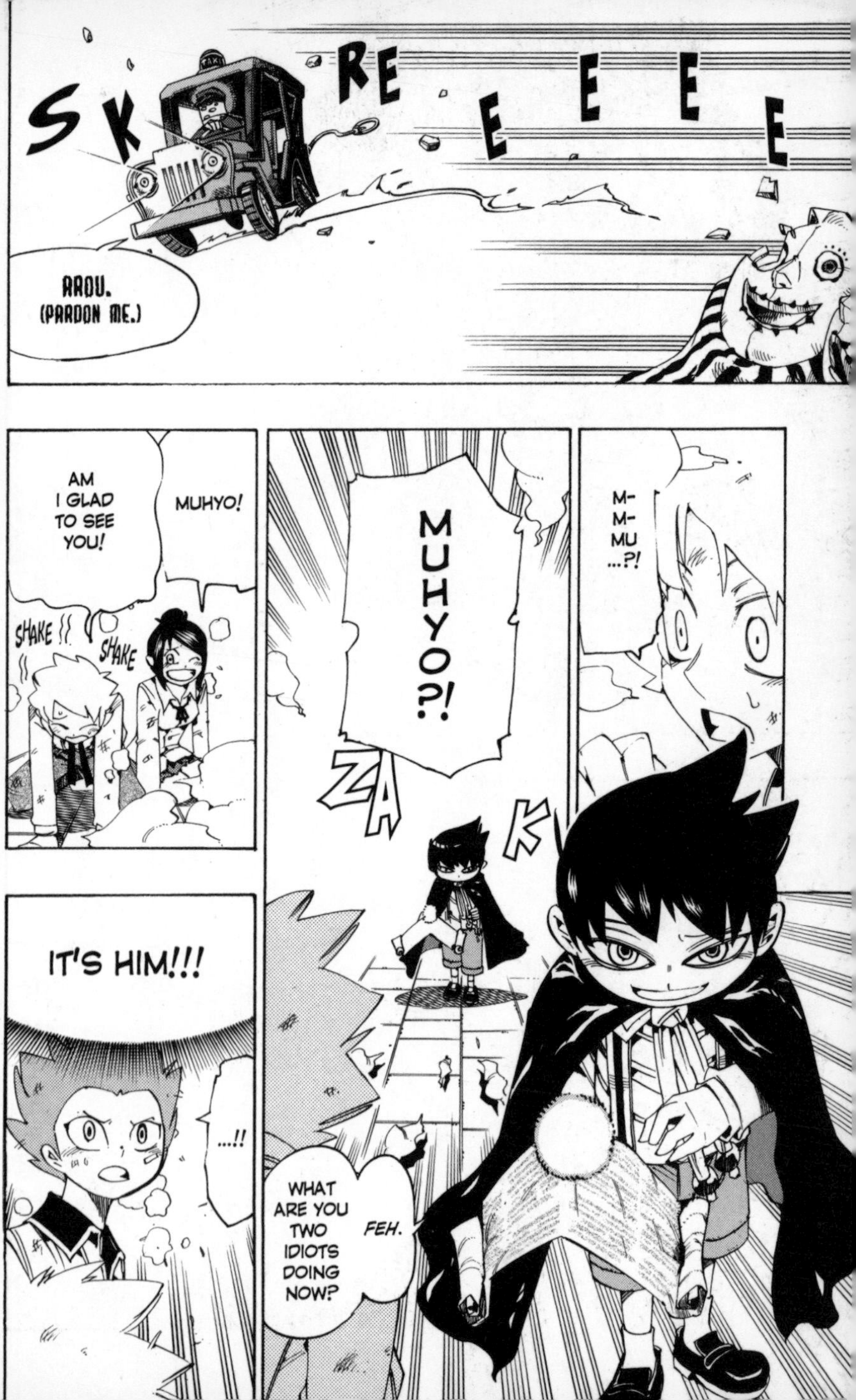
SKREEEEEE
ARDU. (PARDON ME.)
M-M-MU...?!
MUHYO?!
MUHYO!
AM I GLAD TO SEE YOU!
SHAKE SHAKE
ZAK
FEH.
WHAT ARE YOU TWO IDIOTS DOING NOW?
...!!
IT'S HIM!!!

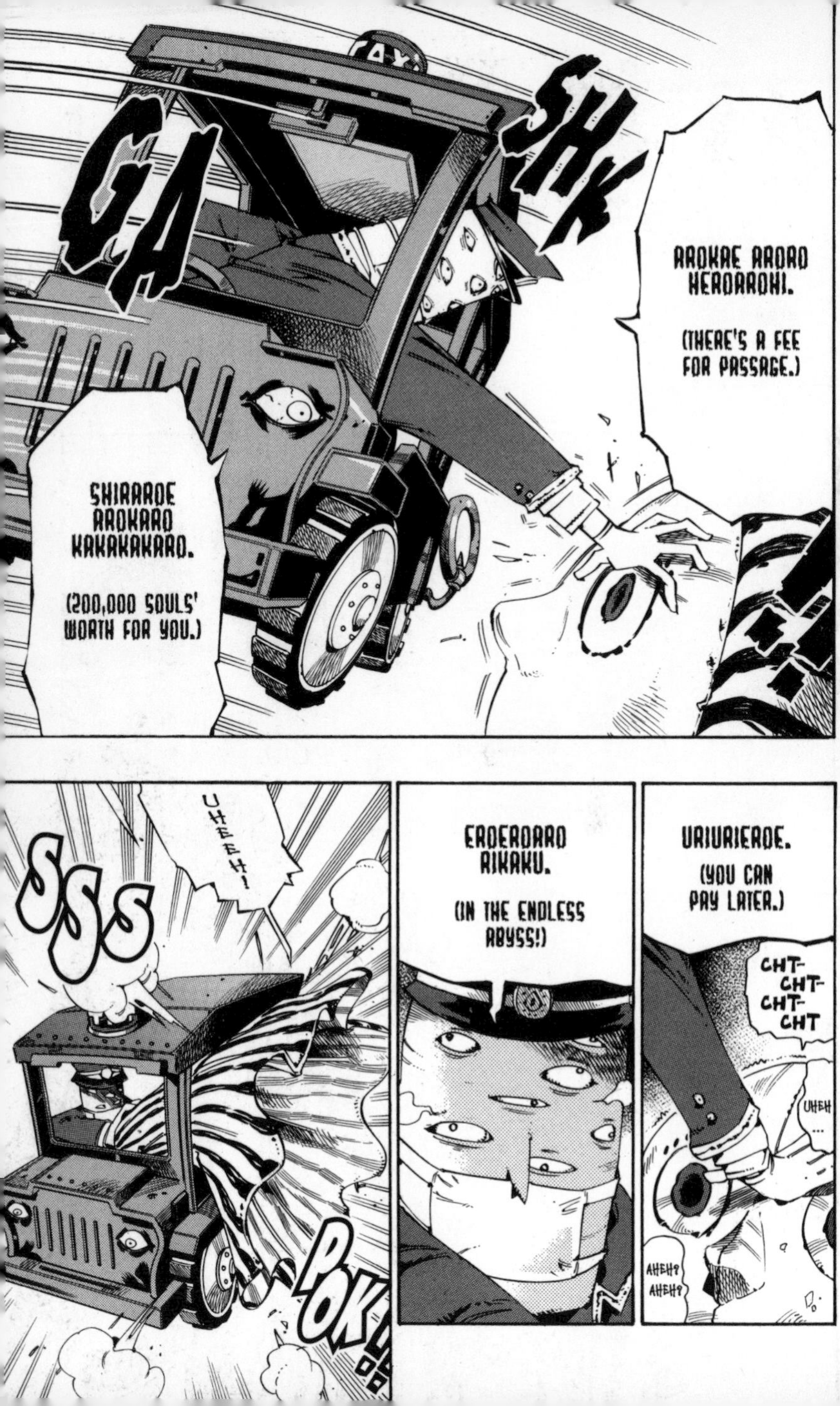
AROKAE ARORO HERORAROHI.
(THERE'S A FEE FOR PASSAGE.)
SHK
GA
SHIRARDE AROKARO KAKAKAKARO.
(200,000 SOULS' WORTH FOR YOU.)
URIURIERDE.
(YOU CAN PAY LATER.)
CHT-CHT-CHT-CHT
UHEH...
AHEH? AHEH?
ERDERORRO RIKAKU.
(IN THE ENDLESS ABYSS!)
UHEEH!
SSS
POK

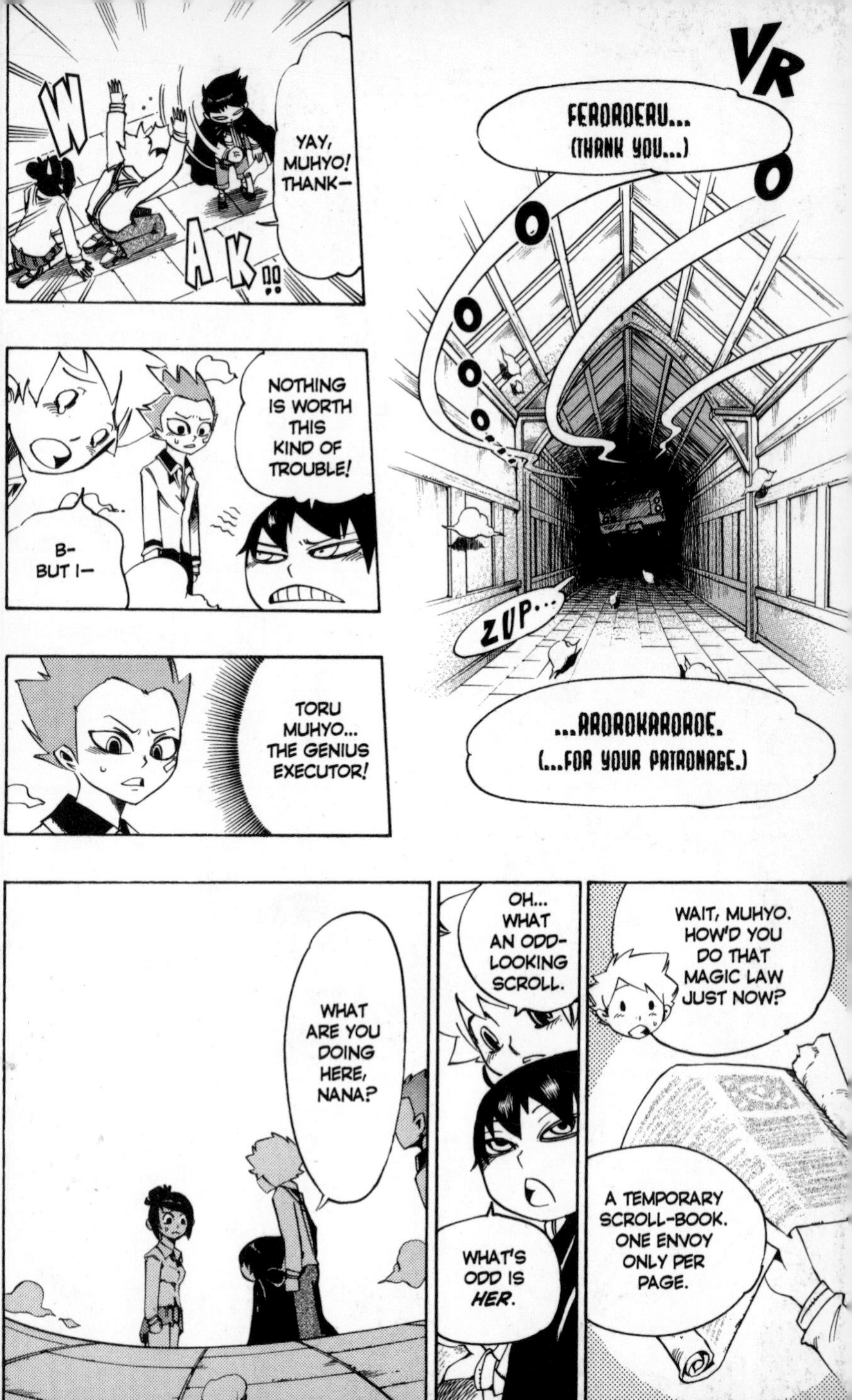
VROOOOOO...
FERORDERU... (THANK YOU...)
ZUP...
...ARORDKARORDE. (...FOR YOUR PATRONAGE.)
YAY, MUHYO! THANK—
WAK!!
NOTHING IS WORTH THIS KIND OF TROUBLE!
B-BUT I—
TORU MUHYO... THE GENIUS EXECUTOR!
WAIT, MUHYO. HOW'D YOU DO THAT MAGIC LAW JUST NOW?
A TEMPORARY SCROLL-BOOK. ONE ENVOY ONLY PER PAGE.
OH... WHAT AN ODD-LOOKING SCROLL.
WHAT'S ODD IS *HER*.
WHAT ARE YOU DOING HERE, NANA?

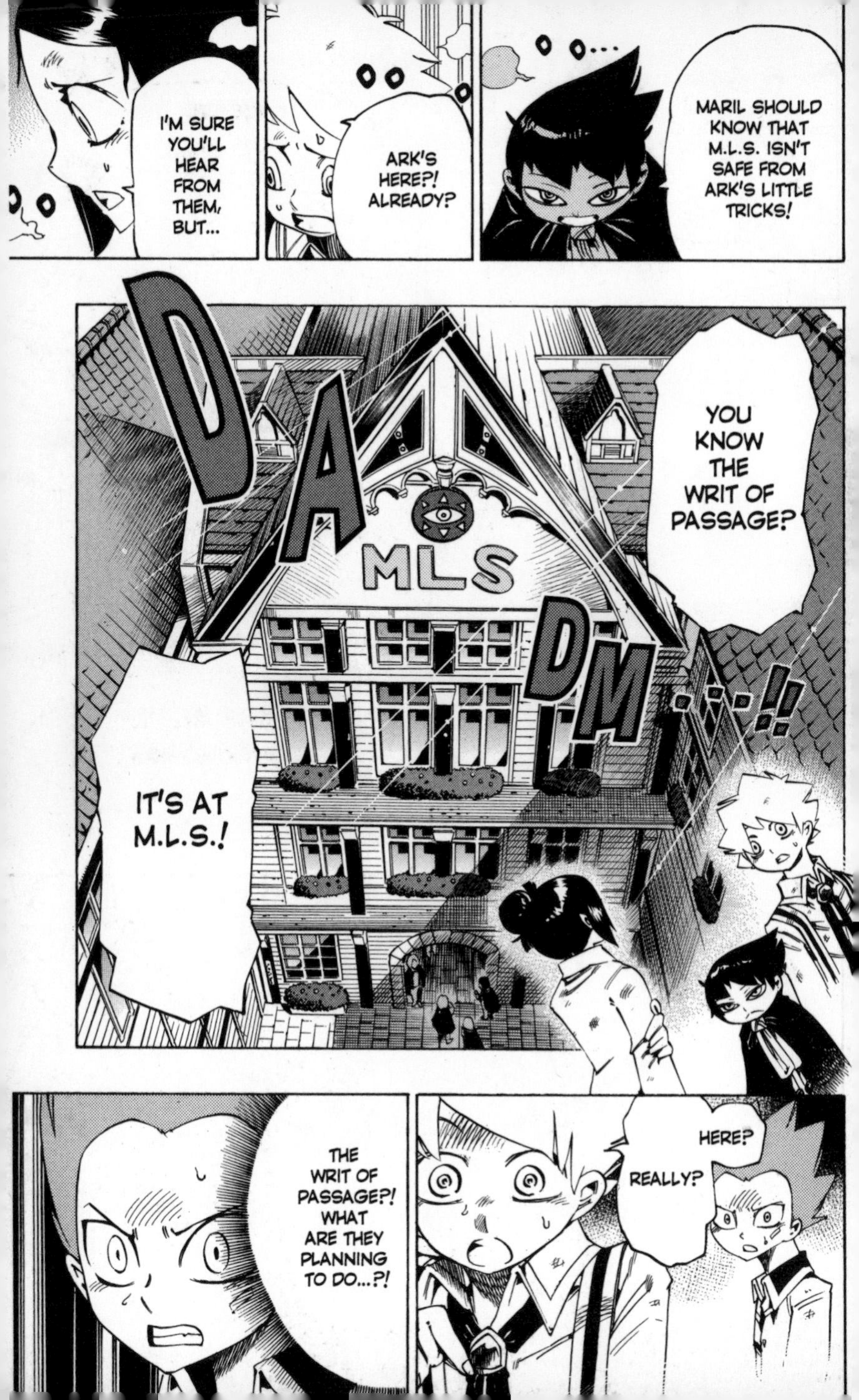
MARIL SHOULD KNOW THAT M.L.S. ISN'T SAFE FROM ARK'S LITTLE TRICKS!
ARK'S HERE?! ALREADY?
I'M SURE YOU'LL HEAR FROM THEM, BUT...
YOU KNOW THE WRIT OF PASSAGE?
DA
MLS
DM...!!
IT'S AT M.L.S.!
HERE?
REALLY?
THE WRIT OF PASSAGE?! WHAT ARE THEY PLANNING TO DO...?!

THAT'S
REALLY
ANNOYING.

JUST
UNTIL NANA
GETS BACK,
PLEASE?

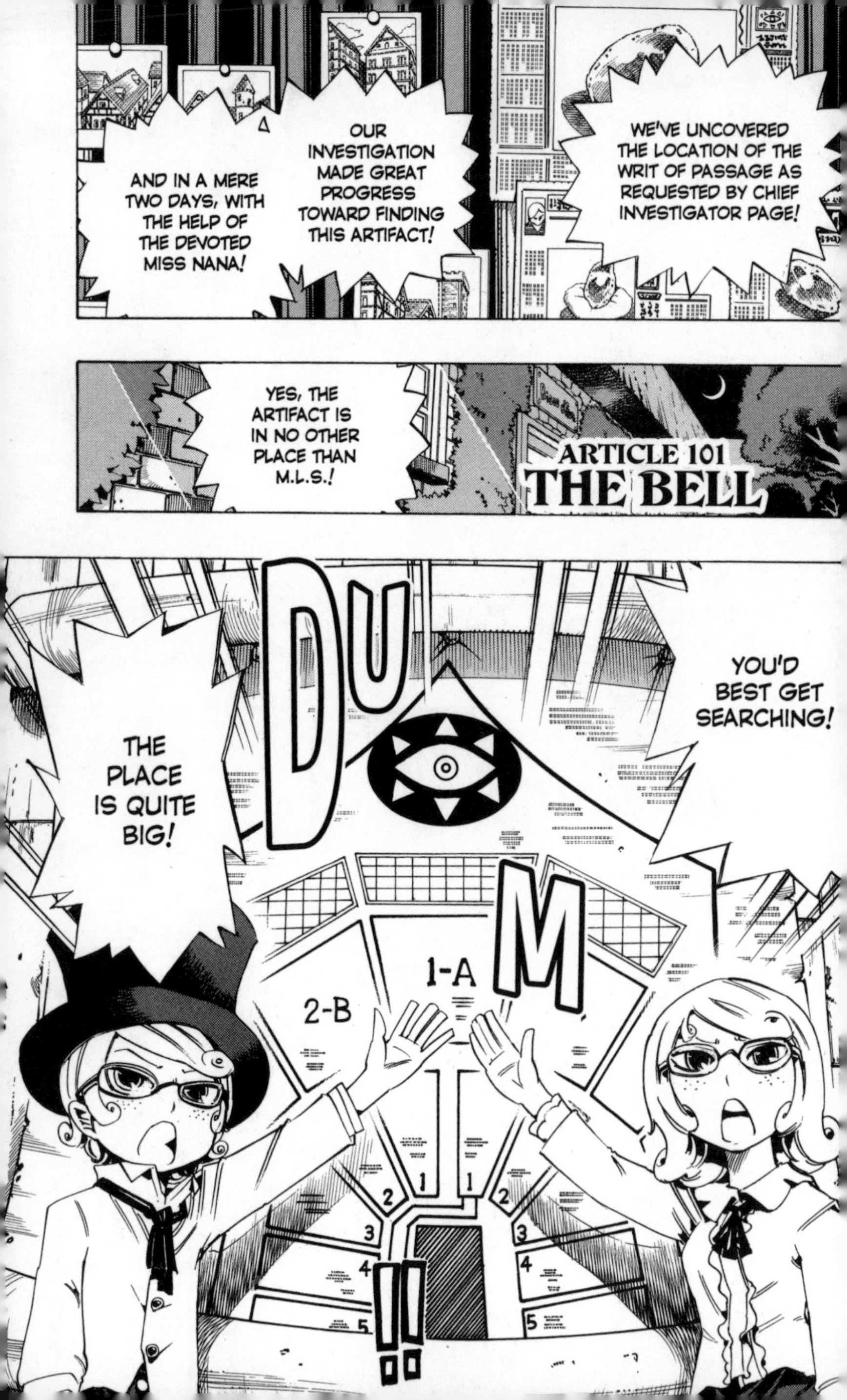
WE'VE UNCOVERED THE LOCATION OF THE WRIT OF PASSAGE AS REQUESTED BY CHIEF INVESTIGATOR PAGE!
OUR INVESTIGATION MADE GREAT PROGRESS TOWARD FINDING THIS ARTIFACT!
AND IN A MERE TWO DAYS, WITH THE HELP OF THE DEVOTED MISS NANA!
YES, THE ARTIFACT IS IN NO OTHER PLACE THAN M.L.S.!
ARTICLE 101
THE BELL
YOU'D BEST GET SEARCHING!
THE PLACE IS QUITE BIG!
DUM!!
1-A
2-B

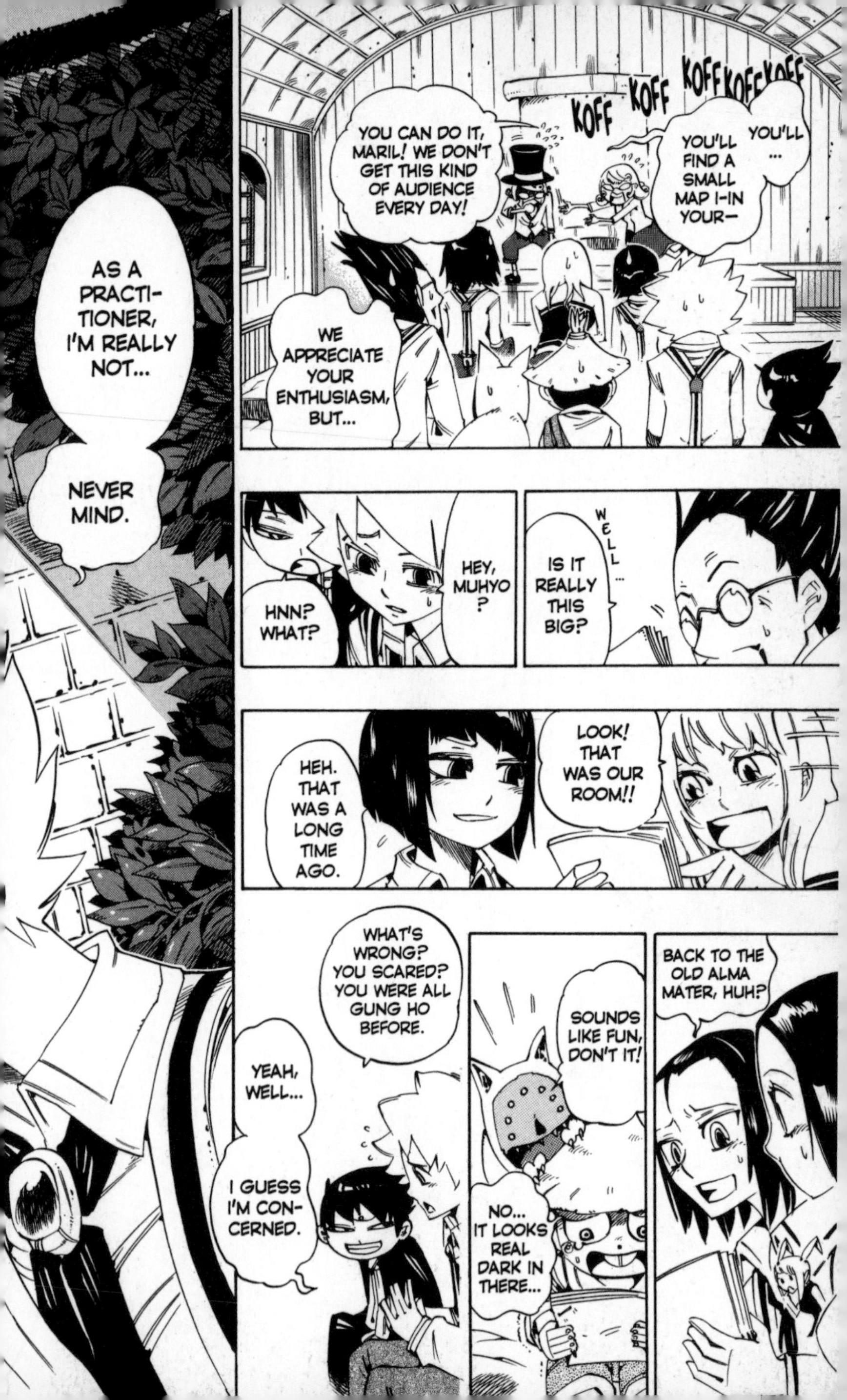
KOFF KOFF KOFF KOFF KOFF
YOU'LL ...
YOU'LL FIND A SMALL MAP I-IN YOUR—
YOU CAN DO IT, MARIL! WE DON'T GET THIS KIND OF AUDIENCE EVERY DAY!
WE APPRECIATE YOUR ENTHUSIASM, BUT...
WELL...
IS IT REALLY THIS BIG?
HEY, MUHYO?
HNN? WHAT?
LOOK! THAT WAS OUR ROOM!!
HEH. THAT WAS A LONG TIME AGO.
BACK TO THE OLD ALMA MATER, HUH?
SOUNDS LIKE FUN, DON'T IT!
NO... IT LOOKS REAL DARK IN THERE...
WHAT'S WRONG? YOU SCARED? YOU WERE ALL GUNG HO BEFORE.
YEAH, WELL...
I GUESS I'M CON-CERNED.
AS A PRACTI-TIONER, I'M REALLY NOT...
NEVER MIND.

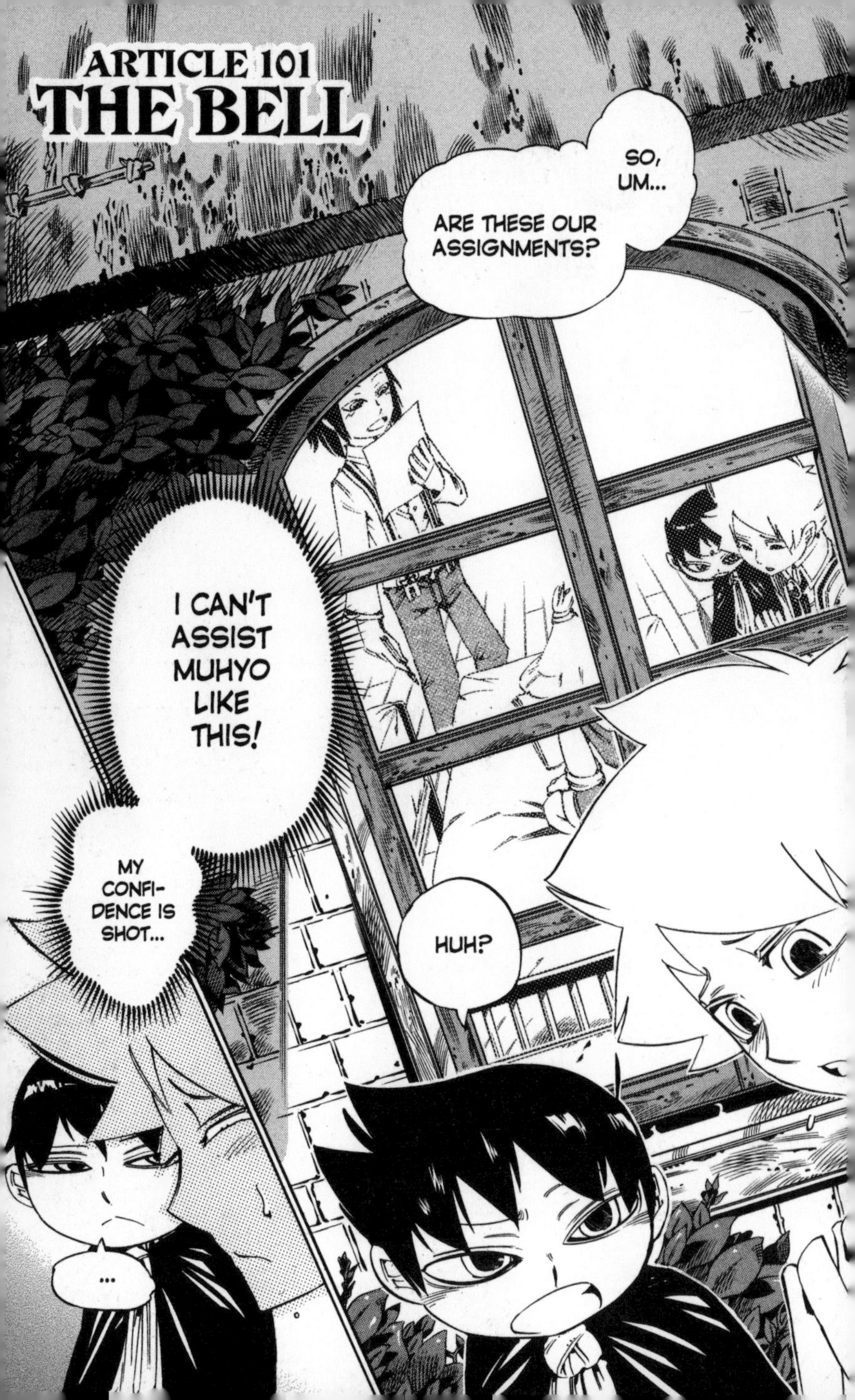
ARTICLE 101
THE BELL
SO, UM...
ARE THESE OUR ASSIGNMENTS?
I CAN'T ASSIST MUHYO LIKE THIS!
MY CONFI- DENCE IS SHOT...
HUH?
...

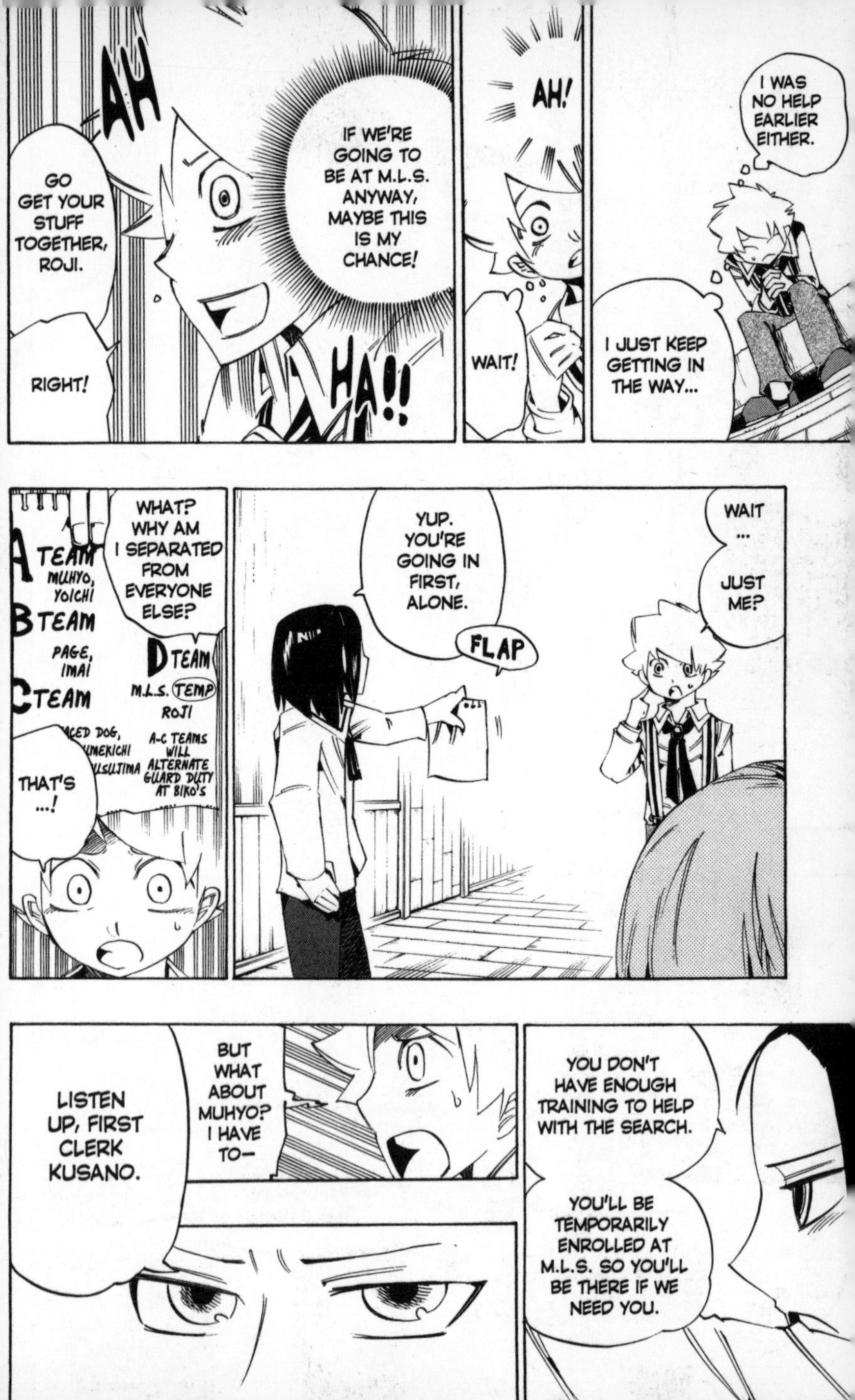
I WAS NO HELP EARLIER EITHER.
I JUST KEEP GETTING IN THE WAY...
AH!
WAIT!
IF WE'RE GOING TO BE AT M.L.S. ANYWAY, MAYBE THIS IS MY CHANCE!
AH
HA!!
GO GET YOUR STUFF TOGETHER, ROJI.
RIGHT!
WAIT ... JUST ME?
YUP. YOU'RE GOING IN FIRST, ALONE.
FLAP
WHAT? WHY AM I SEPARATED FROM EVERYONE ELSE?
A TEAM MUHYO, YOICHI
B TEAM PAGE, IMAI
C TEAM
D TEAM M.L.S. TEMP ROJI
A-C TEAMS WILL ALTERNATE GUARD DUTY AT BIKO'S
THAT'S ...!
YOU DON'T HAVE ENOUGH TRAINING TO HELP WITH THE SEARCH.
YOU'LL BE TEMPORARILY ENROLLED AT M.L.S. SO YOU'LL BE THERE IF WE NEED YOU.
BUT WHAT ABOUT MUHYO? I HAVE TO—
LISTEN UP, FIRST CLERK KUSANO.

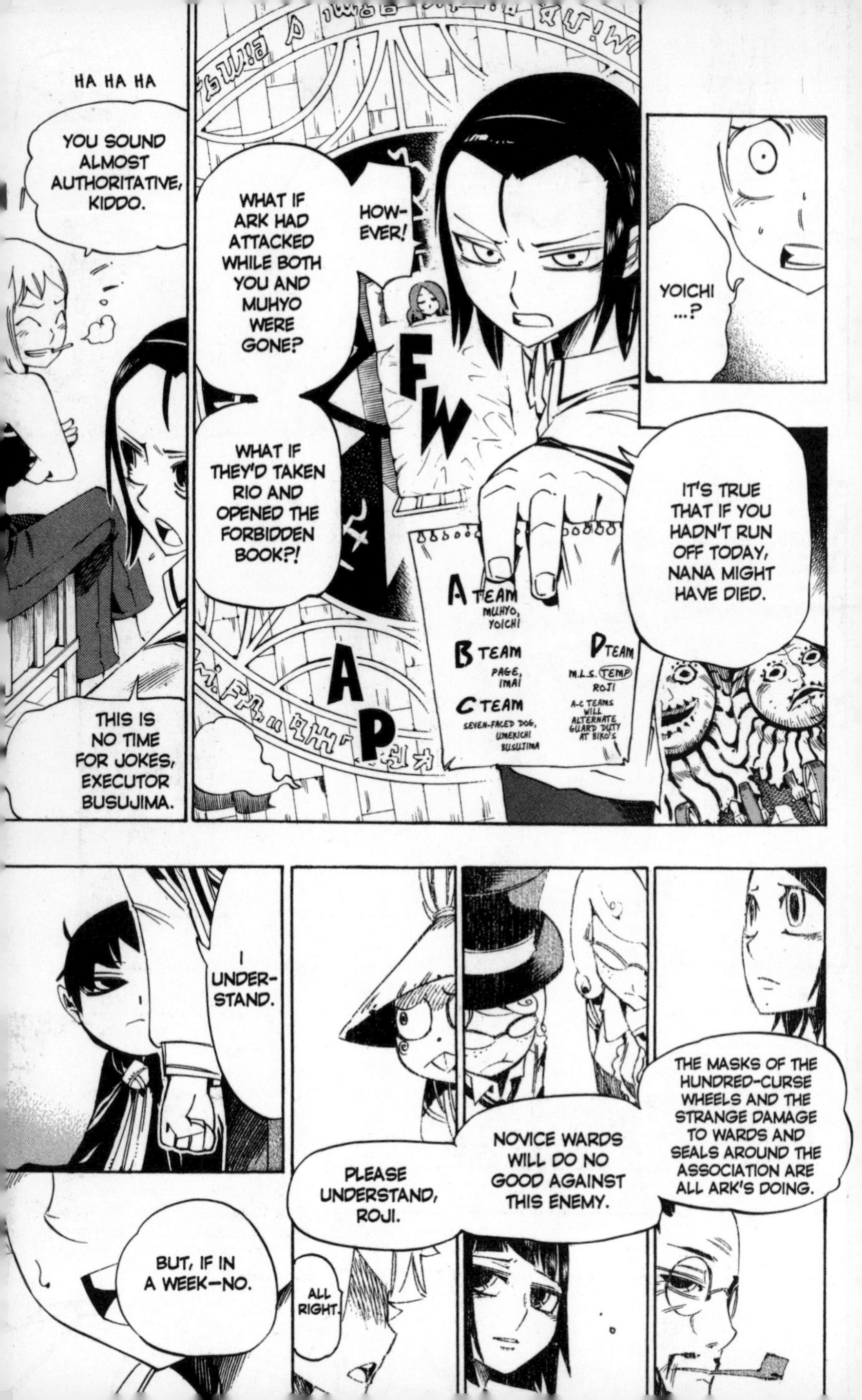
YOICHI ...?
IT'S TRUE THAT IF YOU HADN'T RUN OFF TODAY, NANA MIGHT HAVE DIED.
HOW-EVER!
WHAT IF ARK HAD ATTACKED WHILE BOTH YOU AND MUHYO WERE GONE?
WHAT IF THEY'D TAKEN RIO AND OPENED THE FORBIDDEN BOOK?!
FW
AP
A TEAM MUHYO, YOICHI
B TEAM PAGE, IMAI
C TEAM SEVEN-FACED DOG, UMEKICHI BUSUJIMA
D TEAM M.L.S. TEMP ROJI
A-C TEAMS WILL ALTERNATE GUARD DUTY AT BIKO'S
HA HA HA
YOU SOUND ALMOST AUTHORITATIVE, KIDDO.
THIS IS NO TIME FOR JOKES, EXECUTOR BUSUJIMA.
THE MASKS OF THE HUNDRED-CURSE WHEELS AND THE STRANGE DAMAGE TO WARDS AND SEALS AROUND THE ASSOCIATION ARE ALL ARK'S DOING.
NOVICE WARDS WILL DO NO GOOD AGAINST THIS ENEMY.
PLEASE UNDERSTAND, ROJI.
I UNDER-STAND.
ALL RIGHT.
BUT, IF IN A WEEK—NO.

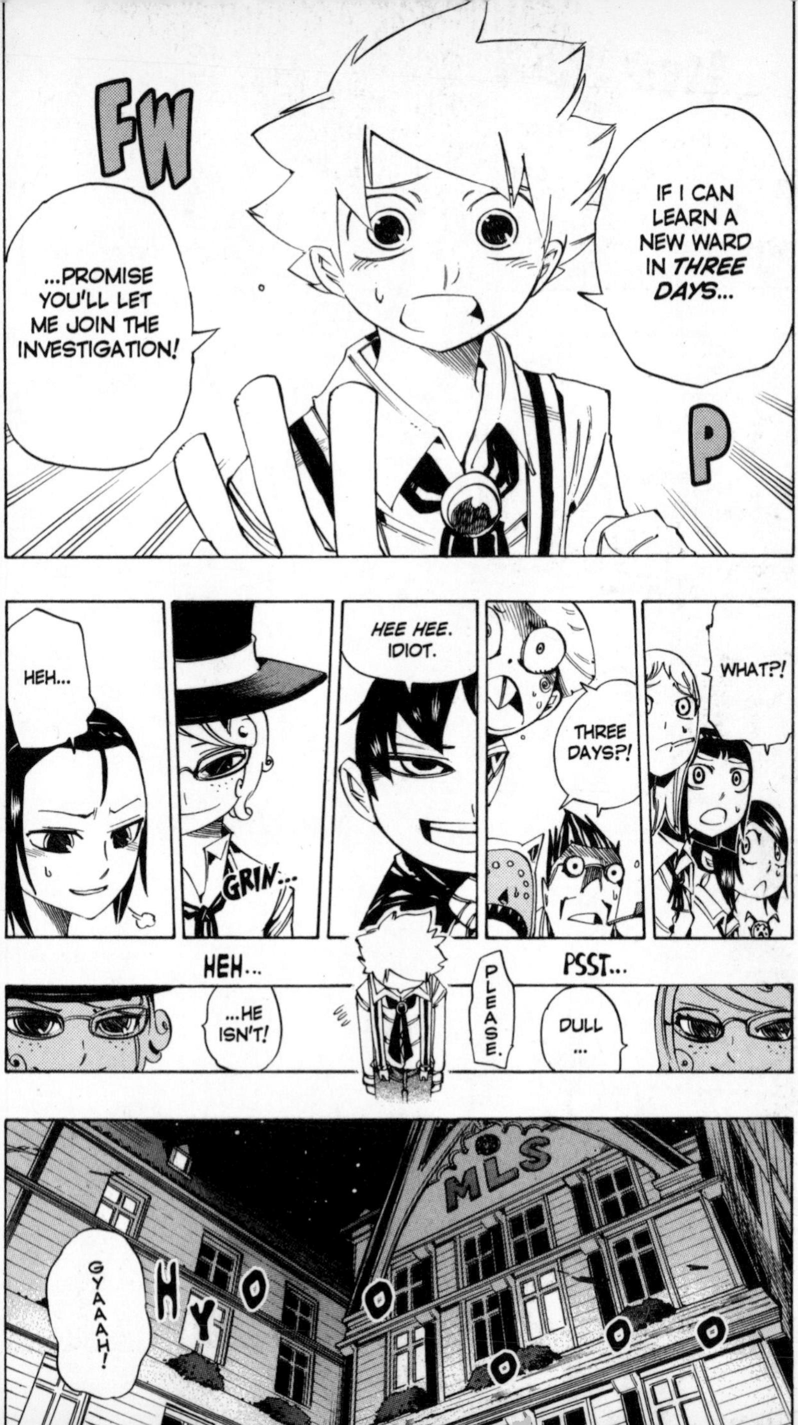
IF I CAN LEARN A NEW WARD IN *THREE DAYS*...
P
FW
...PROMISE YOU'LL LET ME JOIN THE INVESTIGATION!
WHAT?!
THREE DAYS?!
HEE HEE. IDIOT.
GRIN...
HEH...
PSST...
DULL ...
PLEASE.
...HE ISN'T!
HEH...
MLS
O
O
O
O
O
HYO
GYAAAH!

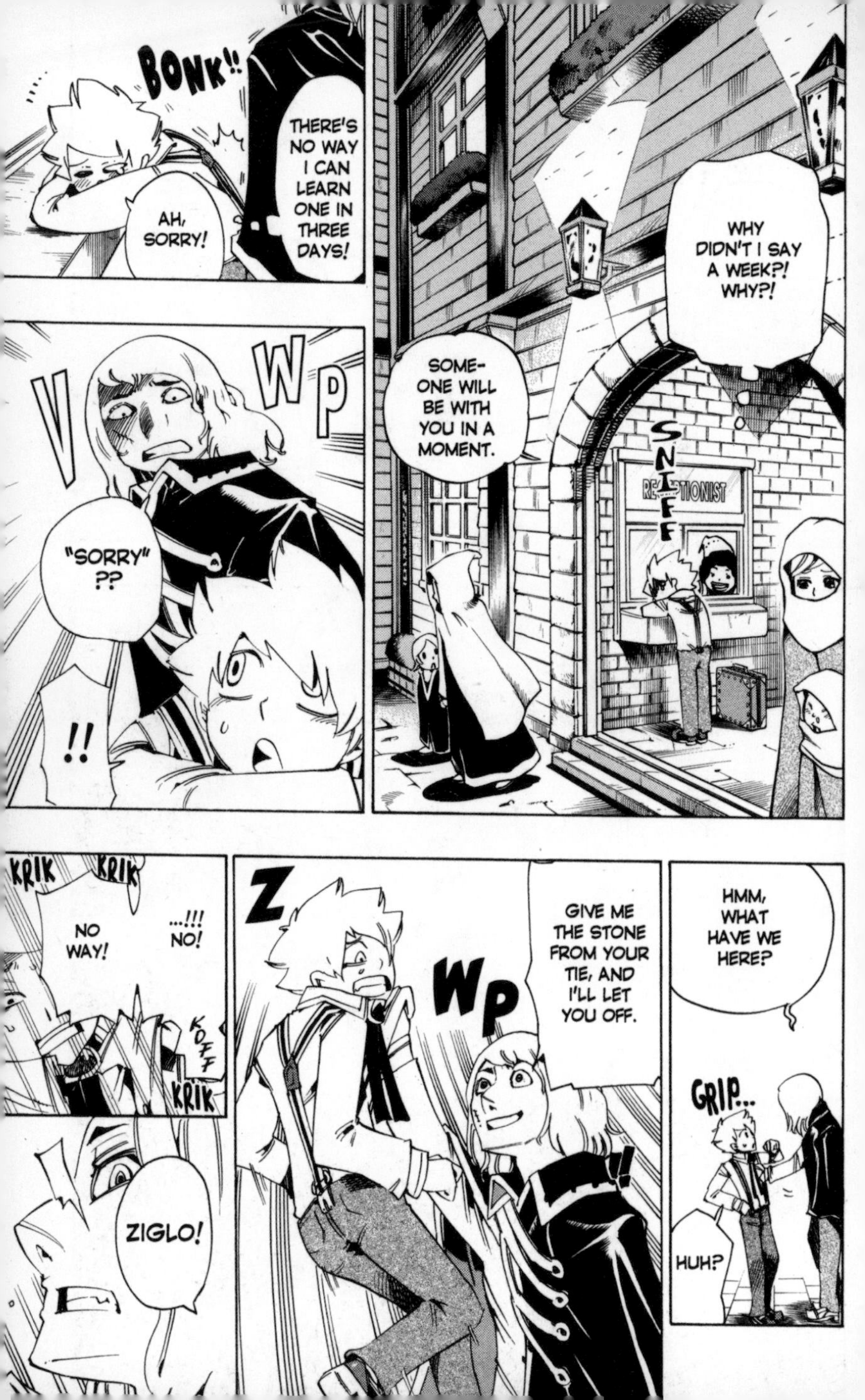
WHY DIDN'T I SAY A WEEK?! WHY?!
SOME-ONE WILL BE WITH YOU IN A MOMENT.
SNIFF
THERE'S NO WAY I CAN LEARN ONE IN THREE DAYS!
BONK!!
AH, SORRY!
...
V
WP
"SORRY" ??
!!
HMM, WHAT HAVE WE HERE?
GRIP...
HUH?
Z
WP
GIVE ME THE STONE FROM YOUR TIE, AND I'LL LET YOU OFF.
KRIK
KRIK
...!!! NO!
NO WAY!
KOFF
KRIK
ZIGLO!

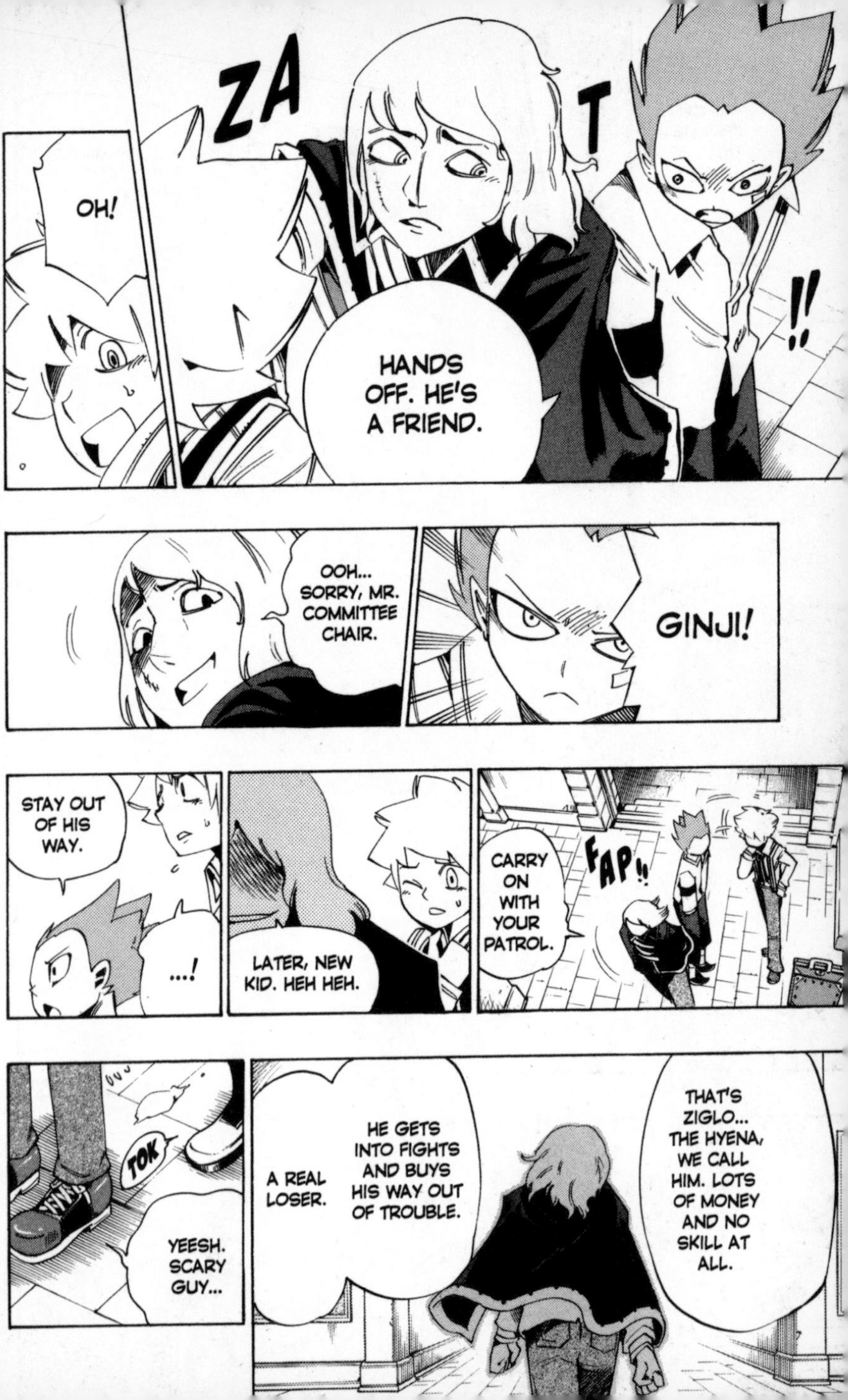
ZAT
!!
HANDS OFF. HE'S A FRIEND.
OH!
GINJI!
OOH... SORRY, MR. COMMITTEE CHAIR.
FAP!!
CARRY ON WITH YOUR PATROL.
LATER, NEW KID. HEH HEH.
STAY OUT OF HIS WAY.
...!
THAT'S ZIGLO... THE HYENA, WE CALL HIM. LOTS OF MONEY AND NO SKILL AT ALL.
HE GETS INTO FIGHTS AND BUYS HIS WAY OUT OF TROUBLE.
A REAL LOSER.
TOK
YEESH. SCARY GUY...

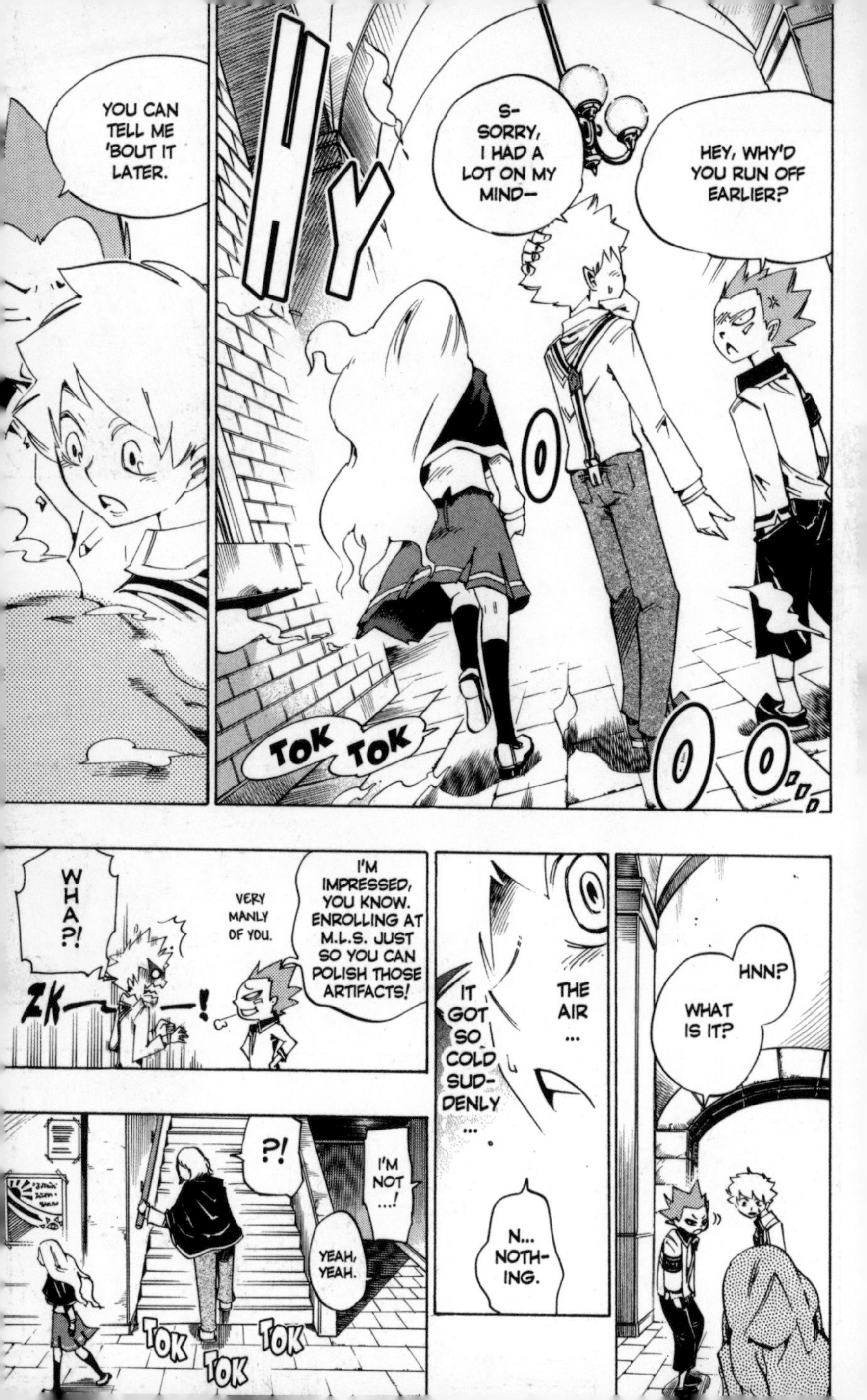
HEY, WHY'D YOU RUN OFF EARLIER?
S-SORRY, I HAD A LOT ON MY MIND—
HY
TOK TOK
YOU CAN TELL ME 'BOUT IT LATER.
HNN? WHAT IS IT?
THE AIR ...
IT GOT SO COLD SUD-DENLY ...
N... NOTH-ING.
I'M IMPRESSED, YOU KNOW. ENROLLING AT M.L.S. JUST SO YOU CAN POLISH THOSE ARTIFACTS!
VERY MANLY OF YOU.
WHA?!
ZK—!
?!
I'M NOT ...!
YEAH, YEAH.
TOK TOK TOK

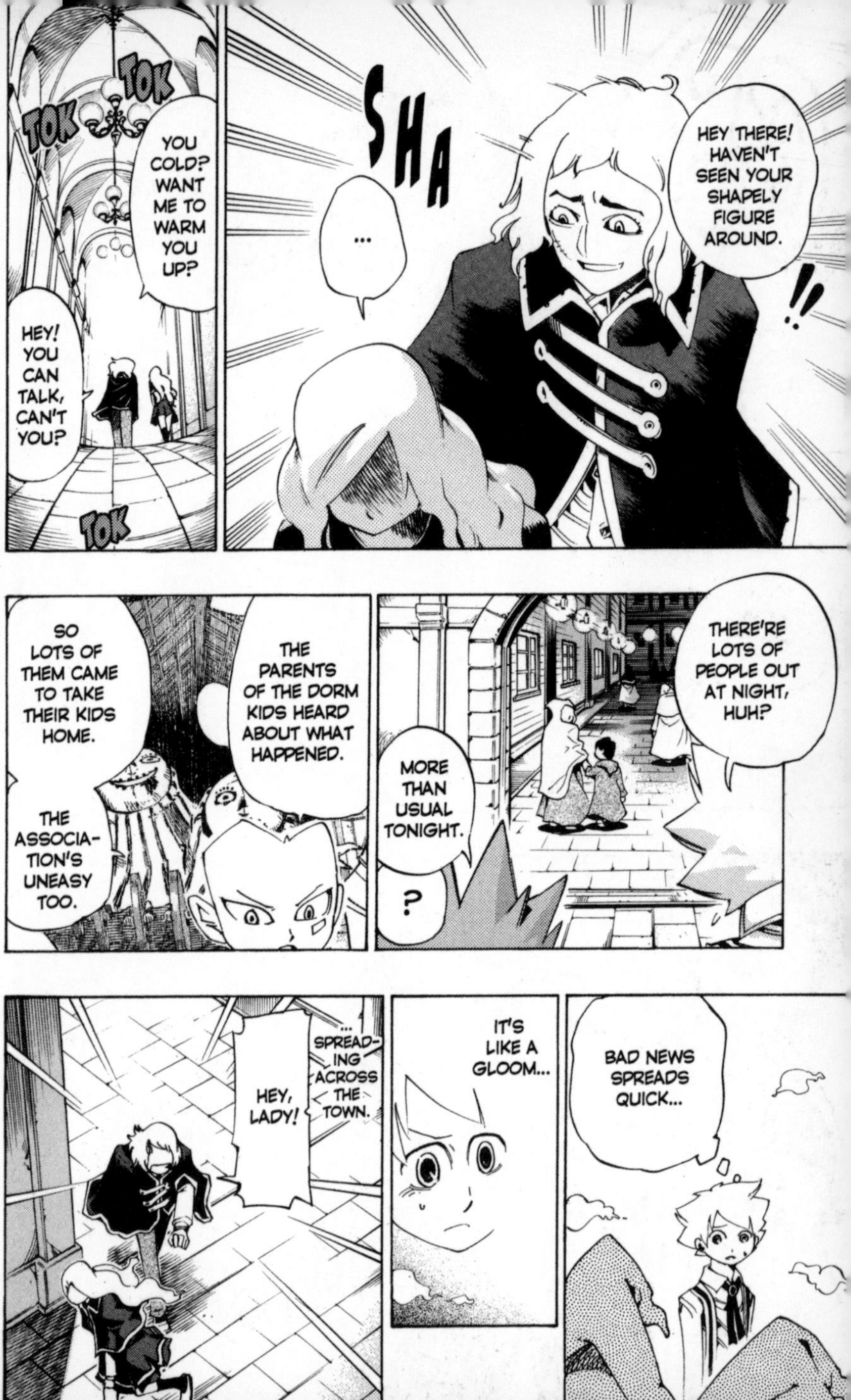
HEY THERE! HAVEN'T SEEN YOUR SHAPELY FIGURE AROUND.
!!
SHA
...
TOK TOK
YOU COLD? WANT ME TO WARM YOU UP?
HEY! YOU CAN TALK, CAN'T YOU?
TOK
THERE'RE LOTS OF PEOPLE OUT AT NIGHT, HUH?
MORE THAN USUAL TONIGHT.
?
THE PARENTS OF THE DORM KIDS HEARD ABOUT WHAT HAPPENED.
SO LOTS OF THEM CAME TO TAKE THEIR KIDS HOME.
THE ASSOCIATION'S UNEASY TOO.
BAD NEWS SPREADS QUICK...
IT'S LIKE A GLOOM...
...SPREADING ACROSS THE TOWN.
HEY, LADY!

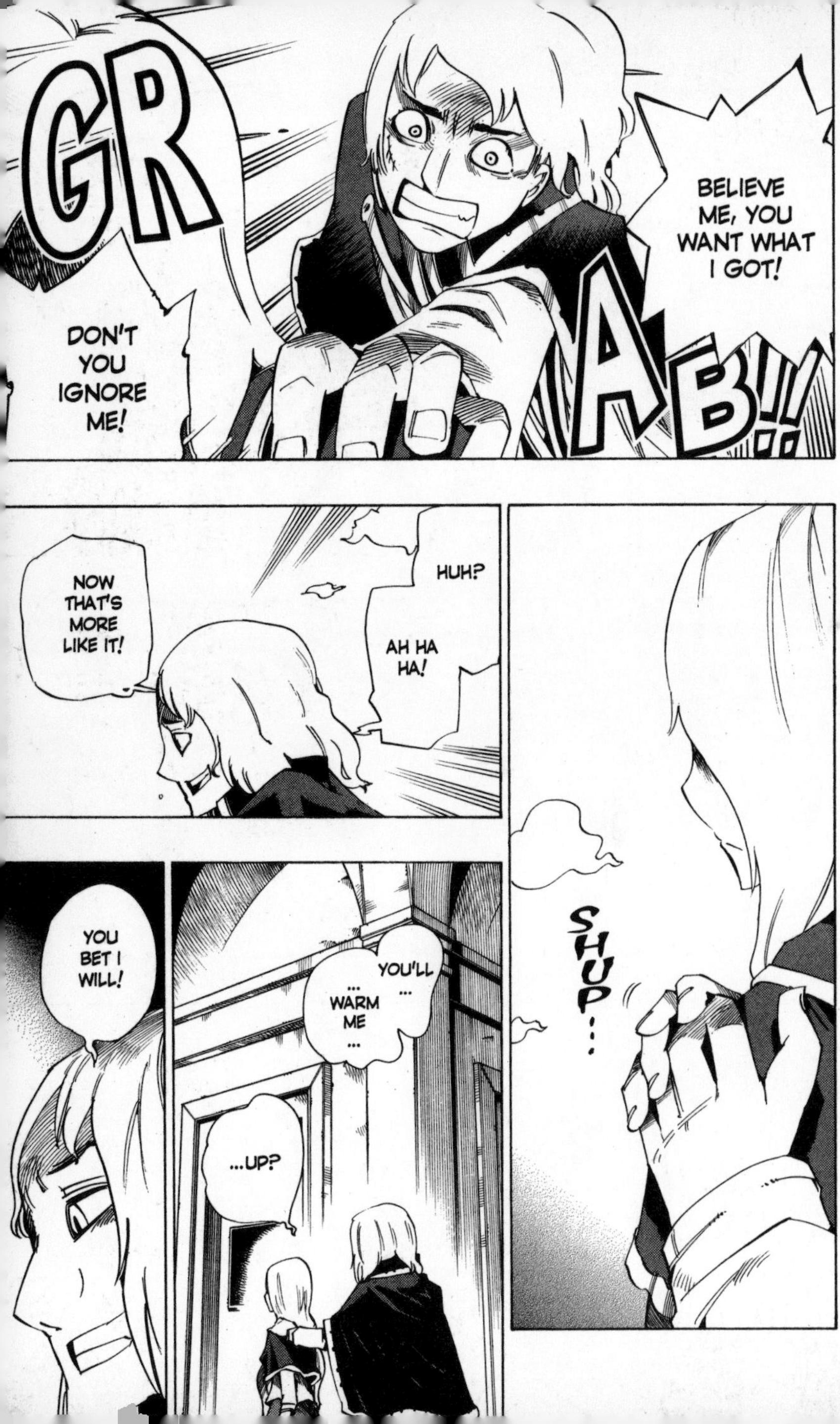
BELIEVE ME, YOU WANT WHAT I GOT!
GRAB!!
DON'T YOU IGNORE ME!
SHUP...
HUH?
AH HA HA!
NOW THAT'S MORE LIKE IT!
YOU'LL... WARM ME...
...UP?
YOU BET I WILL!

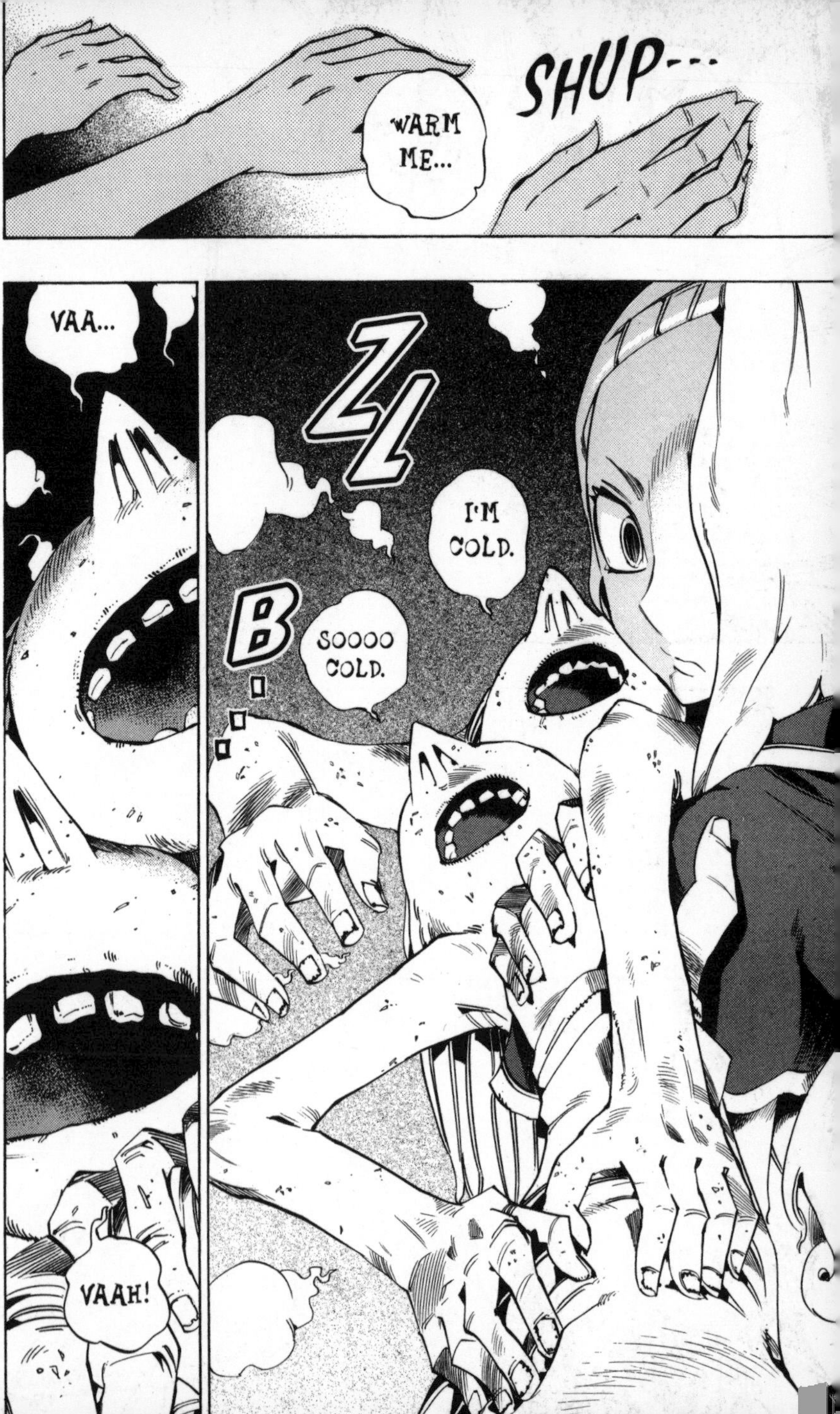
SHUP...
WARM ME...
ZZB...
I'M COLD.
SOOOO COLD.
VAA...
VAAH!

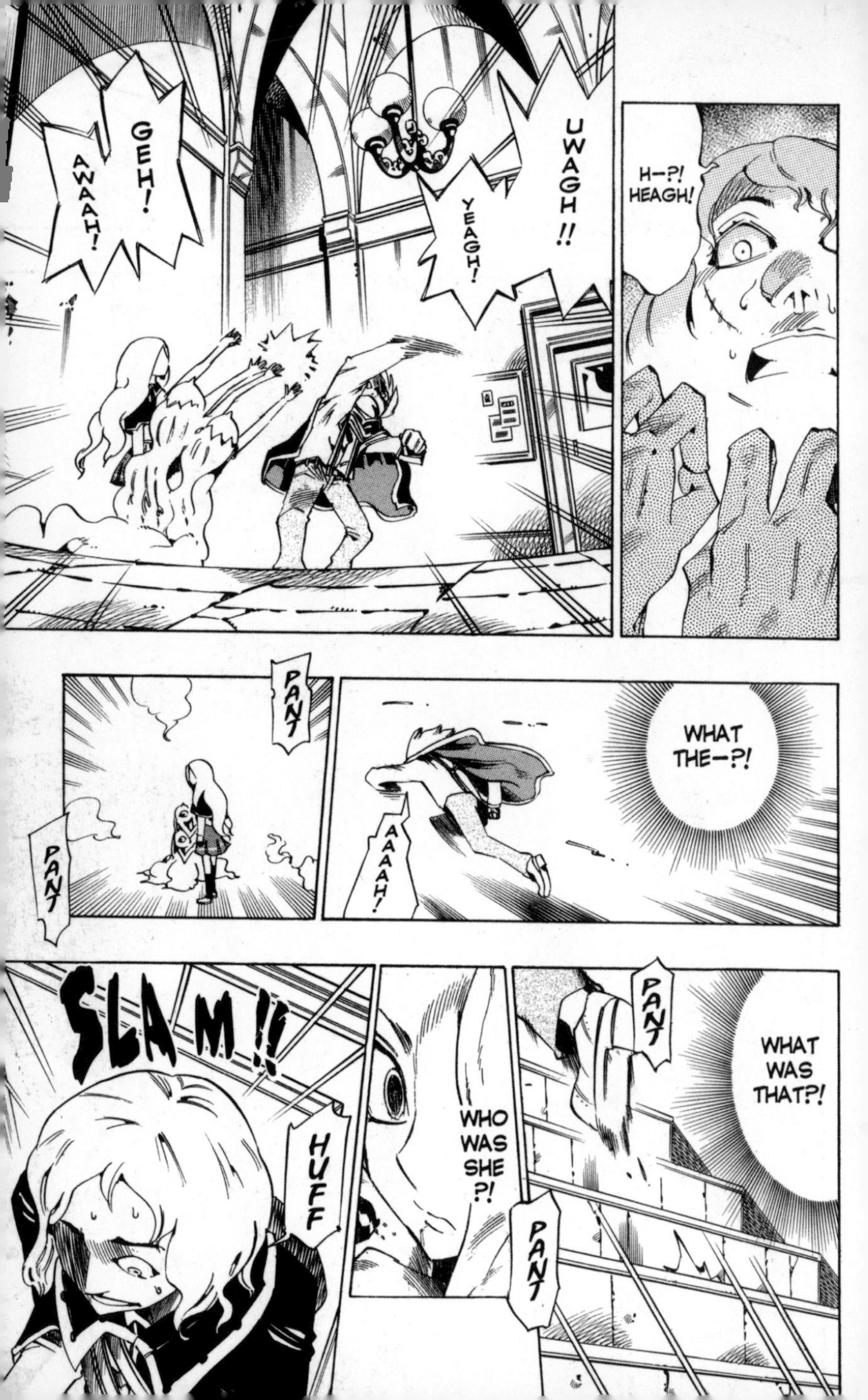

H-?! HEAGH!
UWAGH!!
YEAGH!
GEH!
AWAAH!
WHAT THE-?!
AAAAH!
PANT
PANT
WHAT WAS THAT?!
PANT
PANT
WHO WAS SHE?!
SLAM!!
HUFF

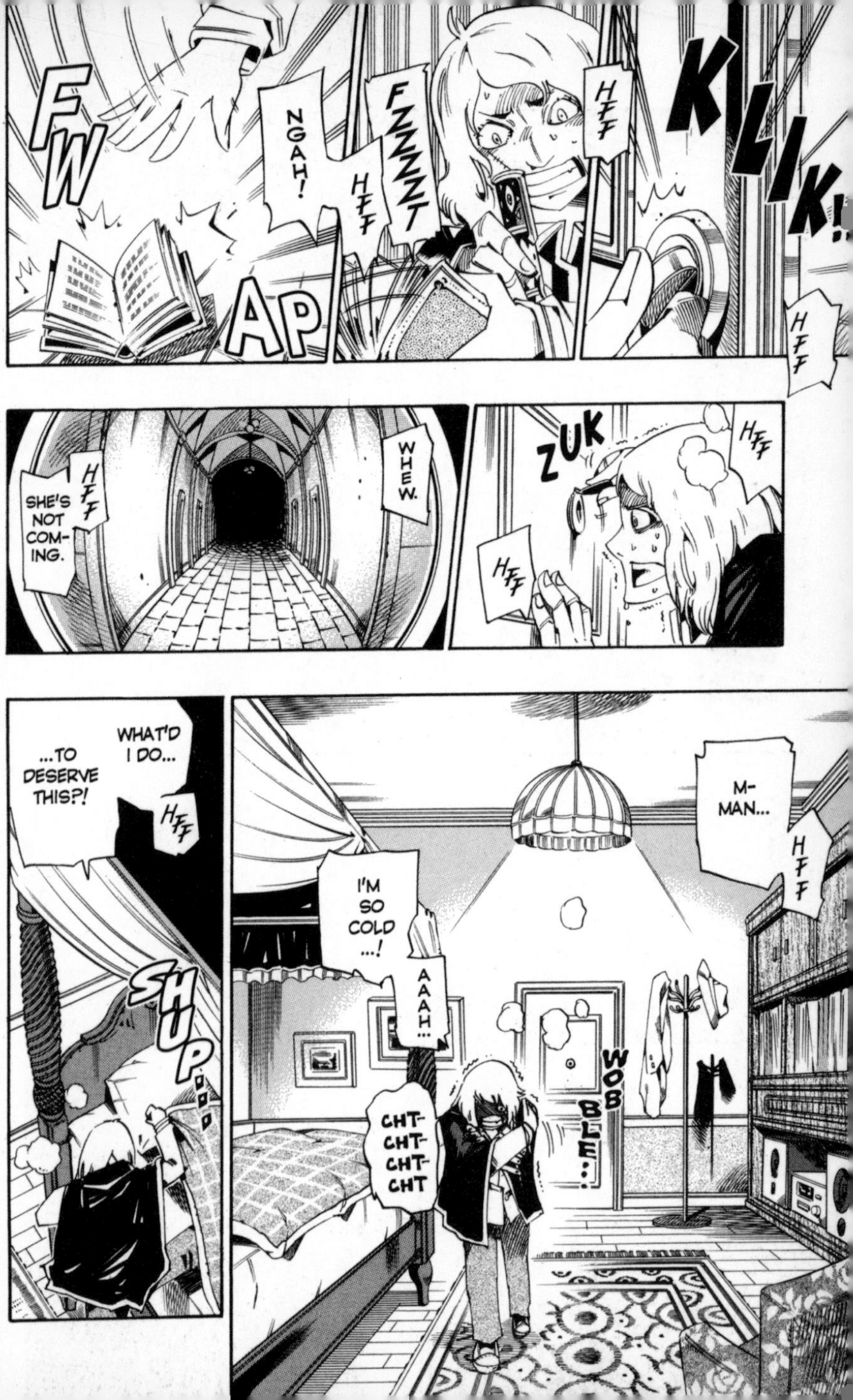
KLIK!!
HFF
HFF
FZZZZT
HFF
NGAH!
FW
AP
HFF
ZUK
HFF
WHEW.
HFF
SHE'S NOT COMING.
M-MAN...
HFF
I'M SO COLD ...!
AAAH...
WOB BLE...
CHT-CHT-CHT-CHT
WHAT'D I DO...
...TO DESERVE THIS?!
HFF
SHUP

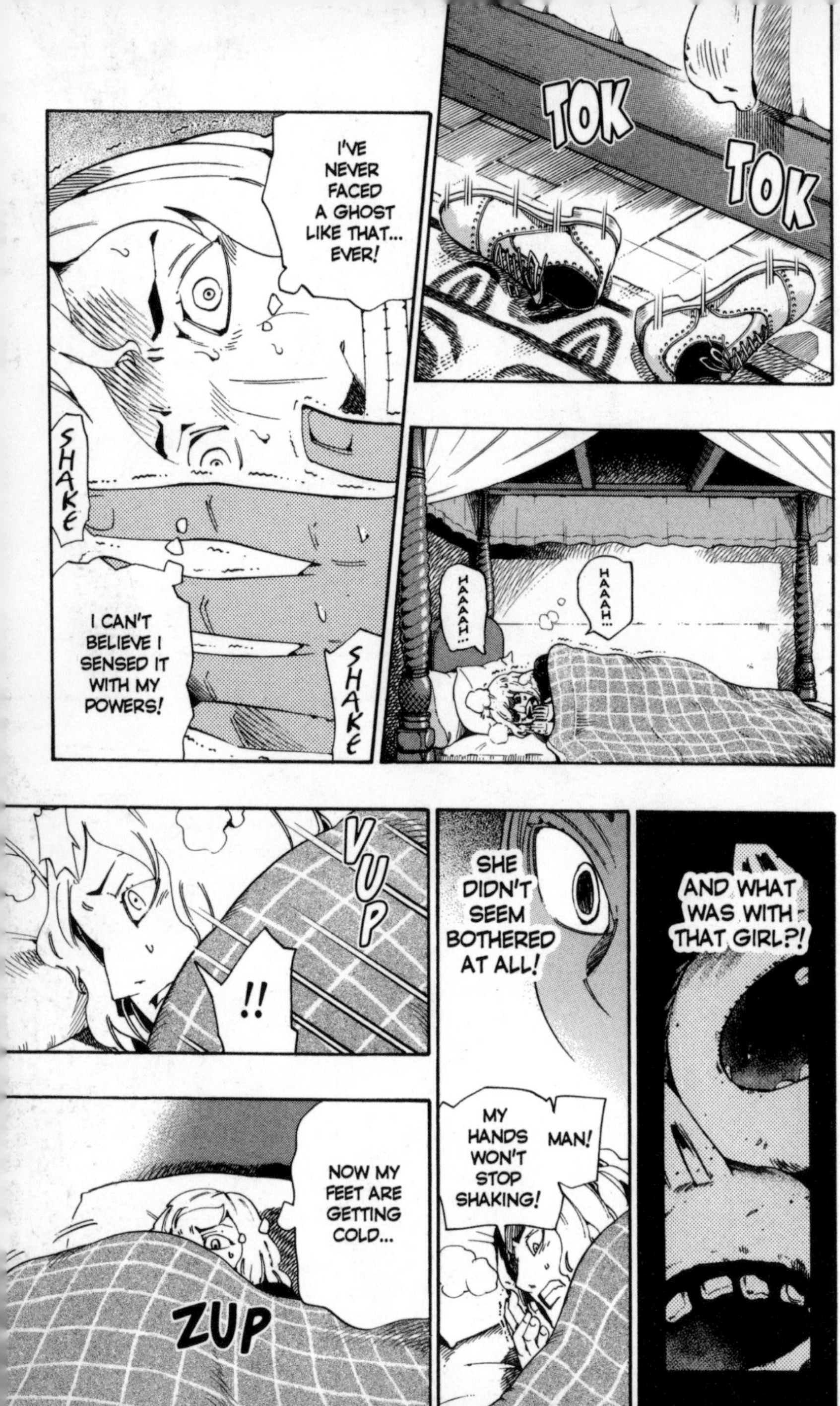
TOK
TOK
HAAAAH...
HAAAAH...
I'VE NEVER FACED A GHOST LIKE THAT... EVER!
SHAKE
I CAN'T BELIEVE I SENSED IT WITH MY POWERS!
SHAKE
AND WHAT WAS WITH THAT GIRL?!
SHE DIDN'T SEEM BOTHERED AT ALL!
MAN!
MY HANDS WON'T STOP SHAKING!
VUP
!!
NOW MY FEET ARE GETTING COLD...
ZUP

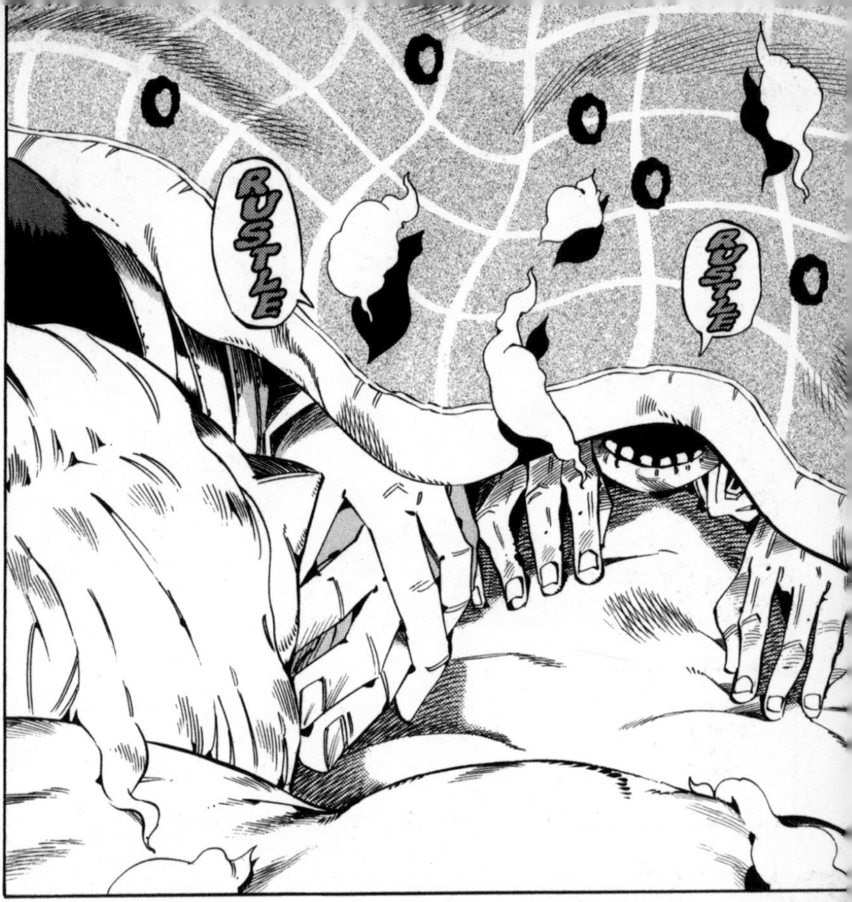
RUSTLE
RUSTLE
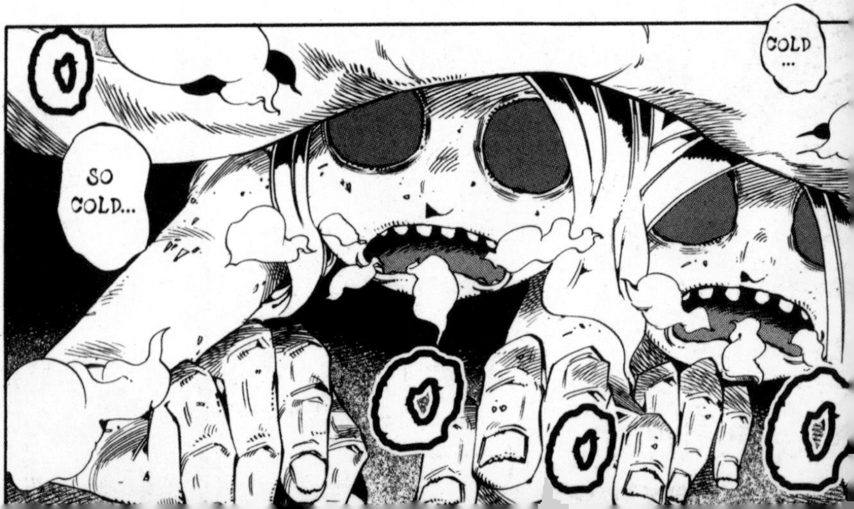
COLD...
SO COLD...

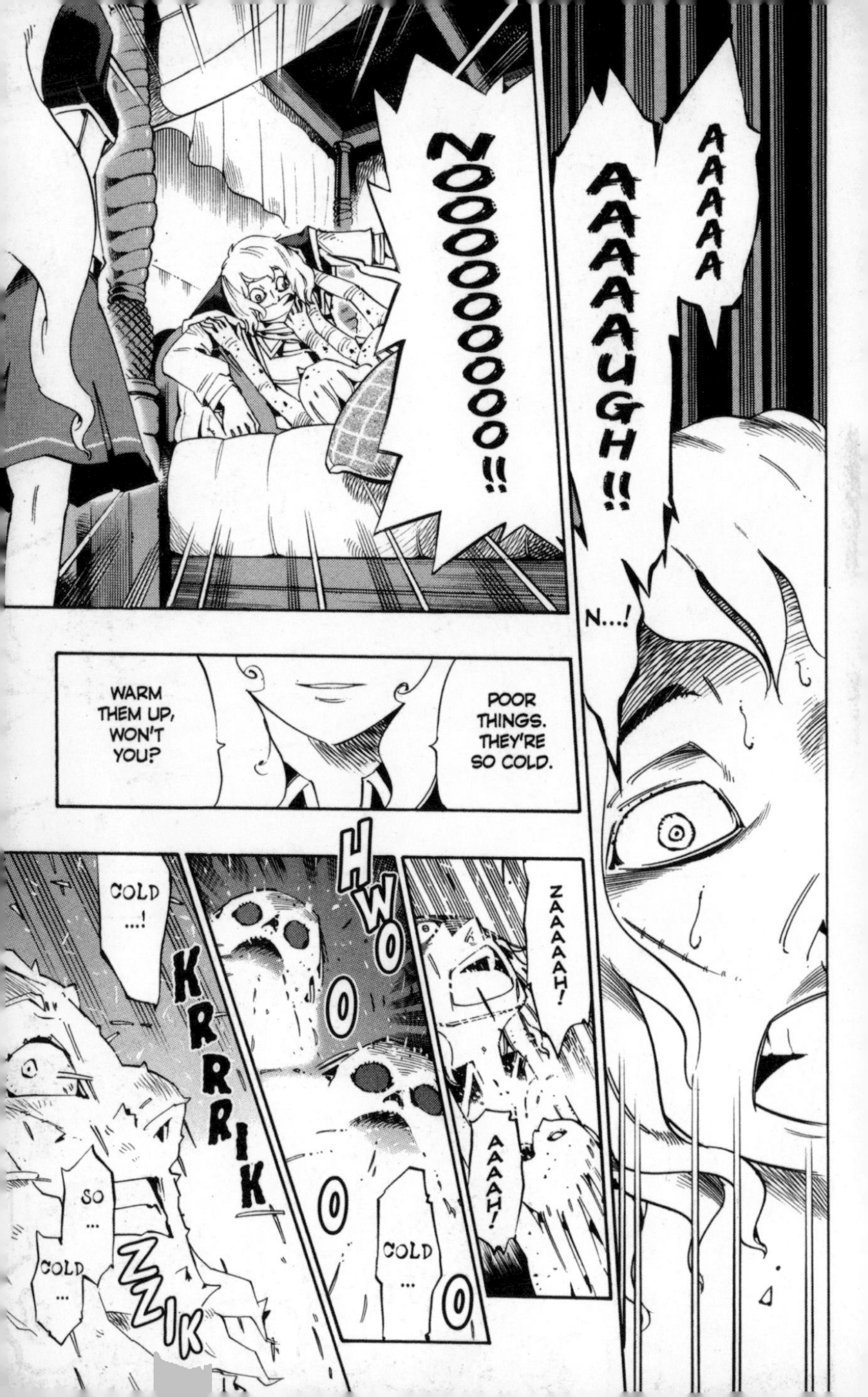
AAAAA AAAAAAUGH!!
N...!
NOOOOOOOOOO!!
POOR THINGS. THEY'RE SO COLD.
WARM THEM UP, WON'T YOU?
ZAAAAAH!
AAAAH!
HWOOOOO
COLD ...
COLD ...!
KRRRIK
SO ...
COLD ...
ZZIK

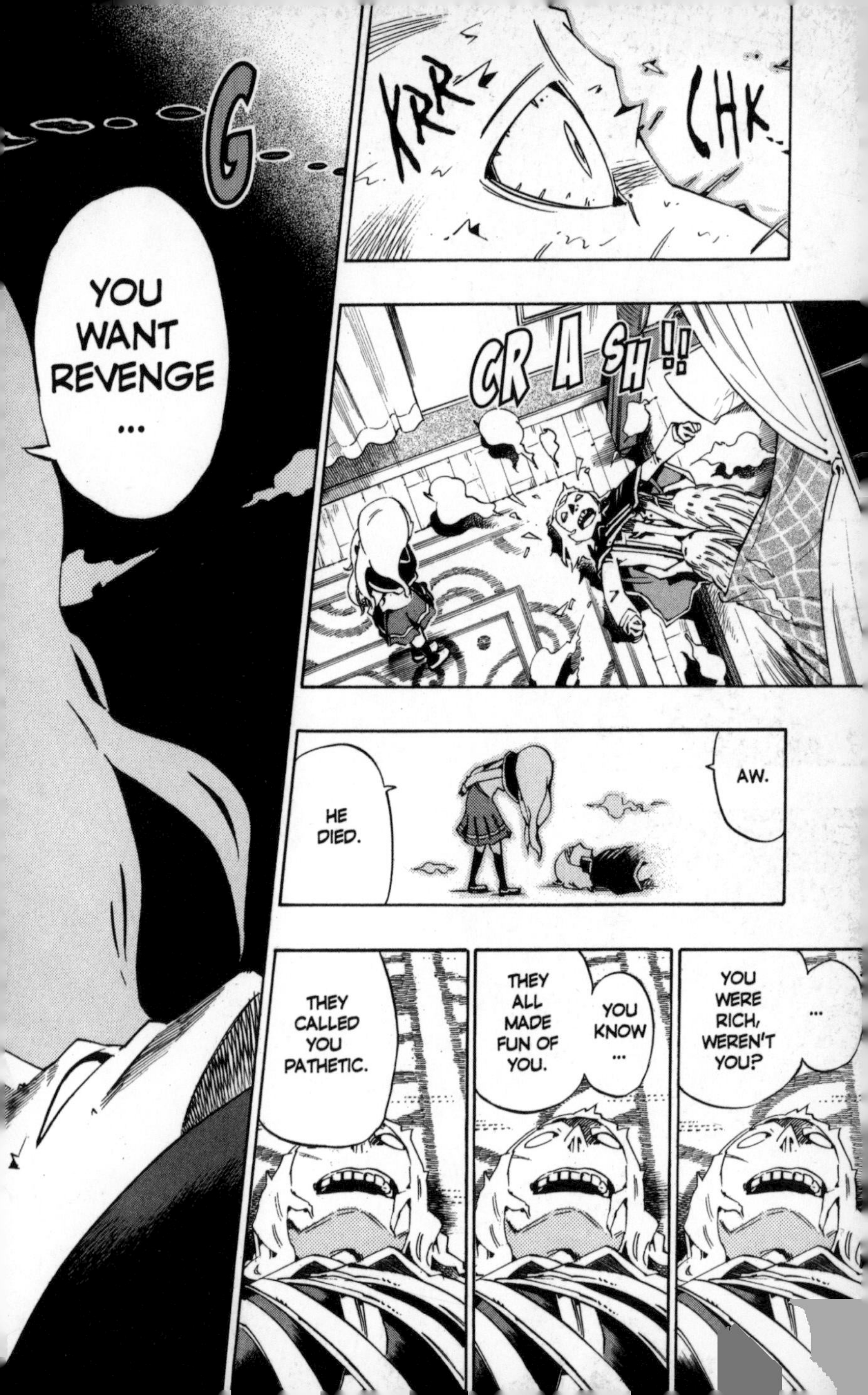
KRR
CHK
CRASH!!
AW.
HE DIED.
...
YOU WERE RICH, WEREN'T YOU?
YOU KNOW ...
THEY ALL MADE FUN OF YOU.
THEY CALLED YOU PATHETIC.
G
YOU WANT REVENGE ...

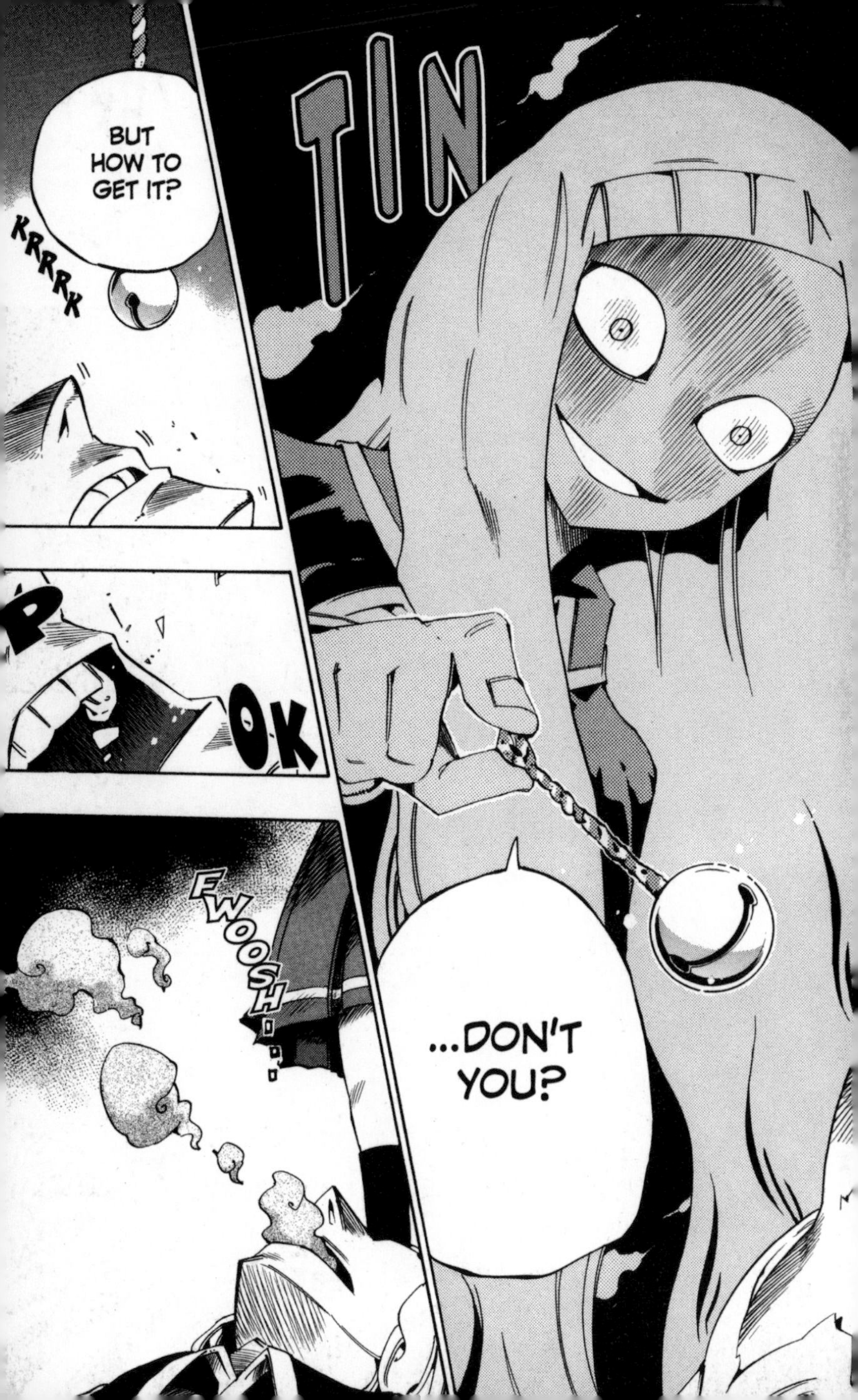
TIN
...DON'T YOU?
BUT HOW TO GET IT?
KRRRRK
POK
FWOOSH

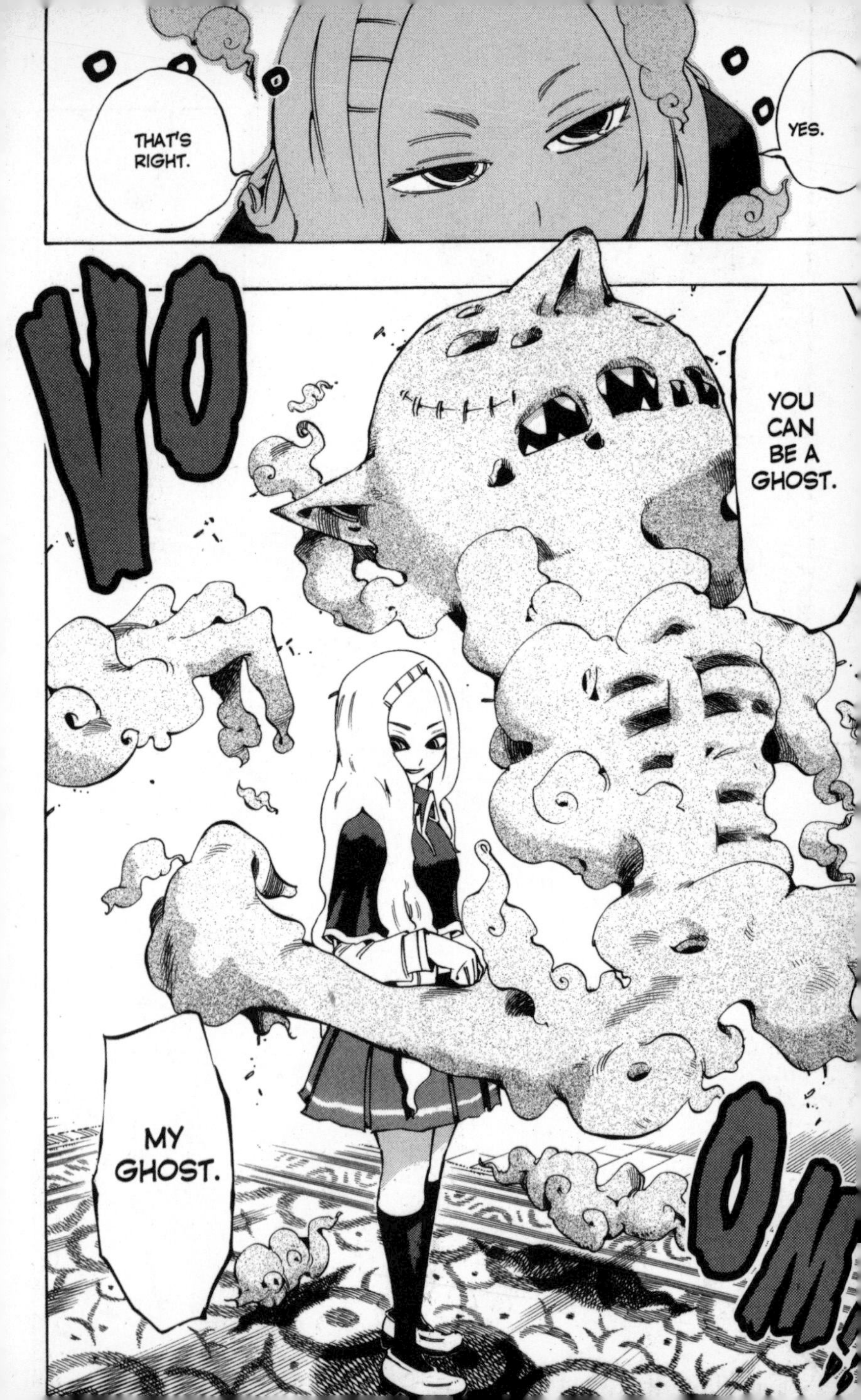
YES.
THAT'S RIGHT.
YOU CAN BE A GHOST.
VO
MY GHOST.
OM

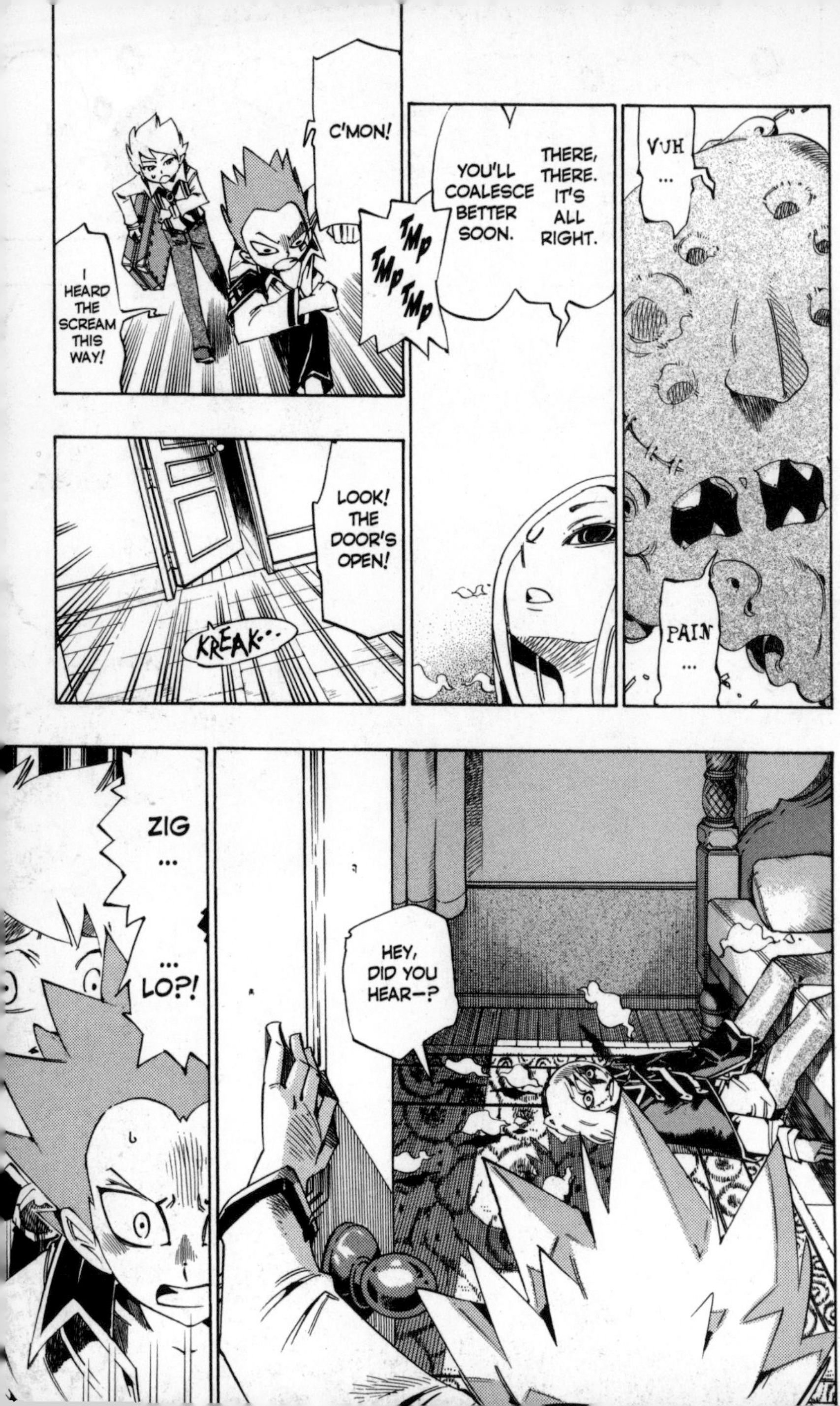
VUH ...
PAIN ...
THERE, THERE. IT'S ALL RIGHT.
YOU'LL COALESCE BETTER SOON.
C'MON!
TMP TMP TMP TMP
I HEARD THE SCREAM THIS WAY!
LOOK! THE DOOR'S OPEN!
KREAK...
HEY, DID YOU HEAR—?
ZIG ...
... LO?!

Muhyo & Roji's
Bureau of Supernatural Investigation
BSI

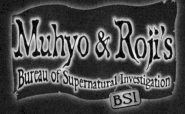

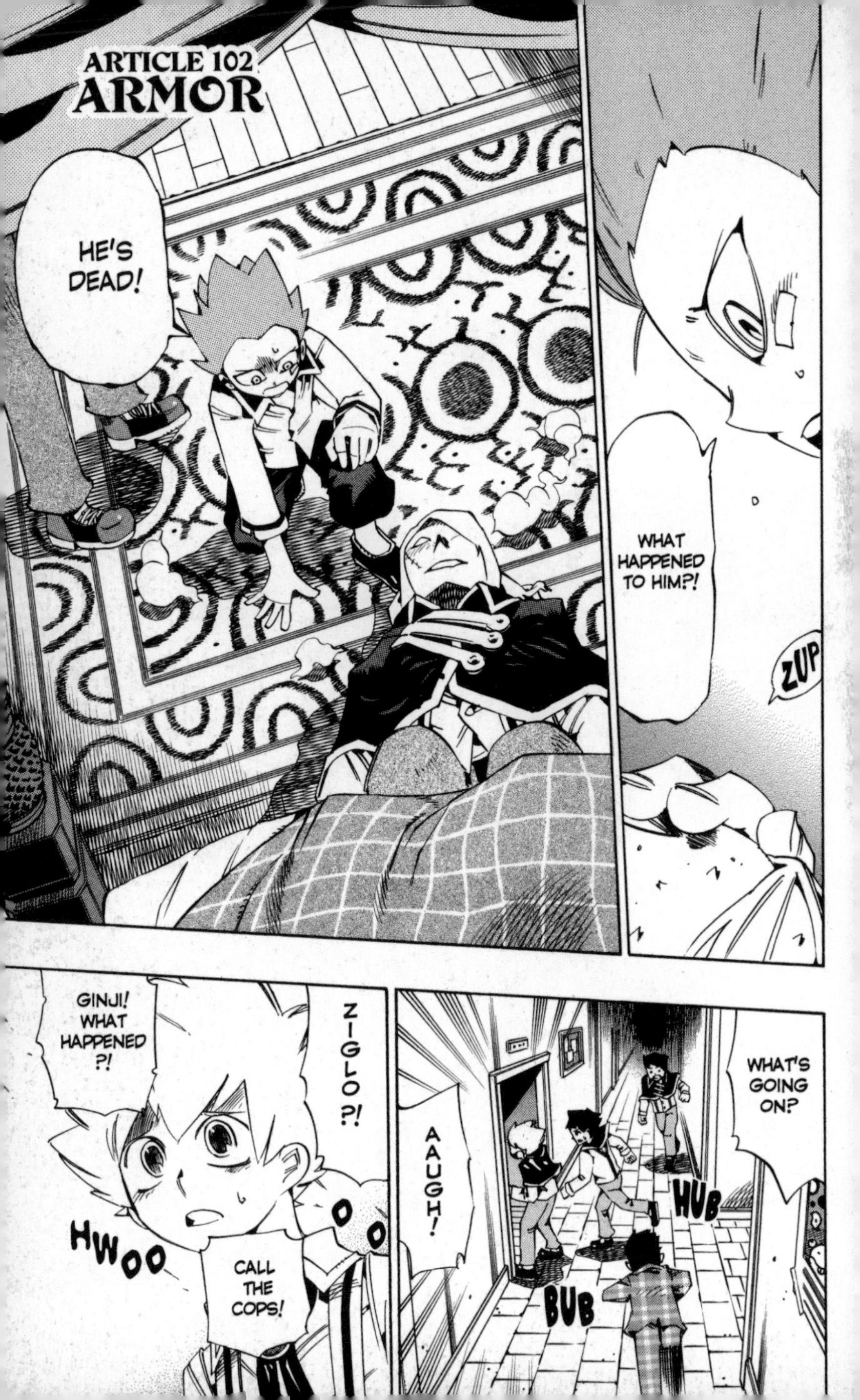
WHAT HAPPENED TO HIM?!
ZUP
ARTICLE 102
ARMOR
HE'S DEAD!
WHAT'S GOING ON?
HUB
AAUGH!
BUB
ZIGLO?!
GINJI! WHAT HAPPENED?!
OO
HWOO
CALL THE COPS!

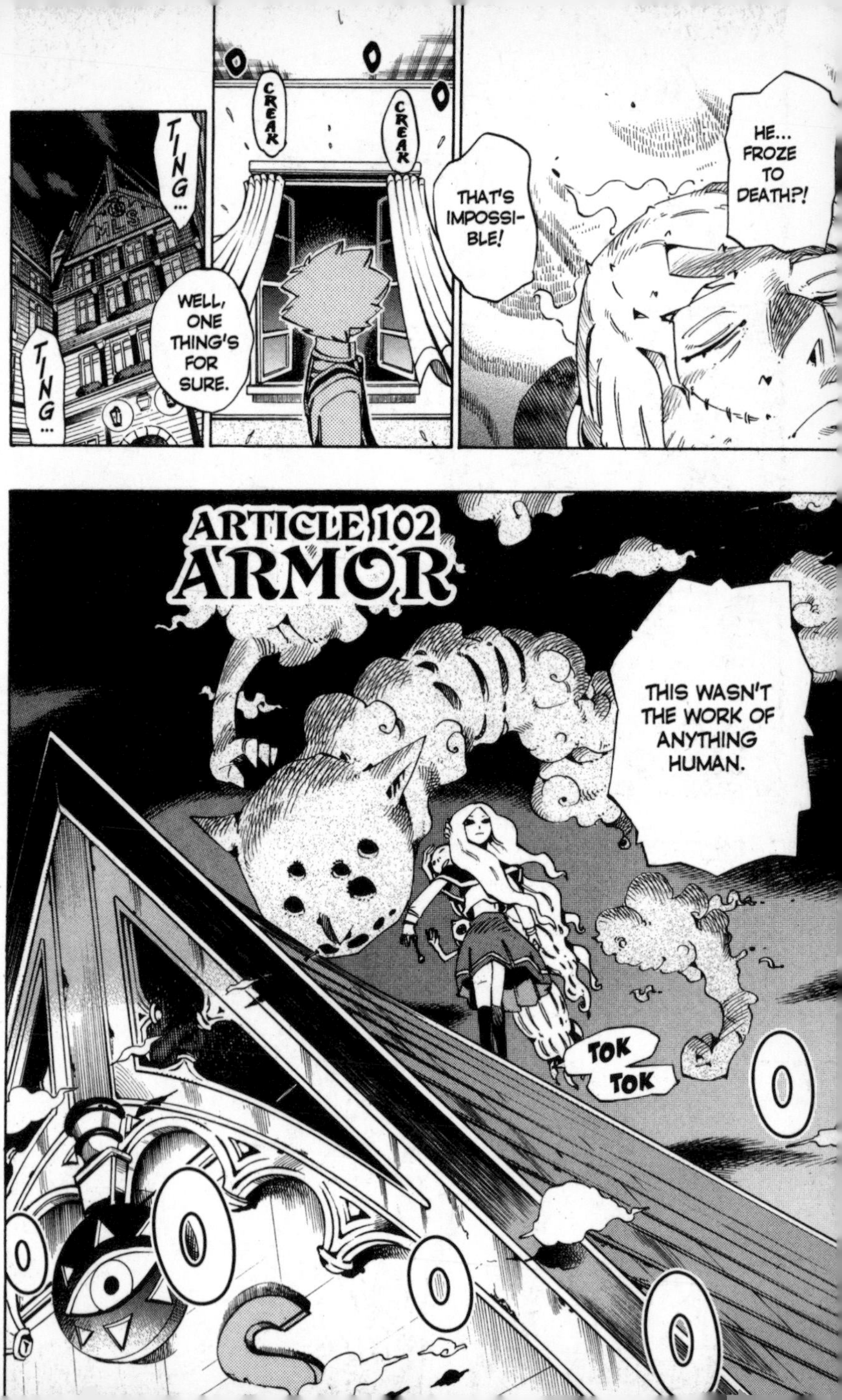
HE... FROZE TO DEATH?!
THAT'S IMPOSSI-BLE!
CREAK
CREAK
WELL, ONE THING'S FOR SURE.
TING...
TING...
ARTICLE 102 ARMOR
THIS WASN'T THE WORK OF ANYTHING HUMAN.
TOK TOK

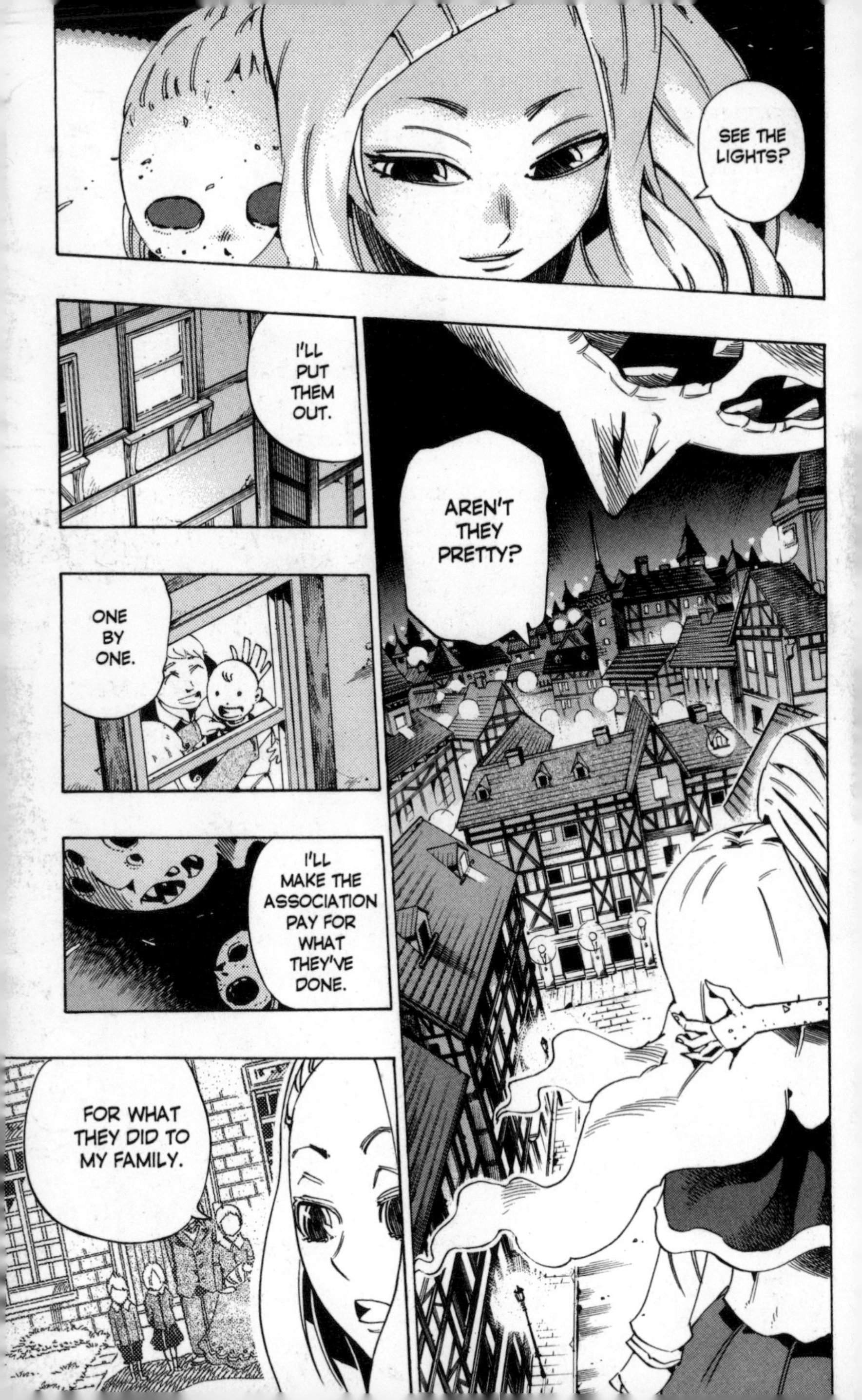
SEE THE LIGHTS?
AREN'T THEY PRETTY?
I'LL PUT THEM OUT.
ONE BY ONE.
I'LL MAKE THE ASSOCIATION PAY FOR WHAT THEY'VE DONE.
FOR WHAT THEY DID TO MY FAMILY.

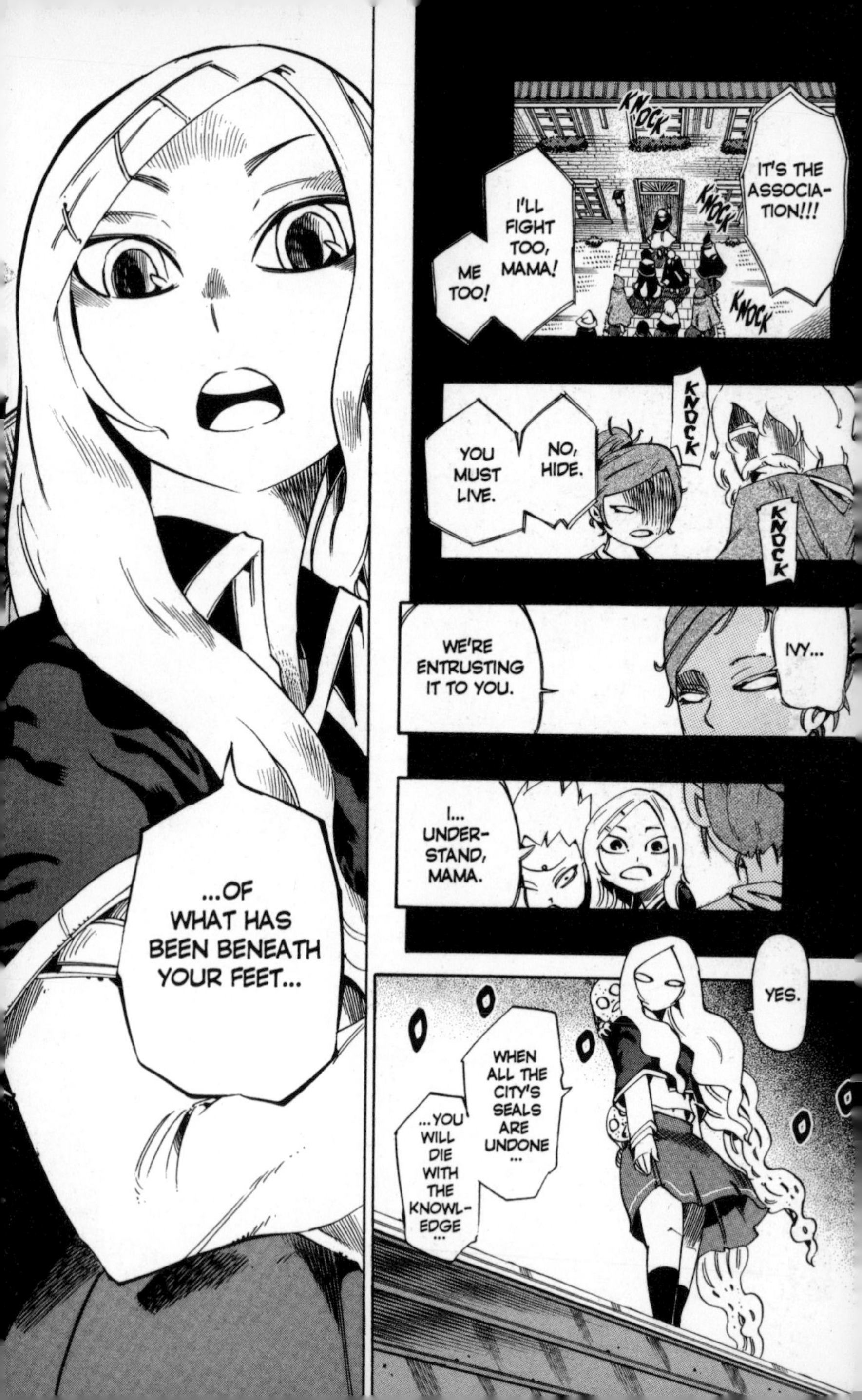
KNOCK
IT'S THE ASSOCIATION!!!
KNOCK
KNOCK
I'LL FIGHT TOO, MAMA!
ME TOO!
KNOCK
KNOCK
NO, HIDE.
YOU MUST LIVE.
IVY...
WE'RE ENTRUSTING IT TO YOU.
I... UNDERSTAND, MAMA.
YES.
WHEN ALL THE CITY'S SEALS ARE UNDONE...
...YOU WILL DIE WITH THE KNOWLEDGE...
...OF WHAT HAS BEEN BENEATH YOUR FEET...

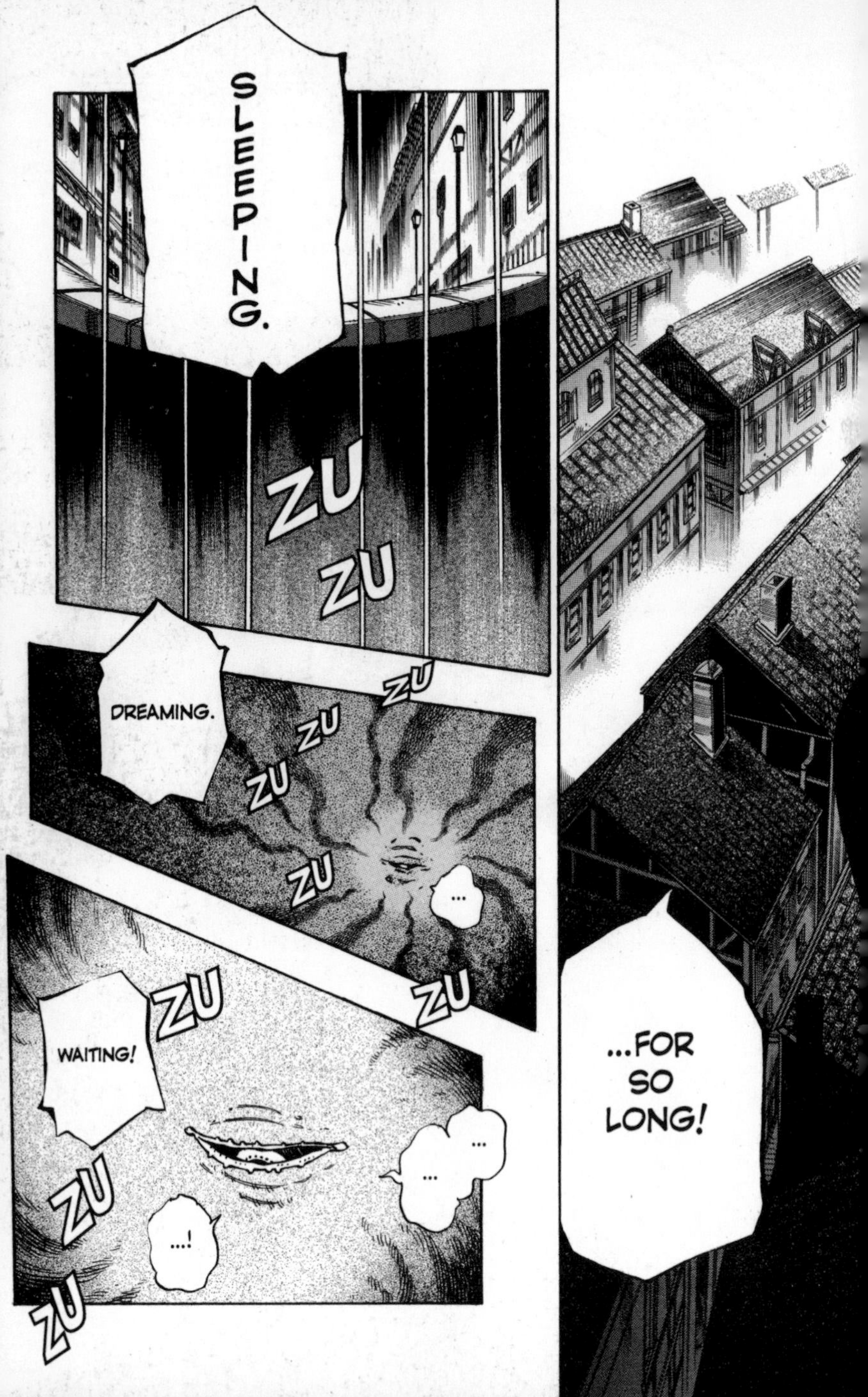
SLEEPING.
ZU
ZU
DREAMING.
ZU
ZU
ZU
ZU
...
ZU
WAITING!
ZU
...
...
...!
ZU
ZU
...FOR SO LONG!

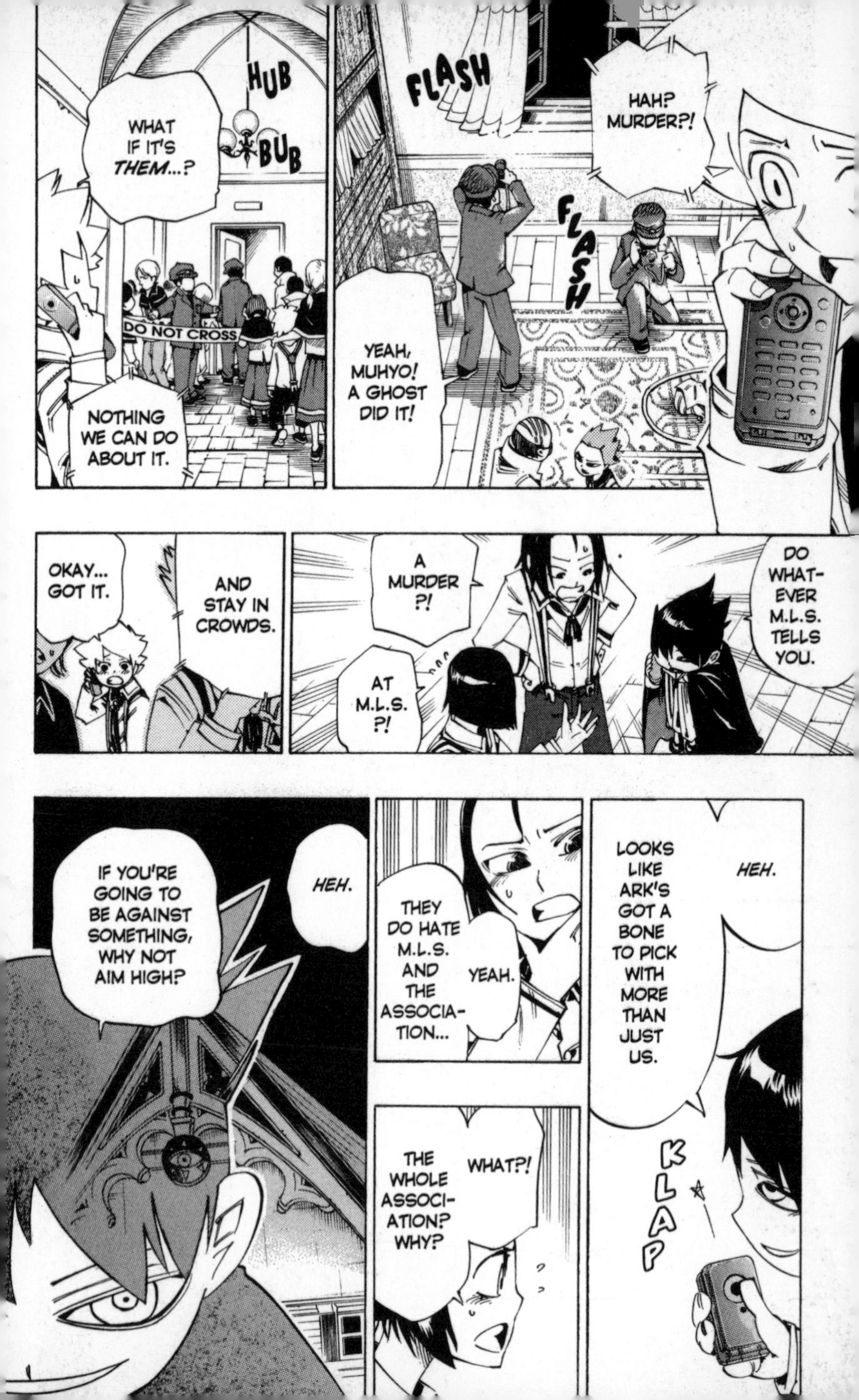
HAH? MURDER?!
FLASH
FLASH
YEAH, MUHYO! A GHOST DID IT!
HUB BUB
WHAT IF IT'S *THEM*...?
DO NOT CROSS
NOTHING WE CAN DO ABOUT IT.
DO WHATEVER M.L.S. TELLS YOU.
A MURDER?!
AT M.L.S.?!
AND STAY IN CROWDS.
OKAY... GOT IT.
HEH.
LOOKS LIKE ARK'S GOT A BONE TO PICK WITH MORE THAN JUST US.
KLAP
YEAH.
THEY DO HATE M.L.S. AND THE ASSOCIATION...
WHAT?!
THE WHOLE ASSOCIATION? WHY?
HEH.
IF YOU'RE GOING TO BE AGAINST SOMETHING, WHY NOT AIM HIGH?

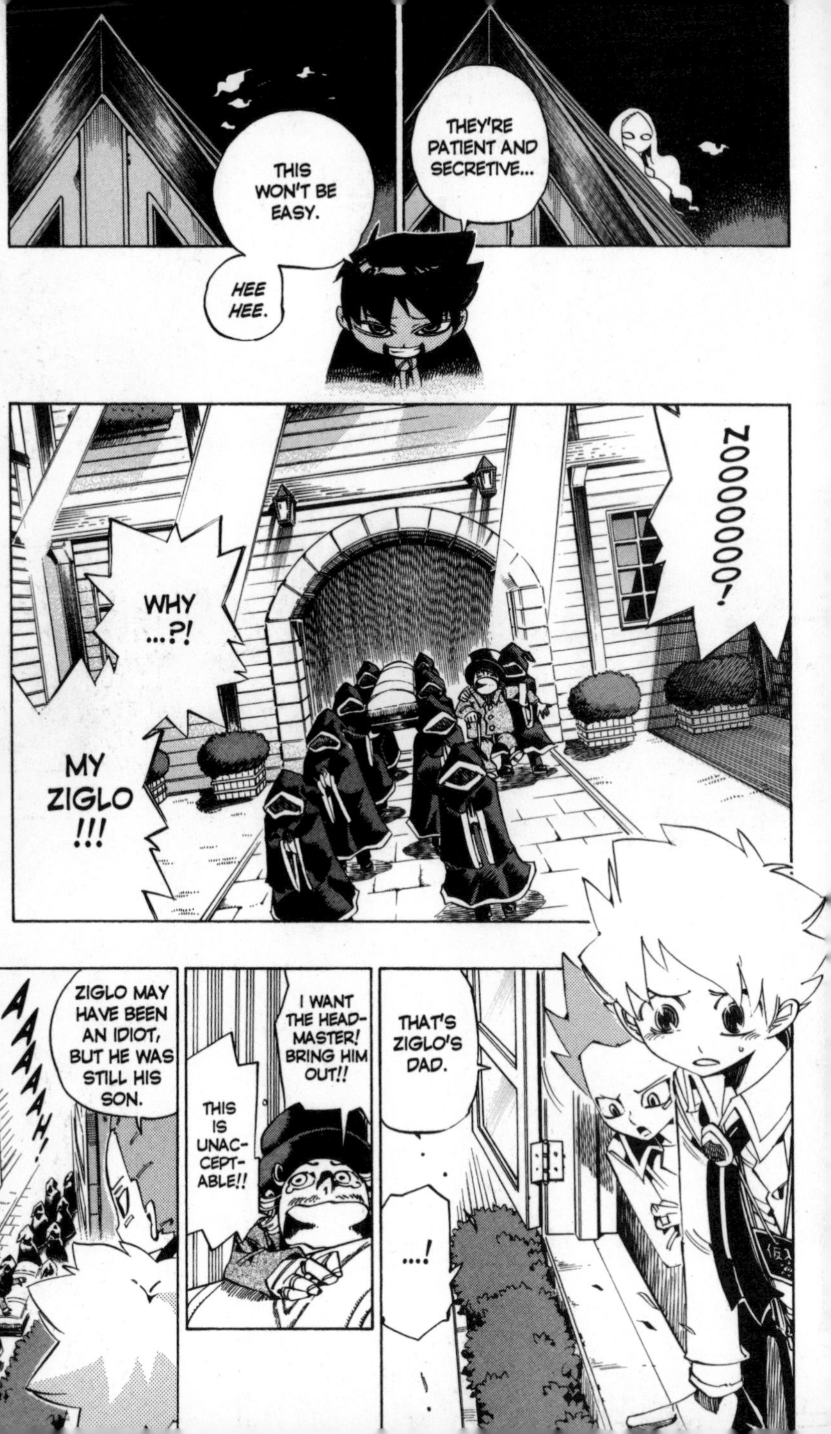
THEY'RE PATIENT AND SECRETIVE...
THIS WON'T BE EASY.
HEE HEE.
ZOOOOOOOO!
WHY ...?!
MY ZIGLO !!!
THAT'S ZIGLO'S DAD.
...!
I WANT THE HEAD-MASTER! BRING HIM OUT!!
THIS IS UNAC-CEPT-ABLE!!
ZIGLO MAY HAVE BEEN AN IDIOT, BUT HE WAS STILL HIS SON.
AAAAAAH!

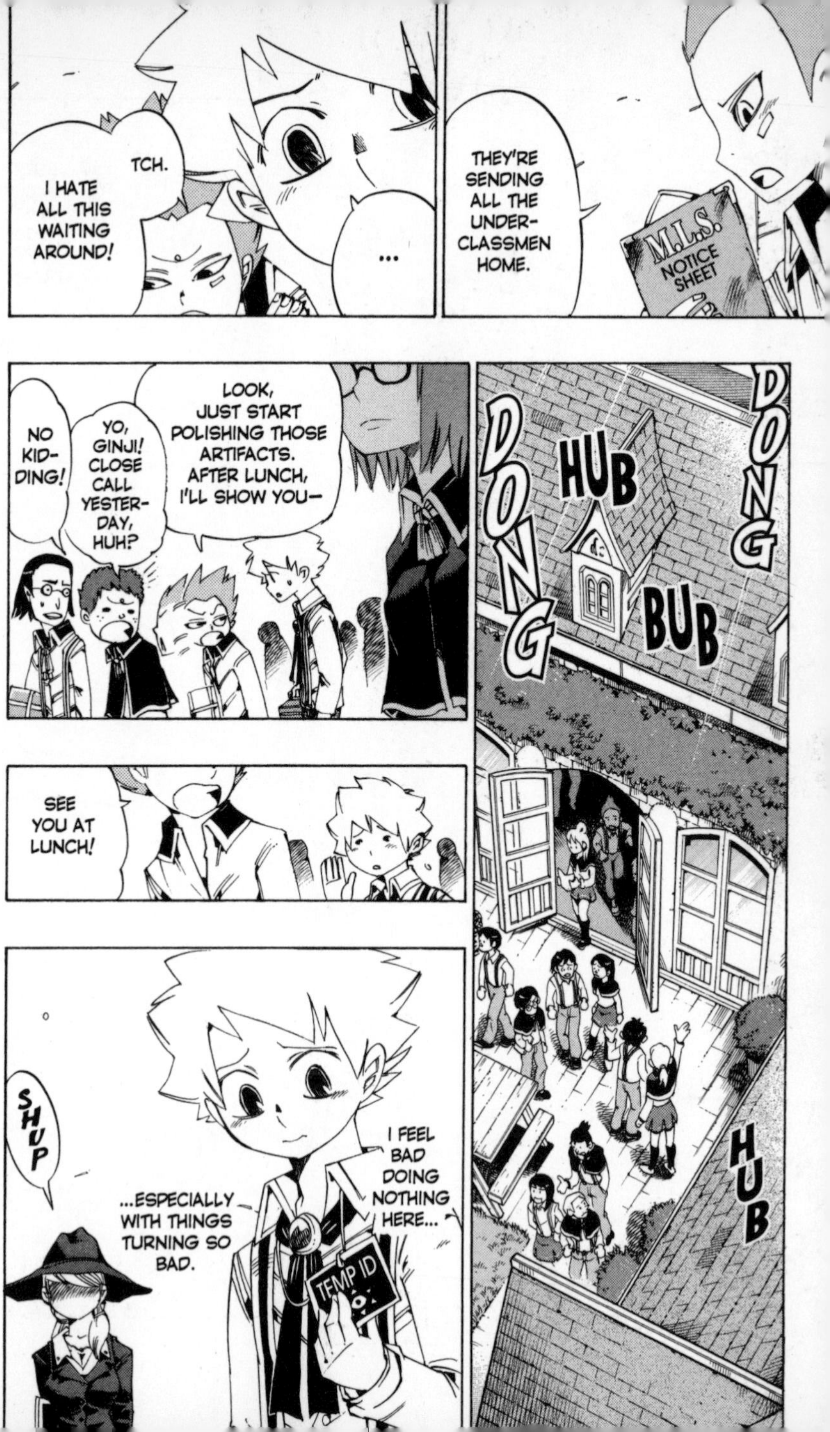
THEY'RE SENDING ALL THE UNDER-CLASSMEN HOME.
M.L.S. NOTICE SHEET
TCH.
I HATE ALL THIS WAITING AROUND!
...
DONG
DONG
HUB
BUB
HUB
LOOK, JUST START POLISHING THOSE ARTIFACTS. AFTER LUNCH, I'LL SHOW YOU—
YO, GINJI! CLOSE CALL YESTER-DAY, HUH?
NO KID-DING!
SEE YOU AT LUNCH!
I FEEL BAD DOING NOTHING HERE...
...ESPECIALLY WITH THINGS TURNING SO BAD.
TEMP ID
SHUP

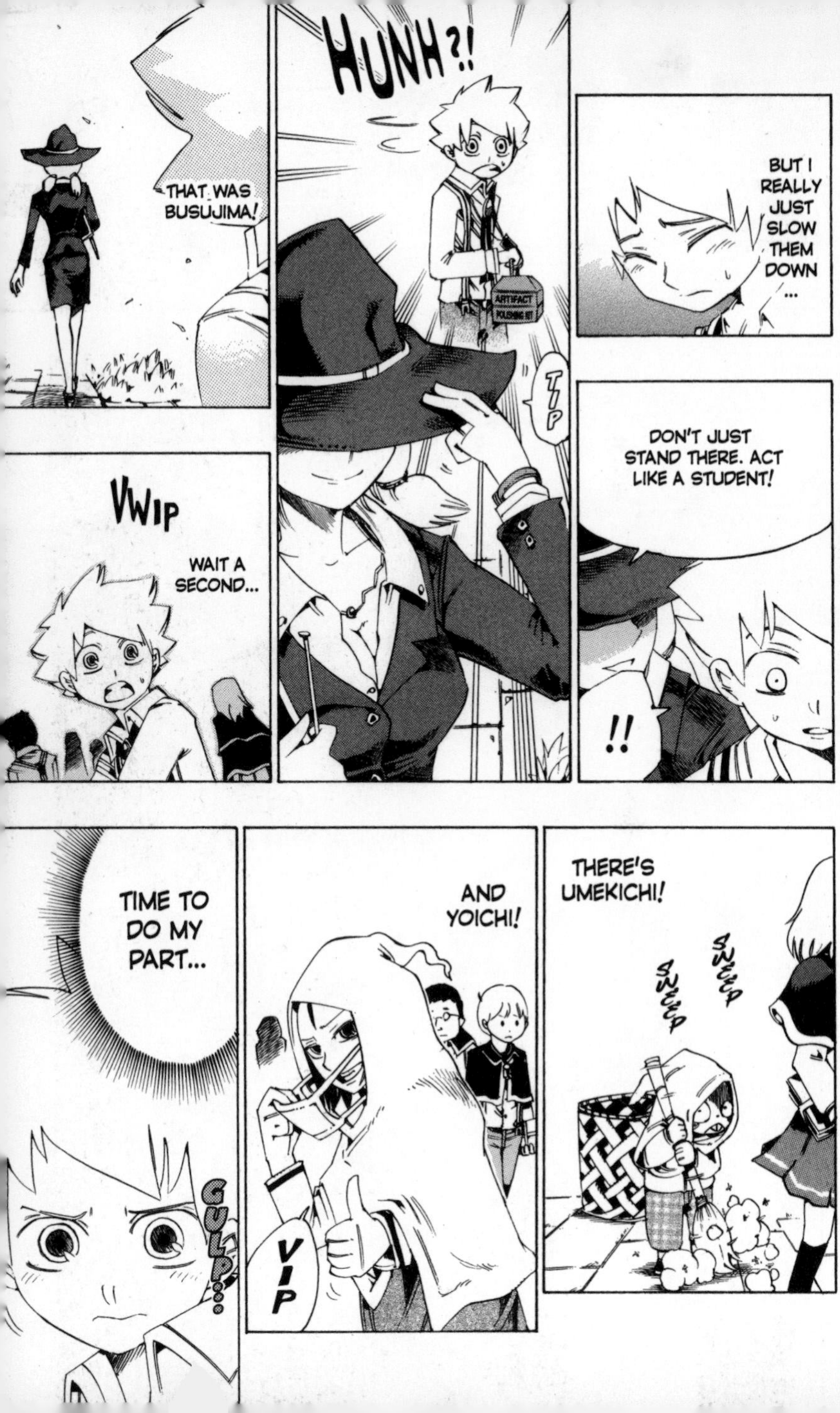
BUT I REALLY JUST SLOW THEM DOWN...
DON'T JUST STAND THERE. ACT LIKE A STUDENT!
!!
HUNH?!
ARTIFACT POLISHING KIT
TIP
THAT WAS BUSUJIMA!
VWIP
WAIT A SECOND...
THERE'S UMEKICHI!
SWEEP
SWEEP
AND YOICHI!
VIP
TIME TO DO MY PART...
GULP...

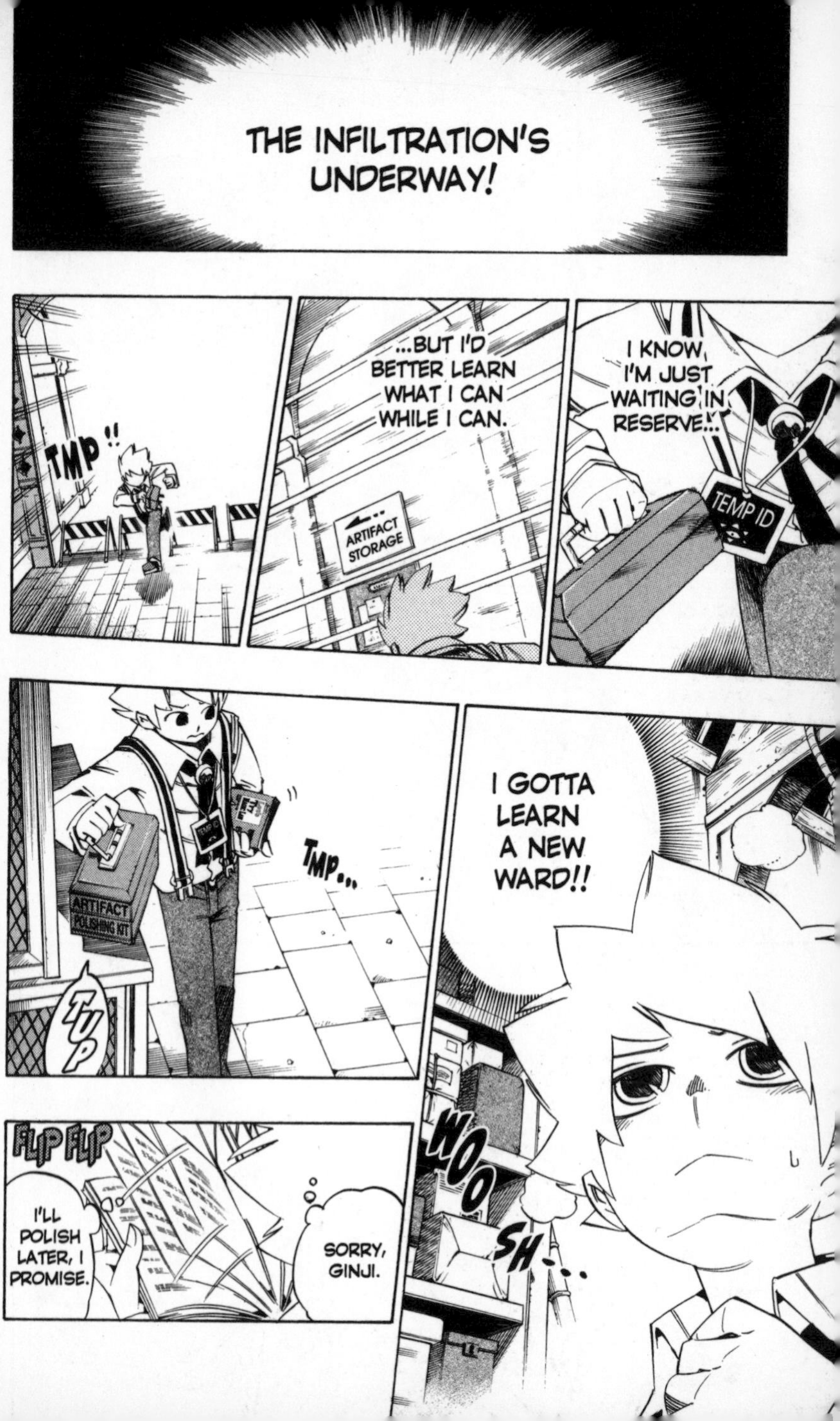
THE INFILTRATION'S UNDERWAY!
I KNOW, I'M JUST WAITING IN RESERVE...
TEMP ID
...BUT I'D BETTER LEARN WHAT I CAN WHILE I CAN.
ARTIFACT STORAGE
TMP!!
I GOTTA LEARN A NEW WARD!!
WOOSH...
TMP...
ARTIFACT POLISHING KIT
TUP
FLIP FLIP
SORRY, GINJI.
I'LL POLISH LATER, I PROMISE.

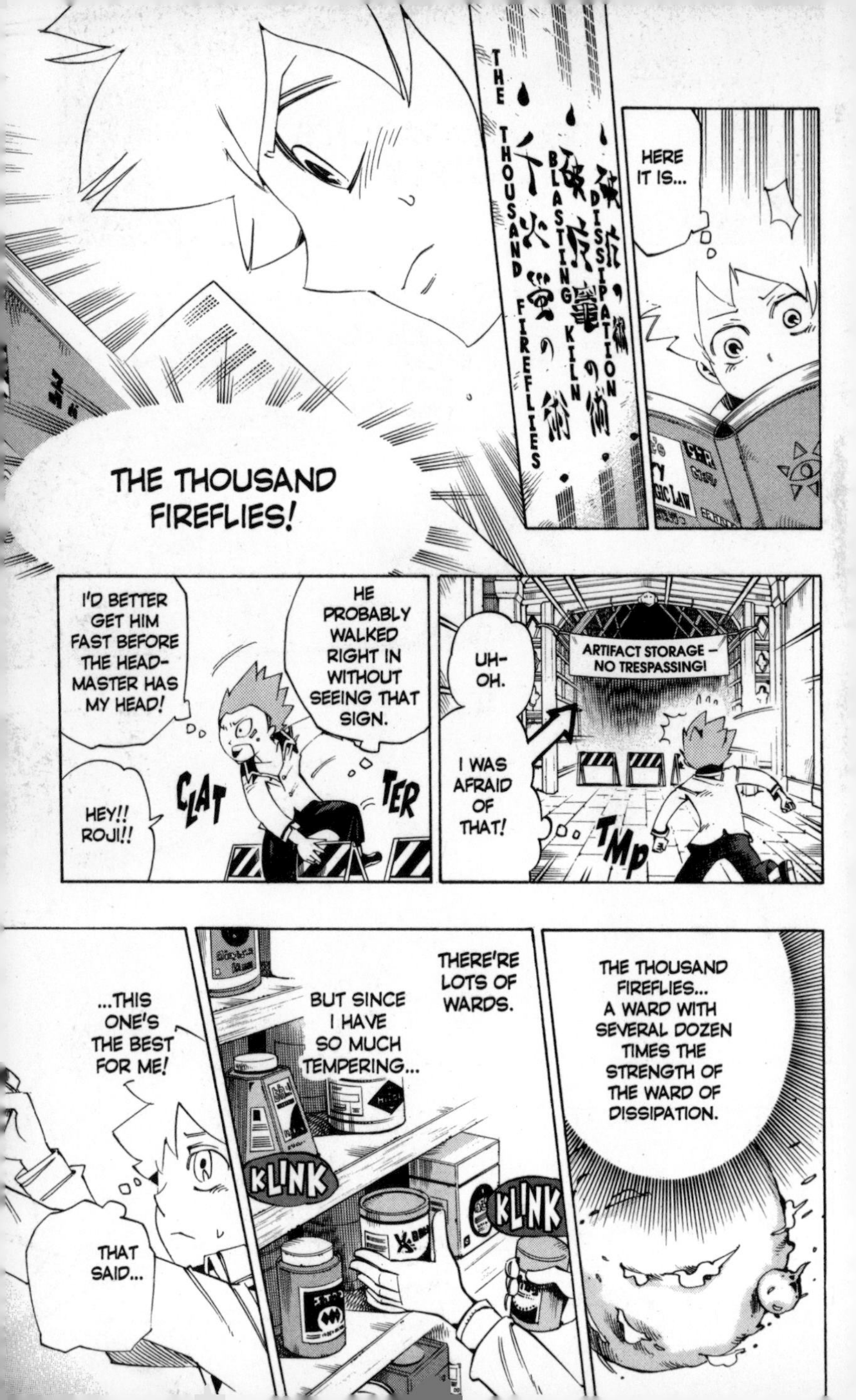
HERE IT IS...
DISSIPATION
BLASTING KILN
THE THOUSAND FIREFLIES
THE THOUSAND FIREFLIES!
ARTIFACT STORAGE – NO TRESPASSING!
UH-OH.
I WAS AFRAID OF THAT!
TMP
HE PROBABLY WALKED RIGHT IN WITHOUT SEEING THAT SIGN.
I'D BETTER GET HIM FAST BEFORE THE HEADMASTER HAS MY HEAD!
CLATTER
HEY!! ROJI!!
THE THOUSAND FIREFLIES... A WARD WITH SEVERAL DOZEN TIMES THE STRENGTH OF THE WARD OF DISSIPATION.
THERE'RE LOTS OF WARDS.
BUT SINCE I HAVE SO MUCH TEMPERING...
KLINK
KLINK
...THIS ONE'S THE BEST FOR ME!
THAT SAID...

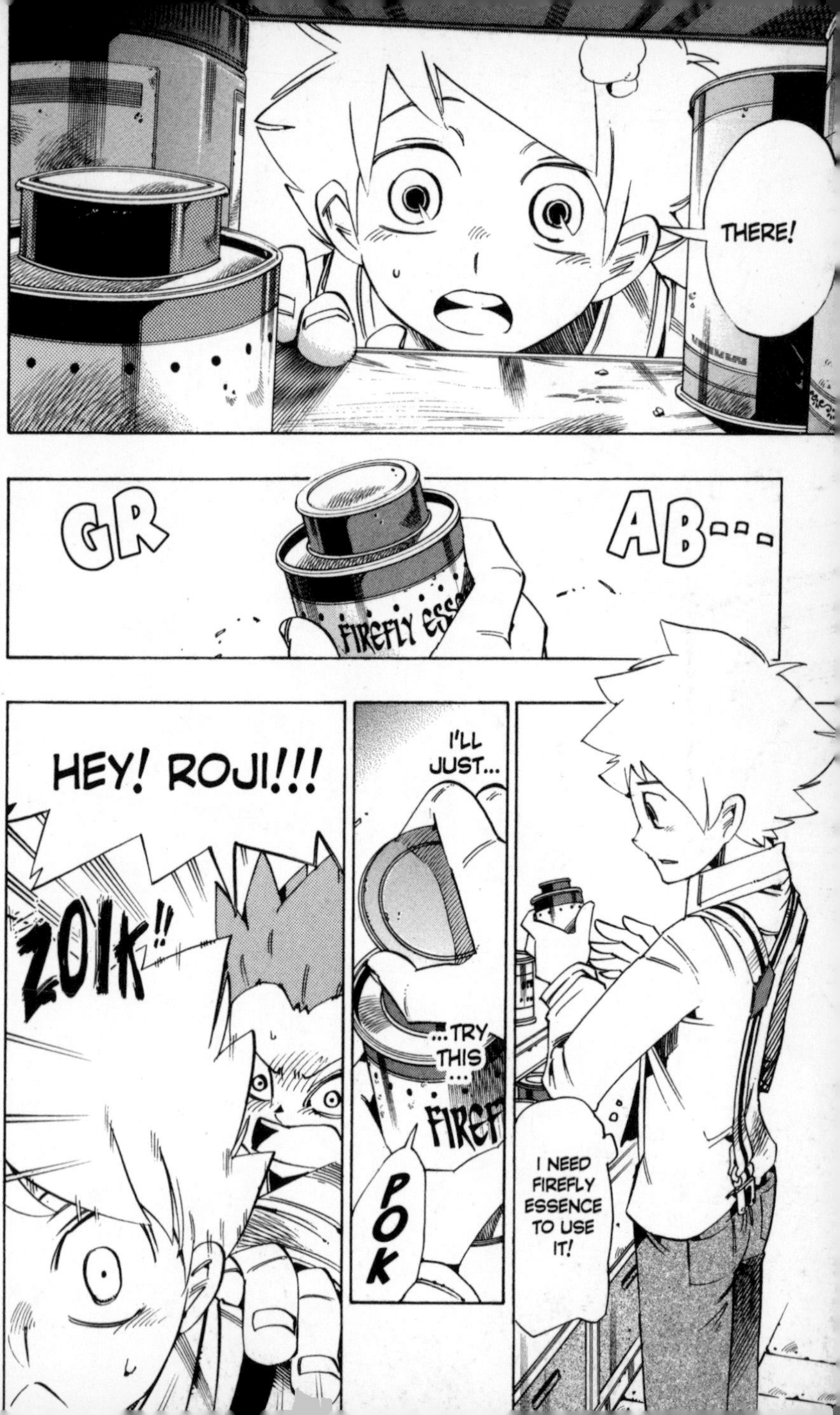
THERE!
GR AB...
I NEED FIREFLY ESSENCE TO USE IT!
I'LL JUST...
...TRY THIS...
POK
HEY! ROJI!!!
ZOIK!!

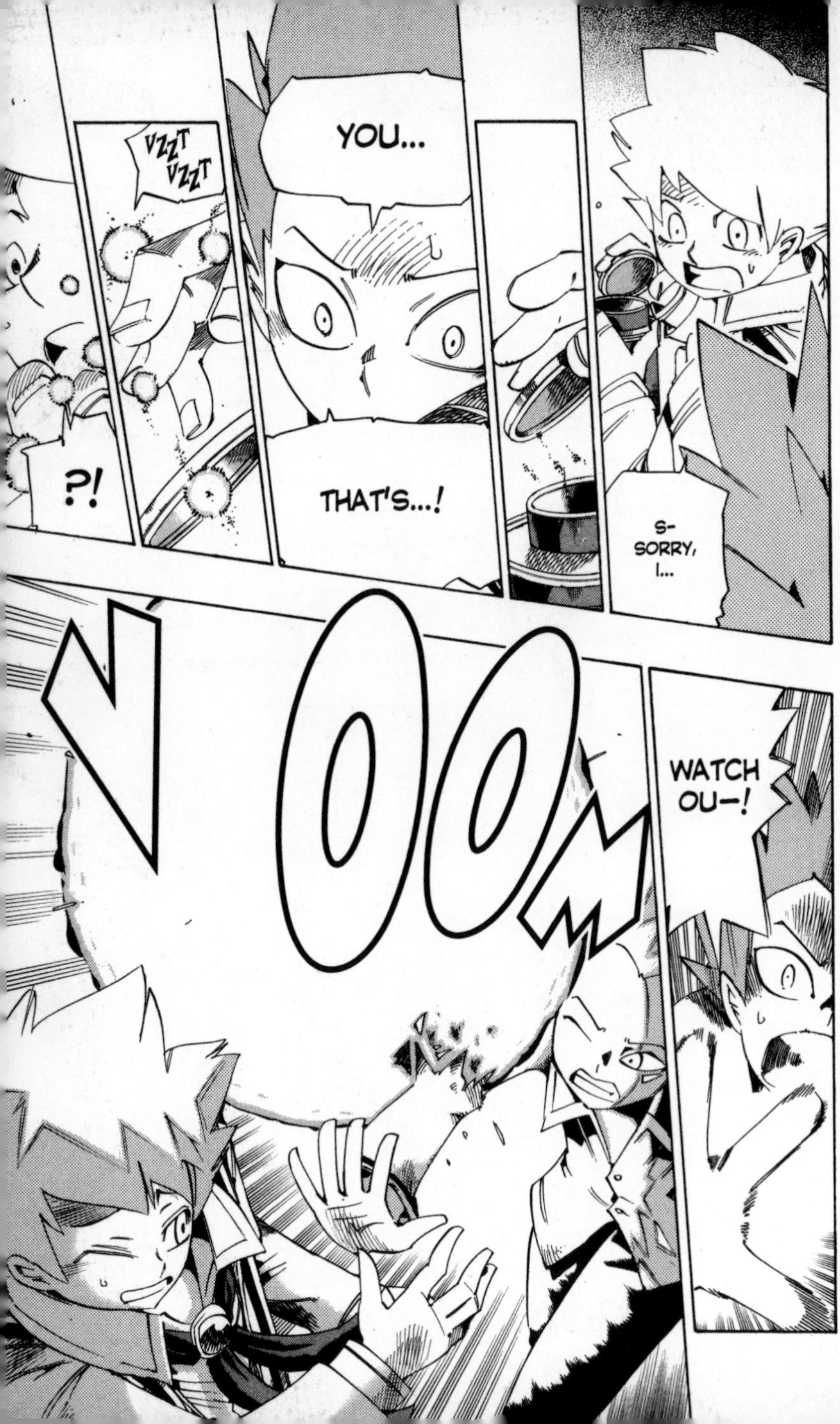
S-
SORRY,
I...
YOU...
THAT'S...!
VZZT
VZZT
?!
WATCH
OU—!
NOO

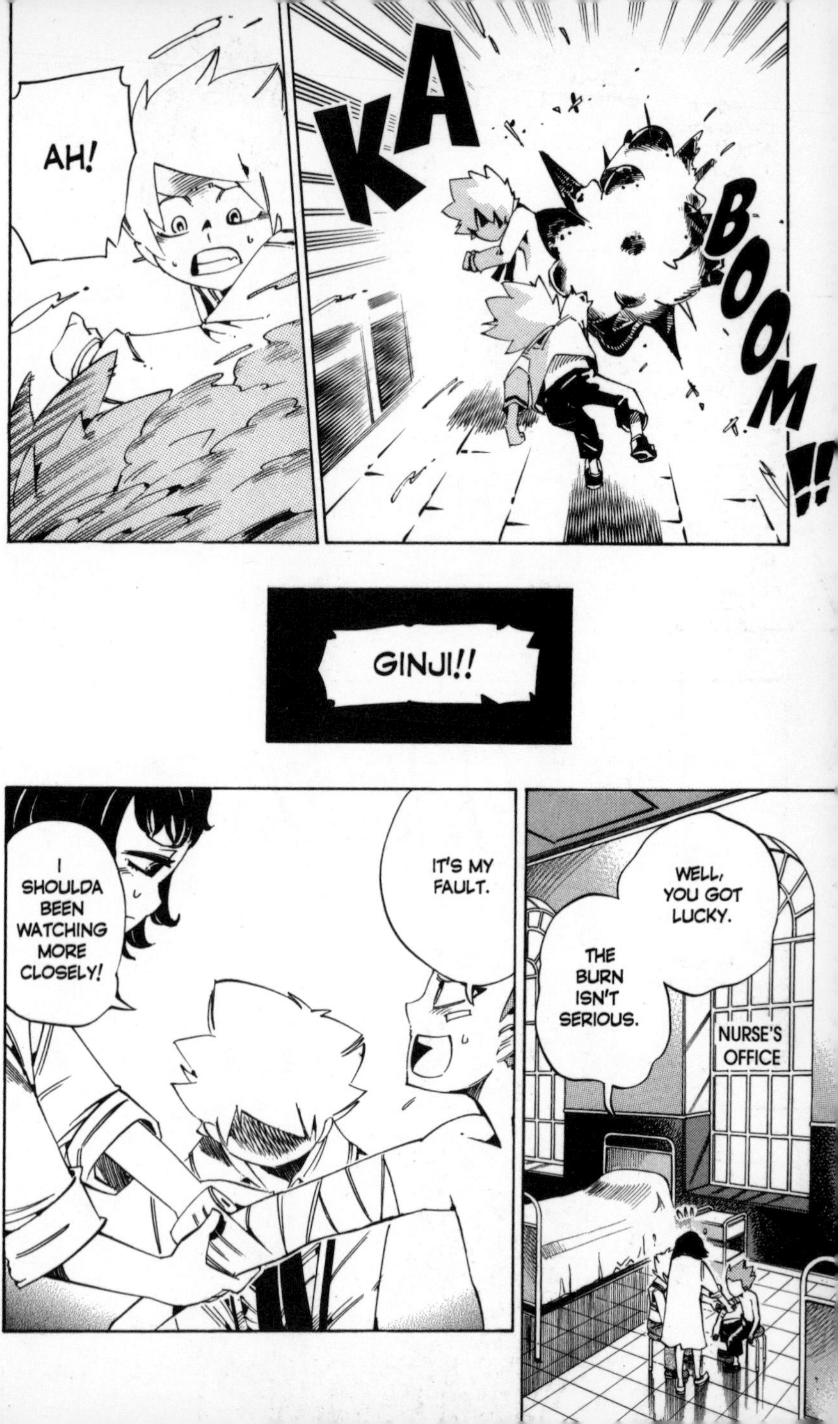
KA
BOOM!!
AH!
GINJI!!
WELL, YOU GOT LUCKY.
THE BURN ISN'T SERIOUS.
NURSE'S OFFICE
IT'S MY FAULT.
I SHOULDA BEEN WATCHING MORE CLOSELY!

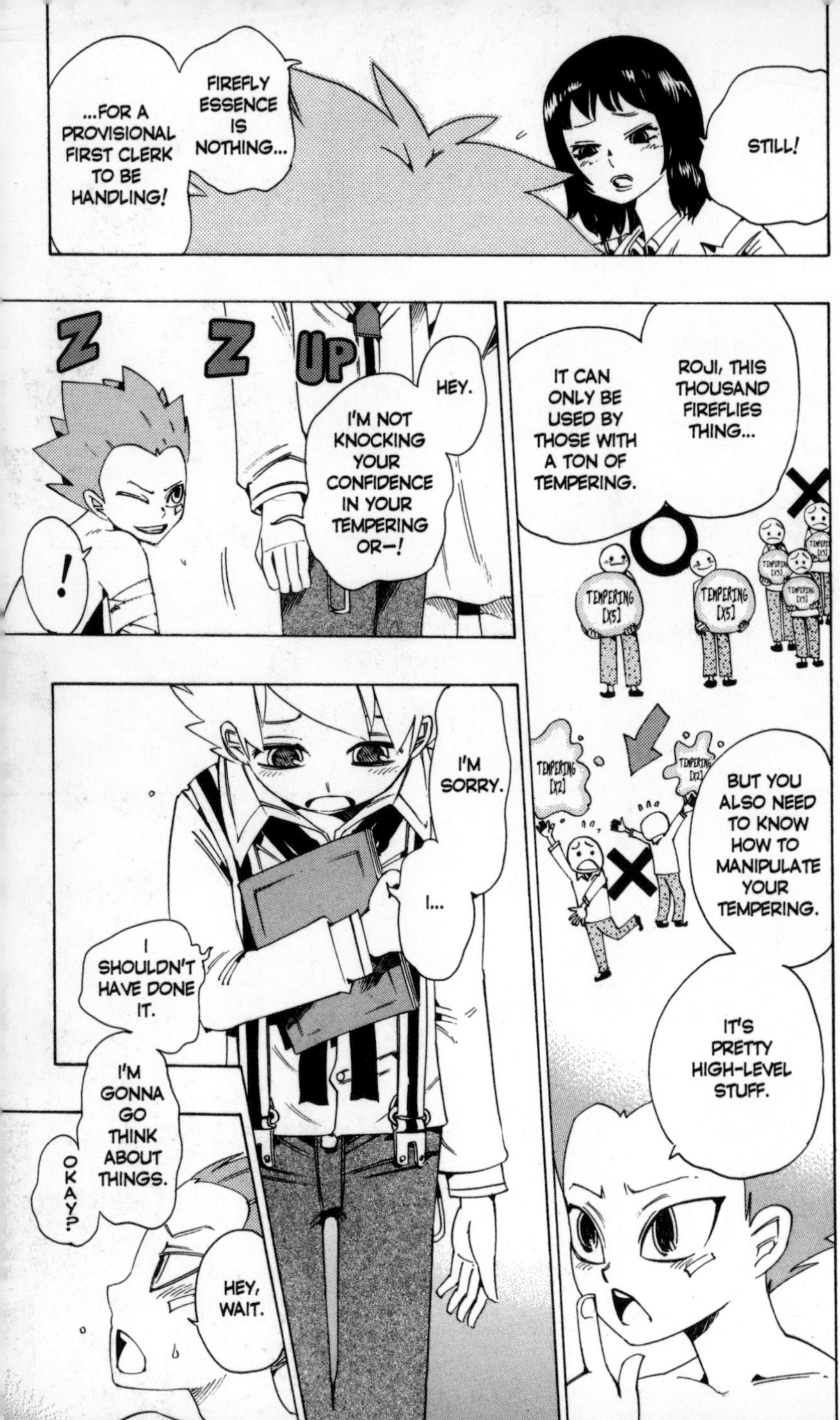
STILL!
FIREFLY ESSENCE IS NOTHING...
...FOR A PROVISIONAL FIRST CLERK TO BE HANDLING!
ROJI, THIS THOUSAND FIREFLIES THING...
IT CAN ONLY BE USED BY THOSE WITH A TON OF TEMPERING.
TEMPERING [X5]
TEMPERING [X5]
TEMPERING [X2]
TEMPERING [X2]
BUT YOU ALSO NEED TO KNOW HOW TO MANIPULATE YOUR TEMPERING.
IT'S PRETTY HIGH-LEVEL STUFF.
Z Z UP
HEY.
I'M NOT KNOCKING YOUR CONFIDENCE IN YOUR TEMPERING OR—!
!
I'M SORRY.
I...
I SHOULDN'T HAVE DONE IT.
I'M GONNA GO THINK ABOUT THINGS.
OKAY?
HEY, WAIT.

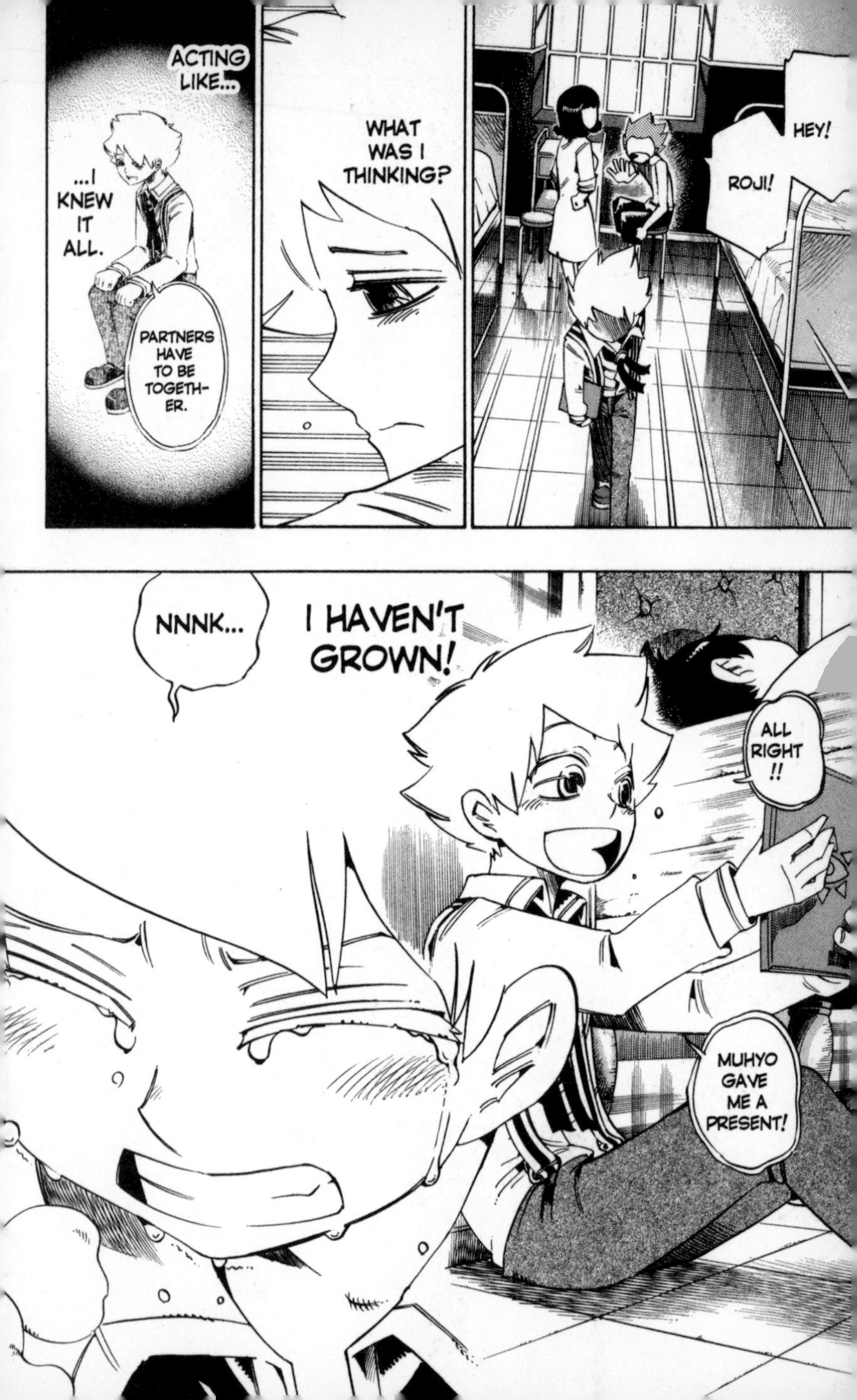
HEY!
ROJI!
WHAT WAS I THINKING?
ACTING LIKE...
...I KNEW IT ALL.
PARTNERS HAVE TO BE TOGETH-ER.
ALL RIGHT!!
MUHYO GAVE ME A PRESENT!
I HAVEN'T GROWN!
NNNK...

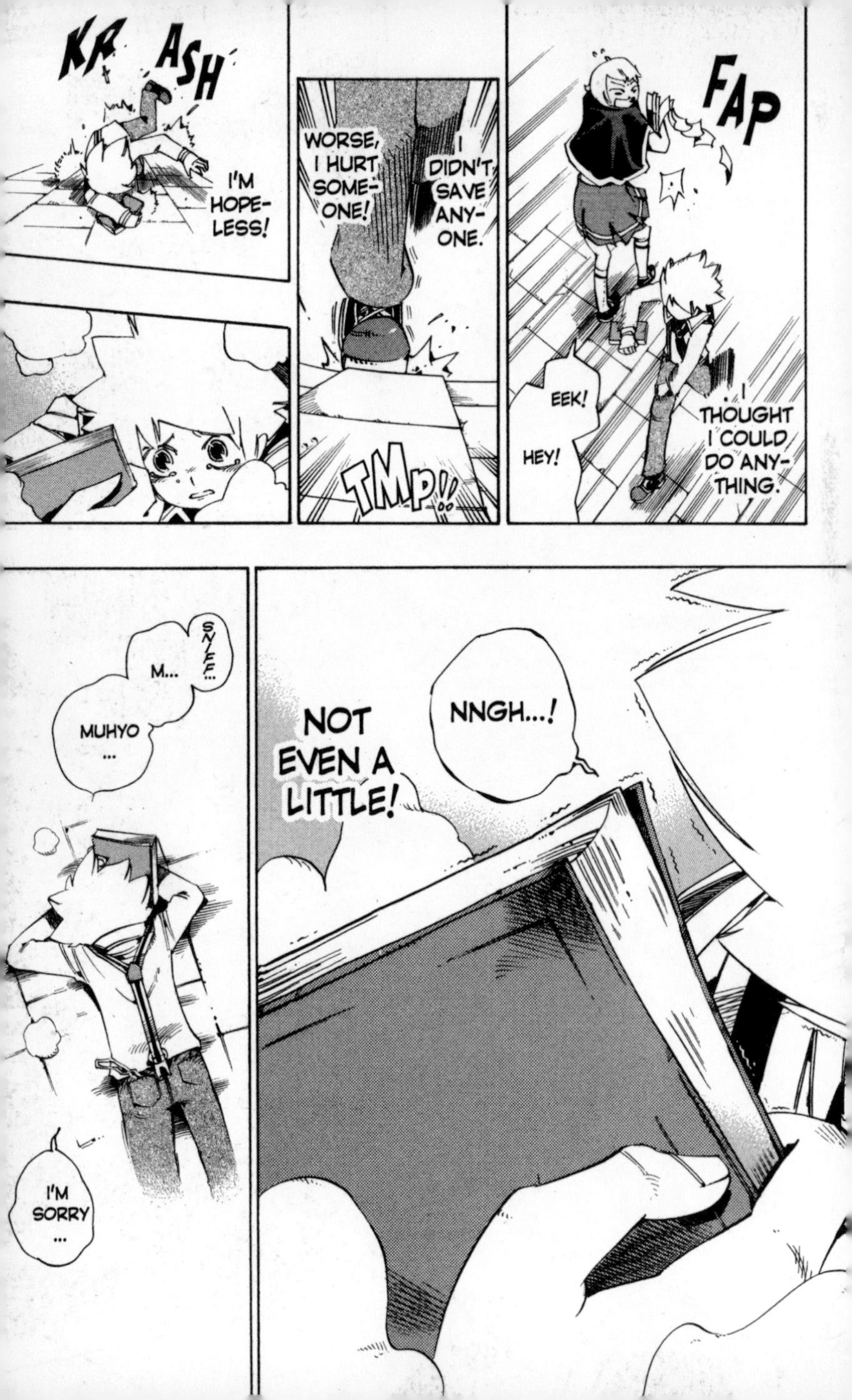
FAP
I THOUGHT I COULD DO ANY-THING.
EEK!
HEY!
I DIDN'T SAVE ANY-ONE.
WORSE, I HURT SOME-ONE!
TMP!!
KRASH
I'M HOPE-LESS!
NNGH...!
NOT EVEN A LITTLE!
SNIFF...
M...
MUHYO...
I'M SORRY...

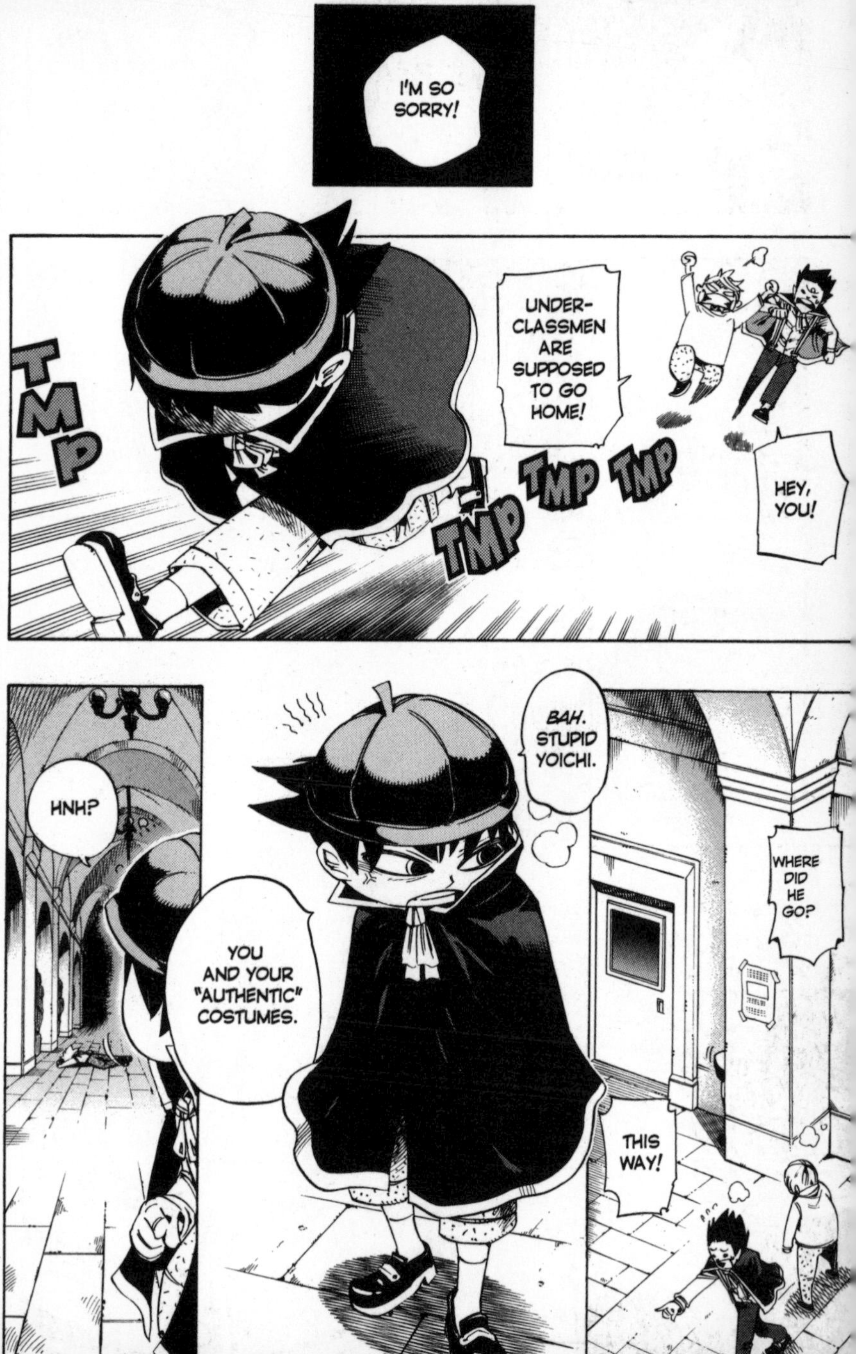
I'M SO SORRY!
HEY, YOU!
UNDER-CLASSMEN ARE SUPPOSED TO GO HOME!
TMP TMP TMP
TMP
WHERE DID HE GO?
THIS WAY!
BAH. STUPID YOICHI.
YOU AND YOUR "AUTHENTIC" COSTUMES.
HNH?

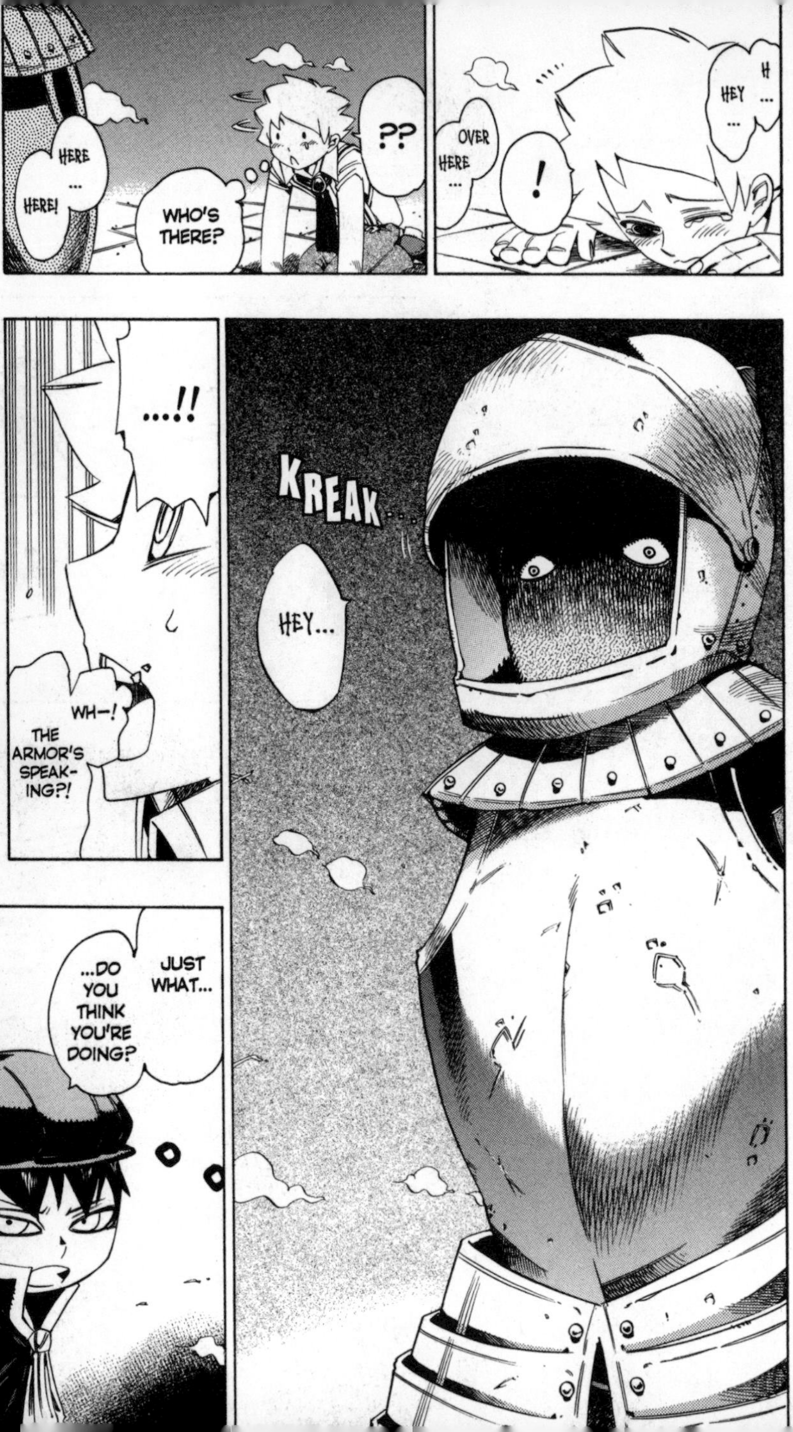
H
HEY ... ...
OVER HERE ...
!
??
WHO'S THERE?
HERE ... HERE!
KREAK...
HEY...
...!!
WH—! THE ARMOR'S SPEAK-ING?!
JUST WHAT...
...DO YOU THINK YOU'RE DOING?

Muhyo & Roji's
Bureau of Supernatural Investigation
BSI

ARTICLE 103 BOBBY

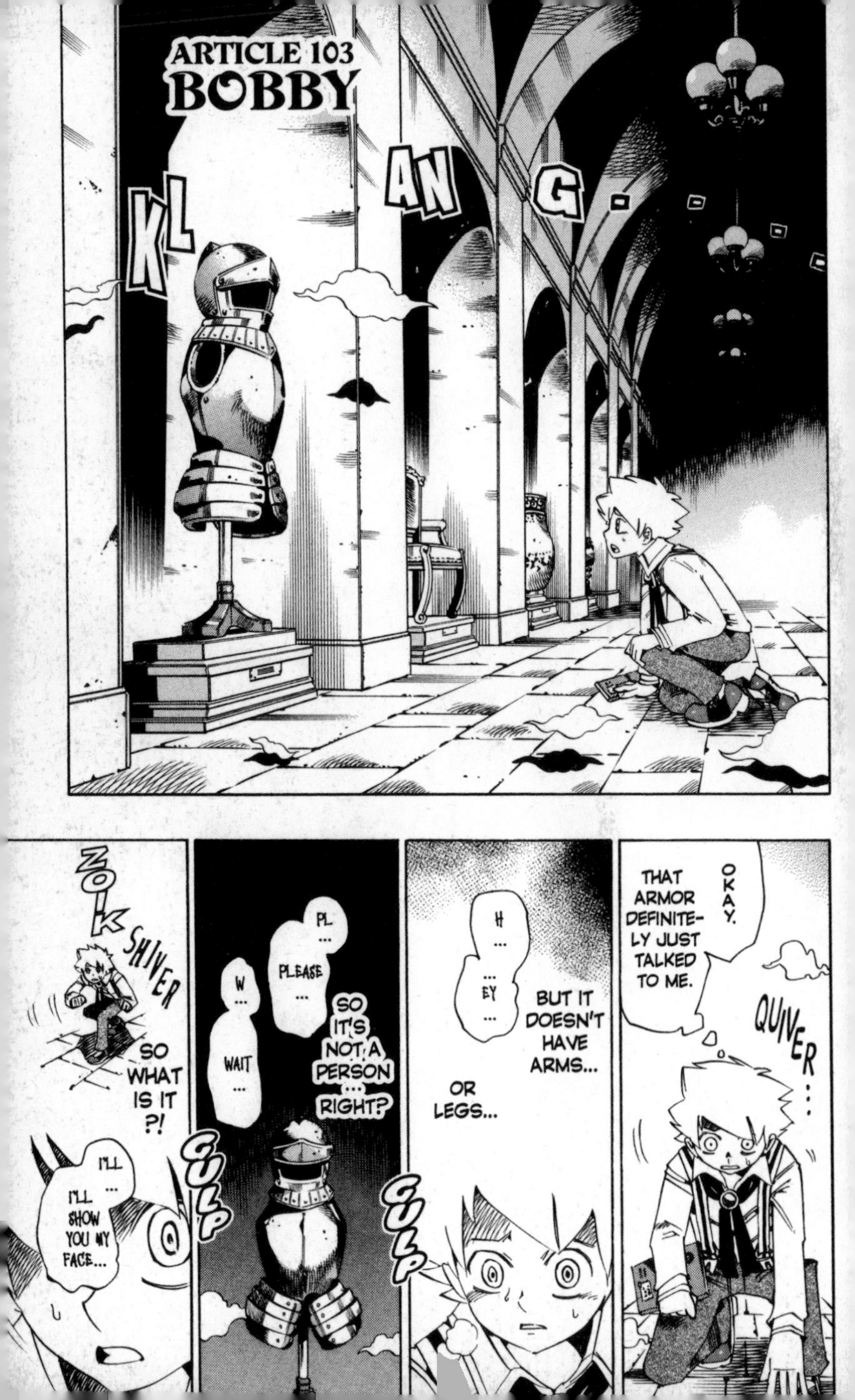
KL AN G...
OKAY.
THAT ARMOR DEFINITE-LY JUST TALKED TO ME.
QUIVER...
H... ...EY...
BUT IT DOESN'T HAVE ARMS...
OR LEGS...
GULP
PL... PLEASE...
W... WAIT...
SO IT'S NOT A PERSON... RIGHT?
GULP
ZOIK
SHIVER
SO WHAT IS IT ?!
I'LL... I'LL SHOW YOU MY FACE...

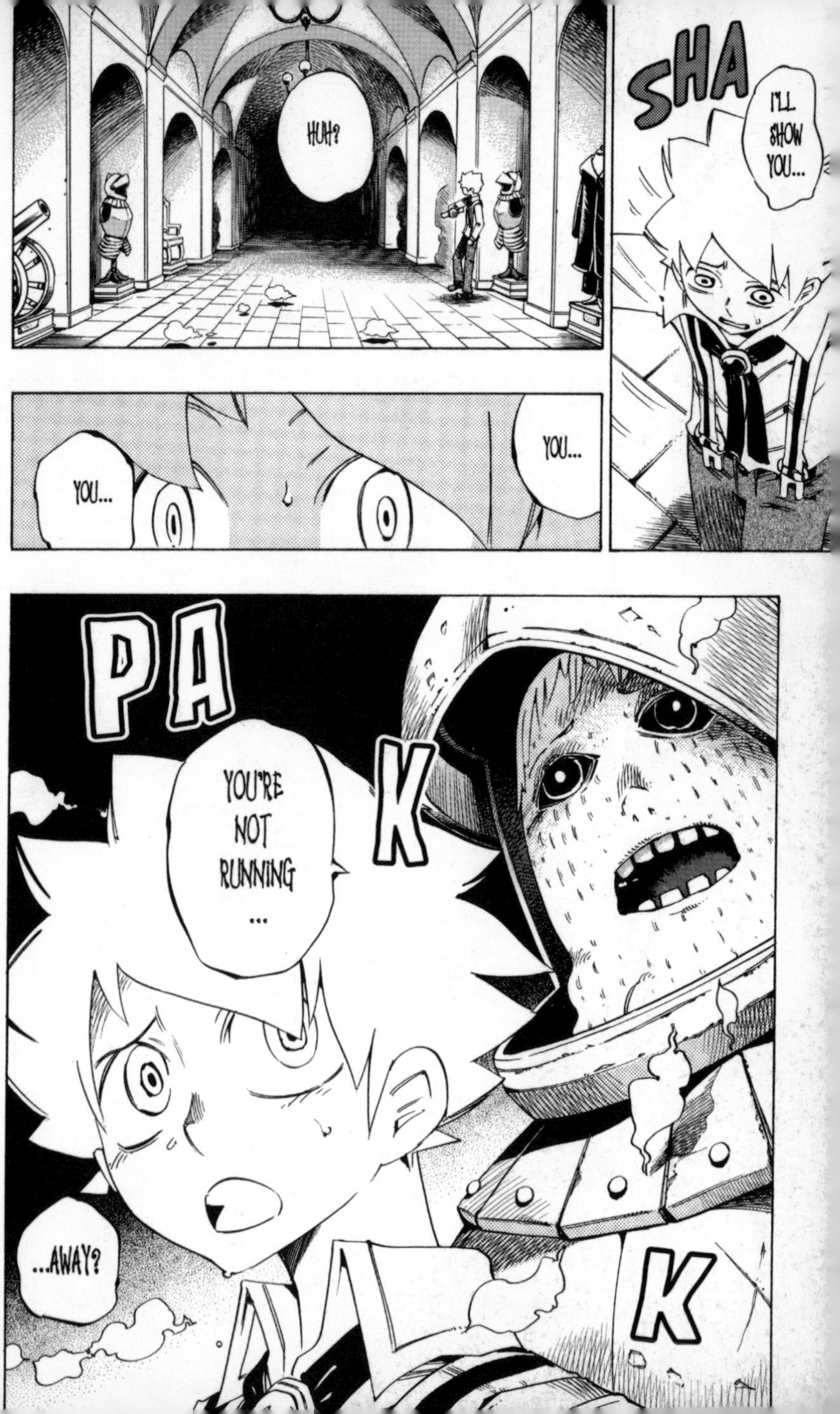
SHA
I'LL SHOW YOU...
HUH?
YOU...
YOU...
PA
K
YOU'RE NOT RUNNING ...
...AWAY?
K

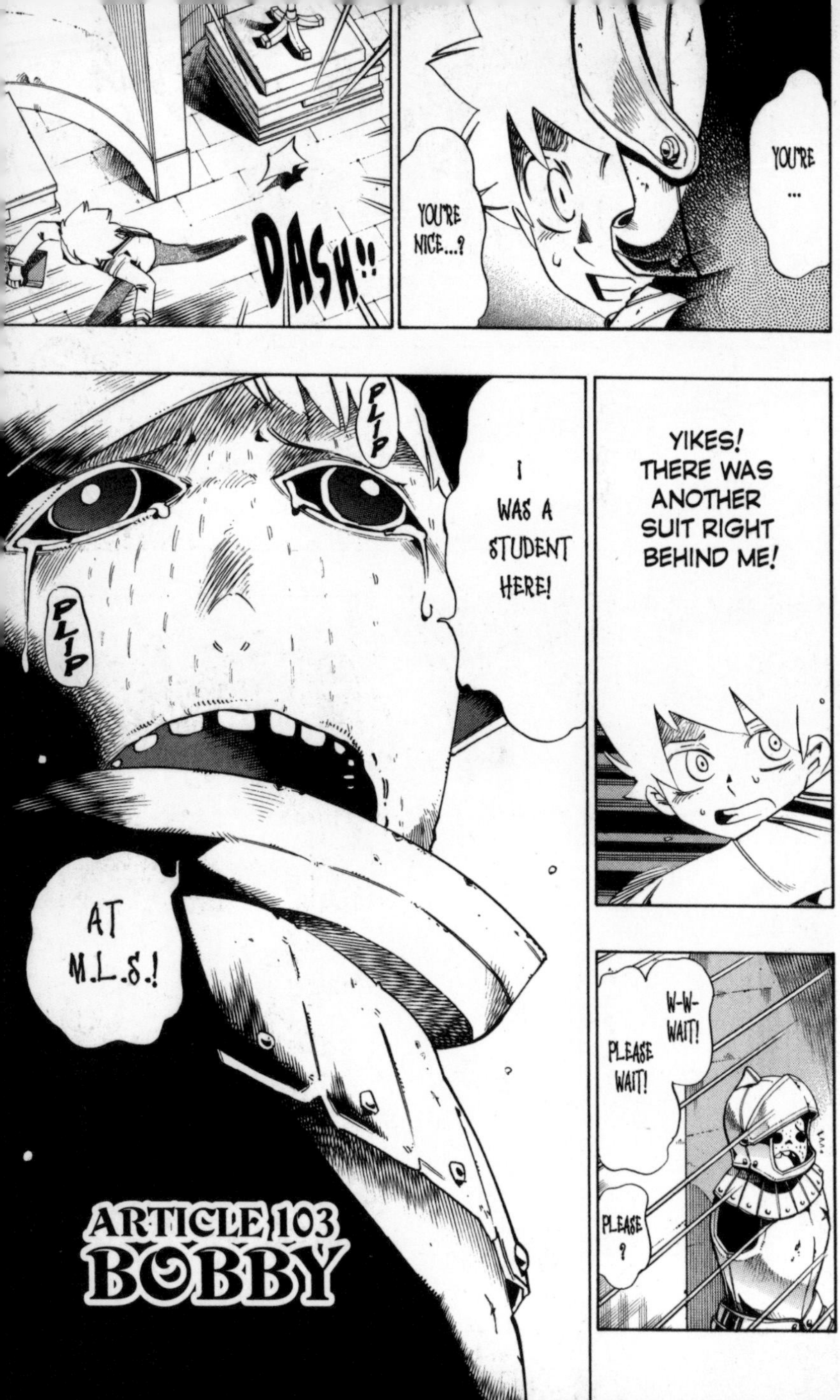
YOU'RE ...
YOU'RE NICE...?
DASH!!
YIKES! THERE WAS ANOTHER SUIT RIGHT BEHIND ME!
W-W-WAIT!
PLEASE WAIT!
PLEASE ?
PLIP
I WAS A STUDENT HERE!
PLIP
AT M.L.S.!
ARTICLE 103
BOBBY

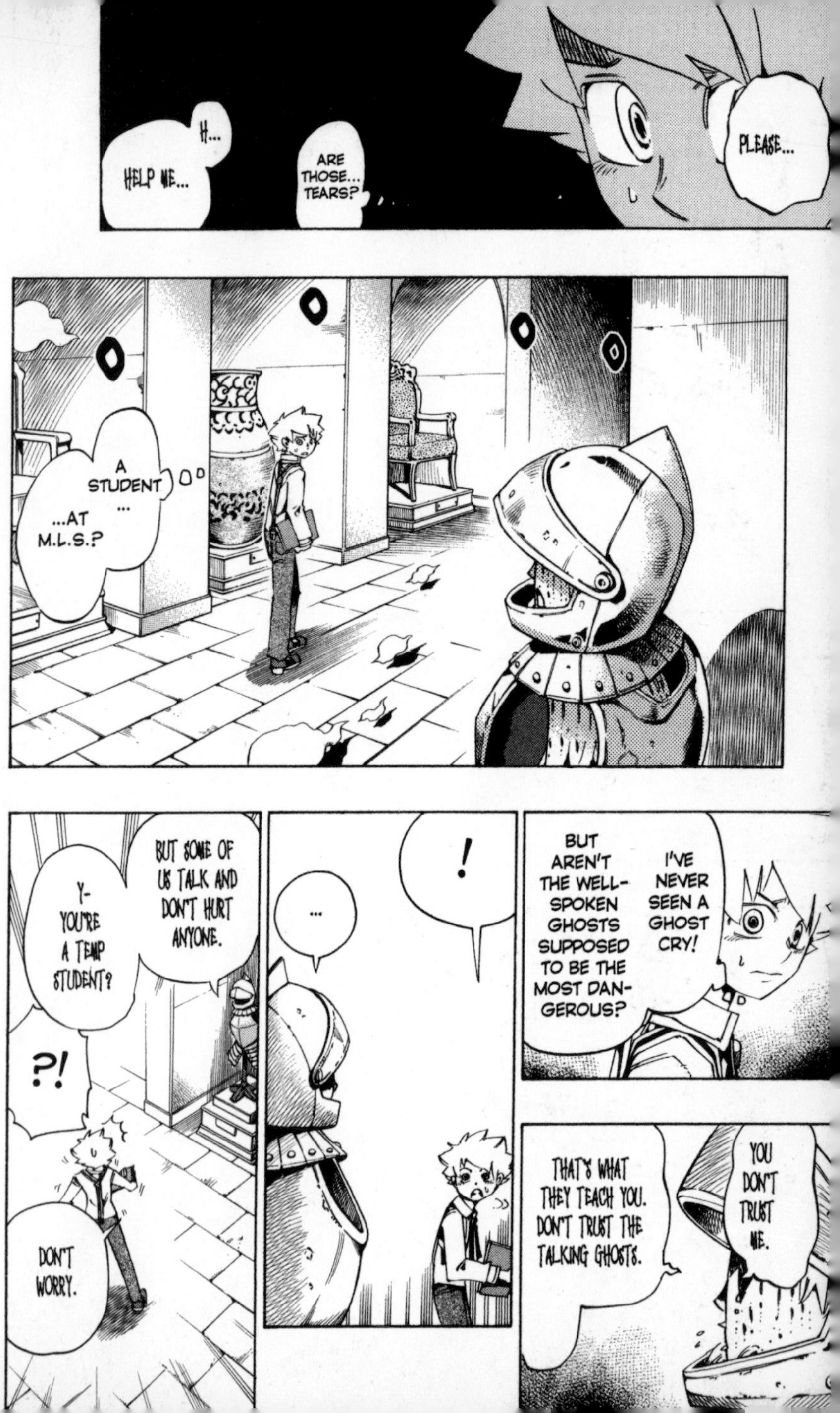
PLEASE...
ARE THOSE... TEARS?
H... HELP ME...
A STUDENT ... ...AT M.L.S.?
I'VE NEVER SEEN A GHOST CRY!
BUT AREN'T THE WELL-SPOKEN GHOSTS SUPPOSED TO BE THE MOST DANGEROUS?
YOU DON'T TRUST ME.
THAT'S WHAT THEY TEACH YOU. DON'T TRUST THE TALKING GHOSTS.
!
...
BUT SOME OF US TALK AND DON'T HURT ANYONE.
Y-YOU'RE A TEMP STUDENT?
?!
DON'T WORRY.

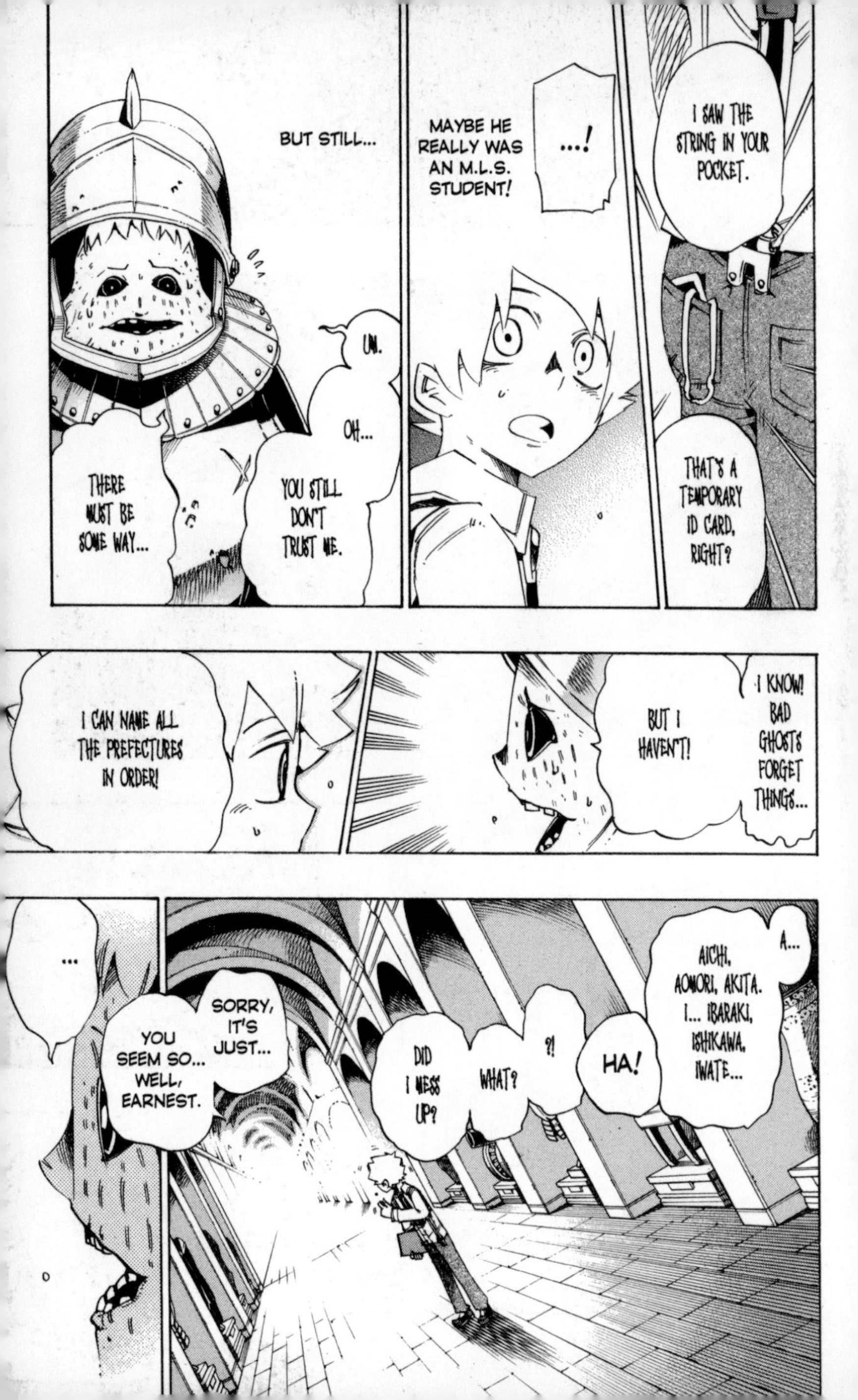
I SAW THE STRING IN YOUR POCKET.
THAT'S A TEMPORARY ID CARD, RIGHT?
...!
MAYBE HE REALLY WAS AN M.L.S. STUDENT!
BUT STILL...
UM.
OH...
YOU STILL DON'T TRUST ME.
THERE MUST BE SOME WAY...
I KNOW! BAD GHOSTS FORGET THINGS...
BUT I HAVEN'T!
I CAN NAME ALL THE PREFECTURES IN ORDER!
A...
AICHI, AOMORI, AKITA. I... IBARAKI, ISHIKAWA, IWATE...
HA!
?!
WHAT?
DID I MESS UP?
SORRY, IT'S JUST...
YOU SEEM SO... WELL, EARNEST.
...

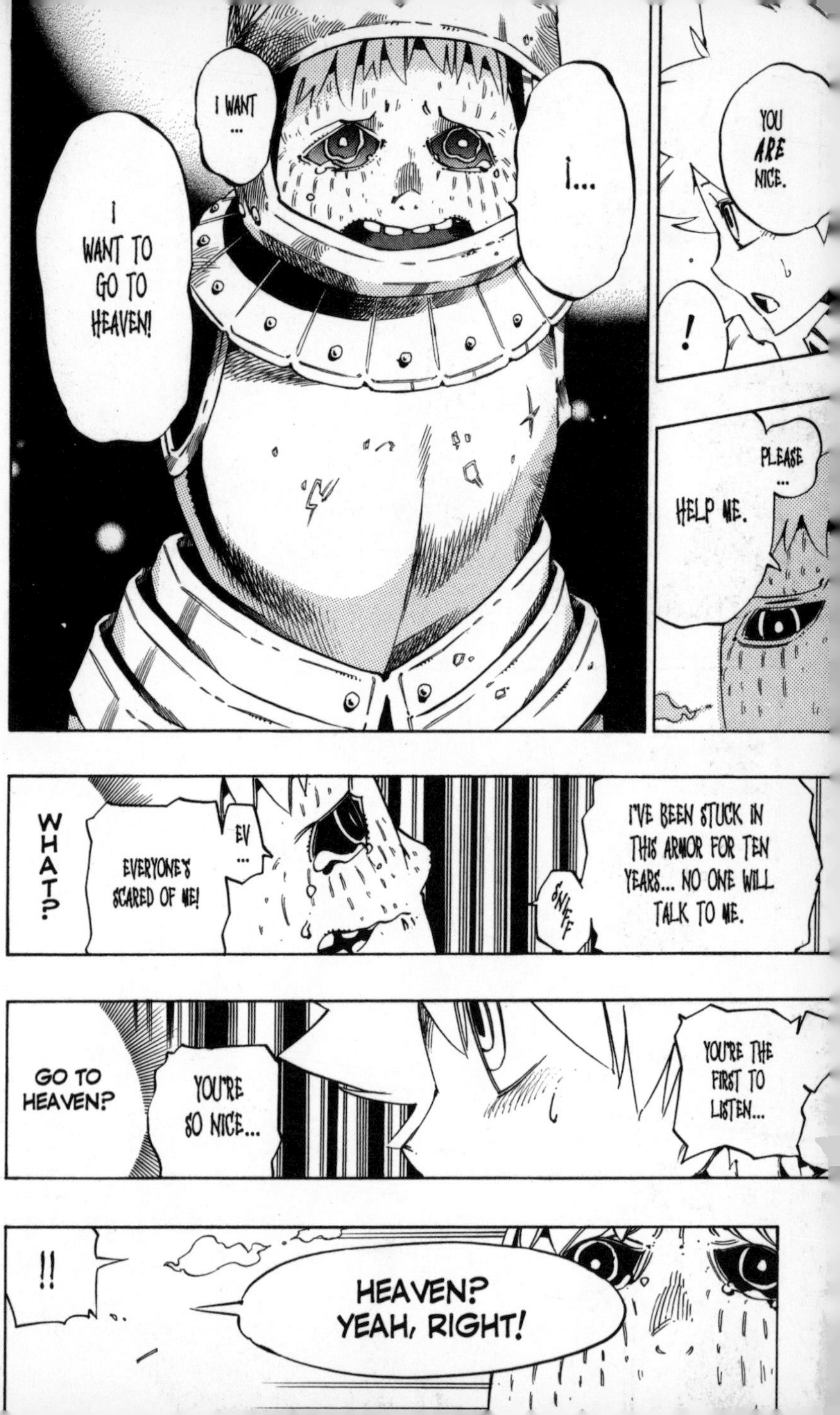
YOU ARE NICE.
!
PLEASE ...
HELP ME.
I...
I WANT ...
I WANT TO GO TO HEAVEN!
I'VE BEEN STUCK IN THIS ARMOR FOR TEN YEARS... NO ONE WILL TALK TO ME.
SNIFF
EV ...
EVERYONE'S SCARED OF ME!
WHAT?
YOU'RE THE FIRST TO LISTEN...
YOU'RE SO NICE...
GO TO HEAVEN?
HEAVEN? YEAH, RIGHT!
!!

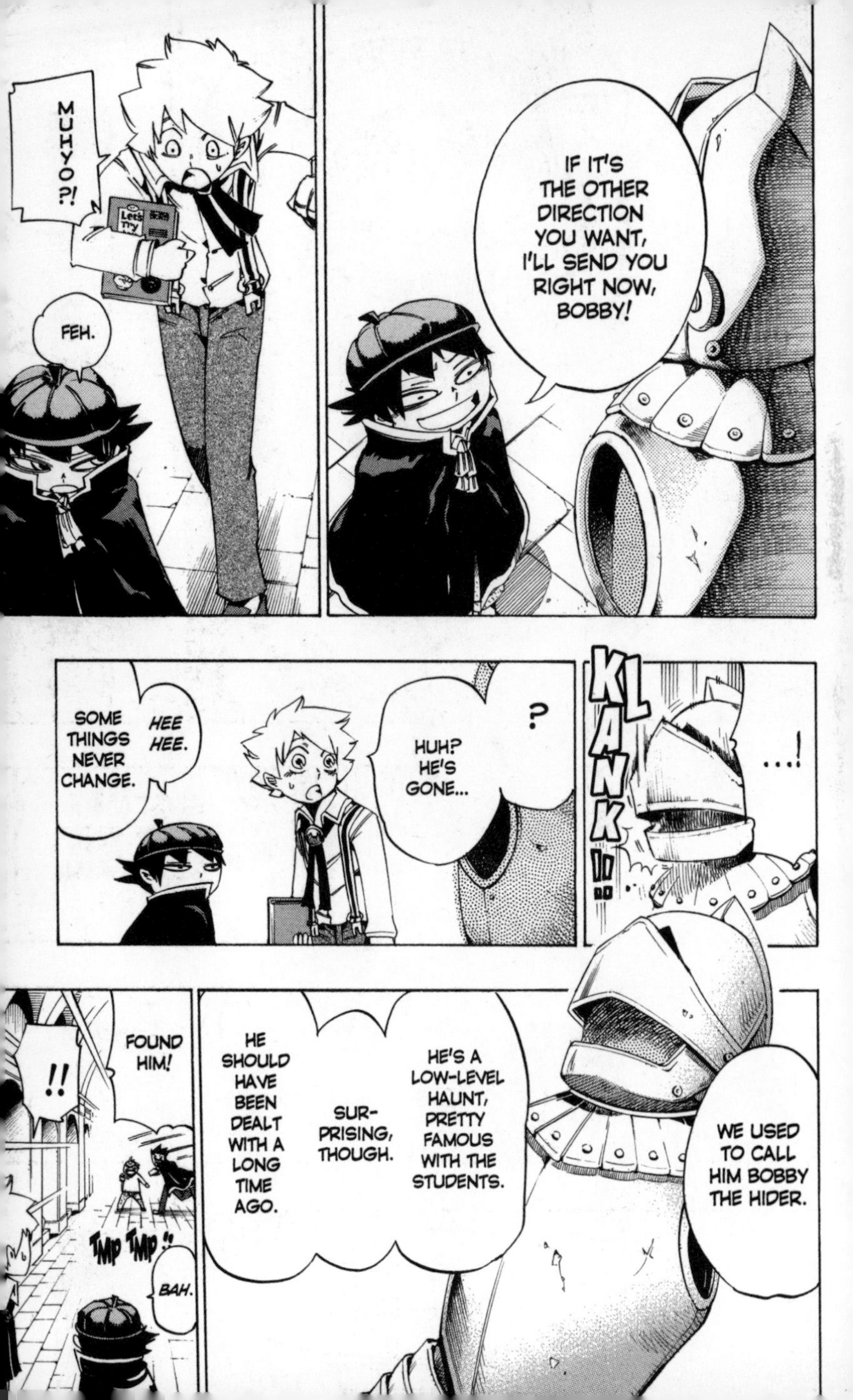
IF IT'S THE OTHER DIRECTION YOU WANT, I'LL SEND YOU RIGHT NOW, BOBBY!
MUHYO?!
FEH.
KLANK!!
...!
?
HUH? HE'S GONE...
HEE HEE.
SOME THINGS NEVER CHANGE.
WE USED TO CALL HIM BOBBY THE HIDER.
HE'S A LOW-LEVEL HAUNT, PRETTY FAMOUS WITH THE STUDENTS.
SUR-PRISING, THOUGH.
HE SHOULD HAVE BEEN DEALT WITH A LONG TIME AGO.
!!
FOUND HIM!
TMP TMP!!
BAH.

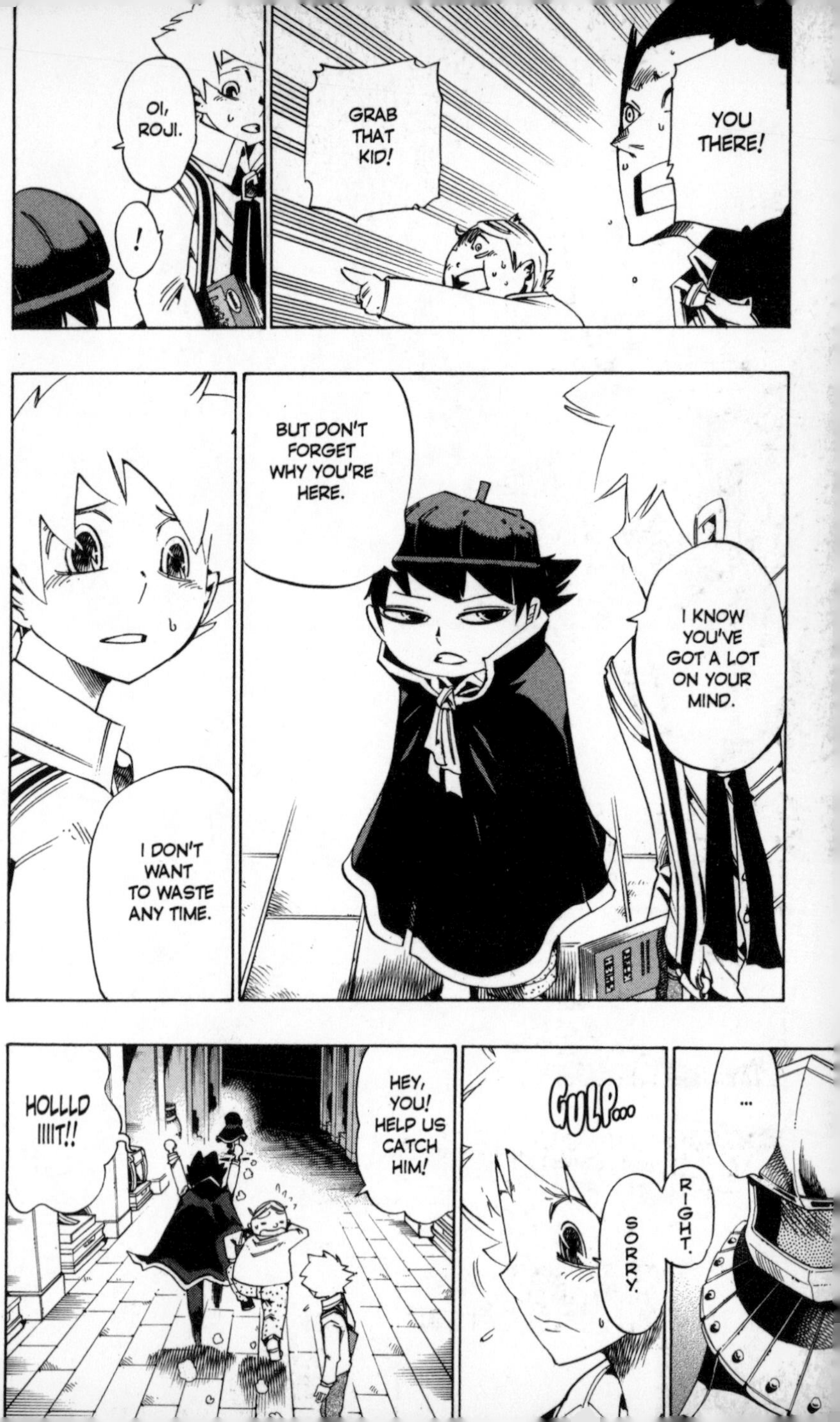
YOU THERE!
GRAB THAT KID!
OI, ROJI.
!
I KNOW YOU'VE GOT A LOT ON YOUR MIND.
BUT DON'T FORGET WHY YOU'RE HERE.
I DON'T WANT TO WASTE ANY TIME.
...
RIGHT.
GULP...
SORRY.
HEY, YOU! HELP US CATCH HIM!
HOLLLD IIIIT!!

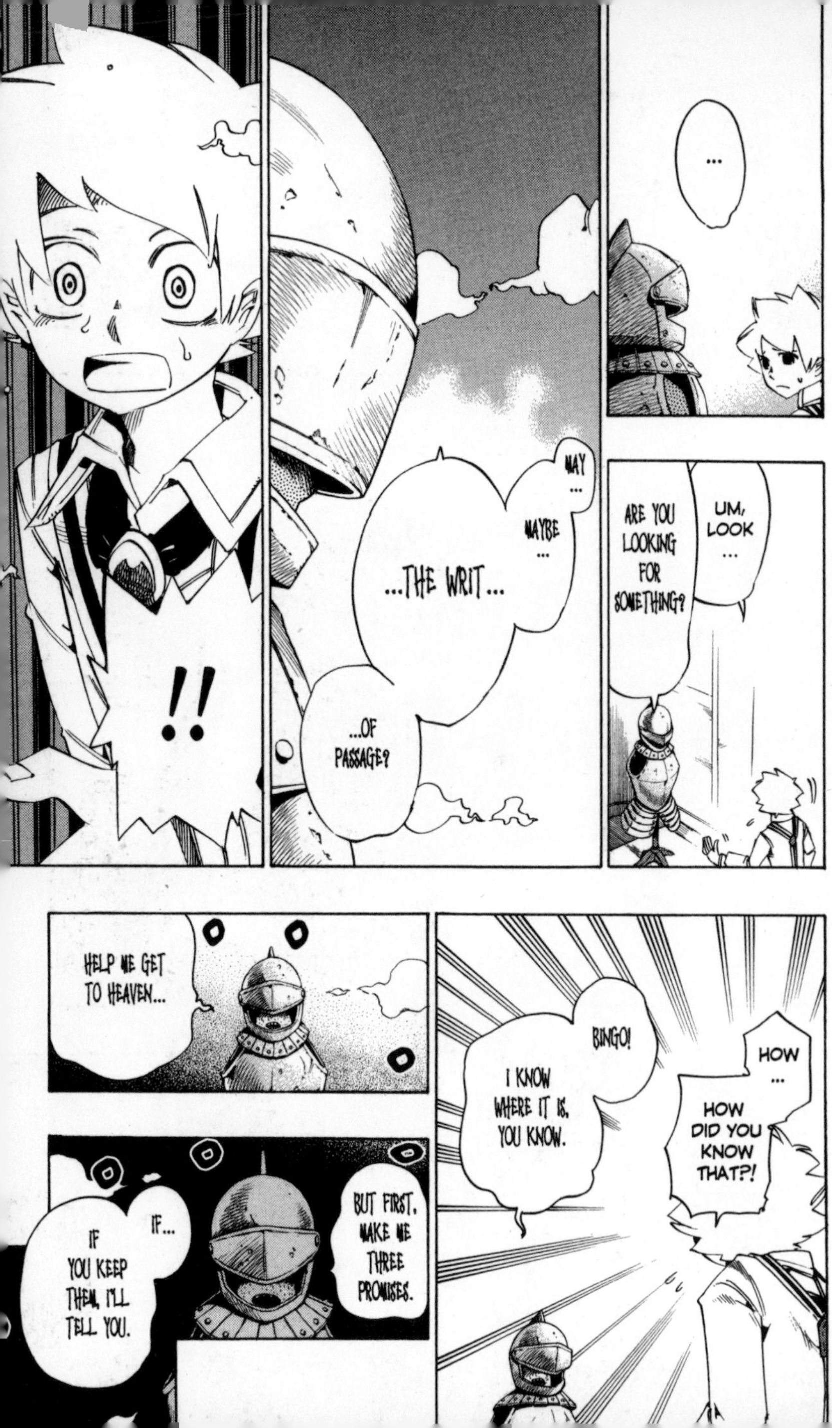
...
UM, LOOK...
ARE YOU LOOKING FOR SOMETHING?
MAY...
MAYBE...
...THE WRIT...
...OF PASSAGE?
!!
HOW...
HOW DID YOU KNOW THAT?!
BINGO!
I KNOW WHERE IT IS, YOU KNOW.
HELP ME GET TO HEAVEN...
BUT FIRST, MAKE ME THREE PROMISES.
IF...
IF YOU KEEP THEM, I'LL TELL YOU.

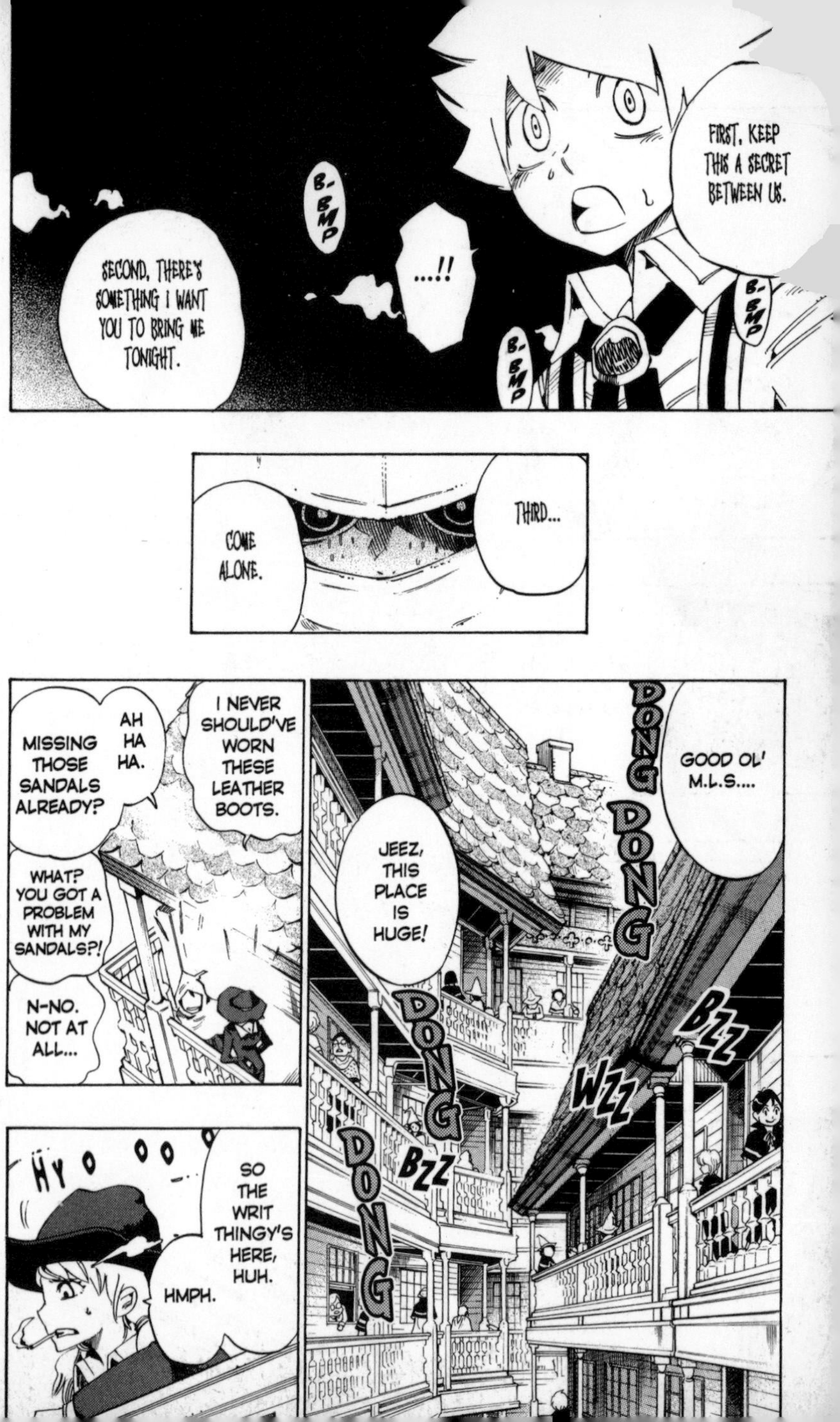
FIRST, KEEP THIS A SECRET BETWEEN US.
B-BMP
B-BMP
...!!
B-BMP
SECOND, THERE'S SOMETHING I WANT YOU TO BRING ME TONIGHT.
THIRD...
COME ALONE.
GOOD OL' M.L.S....
DONG DONG
JEEZ, THIS PLACE IS HUGE!
BZZ
WZZ
DONG DONG
BZZ
I NEVER SHOULD'VE WORN THESE LEATHER BOOTS.
AH HA HA.
MISSING THOSE SANDALS ALREADY?
WHAT? YOU GOT A PROBLEM WITH MY SANDALS?!
N-NO. NOT AT ALL...
HYOOOO
SO THE WRIT THINGY'S HERE, HUH.
HMPH.

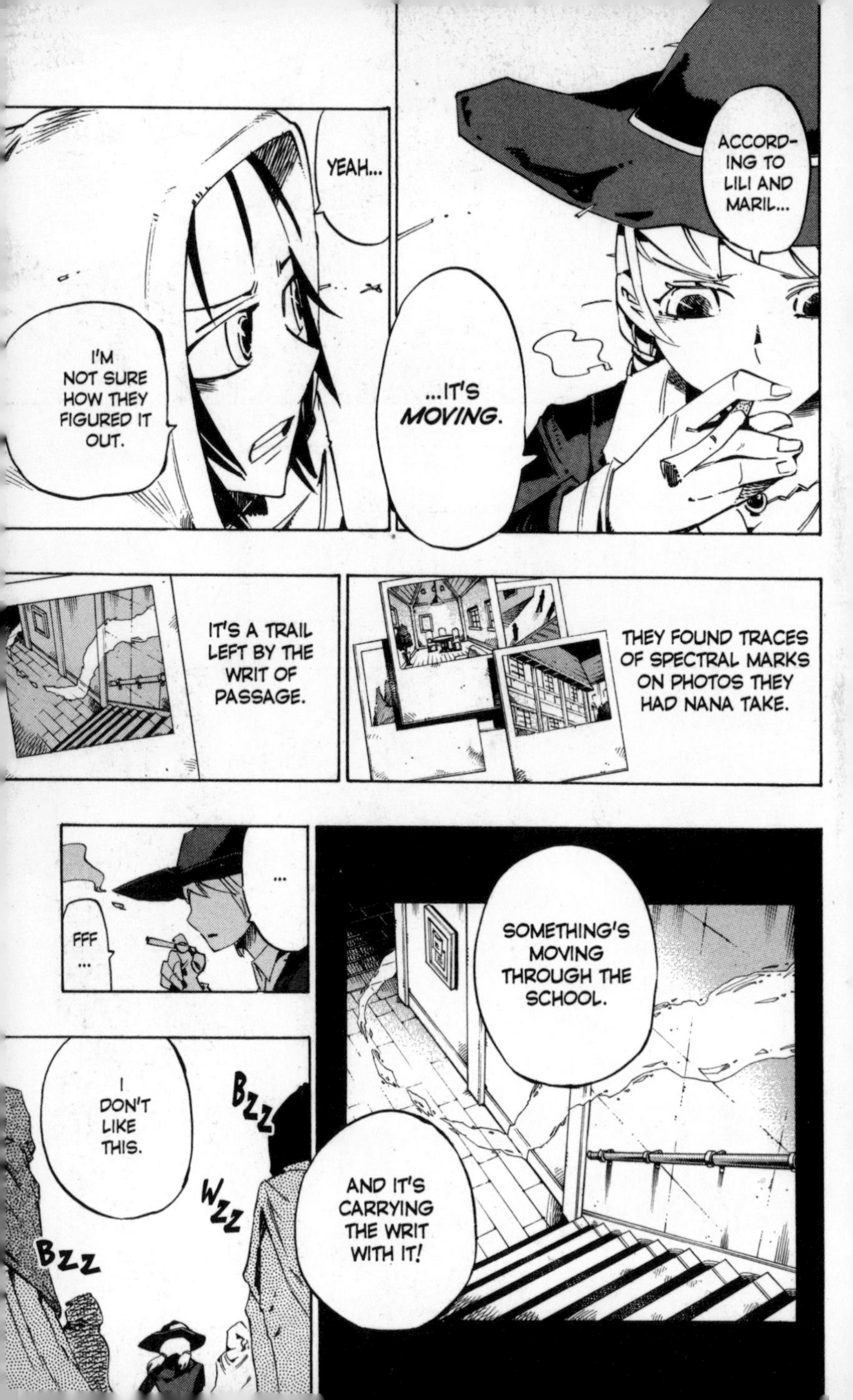
ACCORDING TO LILI AND MARIL...
...IT'S *MOVING*.
YEAH...
I'M NOT SURE HOW THEY FIGURED IT OUT.
THEY FOUND TRACES OF SPECTRAL MARKS ON PHOTOS THEY HAD NANA TAKE.
IT'S A TRAIL LEFT BY THE WRIT OF PASSAGE.
SOMETHING'S MOVING THROUGH THE SCHOOL.
AND IT'S CARRYING THE WRIT WITH IT!
...
FFF...
I DON'T LIKE THIS.
BZZ
WZZ
BZZ

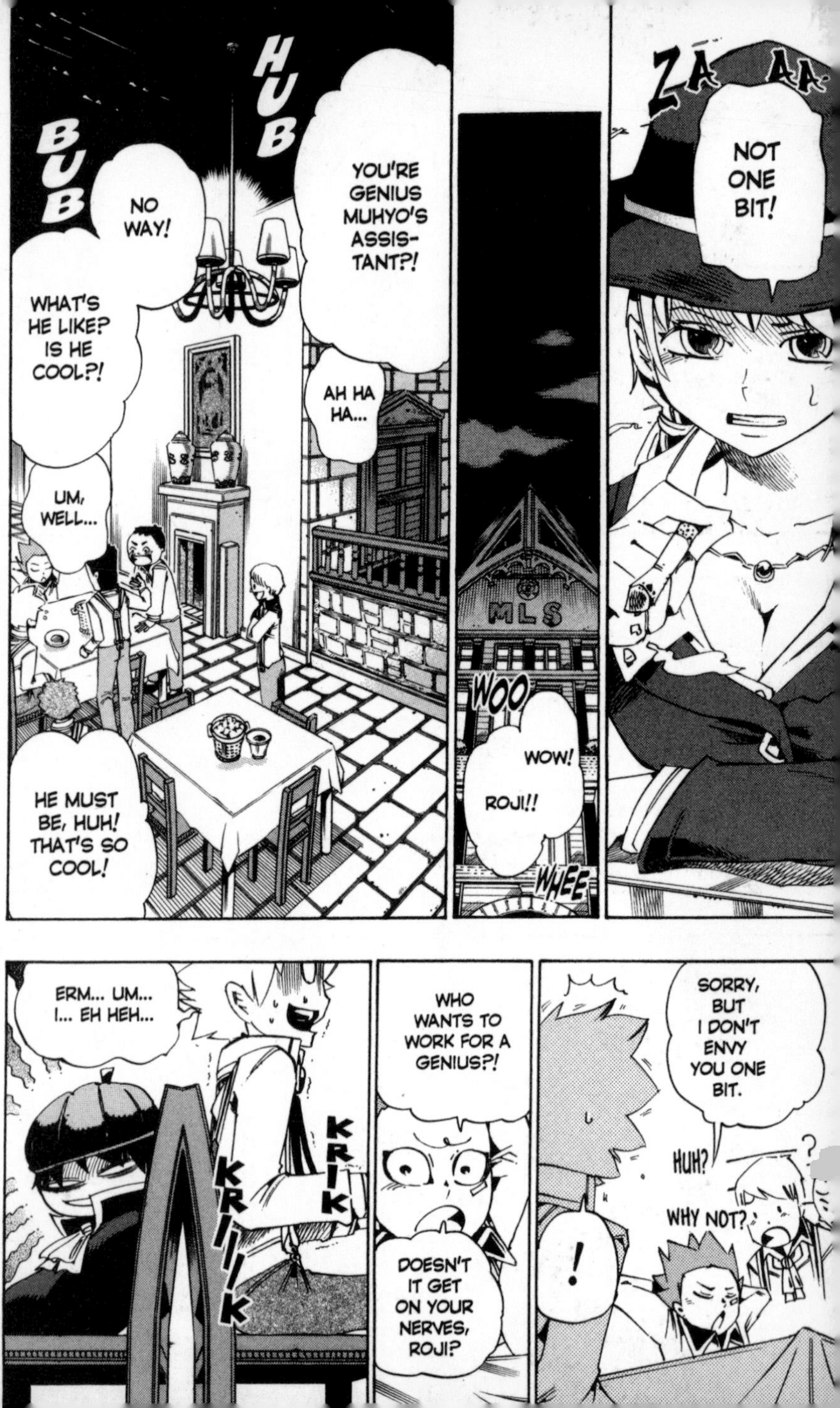
ZAAA
NOT ONE BIT!
WOO
WOW!
ROJI!!
WHEE
HUB HUB
YOU'RE GENIUS MUHYO'S ASSIS-TANT?!
BUB BUB
NO WAY!
WHAT'S HE LIKE? IS HE COOL?!
AH HA HA...
UM, WELL...
HE MUST BE, HUH! THAT'S SO COOL!
SORRY, BUT I DON'T ENVY YOU ONE BIT.
HUH?
WHY NOT?
!
WHO WANTS TO WORK FOR A GENIUS?!
DOESN'T IT GET ON YOUR NERVES, ROJI?
ERM... UM... I... EH HEH...
KRIK
KRIIIIK

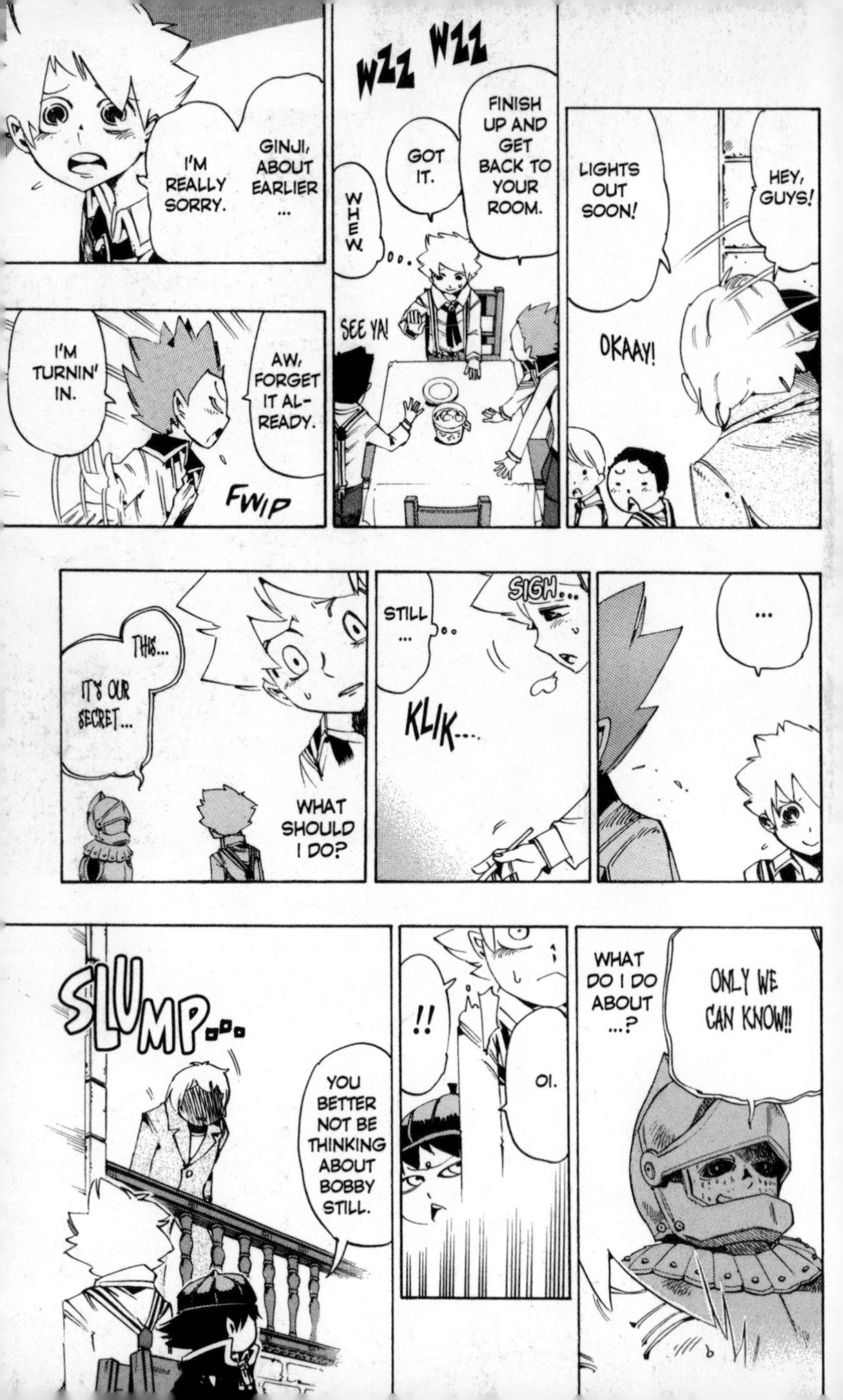
HEY, GUYS!
LIGHTS OUT SOON!
OKAAY!
WZZ WZZ
FINISH UP AND GET BACK TO YOUR ROOM.
GOT IT.
WHEW.
SEE YA!
GINJI, ABOUT EARLIER...
I'M REALLY SORRY.
AW, FORGET IT AL-READY.
I'M TURNIN' IN.
FWIP
...
SIGH...
STILL...
KLIK...
THIS...
IT'S OUR SECRET...
WHAT SHOULD I DO?
ONLY WE CAN KNOW!!
WHAT DO I DO ABOUT ...?
OI.
!!
SLUMP...
YOU BETTER NOT BE THINKING ABOUT BOBBY STILL.

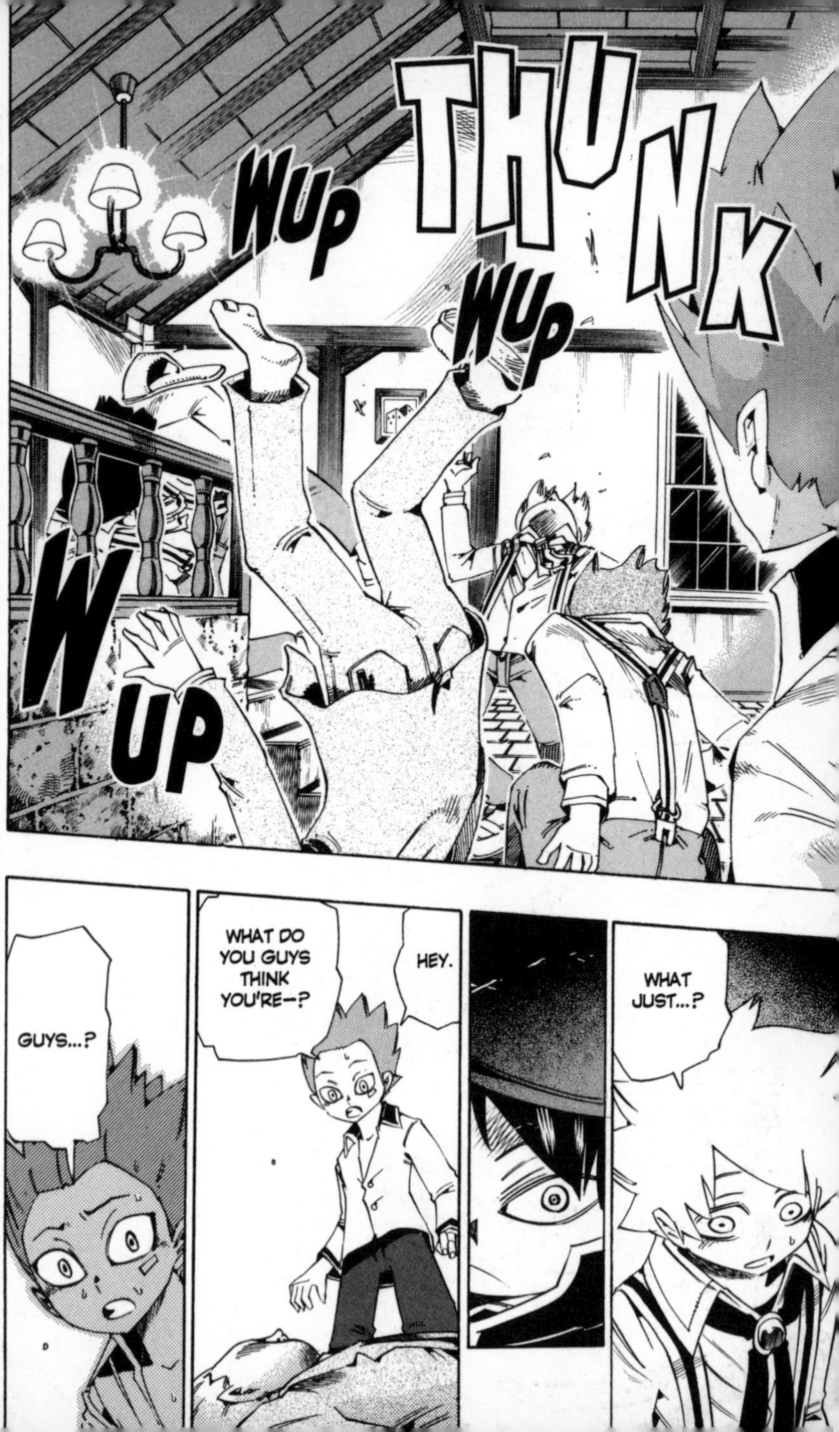
THUNK
WUP
WUP
W UP
WHAT JUST...?
HEY.
WHAT DO YOU GUYS THINK YOU'RE--?
GUYS...?

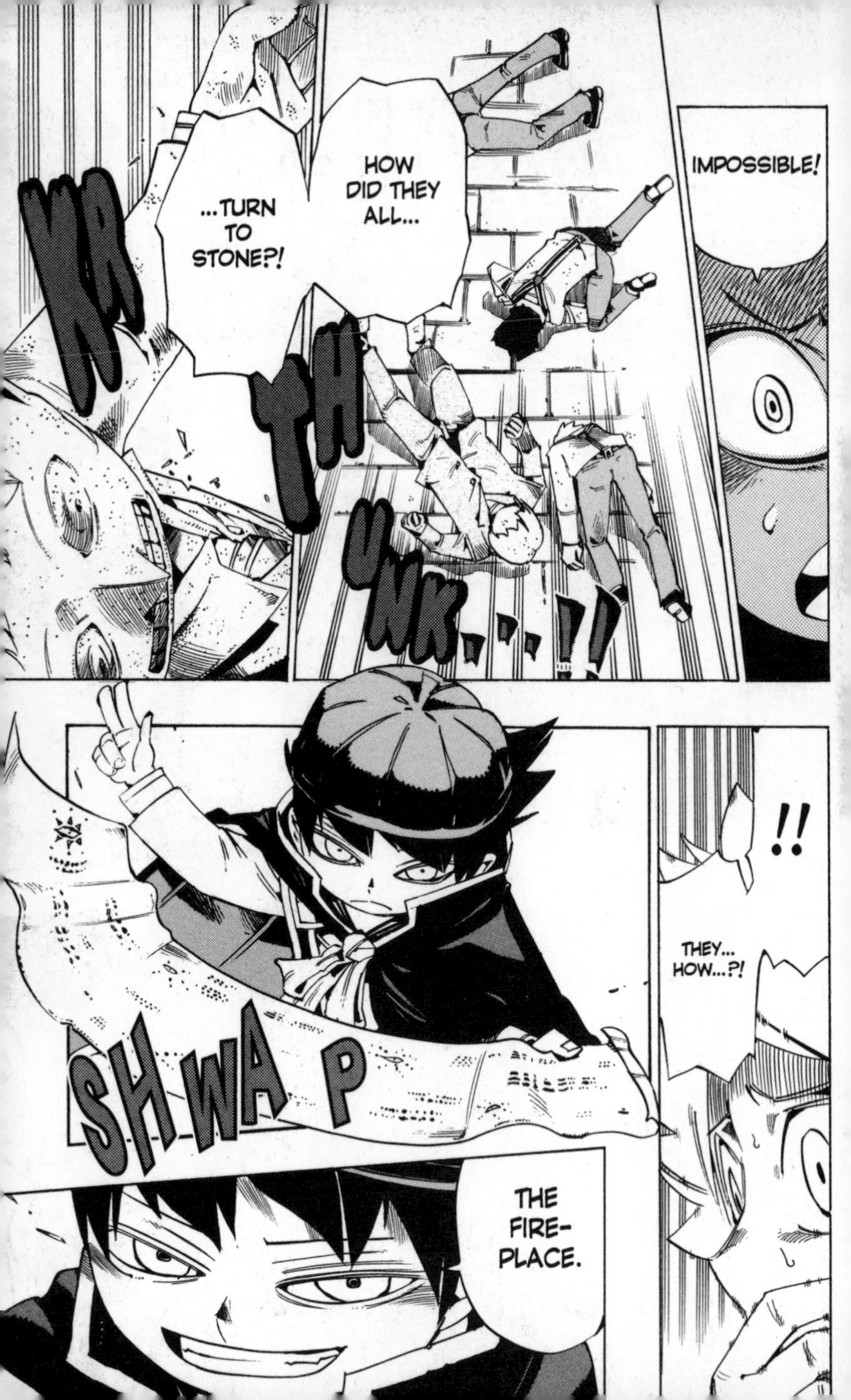
IMPOSSIBLE!
HOW DID THEY ALL...
...TURN TO STONE?!
KRTHUNK..!!
!!
THEY... HOW...?!
SHWAP
THE FIRE-PLACE.

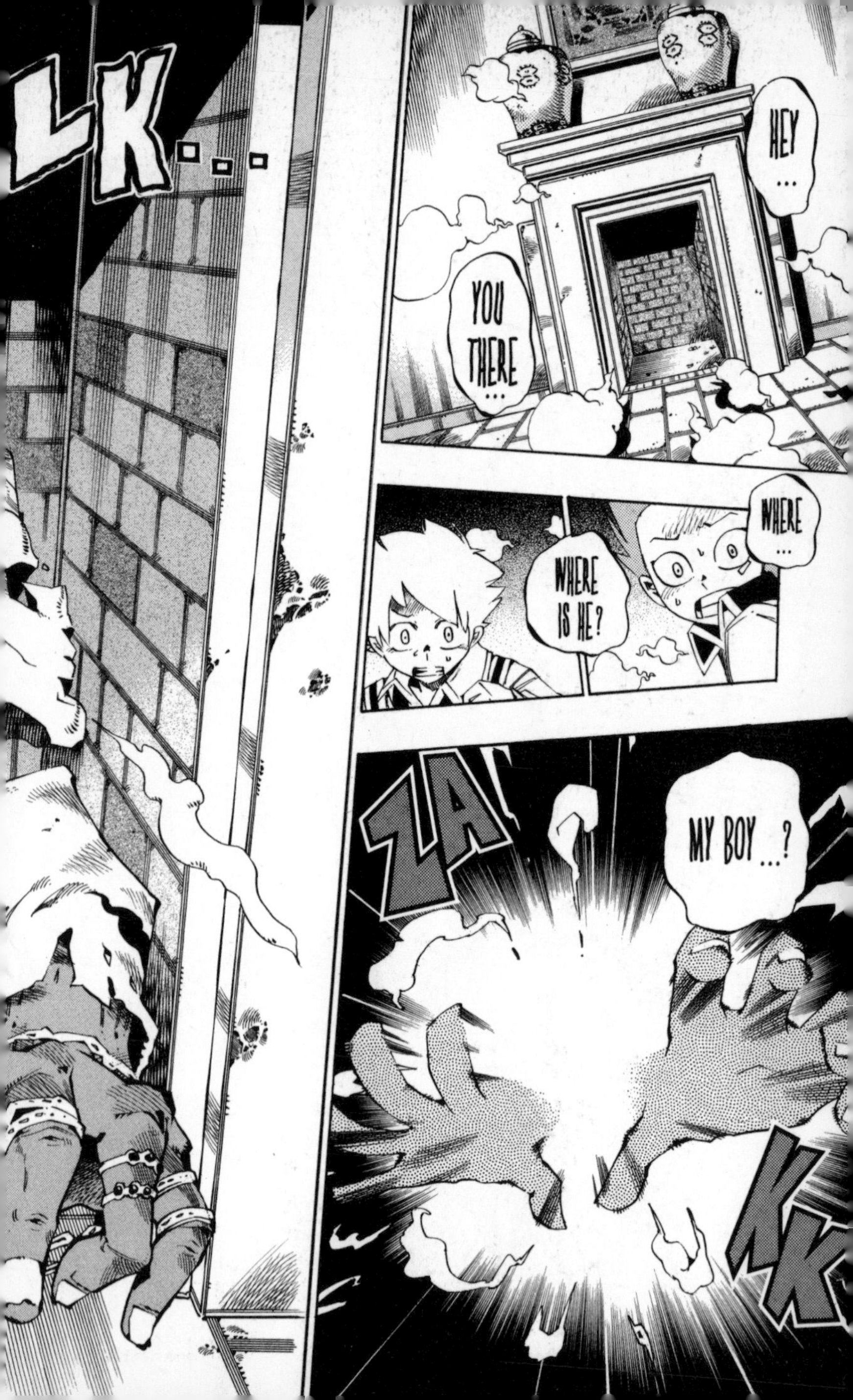
HEY ...
YOU THERE ...
WHERE ...
WHERE IS HE?
MY BOY ...?
ZA
KK
LK...

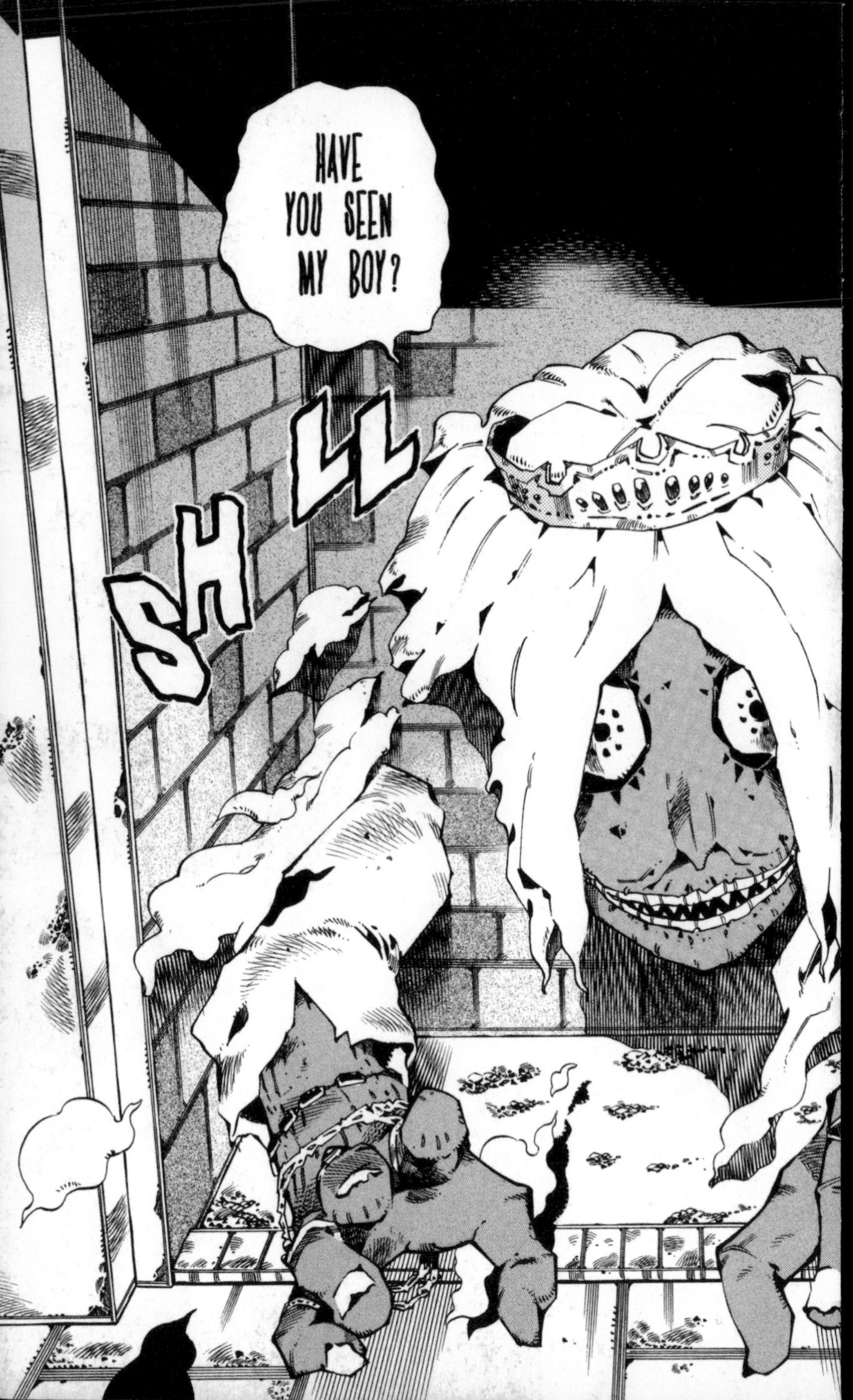
HAVE YOU SEEN MY BOY?
SHLL

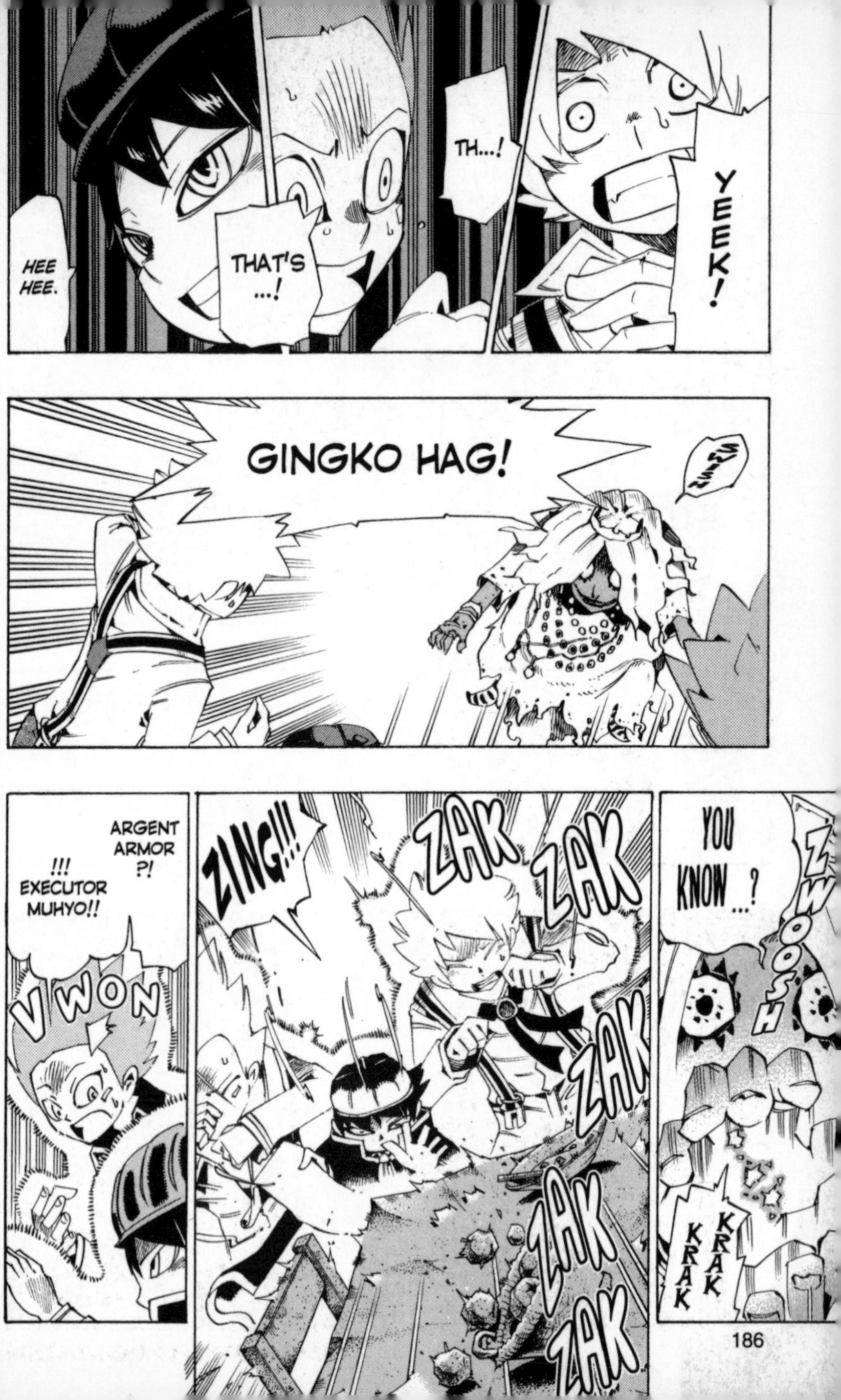
YEEK!
TH...!
THAT'S ...!
HEE HEE.
GINGKO HAG!
YOU KNOW...?
ZWOOSH
KRAK KRAK
ZAK ZAK ZAK ZAK ZAK ZAK
ZING!!!
ARGENT ARMOR ?!
!!! EXECUTOR MUHYO!!
VWON

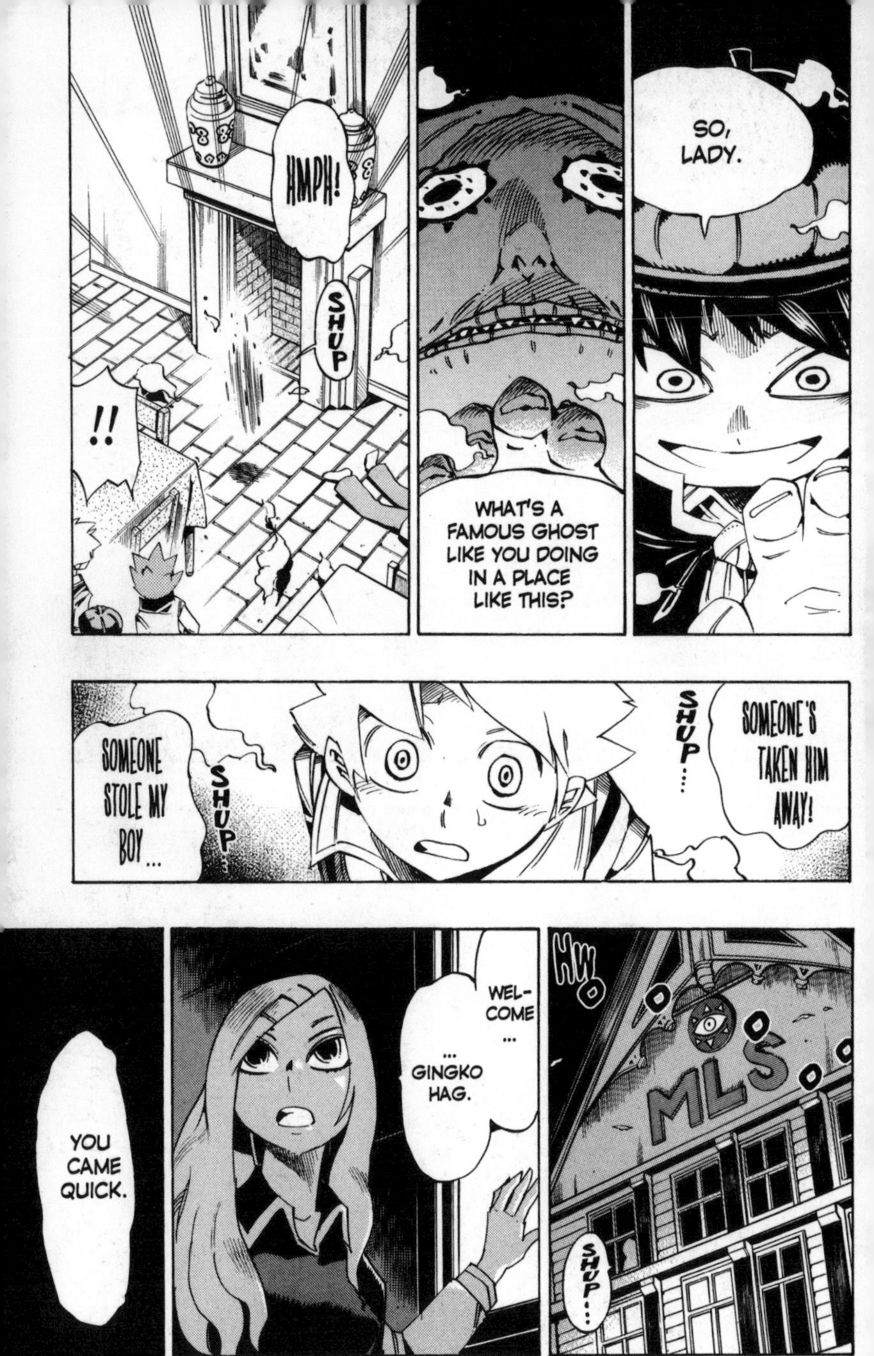
SO, LADY.
WHAT'S A FAMOUS GHOST LIKE YOU DOING IN A PLACE LIKE THIS?
HMPH!
SHUP
!!
SHUP...
SOMEONE'S TAKEN HIM AWAY!
SHUP...
SOMEONE STOLE MY BOY...
HWOO
MLS
SHUP...
WEL-COME...
...GINGKO HAG.
YOU CAME QUICK.

VOLUME 12: HOMECOMING (THE END)

In The Next Volume...

Looks like there's a new envoy in town!

Available October 2009!

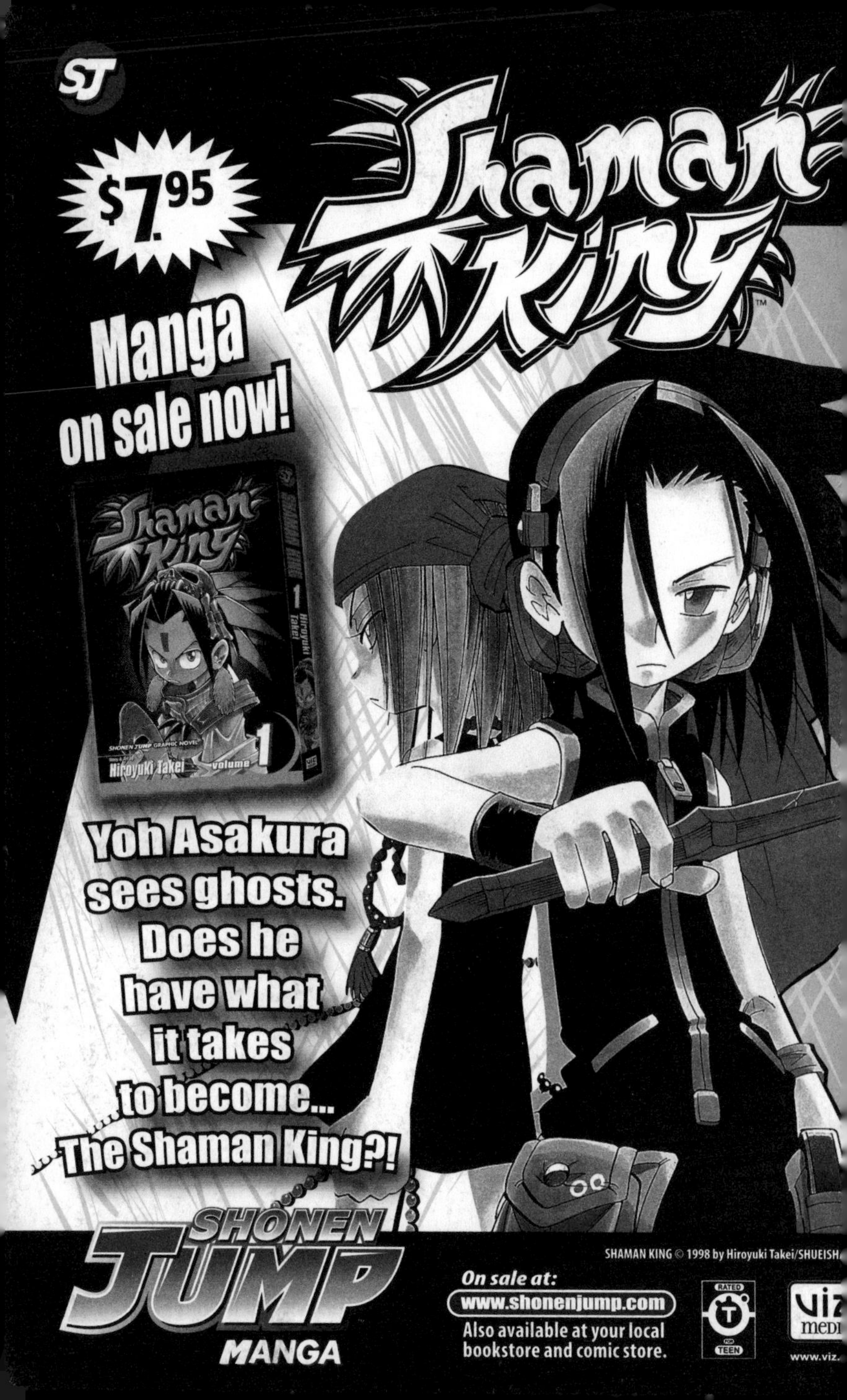
SJ
$7.95
Shaman King™
Manga on sale now!
Shaman King
SHONEN JUMP GRAPHIC NOVEL
Hiroyuki Takei
volume 1
Yoh Asakura sees ghosts. Does he have what it takes to become... The Shaman King?!
SHONEN JUMP MANGA
SHAMAN KING © 1998 by Hiroyuki Takei/SHUEISH
On sale at:
www.shonenjump.com
Also available at your local bookstore and comic store.
RATED T TEEN
viz media
www.viz.

SAVE 50% OFF
HE COVER PRICE!

'S LIKE GETTING 6 ISSUES
FREE!

VER 350+ PAGES PER ISSUE

This monthly magazine contains 7 of the coolest manga available in the U.S., PLUS anime news, and info about video & card games, toys AND more!

❑ **I want 12 HUGE issues of SHONEN JUMP for only $29.95*!**

NAME

ADDRESS

CITY/STATE/ZIP

EMAIL ADDRESS   **DATE OF BIRTH**

❑ **YES**, send me via email information, advertising, offers, and promotions related to VIZ Media, SHONEN JUMP, and/or their business partners.

❑ **CHECK ENCLOSED** (payable to SHONEN JUMP)   ❑ **BILL ME LATER**

CREDIT CARD: ❑ **Visa** ❑ **Mastercard**

ACCOUNT NUMBER   **EXP. DATE**

SIGNATURE

CLIP&MAIL TO:
SHONEN JUMP Subscriptions Service Dept.
P.O. Box 515
Mount Morris, IL 61054-0515

P9GNC1

anada price: $41.95 USD, including GST, HST, and QST. US/CAN orders only. Allow 6-8 weeks for delivery.
JE PIECE © 1997 by Eiichiro Oda/SHUEISHA Inc. BLEACH © 2001 by Tite Kubo/SHUEISHA Inc.
ARUTO © 1999 by Masashi Kishimoto/SHUEISHA Inc.

RATED
T
TEEN
ratings.viz.com

VIZ
media
www.viz.com